The Programmer's Guide to SQL

CRISTIAN DARIE, KARLI WATSON
WITH CHRIS HART, KEVIN HOFFMAN, JULIAN SKINNER

The Programmer's Guide to SQL
Copyright ©2003 by Cristian Darie, Karli Watson with Chris Hart,
Kevin Hoffman, Julian Skinner

ISBN (pbk): 1-59059-218-2

Printed and bound in the United States of America 10987654321

Trademarked names may appear in this book. Rather than use a trademark symbol with every occurrence of a trademarked name, we use the names only in an editorial fashion and to the benefit of the trademark owner, with no intention of infringement of the trademark.

Technical Reviewers: Cristof Falk, Slavomir Furman, Brad Maiani, Judith M. Myerson, Johan Normén, David Schultz

Editorial Board: Dan Appleman, Craig Berry, Gary Cornell, Steven Rycroft, Julian Skinner, Martin Streicher, Jim Sumser, Karen Watterson, Gavin Wray, John Zukowski

Lead Editor: Tony Davis

Assistant Publisher: Grace Wong

Project Manager: Darren Murphy

Copy Editor: Kim Wimpsett

Production Manager: Kari Brooks

Production Editor: Kelly Winquist

Proofreader: Thistle Hill Publishing Services

Compositor: Kinetic Publishing Services, LLC

Indexer: John Collin

Artist: Kinetic Publishing Services, LLC

Cover Designer: Kurt Krames

Manufacturing Manager: Tom Debolski

Distributed to the book trade in the United States by Springer-Verlag New York, Inc., 175 Fifth Avenue, New York, NY, 10010 and outside the United States by Springer-Verlag GmbH & Co. KG, Tiergartenstr. 17, 69112 Heidelberg, Germany.

In the United States: phone 1-800-SPRINGER, email orders@springer-ny.com, or visit http://www.springer-ny.com. Outside the United States: fax +49 6221 345229, email orders@springer.de, or visit http://www.springer.de.

For information on translations, please contact Apress directly at 2560 Ninth Street, Suite 219, Berkeley, CA 94710. Phone 510-549-5930, fax 510-549-5939, email info@apress.com, or visit http://www.apress.com.

The information in this book is distributed on an "as is" basis, without warranty. Although every precaution has been taken in the preparation of this work, neither the author(s) nor Apress shall have any liability to any person or entity with respect to any loss or damage caused or alleged to be caused directly or indirectly by the information contained in this work.

The source code for this book is available to readers at http://www.apress.com in the Downloads section.

Contents at a Glance

Contents

About the Authors

CRISTIAN DARIE is an independent IT consultant specializing in Microsoft technologies. Having worked with computers since he was a child, he won his first prize at the age of 12 in the first programming contest he ever entered. He was actively involved with the former Wrox Press as a technical reviewer and author, having contributed the OOP parts of *Visual C# .NET: A Guide for VB6 Developers* and coauthored *Beginning ASP.NET E-Commerce with Visual Basic .NET and Visual Studio .NET*. He has authored MCAD preparation material and various SkillDrill tests, such as C# Programming, Microsoft COM+, and DB2 Development, which can be taken at http://www.skilldrill.com.

Cristian is at Politehnica University of Bucharest, studying automatic control and industrial informatics. He can be contacted through http://www.ChristianDarie.ro.

My big thanks go to Dave, Julian, and Chris for being such great people to work with.

KARLI WATSON is a freelance author and IT specialist with a penchant for multicolored clothing. He started out with the intention of becoming a world-famous nanotechnologist, so perhaps one day you might recognize his name as he receives a Nobel Prize. For now, though, Karli's computing interests include all things mobile and everything .NET. Karli is also a snowboarding enthusiast and wishes he had a cat.

JULIAN SKINNER studied Germanic etymology before joining the former Wrox Press. He has consequently spent most of the last four-and-a-half years reading, editing, and writing books about programming, focusing on Microsoft technologies and, in particular, on C# and the .NET Framework. He contributed many sections and code samples, and often entire chapters, for the books he worked on at Wrox, mostly hiding behind the relative anonymity of an "additional material" credit, but he is credited as a coauthor of, among other titles, *Professional ADO.NET*.

CHRIS HART is a developer and author based in Birmingham (in the United Kingdom, not Alabama). Chris spent most of the last four years as a member of the technical editorial team at the former Wrox Press and has been programming on a variety of systems since the age of 10. She spends most of her time working with Microsoft technologies and has been heavily involved with .NET since it was first released as an early alpha preview. She's currently working for Business Post and is developing .NET Compact Framework/SQL CE applications and 2D barcode scanning components in Delphi.

KEVIN HOFFMAN started programming at the age of 10 when his grandfather gave him a Commodore VIC-20 that he refurbished, and he's been addicted to programming ever since. He has worked on everything from writing interfaces for scientific instruments to building e-commerce Web sites to providing second-tier technical support for Unix. He got hold of .NET when it was first handed out in early pre-beta form and has been coding with it ever since. He's currently employed in Houston, Texas, where he creates enterprise applications with the .NET Framework for a financial services company.

Introduction

STRUCTURED QUERY LANGUAGE (SQL) is the language of the database. It's a standard that defines how to manipulate almost every aspect of database, from creating the database and tables themselves to creating, reading, inserting, updating, and deleting data in the database. This standard is then implemented and extended differently by each database system vendor.

The current version of the SQL standard is SQL-99. Most major database platforms now adhere fairly closely to this standard with a couple of exceptions. Microsoft Access, for example, has only recently (with Access XP) adopted the SQL-92 standard. Previous editions of Access supported only SQL-89.

In this book, we'll walk through all the major SQL statements you're likely to need when programming databases. We'll highlight differences between the standard and implementations used in five major database systems:

- SQL Server

- Oracle

- DB2

- MySQL

- Access

Who Is This Book For?

This book is designed to meet the needs of both the novice SQL programmer who needs a bit of syntactical help and the developer using SQL day to day who needs a handy desktop SQL reference. You don't need to have done much database programming before, but some experience with databases will be useful. You should also have one of the five database systems mentioned earlier to gain the most benefits from this book.

What Does This Book Cover?

This book covers the following topics:

Chapter 1, **"Understanding SQL and Relational Databases"**: Introduces and clarifies key concepts you'll use throughout the book. This chapter also looks at relational database design theory.

Chapter 2, **"Retrieving Data with SQL"**: Discusses the use of simple SELECT statements to retrieve data from a table.

Chapter 3, **"Modifying Data"**: Covers modifying data in a table using INSERT and UPDATE statements.

Chapter 4, **"Summarizing and Grouping Data"**: Shows how to use some built-in functions for counting rows and averaging columns and then moves on to look at the GROUP BY and HAVING statements. This chapter also highlights differences between platforms when it comes to display-ing selected rows.

Chapter 5, **"Performing Calculations and Using Functions"**: Describes many more available functions that can be used for performing calcula-tions, manipulating strings, working with dates and times, and so on. It also covers creating your own functions.

Chapter 6, **"Combining SQL Queries"**: Talks about subqueries and how to refine queries by combining data from different queries.

Chapter 7, **"Querying Multiple Tables"**: Introduces joins between tables and using the built-in relationships defined in the database to present the correct results when building up a query.

Chapter 8, **"Hiding Complex SQL with Views"**: Discusses creating views for storing queries. It also discusses how you can use views to grant restricted access to data to users without having to worry about them harming the underlying data.

Chapter 9, **"Using Stored Procedures"**: Shows how to create and work with stored procedures on each of the supporting database platforms. It also shows how to use conditional execution, loops, and cursors, and how to handle errors.

Chapter 10, **"Transactions"**: Covers the topic of transactions and how they're implemented on different platforms to handle updates to a data-base. This chapter also covers different locking methods that can be applied to data while a transaction is processed.

Chapter 11, **"Users and Security"**: Discusses the key concepts of user authentication and authorization, focusing on the use of roles and per-missions to restrict or enable certain database functionality.

Chapter 12, **"Working with Database Objects"**: Discusses how to create (and delete) databases, tables, temporary tables, sequences, and indexes and how to apply constraints to columns in a table.

Chapter 13, **"Triggers"**: Discusses how to create and use triggers to react to events in databases; for example, the insertion of a row or the deletion of a table.

Chapter 14, **"Case Study: Building a Product Catalog"**: Drawing on much of the knowledge gained throughout the rest of the book, this case study demonstrates how to create and query the underlying database for a real e-commerce application

Chapter 15, **"Case Study: Implementing Role-Based Security"**: Examines how to use SQL and stored procedures to implement a role-based security system.

Also in this book are three appendixes that cover the following:

Appendix A, **"Executing SQL Statements"**: Provides an overview of how to get up and running so that you're ready to start executing SQL statements against each of the database platforms.

Appendix B, **"Setting Up the InstantUniversity Database"**: Describes how to create and populate the InstantUniversity sample database that's used throughout the examples in this book.

Appendix C, **"Data Types"**: Lists the different data types available to SQL programmers on each of the different database platforms.

What You Need to Use This Book

To run the code in this book, you'll need to have one of the following database platforms installed on a compatible operating system:

- SQL Server

- Oracle

- DB2 UDB

- MySQL

- Access

All the SQL code in the book has been tested against each of these systems. Specifically, the versions we used to test the code were as follows:

- SQL Server 2000

- Oracle 9i R2

- DB2 8.1 beta

- MySQL 4.0 gamma

- Access 2000

Customer Support and Feedback

We always value hearing from our readers, and we want to know what you think about this book: what you liked, what you didn't like, and what you think we can do better next time.

How to Tell Us Exactly What You Think

You might just want to tell us how much you liked or loathed the book in question. Or you might have ideas about how this whole process could be improved. In either case, you should e-mail support@apress.com. Please be sure to mention the book's ISBN and title in your message. You'll always find a sympathetic ear, no matter what the problem is. Above all you should remember that we do care about what you have to say, and we will do our utmost to act upon it.

What We Can't Answer

Obviously with an ever-growing range of books and an ever-changing technology base, there's an increasing volume of data requiring support. Although we endeavor to answer all questions about the book, we can't solve bugs in your own programs that you've adapted from our code. However, do tell us if you're especially pleased with the routine you developed with our help.

Downloading the Source Code for the Book

The source code for this book is available to readers at http://www.apress.com in the Downloads section.

Finding Support and Errata on www.apress.com

We understand that errors can destroy the enjoyment of a book and can cause many wasted and frustrated hours, so we seek to minimize the distress they can cause. The following sections will explain how to find and post errata on our Web site to get book-specific help.

Finding Errata

Before you send in a query, you might be able to save time by finding the answer to your problem on our Web site at http://www.apress.com. Locate this book in the online catalog or within the book's category and go to the book's Web page. Check to see if there is a Corrections link. If there is, click the link to see the posted errata.

Adding an Erratum to the Web Site

If you want to point out an erratum or directly query a problem in the book, then click the Submit Errata link on the book's Web page. Please be sure to include your name and e-mail and the chapter number, page number, and a brief description of the problem, as requested.

We won't send you junk mail. We need the details to save your time and ours.

Queries will be forwarded to the book's authors and editor. You may receive a direct e-mail reply, and/or the erratum will be posted to the Web site so all readers can benefit.

Participating in Peer-to-Peer Forums

For author and peer discussion, join the Apress discussion groups. If you post a query to our forums, you can be confident that many Apress authors, editors, and industry experts are examining it. At forums.apress.com you'll find a number of different lists that will help you, not only while you read this book but also as you develop your own applications. To sign up for the Apress forums, go to forums.apress.com and select the New User link.

CHAPTER 1

Understanding SQL and Relational Databases

AT THE HEART OF ALMOST every large-scale application, whether it be a Web application or a corporate intranet, is the database. The modern database has moved on a long way from the flat-file address-card style of database storage, and you now have the ability to store terabytes of information about customers, products, contacts, and so on. It's all very well storing all of this data in a central database, but simply storing data doesn't give you much in return if you can't find some way to organize, access, and work with this data. Structured Query Language (SQL) is a standardized language designed to access and manipulate data stored in relational databases and to work with the databases themselves.

This chapter explains what SQL is and how it works. You'll also be looking at some relational database theory because to be able to work confidently with SQL, you need to understand some of these core concepts.

What Is SQL?

SQL is a language that's used for accessing and manipulating databases and, more importantly for the programmer, the data that's contained in databases. SQL statements give you the power to manipulate all aspects of your database using code instead of visual tools.

 NOTE *SQL is pronounced either "ess-kue-ell" or "see-kwell" depending on your preference. We go for the latter, so no complaints about us writing "a SQL statement" rather than "an SQL statement," please!*

In essence, what you have is a "front end" that sends a SQL statement (or a set of SQL statements) to a "back-end" data store. For a programmer, this SQL statement will most commonly contain coded instructions to perform one or more of the following operations:

- Extracting specific data from the database

- Inserting new data into the database

- Modifying existing data

- Deleting data

Many commercial vendors supply relational databases, including Microsoft (SQL Server and Access), Oracle Corporation (Oracle), and IBM (DB2). There are also several freely available open-source products such as MySQL and PostgresSQL. No matter what platform you're using, several features are common to all relational databases, whatever they contain. All data in these databases is held in *rows* (also known as *records*) that span the *columns* (*fields*) of a *table* within the database, and the values for each column are of a specified *data type*. Because the data is stored in a similar structure on different platforms, you can use similar techniques to access and manipulate the data. Furthermore, each of these platforms uses SQL as the universal language to implement these techniques. In other words, *SQL is the language that every relational database understands.*

What about your "front end"? Well, you have a variety of options here, too. For example, your front end might be one of the following:

- **A Web page** that allows a customer to enter information into a Search box. Based on the data entered, a SQL statement will be constructed, sent to the back-end data store, and executed, and the specific data that the customer requested will be returned and displayed on the Web page.

- **A business application** that allows employees to query a data store for information about employees, product sales, or any number of things.

- **A simple SQL editing tool**, as provided by every relational database product, that allows you to execute SQL statements against a database on your own computer or a computer to which you're networked.

And here you have the real beauty of SQL: Regardless of the language used to create the front end—be it ASP.NET, Java, Visual Basic, C#, or virtually any other language—SQL is the language that all of these front ends will use to communicate with a relational database.

In addition to all this, you can also use SQL to administer the relational database itself—for example, to create or remove new database storage structures or to access and modify the security settings for that database.

The bottom line is that regardless of the language in which you program or the particular database in which you store your data, knowledge of SQL is an essential skill.

Introducing the SQL Standard

SQL has quite a long history. It was first invented at IBM in 1974–75 and was used to communicate with mainframe databases. Later, in 1979, the first commercial relational database product that supported SQL was released by Oracle, and in 1986–87 the ANSI and ISO standards organizations worked on a SQL standard that was released two years later, known as *SQL-89*. This standard was updated in 1991 to a new version, SQL-92, and subsequently to another version, SQL-99 (also referred to as *SQL:1999* and *SQL3*). This book concentrates on this SQL-99 standard.

The standard defines techniques for a variety of operations on relational databases and the data that they contain. Essentially, the SQL standard splits down into three key components:

- **Data Manipulation Language (DML)**: This is the component of the language with which this book is most concerned. It provides four basic SQL statements:

  - SELECT statements that are used to read and extract data from the database. This portion of the language is often given a subheading all its own, namely Data Query Language (DQL); these SQL statements can correctly be referred to as *SQL queries*.

  - INSERT statements that are used to insert new rows of data into the database.

  - UPDATE statements that are used to modify existing rows of data.

  - DELETE statements that are used to remove rows of data from the database.

- **Data Definition Language (DDL)**: This is used to create, modify, or remove tables and other database objects. It includes such statements as CREATE TABLE, ALTER TABLE, DROP TABLE, CREATE INDEX, and so on. You'll investigate this component of the language in Chapter 12, "Working with Database Objects."

- **Data Control Language (DCL)**: This is used to manage database security, manage which users have access to which tables and what data, and so on. You'll investigate this in Chapter 11, "Users and Security."

The majority of this book is devoted to the DML component of SQL and more specifically to writing SQL queries.

How SQL Works

As its name suggests, a large part of the Structured *Query* Language is dedicated to the process of *querying* a relational database. That is, you can use SQL to ask certain "questions" of the database and have the "answer" (a row or rows of data) returned. For example, say you have a database that stores information about a particular university and the courses it runs, the people who teach those courses, and so on. You might ask the question "Which courses are offered by the university?" A SQL query such as the following might do the trick:

```
SELECT * FROM Courses
```

What this query is basically saying in database-speak is "Give me a list of all of the information stored for all of the courses in the Courses table." This query would work against any relational database as long as it contained a Courses table. Now, the Courses table might hold a variety of different information, and perhaps you're only interested in the name of the courses offered. Then you might modify your SQL query as follows:

```
SELECT CourseName FROM Courses
```

Now, this query would work against any relational database as long as it had a Courses table that contained a column called CourseName. What it's saying is "Give me only the names of all the courses in the Courses table." In other words, give you all the rows stored in the database but only return the values stored in the CourseName column. Any other information stored in the table, such as the number of credits required to pass each course (perhaps stored in a Credits column) would be ignored. Finally, suppose you wanted to see data from all of the columns in the Courses table but only for Chemistry courses:

```
SELECT * FROM Courses WHERE CourseName = 'Chemistry'
```

We won't go any further now, but we hope you can see that, in some circumstances, a line of SQL can often look much the same as a line of English. Of course, there's a bit more to it than that, and complex operations will require far more complex SQL code! Like any language, you have a lot of syntax and usage information to learn, but SQL does have one important advantage: Once you get used to it, the syntax is simple indeed and can often be interpreted even by people who have never seen it before.

One important point to take home from this discussion is that your SQL statements merely define which data you want to retrieve. You don't specify *how* your database should go about retrieving them. SQL is a declarative language, not a procedural language (such as Java, Visual Basic, and so on). You just specify what you want to do in SQL and let your Relational Database Management System (RDBMS) decide the best way to actually do it.

Introducing Relational Database Management Systems

The term *database* is often confused with "the software that makes data storage possible." For example, you've probably heard SQL Server, Access, and Oracle referred to as *databases*. More accurately, they should be referred to as *Relational Database Management Systems* (RDBMSs). They're applications that are responsible for the storage of data as well as providing an interface that can be used to access the database(s) they contain. Typically, as well as some kind of user interface, RDBMSs include an Application Programming Interface (API) that can be used by other applications to access data.

Each RDBMS will be capable of maintaining a large number of individual databases (in other words, the data storage constructs and the actual data).

One crucial part of RDBMSs is the *database engine*. This part of an RDBMS is responsible for accessing data, as opposed to other parts that may relate to manipulating database manipulation more abstractly, dealing with user input, displaying results, and so on. As such, when you programmatically access databases stored by RDBMSs, you're really using the database engine of the RDBMS via the API. It's the database engine that decides how best to carry out the instructions contained in your SQL statements.

Often you'll use an additional layer of abstraction between your applications and the database engine, that is called a *data provider*. A data provider is usually a service available to all code running on a computer that mediates between your applications and the database engine you're using, making it easier to execute queries. In some cases this can be a great advantage because swapping between databases can be as simple as using a different provider (one for SQL Server instead of one for Oracle, for example). However, this isn't always the case because there may be fundamental differences to overcome with such a migration.

Different RDBMSs are optimized in different ways, and they provide a variety of functionality depending on their purpose. More powerful (and therefore more expensive) RDBMSs will provide better support for concurrency (coping with multiple users accessing data at the same time), provide more simultaneous connections, provide better performance, provide stronger security, provide more versatile backup and failsafe procedures, allow transactions (where single operations may involve several database accesses, and that operation is only successful if all accesses complete), and generally just be a little more robust.

Luckily, mastering the basic use of databases is a bit like learning to drive a car. Unless you learn on an automatic before switching to a manual, you'll be able to drive most vehicles. You might not have the in-car stereo you're used to, but you'll get by. The main reason for all this is that pretty much all RDBMSs that are currently available support SQL, which is of course what this book is all about. You only need to learn SQL once, and you should find that everything is fine regardless of the RDBMS you use.

Introducing SQL Dialects

The idea that you only need to learn SQL once pretty much holds true for all basic data manipulations. Nevertheless, you'll notice differences as you move from RDBMS to RDBMS. For example, you should note that although the current global standard for SQL is SQL-99, most RDBMSs only fully support the earlier standard, SQL-92. This means that certain parts of the SQL-99 standard may not be supported by your RDBMS. There are also subtle differences in the way the standard is implemented on each RDBMS. One minor difference is that MySQL, DB2, and Oracle require semicolons at the end of SQL statements, but SQL Server doesn't (however, including a semicolon at the end of a statement won't cause any negative effects in SQL Server). This book includes these characters at the end of every statement because omitting them would break the code on the other platforms.

Other times, it'll mean that the statement required to perform a certain task is written slightly differently, depending on the RDBMS. On these occasions, the code in this book may be presented more than once to highlight differences between database platforms.

 NOTE　*The downloadable code for this book includes separate directories containing SQL formatted for use in these different environments. You can access this code from the Downloads section of the Apress Web site (*http://www.apress.com*).*

You may also find that your RDBMS provides additional statements and functions that allow you to do some complex calculation in SQL, which you would otherwise have had to do in another language (obviously, this helps a particular vendor market its own product). In general, this book covers these only where it's the only way (or only sensible way) to achieve a certain task for that RDBMS.

Furthermore, you'll find that some of the RDBMSs provide a language all their own, which you can use to program on that particular platform. For example, Oracle provides the PL/SQL language, and SQL Server provides the Transact-SQL language. As you can probably tell from the names, these languages encapsulate SQL but at the same time provide procedural extensions to the language that allow you to perform more powerful data operations. You can "wrap" your SQL code in these languages, which can perform any related business logic required to make sure that the data manipulation conforms to your particular rules. You can then store this code in the database as a distinct programming unit. Examples of such programming units are *stored procedures* and triggers, which are covered in Chapters 9 and 13, respectively.

Obviously in these cases, the code is RDBMS specific and must be presented separately for each RDBMS—though MySQL and Access don't support stored procedures or triggers.

To fully understand how SQL works, you need to look at how relational databases work, so now you'll take a step back from SQL for a moment and explore relational databases in a bit more detail.

Introducing Relational Databases

A *database* is an organized store of data. Many applications, created in any language, need access to a database. For example, without a database of customers and products, e-commerce applications simply aren't possible.

From the point of view of applications using data in a database, the actual mechanism of storage is usually not important. Whether the data is stored on disk, in memory, or in arrangements of trees on a desert island somewhere, the usage will be the same. What we mean by this is that if an application requests some data concerning a customer and subsequently obtains that data, then where it came from doesn't matter. Of course, performance might be increased if you don't have to keep planting trees. . . .

Three concepts you need to understand before learning about how data is stored in a relational database are *entities*, *attributes*, and *values*. An entity represents some object in reality, such as a person or a product. Entities, as objects, represent a class of "things." A Customers entity describes all possible customers, and then each instance of that object represents a specific customer. Each instance of your Customers entity will have identical attributes that define the meaning of that entity. Consider the following collection of attributes:

- Customer first name

- Customer last name

- Postal address

- E-mail address

- Phone number

Each of these attributes will store values, and these values are generally different from one `Customer` instance to another. One `Customer` instance could store the values `Joe`, `Bloggs`, `12 SQL Street`, `jbloggs@email.com`, and `012-456-789`. Another instance might store completely different values in each attribute.

In the relational database world, roughly speaking, the following is true:

- An entity is a *table*.

- An attribute is a *column* in that table.

- A *row* describes a particular instance of the entity (it contains values for the various columns that comprise the table).

Understanding Database Tables

The fundamental data storage unit in a relational database is the *table*. A single database contains one or more tables. Tables are used to group related data into a single, named unit. For example, an e-commerce application will need to keep track of customers and products. To cater to this, you could use two separate tables, perhaps one called `Customers` and one called `Products`, which store relevant information with regard to each entity.

NOTE *There's a general disagreement in the programming community concerning whether table names should have plural names. We tend to think they should be because they're likely to contain multiple data entries, but others have told us they like referring to, say, "the* `Customer` *table" because it sounds better. Quite honestly, though, you shouldn't worry about any of this too much as long as the name you choose relates to the table content in a reasonably sensible way.*

Obviously, tables require more than just a name before you can store data in them. What data can and can't go into a table, and in what form it's stored, is defined by the *schema* information for the table. A database will typically include a single schema defining all the tables it contains, including information concerning columns and data types as described next, relationships between tables, and so on. Schemas are usually stored in the RDBMS in some proprietary format, which is fine because you're unlikely to want to manipulate table schemas directly. Instead, higher-level modifications to table structure will be reflected in schema changes.

Tables consist of a series of columns and rows. Columns define what data can be stored in the table, and rows are where you store the actual data.

Columns

Each table in a database is made up of one or more named *columns* (also known as *fields*). Each column describes one particular facet of your entity (for example, the name of a customer). For example, an entry in the previous Customers table is likely to have the following columns:

- FirstName

- LastName

- Address

- Email

- TelephoneNumber

And so on. Columns might be marked as required, in which case they *must* contain data for a given data item (for example, you'll probably always want to store the customer's name, address, and e-mail), but they might also allow NULL values (where no data is specified) in some circumstances—you don't necessarily need a customer phone number, for example. In most RDBMSs it's also possible to have columns that aren't maintained by you, such as a column that receives an automatically generated value for each data item, for example. You'll learn more about these topics later in this chapter.

Bear in mind that the columns that make up a table uniquely define that table. If you were to take data from somebody else's Customers table (that is, a Customers table in another database), things might not fit right. Instead of an Address column, for example, a different database might contain multiple columns, columns for each line of the address, like City, ZipCode, and others. This is an excellent example of a common problem—deciding which columns you require in a table. With addresses, the single-column model is more versatile because you could put anything you like in there, but using multiple columns makes more sense in terms of identifying and using the different strings that make up a complete address. However, the exact columns used might not fit in with the methods of addressing used worldwide. For example, United Kingdom addresses use postcodes rather than ZIP codes, which, while serving the same purpose, are formatted differently. This could cause problems both for users (who might not know how to enter data in columns with unfamiliar names) and administrators (who might rely on the validation of address information prior to shipment).

Once the columns in a table have been defined, it can be awkward to add more or remove redundant ones while maintaining data integrity, so a well-planned design at the start is essential.

Each column in a database table has a specific *data type*. This data type determines what information can be stored in the column. We'll return to this topic shortly.

Rows

Data in a database table takes the form of individual *rows*. Each row in a database is a single data entry, or item, and is often referred to as a *record*. A single row includes information for each column in a table that requires a value.

So, in the Customer table described earlier, a single row will represent a single customer. Joe Bloggs gets his own row, as would Bridget Jones.

Primary Keys

A fundamental tenet of storing data in a relational database is that you must be able to uniquely identify each row of data that you store. As such, each table is required to have a column that's known as the *primary key* for the table. The data in this column is used to uniquely identify rows in a table, so if you ask for the row with a primary key value of seven (or row 2f7dh—keys don't necessarily have to be integers although they tend to be for simplicity), you'll receive one and only one row. It's usual for RDBMSs to keep track of key values, so if you try to add a row with a duplicate key, you'll probably raise an error.

 NOTE *Primary keys only need to be unique across a single table. It's perfectly okay to have several tables using the same primary key values.*

Say you had a Friend table where you stored phone numbers for each of your friends. Without primary keys, you could have a Friend table with the following contents:

```
Name                       PhoneNumber
-------------------------  ------------
Johnny                     8989189
Johnny                     2328014
Emilio                     4235427
Girl nextdoor              ???
```

Of course, this table has a problem. If we were to ask you what Johnny's phone number is, you couldn't answer because you have two records with the same Name value.

The solution is to either make Name a primary key (in which case the database will not allow duplicate values) or add a new column (an ID column) to act as a primary key. With an ID column, the Friend table would look like this:

```
FriendID    Name                       PhoneNumber
----------  -------------------------  ---------------
1           Johnny                     8989189
2           Johnny                     2328014
3           Emilio                     4235427
4           Girl nextdoor              ???
```

In this example, even if you have two people named Johnny, they're regarded as different people because they have different IDs. Because the primary key is FriendID, this is the column on which you'll do the identifying searches on the table.

Although in practice it's easier to say that FriendID is the primary key column of Friend, technically this isn't accurate—a primary key isn't a column but a *constraint* that applies to a column.

Constraints are rules that apply to data tables and that form part of the integrity rules of the database. The database itself takes care of its integrity and makes sure that these rules aren't broken. As with data types (when, for example, the database doesn't allow you to insert a string value on a numeric column), you won't be able to insert two records with the same ID value if the ID column is set to be the primary key.

Sometimes choosing the primary key of a table can be a tough decision to make, especially because, in most cases, it has deep impact on the design of the whole database. The philosophy of database design says that the primary key column should *represent* (uniquely identify) the table rows. It's common to have values assigned to this column automatically by the RDBMS. Alternatively, unique properties of records could be used rather than a random value. You could use the Social Security number of a customer, for example. However, this can make things more complicated, and in general it's better to have a completely separate data facet for the primary key.

Primary keys can be formed by combing more than one column. The groups of columns that form the primary key, taken as a unit, are guaranteed to have unique values, even if the individual columns can have repeating values in the table.

There can be only one primary key on a table. A value must be entered for every row of the primary key (it isn't allowed to contain NULL values—see later), and an index is automatically created on its constituent columns. Indexes affect database performance, and we'll talk more about them in Chapter 12, "Working with Database Objects."

Before moving on, let's recap the terminology you've learned so far (see Figure 1-1).

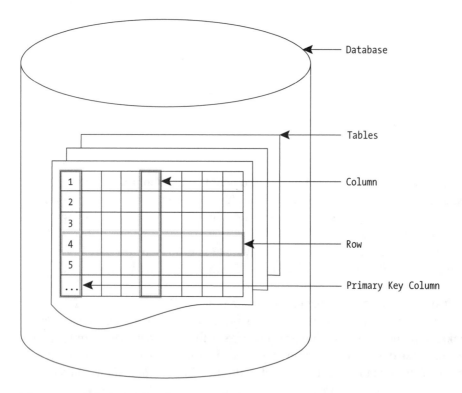

Figure 1-1. Relational database terminology

Enforcing Table Integrity

A table has the power to enforce many rules regarding the data it stores, and it's important that you understand these rules, both when using the DML and when using the DDL portions of SQL. You've already seen what you can achieve by enforcing a primary key constraint on a column. There are many other options available. You'll not look at all of them here (you'll be meeting a fair amount of this when you learn about creating tables in Chapter 12, "Working with Database Objects"), you'll look at some of the most immediately useful areas. Data types are perhaps the most important way to control the stored data, so let's start with them.

Data Types

Data types are a fundamental topic we need to discuss simply because you can't avoid them. It's always necessary to specify a data type when creating a new table field. This might mean that a given column can only hold integer numbers, for example. The data types used in RDBMSs tend to be a little more versatile than this, though, often allowing you to specify how many bytes of storage are allocated to an entry in a column, which will put a restriction on, say, the maximum value of an integer or the precision to which a floating-point number is represented. Alternatively, they might restrict data to positive values (we're still talking integers here—we've yet to see a database that restricts string-type columns to values such as "hardworking," "good sense of humor," or "team player"). Often, you'll want to restrict the number of characters allowed to store strings. For example, you might decide to limit a Password field to eight characters.

Choosing which data types to use for different columns can impact the performance and scalability of your database. By restricting values, you can ensure that less memory is taken up in the database because you don't allocate memory for values that can't be used. Data types also provide a low-level error checking capability because trying to put a "wrong" value in a database is likely to generate an error. As with variable types in some programming languages, though, this won't always be the case. Sometimes a round peg will fit through a square hole even though the square peg won't fit through the round hole, and you can't rely on this aspect of database storage to validate all your data. In any case, you can achieve far better and more powerful validation by other means.

One important (and occasionally annoying) point here is that column data types tend to vary between RDBMSs. This can make it difficult to transfer data between databases and might also result in having to change source code in order to access the same data in a different database. Often the difference is minor—perhaps an integer data type in one RDBMS is called int in another while retaining the same meaning—but it can still break code if you're not careful. Appendix C, "SQL Data Types," of this book provides an overview of the data types supported by each RDBMS and offers advice on "equivalent" types if a specific type in one RDBMS isn't supported (or called the same thing) in another.

Although in some cases the actual names differ, the main data types are supported by all databases. Let's see which these are.

Numbers

Numbers are everywhere and probably are the favorite type of each database. Numbers come in different sizes, shapes, and internal storage formats.

Integers are usually represented by the INT or INTEGER data type. Depending on your database, you may have access to other integer data types (which differ by the minimum and maximum values allowed), such as TINYINT, SMALLINT, MEDIUMINT, and BIGINT.

Floating-point numbers are stored using the FLOAT, REAL, or NUMBER (for Oracle) data type.

A common issue regarding numeric data types concerns accurately storing monetary information. With MySQL and DB2, the DECIMAL data type is the way to go; with Oracle you use the general-purpose NUMBER, and SQL Server has a specialized Money data type, but DECIMAL (or NUMERIC) can also be used.

Text

The second important group of types is the one that stores text and character data.

Usual names for string data types are CHAR, VARCHAR, and TEXT. VARCHAR is a variable-length type for which you specify a maximum size, but the actual size occupied in the database depends on the length of the string you're storing (which might be considerably lower than the maximum size defined for that column).

TEXT usually allows for much longer strings but acts considerably slower than CHAR and VARCHAR.

When creating or altering columns of character data types, you need to specify the maximum length of the string to be stored.

Date and Time

Each database knows how to store dates and times.

The actual data types are SmallDateType and Date for SQL Server, DATE for Oracle, and DATETIME, DATE, TIMESTAMP, TIME, and YEAR for MySQL.

NULLs

Apart from establishing the data types for your columns, you have to decide whether you have to enter a specific value into a column or whether you're allowed to leave it empty. In other words, can a column store NULL values?

What's NULL? Perhaps the best definition of NULL is "undefined"—simply a column for which a value hasn't been specified. The decision of allowing NULL values is a strategic one: Columns that you mark to reject NULL values will always have a value, and the database engine will require you to specify a value for them when adding new rows. On the other hand, if a column is nullable and you don't specify a value for it when adding a new row, NULL will be automatically assigned to it.

NOTE *An empty string (' ') and a numeric value of zero are specific values and aren't the same as NULL values.*

Even saying "NULL value," although used frequently, is a bit misleading because NULL isn't a value. NULL specifies the absence of a value, and the database knows that. If you try to find all rows that have NULL for a specific field, searching with something like the following:

```
SELECT * FROM Customer WHERE PhoneNumber = NULL
```

you won't get any results. SQL works with a tri-valued logic: TRUE, FALSE, and UNKNOWN. For the previous query, the database engine will search through the rows and evaluate the values found in the PhoneNumber column against the search condition WHERE PhoneNumber = NULL. It'll return a row only if the search condition evaluates to TRUE. However, when a NULL value is compared to any other value—a definite value or another NULL—the answer is always UNKNOWN.

Instead, SQL has its own syntax for searching NULLs. You can retrieve all records that don't have a PhoneNumber specified with the following query:

```
SELECT * FROM Customer WHERE PhoneNumber IS NULL;
```

If you want to find all records that do have a value for PhoneNumber, this is the query that does the trick:

```
SELECT * FROM Customer WHERE PhoneNumber IS NOT NULL;
```

Default Values

Often you'll want to create tables that have default values for some columns. In other words, when inserting new records into a table, instead of NULL, the database should insert a predefined value for the columns if the user specified no value.

Most databases support this option, using the DEFAULT constraint, which we'll discuss in detail in Chapter 12, "Working with Database Objects." In some cases you can also supply a function for the default value. With SQL Server, for example, you can supply GETDATE (say, to a column named DateInserted) that always returns the current date and time. This way, when a new row is inserted into the table, GETDATE is called, and the current date and time are supplied as the default value for the DateInserted column.

Unique Constraints

Like a primary key, UNIQUE is also a constraint that doesn't allow columns containing repeating values. However, there are differences. You can have multiple unique columns in a table—as opposed to a single primary key.

NOTE *Unique columns can sometimes be set to accept NULLs on SQL Server (in which case, the column can only accept one NULL value). MySQL and Oracle can accept NULLs on unique columns and can accept more than one row having a NULL for that column, but any data entered into that column on any row must be unique. DB2, on the other hand, won't let you create a table specifying that a column must be both unique and accept NULL values.*

UNIQUE columns are useful in cases where you already have a primary key but you still have columns for which you want to have unique values. This might the case for a column named Email or MobilePhone in the Customer table, in a scenario where CustomerID is the primary key.

Defining Relationships Between Tables

Of course, databases are about much more than stuffing specific types of data in specific columns of a particular table and being able to identify each row. The power of relational databases comes, as the name suggests, from the ability to define relationships between data in different tables. These related tables form the relational database (the database object), which becomes an object with a significance of its own, rather than simply being a group of unrelated data tables. Relational databases store information. It's said that data becomes information only when you give significance to it, and establishing relations with other pieces of data is a good means of doing that. Moving from the concept of a table to that of relational databases isn't a huge leap, but it's a crucial step for any serious SQL programmer.

It helps to think of the entities (the real "things") that database tables need to describe. For example:

You have *customers* who place *orders* for certain *products.*

Straight away, you start to see the sort of entities that you must describe and the relationships that exist between them. You might be able to map these entities directly to tables, creating a Customers table, an Orders table, and a Products table.

In reality, although the underlying concept of identifying entities and their interrelationship is valid, it's likely to be slightly more complex than that. For example, how much information do you store in the Customers table? Do you store customers' billing addresses there? What if they have more than one address?

In fact, there exists a whole bunch of rules that define how you can most effectively store your data to avoid repetition (storing the same information over and over again) and to safeguard against any possible infringement on the integrity of the data. The process is called *normalization,* and the rules are called *normal forms*. We aren't going to discuss this in detail in this book because we want to focus on SQL, not on the optimum design for relational databases.

NOTE *You can find a good treatment of normal forms in the book* Joe Celko's SQL for Smarties: Advanced SQL Programming, *Second Edition (Morgan Kaufmann, 1999).*

However, we do need to introduce some of the fundamental relational data storage concepts that you simply must understand in order to write effective SQL queries against relational databases. For example, you'll investigate how to do the following:

- **Create relationships between tables (*one* customer may create *many* orders...)**: You can then use SQL to retrieve data that's spread across more than one table (for example, to retrieve all of the orders made by a specific customer).

- **Safeguard against fundamental data integrity issues**: For example, you can ensure that you don't enter the same order twice (the customer would be unhappy to be billed twice for the same purchase) or enter an order for a customer who doesn't exist.

Primary keys are central to your ability to define relationships. For example, a customer row in your Customer table might refer to credit card details stored in a `CreditCards` table rather than including the information in a single place. The advantage is that is becomes much easier to make more complex associations between data.

Because one customer may own multiple credit cards, it's important to be able to link those cards to that exact customer who owns them, and primary keys help to ensure that this happens. However, there's more to it than this.

Relational Integrity and Data Normalization

As we've discussed, information is rarely stored in a single data table. Most of the time, you try to store relatively independent pieces of information in separate tables—in something that you name to be a *normalized* form of the data.

Say that you want to create a database where you need to store information about some products and about the departments to which they belong. In a non-normalized database, you might simply create a table named `ProductDepartment`, containing the data shown in Figure 1-2.

Product Name	Department Name
Warcraft III	Games
Need for Speed	Games
Beginning ASP.NET E-commerce	Books
Matrix	Movies
Me, Myself and Irene	Movies
ABBA - Greatest Hits	Music
Ice Age	Movies
Motorola V60	Electronics
Aerosmith - Just Push Play	Music

Figure 1-2. The `ProductDepartment` *table*

Having data stored like this generates more problems than it solves—storing information this way is, most importantly, hard to maintain. Imagine that you had also stored descriptions and other attributes for departments and products.

Also, you're storing repeating groups of information. If you want to change the name of a department, instead of changing it in one place, you need to change it in every place it was used. If you want to get a list of all the different departments, you need to do a resources-heavy query on the `ProductDepartment` table. And the list of potential problems has just begun....

In the process of *data normalization*, you split tables such as `ProductDepartment` into separate tables to eliminate repeating groups of information.

The `ProductDepartment` table shown earlier contains data about products and departments. In a normalized data structure, you would store them in separate tables, as shown in Figure 1-3.

Department		Product	
DepartmentID	Name	ProductID	Name
1	Books	1	Warcraft III
2	Games	2	Need for Speed
3	Music	3	Beginning ASP.NET E-commerce
4	Movies	4	Matrix
5	Electronics	5	Me, Myself and Irene
		6	ABBA - Greatest Hits
		7	Ice Age
		8	Motorola V60
		9	AeroSmith - Just Push Play

Figure 1-3. The Department *table and the* Product *table*

In a normalized database, having primary keys that uniquely identify the records is a fundamental necessity. The problem with the previous tables is that, based on the data they offer, you can't find out which departments relate to which products.

Depending on the kind of relationship you want between departments and products, you may need to do further modifications to the tables' structures. Let's continue the journey by taking a closer look at table relationships and how you implement them in the database.

Types of Table Relationships

So, what types of table relationships are there, after all? You always need to decide how your data relates before designing the database.

Let's continue with the example. Again, the problem is that, with the current structure, you have no way of knowing which departments relate to which products, as shown in Figure 1-4.

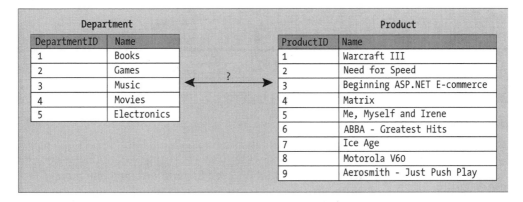

Figure 1-4. Two tables without a relationship

Two tables like the ones you see here can't be very helpful because they don't tell you which products belong to which departments. However, having a figure such as this containing the individual rows without the relationships helps you see what kind of relations should be implemented.

There are two main kinds of table relationships:

- **The one-to-many relationship**: One row in a table is related to one or more rows in the related table.

- **The many-to-many relationship**: Multiple rows in one table match multiple rows in the related table.

Although relatively rare, there's also a one-to-one relationship, whereby one and only one row in a table is matched with a single row in its related table. For example, in a database that allowed patients to be assigned to beds, you would hope that there would be a one-to-one relationship between patients and beds!

The One-to-Many Relationship

With the one-to-many relationship, one record in a table can be associated with multiple records in the related table, but not vice versa.

If you decide that each department can contain more products, but a product belongs to exactly one department (a product can't belong to more departments), then the one-to-many relationship is the best choice for your tables.

This becomes clearer after visualizing the relationship (see Figure 1-5).

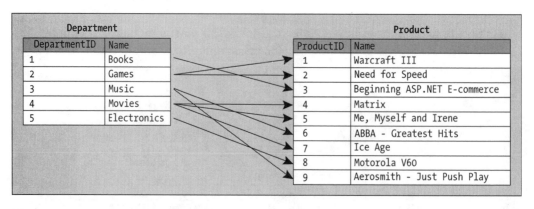

Figure 1-5. A one-to-many relationship

With this graphic, you can see that for each department there are more related products: *One* department relates to *many* products, and thus you have a one-to-many relationship.

NOTE *The opposite must not be true: A product shouldn't relate to many departments. If it did, you'd have a many-to-many relationship (discussed in the next section).*

Figure 1-5 showed which products belong to which departments using arrows—it's time to see how you can tell the database to store this information.

TIP *You implement the one-to-many relationship by adding a column to the table in the* many *side of the relationship. The new column will store the ID (the primary key value) of the record in the* one *part of the relationship to which it relates.*

In the sample scenario, you need to add a DepartmentID column to the Product table, as shown in Figure 1-6.

Department			Product		
DepartmentID	Name		ProductID	DepartmentID	Name
1	Books		1	2	Warcraft III
2	Games		2	2	Need for Speed
3	Music		3	1	Beginning ASP.NET E-commerce
4	Movies		4	4	Matrix
5	Electronics		5	4	Me, Myself and Irene
			6	3	ABBA - Greatest Hits
			7	4	Ice Age
			8	5	Motorola V60
			9	3	Aerosmith - Just Push Play

Figure 1-6. Adding a DepartmentID column to the Product table

NOTE *The table at the* many *part of the relation (*Product *in this case) is called the* referencing table, *and the other table is called the* referenced table.

You can visual this relationship in the form of a database diagram in different ways. For example, Figure 1-7 shows how SQL Server's Enterprise Manager shows the relationship.

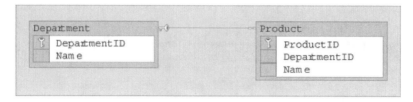

Figure 1-7. Illustrating primary key relationships

The golden key located next to column names show the primary key of the table. When the primary key is formed using a combination of more than one column, all the columns forming the primary key will be marked with the golden keys; remember that you can't have more than one primary key in a table, but a primary key can be formed from more than one column.

In the relationship line, the golden key shows the table whose primary key is involved in the relationship—in other words, it points to the table on the *one* side of the relationship. The infinity sign shows the table in the *many* side of the relationship.

Note that the relationship signs don't also show the table columns involved in the relationship—they only show the kind and direction of the relationship.

The same diagram looks like Figure 1-8 when drawn differently.

Department	
PK	**Department ID**
	Name

Product	
PK	**Product ID**
FK1	Department ID
	Name

Figure 1-8. A full representation of the primary key/foreign key relationship

In this figure, primary keys are marked with *PK* and are listed separately at the beginning of the list, and the foreign keys with *FK* (foreign keys are discussed in the next section) are listed next. Because there can be more than one foreign key, they're numbered. Columns that don't allow NULLs are displayed in bold. The arrow points to the table at the *one* side of the relationship.

After DepartmentID is added to Product, the database has all the information it needs to find out which products belong to which departments. You can then query these two tables to see combined information from both tables. You could use the following SQL query to display a list containing the name of each product along with the name of the department to which it belongs:

```
SELECT Product.Name, Department.Name
FROM Product, Department
WHERE Product.DepartmentID = Department.DepartmentID
```

This query returns these results:

```
Name                                 Name

----------------------------------   ------------------
Warcraft III                         Games
Need for Speed                       Games
Beginning ASP.NET E-Commerce         Books
Matrix                               Movies
Me, Myself, and Irene                Movies
ABBA - Greatest Hits                 Music
Ice Age                              Movies
Motorola V60                         Electronics
Aerosmith - Just Push Play           Music
```

Don't worry too much about how the SQL code works from now, but this should help to show how you can still see the same data you listed before, even though it's now stored in two different but related tables.

Enforcing Relationships Using the Foreign Key Constraint

You can enforce the one-to-many relationship by the database using *foreign key constraints*. A column that has a foreign key constraint defined on it is called a *foreign key* in that table. The foreign key is a column or combination of columns used to establish or enforce a link between data in two tables.

TIP *The foreign key constraint is always defined for a column in the* referencing table, *and it references the primary key of the* referenced table.

Remember, the referenc*ing* table is the one at the *many* side of the relationship, and the referenc*ed* table is the one at the *one* side of the relationship. In the products/departments scenario, the foreign key is defined on the DepartmentID column of the Product table, and it references the DepartmentID column of the Department table.

You need to enforce table relationships in order to maintain the database in a consistent state. Without enforcing table relationships using foreign keys, you could end up deleting rows that are being referenced from other tables or referencing nonexistent rows, thus resulting in orphaned records. This is something you need to avoid (for example, you don't want rows in the `Product` table referencing nonexistent departments).

Unlike the constraints you learned about in the first part of the chapter, which apply to the table as an independent database object, the foreign key constraint applies restrictions on both referencing and referenced tables. When establishing a one-to-many relationship between the `Department` and the `Product` tables by using a foreign key constraint, the database will include this relationship as part of its integrity. It won't allow you to add a category to a nonexistent department, and it won't allow you to delete a department if there are categories that belong to it.

The Many-to-Many Relationship

A many-to-many relationship happens when records in both tables of the relationship can have multiple matching records in the other table. While studying the many-to-many relationship, you'll see that depending on how the records in your data tables are related, you may need to implement the database structures to support the relationships differently.

With the one-to-many relationship, one department could contain many products (*one* department/*many* products). With the many-to-many relationship, the opposite is also true: One product can belong to more departments (*one* product/*many* departments).

You'd need this kind of relationship for the scenario if you want to support adding products that can be part of more than one department, such as a product named *Selection of Christmas Games and Music*. This product should be found in both the Games and Music departments. So how do you implement this into the database?

TIP *Although logically the many-to-many relationship happens between two data tables, in practice you need to add a third table to the mix. This third table, named a* junction *table (also known as a* linking *table, associate* table, *or* bridge *table), associates records in the two tables you need to relate by implementing two one-to-many relationships, resulting in the many-to-many relationship.*

The theory might sound a bit complicated, but actually it's quite simple. In Figure 1-9, you can see how the junction table associates the departments and products.

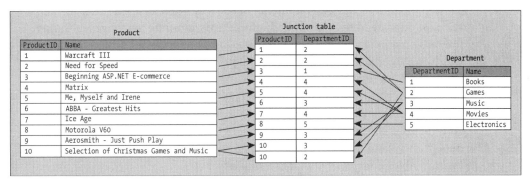

Figure 1-9. A many-to-many relationship

This figure shows how the junction table can be used to link products to departments. You can easily see that each department is linked to more products and that the newly added product is also linked to two departments. So, the magic has been done: The junction table successfully allowed you to implement the many-to-many relationship.

Figure 1-10 presents the new database diagram containing the ProductDepartment junction table.

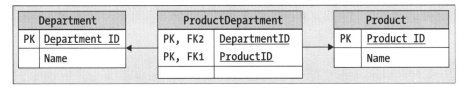

Figure 1-10. A full representation of a many-to-many relationship

Because the many-to-many relationship is implemented as two one-to-many relationships, the foreign key constraint is all you need to enforce it. The junction table is the referencing table, and it references the two tables that form the many-to-many relationship.

In the junction table, both columns form the primary key, so each (ProductID, DepartmentID) pair is guaranteed to be unique. This makes sense because the junction table associates one product with one department— a product can either be or not be associated with a particular department. It wouldn't make sense to associate a product with a department twice.

The Power of SQL

You've covered a fair bit of ground in this chapter, so let's try to round things up by discussing what all this means for the SQL programmer. Mostly, it's good news. As you've seen, SQL statements (including queries) are written in plain text and don't need to be compiled, unlike programming languages (although they'll be parsed in the database to make sure the syntax is correct). The keywords in SQL make it possible for SQL statements to read almost like English, which makes it relatively easy to quickly understand a SQL statement you haven't seen before—when you've grasped the basic syntax.

The fact that you're able to establish sophisticated relationships between your tables means that you can write a single SQL query that extracts and uses data from several tables. You can pull together all of the data you need from the various tables and present it all in a single "report."

In the examples used in this book (based on an InstantUniversity database), you'll see many examples of one-to-many and many-to-many relationships between the tables, and you'll look at example SQL code to extract related data from these and other tables throughout the book. In fact, Chapter 14, "Case Study: Building a Product Catalog," describes a complete product catalog case study. You'll create basic data structures to hold information about products and about their categories and departments, and you'll also see other techniques to gather reports containing related data from your tables.

If you find yourself using the DDL portion of SQL, then, again, you'll find that the syntax is easy to grasp. For example, the following code creates a simple Course table:

```
CREATE TABLE Course (
    CourseID INT NOT NULL PRIMARY KEY,
    Name     VARCHAR(50),
    Credits  INT);
```

As you can see, you've created three columns: CourseID, Name, and Credits. You've specified that CourseID will hold integer data types and is a PRIMARY KEY column, so each value in this column must be unique. You've specified that the Name column (the name of the course) will hold character data of varying length but with a maximum for 50 characters. Finally, you've specified that the Credits column will hold integer data types.

Of course, if you're charged with making the decisions as to how to actually store the data, what tables must be created, how they're related, what data types to use, and so on, then a lot of careful thought needs to go into this before you start executing the SQL. Your choices can dramatically impact the integrity of your data and the performance of the applications that rely on your data.

If you're responsible for controlling access to the data in your database, then you need to have a good understanding of the DCL portion of the language. We haven't covered the SQL statements that fall in this category in this chapter, but you can learn about them in Chapter 11, "Users and Security," and then see them in action in Chapter 15, "Case Study: Implementing Role-Based Security."

Getting Started

Okay, before you really get your hands dirty with SQL, you need to ensure that you're ready to start entering SQL statements and that you have a sample database from which to work. To this end, we've included two appendixes in this book that you'll find useful for these tasks:

- **Appendix A, "Executing SQL Statements"**: This appendix describes how to get each of the RDBMS platforms used in this book (SQL Server, DB2, Oracle, MySQL, and Access) up and running and ready to execute SQL statements.

- **Appendix B, "Setting Up the InstantUniversity Database"**: This appendix describes the sample application you'll use throughout the book, the InstantUniversity database. This appendix describes how to create the database structure and populate it with data.

You can download the sample code for each database platform from the Downloads section of the Apress Web site (`http://www.apress.com`).

A Note on SQL Scripts and Comments

In Appendix B, "Setting Up the InstantUniversity Database," you'll see the basic code you need to create and populate the database tables. However, these processes are RDBMS specific in many cases, so what we've done in the code download is provide separate *scripts* for each database.

A script is simply a document (say, a Notepad document, usually with a `.sql` identifier) that gathers all of the necessary SQL statements required to perform a certain action. Therefore, you'll have all the SQL statements you need for each platform, gathered into separate scripts.

A useful technique when coding SQL in general, and especially when putting together scripts containing lots of SQL statements, is to clearly *comment* your SQL code so that the intent of the code is apparent. A comment is simply some text entered by the creator of the script that doesn't get interpreted as a SQL statement; in fact, RDBMSs ignore comments when processing the SQL statements. As with programming languages, different SQL dialects use different comment syntax; that is, they use different character strings to denote that a block of text is a comment and shouldn't be interpreted as a SQL statement. You'll meet these from time to time as you work through the book, so you'll quickly see how to structure them here.

All RDMBSs, except for Access, use a double dash (--) to indicate a comment:

```
-- This is a comment in RDBMSs other than Access
```

Note, however, that comments marked with -- must be followed by a space to avoid any possible confusion.

In Microsoft Access, you use a single quote (') at the start of a line of text, and everything else on that line is ignored:

```
' This is a comment in Access
```

Some RDBMSs also use other syntaxes; for example, SQL Server allows you to use C++ style /* and */ delimiters, which enable you to write comments that span several lines. Everything between these delimiters is ignored, for example:

```
/*
   This is a comment in SQL Server...

   ...it can span multiple lines!
*/
```

Finally, it's worth noting that older versions of MySQL only support # to mark a line as being a comment. Although more modern implementations of MySQL also support this syntax, they also implement the -- method.

Summary

This chapter covered the basics that are required to understand SQL. We briefly discussed how SQL works and its evolution as a global standard for database access.

The chapter then moved on to look at exactly what's meant by the term *database,* as well as several concepts that together relate to the way data is stored. You saw that databases consist of tables that contain rows of data, where each row contains a single data entry that's made up of entries in several columns. You also saw that a row in a table must have a unique primary key value in order to differentiate it from other rows in the same table.

You then learned how you can relate tables together in a relational database and the types of relationships that can exist between tables.

Finally, you had your first look at the basics of SQL, including comment syntax.

For the rest of this book, you'll look at how to use the SQL introduced in this chapter, and you'll use the terms defined in this chapter continuously. Trust us— give it a few more chapters, and these terms will be indelibly etched in your mind (if they aren't already), so there's no danger of forgetting any of them!

CHAPTER 2

Retrieving Data with SQL

IN THIS CHAPTER, YOU'LL get started with SQL by examining how you can use SQL statements to query a relational database and extract data from it. Here, you'll be querying just one table in a database, but later on in the book (in Chapter 6, "Combining SQL Queries"), you'll see how to query data from multiple tables.

The most important SQL keyword used in querying is SELECT. This chapter introduces the basic syntax for a SQL SELECT query and demonstrates the process with some simple code examples. You'll see how to limit your queries to specific columns in a table, how to create column aliases and calculated columns, and how to sort the data returned by your query by applying an ORDER BY clause to the appropriate column.

We'll then move on to discuss how to *filter* your data—that is, to select or to filter out just the specific rows of data that you're interested in rather than returning every record. You can achieve this by placing various restrictions on the SQL query in a WHERE clause.

To run the code examples in this and every other chapter, you'll need to install one of the five Relational Database Management Systems (RDBMSs) covered in this book and create the InstantUniversity database, all of which is described in Appendix A, "Executing SQL Statements."

Understanding Simple Retrieval

To extract data from a database using SQL, you use a SELECT statement. All SELECT statements start in the same way, using the SELECT keyword. The rest of the statement varies but generally includes the names of the columns in which you're interested and the name of the table from which you want to extract data. The following sections focus on how to retrieve data for every row of every column of a table and how to limit your queries to a specific column (or columns).

Returning All Columns

On the rare occasion that you need to obtain all data from all columns in the table, you can achieve it using the following syntax:

```
SELECT * FROM Table;
```

Here, SELECT and FROM are SQL keywords, * is a wildcard that means "all columns," and *Table* is the name of the table that contains the data you want.

 CAUTION   *Some RDBMSs will add a semicolon to the end of your SQL automatically if you don't include it. In some cases, if you're executing SQL statements from an application through a data-access technology such as ActiveX Data Objects (ADO) or Open Database Connectivity (ODBC), the driver may add a semicolon automatically so an error would be caused if you add one manually.*

So, to retrieve every row of data from every column of a table called Customers, you could use the following SQL query:

```
SELECT * FROM Customers;
```

This statement would work when executed against any database that contained a table called Customers. It's a good idea to try out some simple SELECT * queries against the InstantUniversity database. For example, try executing the following query:

```
SELECT * FROM Student;
```

You should see results that look something like this:

```
StudentID    Name

-----------  ----------------
1            John Jones
2            Gary Burton
3            Emily Scarlett
4            Bruce Lee
...          ...
```

Notice that the column header given to each column in this result set is simply the name of the column as it exists in the database table. The columns are returned in the order they were created in the database.

It's important to note that although this simple SELECT *... syntax is easy to use, it's rarely the best way to go about things. When you use the * wildcard, you actually end up putting far more of a strain on an RDBMS than using one of the methods examined later in this chapter. This is because the RDBMS must examine the table itself to find out how many columns there are and what they're called. Moreover, you can't predict in what order the columns will be returned. As a general rule of thumb, you should only use the * syntax given here for testing.

Specifying the Target Database

You may have noted that, so far, you haven't specified a particular database to use in these queries. This implies that you're executing your statements against, for example, the Customer table in the database (or schema in the case of Oracle) to which you're directly connected.

SQL Server and Access also allow you to specify the database to find the table in by prefixing the database name followed by two dots to the table name:

```
SELECT * FROM pubs..authors;      -- SQL Server
```

With Access, the database name will be the path and filename of the .mdb file:

```
SELECT * FROM C:\NWind.mdb..Employees;
```

MySQL has similar functionality but uses only one dot instead of two:

```
SELECT * FROM InstantUniversity.Student;
```

In SQL Server, Oracle, and DB2, if you want to access a table in a different schema from the one used to connect to the database, you can prefix the schema name to the table name using the syntax Schema.Table. For example:

```
SELECT * FROM scott.EMP;
SELECT * FROM db2admin.Employee;
```

This will, of course, only work if you're currently connected under a user account that has access rights to this table (for example, if you're connected as a database administrator). Chapter 11, "Users and Security," covers security in more detail.

A Note on Table and Column Naming

Occasionally, because of poor initial data design, you may find that you need to access a table or column that contains spaces. If such a situation occurs, then some RDBMSs require you to enclose the names in either square brackets or quotes. In SQL Server and Access, you use square brackets; in Oracle and DB2 (and in MySQL running in ANSI mode), you use double quotes. For example:

```
SELECT * FROM [Valued Customers]; -- SQL Server or Access
```

Or, for example:

```
SELECT * FROM "Valued Customers"; -- DB2 or Oracle
```

Be aware, though, that using the double-quote syntax of Oracle and DB2 means that the table or column name will be treated as case sensitive. Therefore, the following query:

```
SELECT * FROM "Valued Customers";
```

is a different query from this:

```
SELECT * FROM "valued customers";
```

You may also need to use the double-quote or square-bracket syntax if a table or column name is identical to a SQL keyword or a word that your database vendor has "reserved." Again, this is bad design and should be avoided whenever possible, but you may be caught out by future expansions to SQL or by expansions in your database vendor's list of reserved words.

 NOTE *Reserved words have special meaning to the database and can't be redefined. Therefore, they can't be used to name database objects. For example, Oracle doesn't permit the name of the pseudo-column* ROWID *to be used as a column or table name.*

Say, for example, that you are accessing a table called Language and then, at a later date, your vendor adds Language to its list of reserved words. You could still use the table in your queries by using the following:

```
SELECT * FROM [Language];    -- SQL Server or Access
```

or using the following:

```
SELECT * FROM "LANGUAGE";    -- DB2 or Oracle
```

Note the use of capital letters for the table name in the second example. If the Language table was created without using the double-quote syntax, both DB2 and Oracle would create it as LANGUAGE, so chances are that the previous query would succeed but that something such as SELECT * FROM "Language"; would fail. Conversely, if the table was created as "Language" (with quotes), attempting to access it using the statement SELECT * FROM "LANGUAGE"; would fail.

Returning a Single Column

With a simple modification to the SELECT * query used previously, you can obtain all the values from a single-named column. The syntax is as follows:

```
SELECT Column FROM Table;
```

Here, Column is the name of the column you're interested in from Table. You can write this column name in several different ways. The simplest is to include just the name as follows:

```
SELECT CustomerName FROM Customers;
```

To see this working in practice, try executing the following command against the InstantUniversity database:

```
SELECT Name FROM Professor;
```

The results are as follows:

```
Name

----------------

Prof. Dawson
Prof. Williams
Prof. Ashby
Prof. Patel
Prof. Jones
Prof. Hwa
```

You can also enclose the column name within delimiters. The same arguments apply to the use of square-bracket or double-quote delimiters with column names that apply to table names:

```
SELECT [Language] FROM Countries; -- SQL Server or Access
SELECT "LANGUAGE" FROM Countries; -- Oracle or DB2
```

Sometimes it's useful to include information as to what table the column can be found in, as follows:

```
SELECT Customers.CustomerName FROM Customers;
```

Although this is a bit pointless in this example because only the Customers table is being queried, it can be invaluable in more complex scenarios. In later chapters, you'll see how you can extract data from multiple tables simultaneously, and in this case the syntax shown previously serves two purposes. First, it makes it easier for you to see at a glance what information comes from which table. Second, it allows you to differentiate between columns in different tables that have the same name.

Returning Multiple Columns

Getting data from more than one column is just as easy. Rather than specifying simply a column name, you specify multiple column names separated by commas:

```
SELECT ColumnA, ColumnB, ColumnC FROM Table
```

Here *ColumnA*, *ColumnB*, and *ColumnC* are the names of three columns you want from *Table*.

For example, the following query gets the ID for each student and the ID and comments for each exam they took from the InstantUniversity database:

```
SELECT StudentID, ExamID, Comments FROM StudentExam;
```

The first four records in the result set are as follows:

```
StudentID   ExamID    Comments

---------   --------  -------------------------------------------
1           1         Satisfactory
1           2         Good result
2           3         Scraped through
2           5         Failed, and will need to retake this one
                      later...
...         ...       ...
```

Note that the columns are returned in the order you specify them—although in practice this may not be an issue because when you manipulate data such as this in your own application code, you can ignore such structure and impose your own.

Using Aliases

You've now seen how to select specific columns from a table and how to control the order in which those columns are retrieved. In addition, you can supply *aliases* for columns or tables. In other words, you can refer to columns in your returned data set by your own names, not the ones that exist in the database.

This can be useful in making your SELECT statements and the data they return easier to read and understand and in getting data into a form that's more appropriate for your application. In particular, where multiple tables have columns with identical names, you might provide aliases to make it easier for you to differentiate between them.

To do this, you use the AS keyword to provide an alias for a name:

```
SELECT ColumnA AS A, ColumnB AS B, ColumnC AS C
FROM Table AS T;
```

Here you're providing aliases for every name used: *A* is used for *ColumnA*, *B* for *ColumnB*, and so on. These aliases will appear in the results returned by the query. This is another useful technique for combating situations where you have multiple columns with the same name because you can provide an easily identifiable alternative.

When you provide an alias for a table name, you can use that alias within the same SQL statement, for example:

```
SELECT T.ColumnA AS A, T.ColumnB AS B, T.ColumnC AS C
FROM Table AS T;
```

Where there are more complicated queries from multiple tables with lengthy names, this can make SQL queries a lot more readable and take up much less space!

The ANSI specification for SQL-99 allows you to omit this AS keyword:

```
SELECT T.ColumnA A, T.ColumnB B, T.ColumnC C
FROM Table T;
```

This format is supported by most database systems (although not by Access) and in fact is the only format supported by older versions of Oracle. However, the current versions of all the RDBMSs used to test the code in the book support AS, so you'll use this syntax throughout. It also makes for clearer, more readable SQL.

TIP *SQL Server also allows the use of the = operator instead of AS, with the positions of the alias and column reversed. For example, it allows NewColumnName = ExistingColumn.*

As before, you can see how this works in practice by executing the following SQL query against the InstantUniversity database:

```
SELECT Name AS StudentName, StudentID AS ID FROM Student;
```

This query should produce the following results (only the first four records are shown):

```
StudentName      ID

---------------- ----
John Jones       1
Gary Burton      2
Emily Scarlett   3
Bruce Lee        4
...              ...
```

In the database, these two columns are called Name and StudentID. In the result set, you have given them the aliases StudentName and ID, respectively.

Returning Calculated Columns

It's also possible to execute SELECT queries that return *calculated columns*. Retrieving calculated columns means getting data that doesn't necessarily exist in the database but can be constructed or calculated from data that's there. You might, for example, combine the FirstName and LastName columns in a database to a single Name column, built from the content of the two original columns.

To do this, you simply specify the new column name in the usual way but equate it to the result of some processing or other:

```
SELECT Details AS CustomColumn FROM Table;
```

Here you create a column called *CustomColumn* based on the information specified in *Details*, which can include all sorts of mathematical and string operations, as well as calling on certain built-in functions for data processing.

NOTE *You'll be looking at performing calculations and using built-in SQL functions in more detail in Chapter 5, "Performing Calculations and Using Functions."*

Performing Mathematics

For example, you could perform an automatic calculation as follows:

```
SELECT ItemName, Amount, Amount * ItemCost AS TotalCost
FROM Items;
```

Here you create a new column called `TotalCost`, which is the product of the values from two other columns, `Amount` and `ItemCost`, taken from the `Items` table.

As another example, let's return to the `InstantUniversity` database. Consider the following SQL query that combines data from the `Mark` and `IfPassed` columns to give either the actual mark if the exam is passed or zero if not. You place this data in a custom `MarkIfPassed` calculated column:

```
SELECT StudentID, ExamID, Mark * IfPassed AS MarkIfPassed FROM StudentExam;
```

The results from this query are as follows:

StudentID	ExamID	MarkIfPassed
1	1	55
1	2	73
2	3	44
2	5	0
2	6	63
...	...	...

As you can see, the data returned in the result set looks different from that in the original table. Through your result set, you have access to a column of data, `MarkIfPassed`, that doesn't actually exist in the database.

Concatenating String Values

For example, you could perform an automatic calculation as follows:

```
SELECT ItemName, Amount, Amount * ItemCost AS TotalCost
FROM Items;
```

Here you create a new column called TotalCost, which is the product of the values from two other columns, Amount and ItemCost, taken from the Items table.

As another example, let's return to the InstantUniversity database. Consider the following SQL query that combines data from the Mark and IfPassed columns to give either the actual mark if the exam is passed or zero if not. You place this data in a custom MarkIfPassed calculated column:

```
SELECT StudentID, ExamID, Mark * IfPassed AS MarkIfPassed FROM StudentExam;
```

The results from this query are as follows:

StudentID	ExamID	MarkIfPassed
1	1	55
1	2	73
2	3	44
2	5	0
2	6	63
...	...	...

As you can see, the data returned in the result set looks different from that in the original table. Through your result set, you have access to a column of data, MarkIfPassed, that doesn't actually exist in the database.

SQL Server

SQL Server uses the plus sign (+) to perform string concatenation:

```
SELECT FirstName + ' ' + LastName AS FullName FROM People;
```

In this example, you create a full name string in a column called FULLNAME by concatenating the strings in the FirstName and LastName columns of People using the + operator. For neatness, you also put a space in the middle, which is achieved by including a literal string value enclosed in ' or " characters.

However, because the + sign is also used for numeric addition, you can't use it for concatenation if any numeric values are involved. For example, this query:

```
SELECT 'Room ' + RoomID AS RoomName
FROM Room;
```

causes the following error:

```
Syntax error converting the varchar value 'Room ' to a column of data type int.
```

The easiest way around this is to convert the numeric value to a string explicitly using SQL Server's STR() function:

```
SELECT 'Room ' + STR(RoomID) AS RoomName
FROM Room;
```

EXAMPLE: JOINING STRINGS (SQL SERVER)

Enter this query into Query Analyzer and execute it against the InstantUniversity database:

```
SELECT ClassID,
       Time + ', Room ' + STR(RoomID) AS ClassDetails
FROM Class;
```

Here you retrieve the ID for each row in the Class table, together with a new column called ClassDetails, which you create by concatenating the Time field with the string literal ', Room ', followed by the ID for the room where that class is held. Because `RoomID` is an integer field, you need to convert the value to a string before you can use it in a concatenation. The output from this query is as follows:

```
ClassID  ClassDetails

-------- -----------------------------------------
1        Mon 09:00-11:00, Room 6
2        Mon 11:00-12:00, Thu 09:00-11:00, Room 5
3        Mon 14:00-16:00, Room 3
4        Tue 10:00-12:00, Thu 14:00-15:00, Room 2
...      ...
```

MySQL

When run in the default (that is, not ANSI) mode, MySQL also uses + as the concatenation operator:

```
SELECT FirstName + ' ' + LastName AS FullName FROM People;
```

Naturally, using + has the same drawback as in SQL Server—you'll get unpredictable results if any numeric values are involved. MySQL automatically converts numeric values to strings (and vice versa) as necessary, so it doesn't have any direct equivalent to SQL Server's `STR()` function. You therefore need a different solution to this problem.

 NOTE *When run in ANSI mode, MySQL uses the same string concatenation operator as Oracle (||).*

The answer comes in the form of the `CONCAT()` function. This function takes a variable number of arguments and joins them to form a single string. The arguments will automatically be converted to strings, so you can pass in arguments of any data type.

NOTE *This feature allows you to use this function to simulate the SQL Server* STR() *function—you can concatenate an empty string to the value you want to convert (say, a number), and that value will be returned as a string.*

So, to join the string literal 'Room ' and the RoomID into a single value, you'd use this statement:

```
SELECT CONCAT('Room ', RoomID) AS RoomName
FROM Room;
```

You'll look at using SQL functions in more detail in Chapter 5, "Performing Calculations and Using Functions."

EXAMPLE: JOINING STRINGS (MYSQL)

Execute this query against the InstantUniversity database:

```
SELECT ClassID,
       CONCAT(Time, ', Room ', RoomID) AS ClassDetails
FROM Class;
```

Again, you retrieve the ID for each class, together with the calculated ClassDetails that represents the details of where and when the class is held. Again, because RoomID is an integer field, you need to use the CONCAT() function rather than the + operator to perform the concatenation. The output from this query is as follows:

```
ClassID  ClassDetails

-------- -------------------------------------------
1        Mon 09:00-11:00, Room 6
2        Mon 11:00-12:00, Thu 09:00-11:00, Room 5
3        Mon 14:00-16:00, Room 3
4        Tue 10:00-12:00, Thu 14:00-15:00, Room 2
...      ...
```

Oracle

Oracle uses the ANSI standard concatenation operator, ||. Because this operator is reserved for string concatenation, the operands don't need to be cast to a string type—they'll be converted automatically:

```
SELECT FirstName || ' ' || LastName AS FullName FROM People;
```

This operator is also used for MySQL when it's running in ANSI mode.

EXAMPLE: JOINING STRINGS (ORACLE)

Execute this query against the InstantUniversity database:

```
SELECT ClassID,
       Time || ', Room ' || RoomID AS ClassDetails
FROM Class;
```

This query returns the ClassID for each class, together with a calculated column containing the time and room number details for each class:

```
ClassID   ClassDetails

--------  -----------------------------------------
1         Mon 09:00-11:00, Room 6
2         Mon 11:00-12:00, Thu 09:00-11:00, Room 5
3         Mon 14:00-16:00, Room 3
4         Tue 10:00-12:00, Thu 14:00-15:00, Room 2
...       ...
```

DB2

DB2 can use either the ANSI standard || operator or the CONCAT keyword to perform string concatenation:

```
SELECT FirstName || ' ' || LastName AS FullName
FROM People;
```

or:

```
SELECT FirstName CONCAT ' ' CONCAT LastName AS FullName
FROM People;
```

Whichever of these you use, you'll need to convert any numeric data types to strings before performing the concatenation. You can achieve this using the CHAR() function:

```
SELECT 'Room ' CONCAT CHAR(RoomID) AS RoomName FROM Room;
```

You can also use CONCAT() as a standard function. It takes two parameters, which both must be string types:

```
SELECT CONCAT('Room ', CHAR(RoomID)) AS RoomName FROM Room;
```

EXAMPLE: JOINING STRINGS (DB2)

Execute this query against the InstantUniversity database:

```
SELECT ClassID,
       Time CONCAT ', Room ' CONCAT CHAR(RoomID)
          AS ClassDetails
FROM Class;
```

Here you use the CONCAT keyword like an operator to join three values into a single string. If you had used CONCAT() as a function, you would have to nest one call to CONCAT() within another because this function takes two arguments:

```
SELECT ClassID,
       CONCAT(
          CONCAT(Time, ', Room '), CHAR(RoomID)
       ) AS ClassDetails
FROM Class;
```

The output from this query is as follows:

```
ClassID  ClassDetails

-------- -----------------------------------------
1        Mon 09:00-11:00, Room 6
2        Mon 11:00-12:00, Thu 09:00-11:00, Room 5
3        Mon 14:00-16:00, Room 3
4        Tue 10:00-12:00, Thu 14:00-15:00, Room 2
...      ...
```

Access

Finally, Access uses the ampersand (&) to perform concatenation. As with || in Oracle, this operator is used only to join strings, so you don't need to convert the operands to a string type before using it.

EXAMPLE: JOINING STRINGS (ACCESS)

Execute this query against the InstantUniversity database:

```
SELECT ClassID, Time & ', Room ' & RoomID AS ClassDetails
FROM Class;
```

Again, you join the Time and RoomID columns, separated by the literal string ', Room ', into a single column named ClassDetails:

```
ClassID  ClassDetails

-------- -----------------------------------------
1        Mon 09:00-11:00, Room 6
2        Mon 11:00-12:00, Thu 09:00-11:00, Room 5
3        Mon 14:00-16:00, Room 3
4        Tue 10:00-12:00, Thu 14:00-15:00, Room 2
...      ...
```

Sorting Data

By default, rows are stored in the database in an arbitrary order. Using SQL, you can apply a definite order to the set of rows returned by your query. For example, you can get a set of rows that's sorted in reverse alphabetical order. Obviously, a row in its entirety doesn't have an obvious value to sort by, so instead you need to specify a column for sorting.

The syntax is as follows:

```
SELECT ColumnA, ColumnB, ColumnC FROM Table
ORDER BY ColumnA;
```

Here, the ORDER BY clause is used to specify that ColumnA should be used to sort the data. The values in this column are examined according to their type, which might be alphabetic, numeric, timestamp, or whatever, and sorted accordingly.

The default behavior is to sort rows into an ascending order, so if the column to be sorted by is alphabetic, then rows will be returned sorted from A to Z according to the selected column. The previous query is shorthand for the following:

```
SELECT ColumnA, ColumnB, ColumnC FROM Table
ORDER BY ColumnA ASC;
```

Although this is the default behavior so you don't need to explicitly specify the ASC keyword, it's a good idea to include it to ensure that your queries are as easy to read as possible.

Alternatively, you may want to sort your rows in descending order, in which case you use the DESC keyword:

```
SELECT ColumnA, ColumnB, ColumnC FROM Table
ORDER BY ColumnA DESC;
```

For example, if you obtained a list of products from a Products table, you might want to order them according to their names:

```
SELECT ProductID, ProductName, AmountInStock FROM Products
ORDER BY ProductName ASC;
```

The following example shows a query on the InstantUniversity database, which orders the results alphabetically in reverse order:

```
SELECT Name, ProfessorID FROM Professor ORDER BY Name DESC;
```

Here are the results of the query:

```
Name              ProfessorID

---------------   -----------
Prof. Williams    2
Prof. Patel       4
Prof. Jones       5
Prof. Hwa         6
Prof. Dawson      1
Prof. Ashby       3
```

Filtering Data

So far, all the queries you've seen have returned data from *all* the rows in a table. However, there are times when this isn't desirable. Often you'll want to extract only a subset of the rows in a table, or even a single row, based on specific criteria. SQL includes a whole host of tools to enable this kind of query, and in the following sections you'll examine them.

First, you'll look at how you can filter out any duplicate rows in your result set. Next, you'll look at how to extract certain rows based on simple conditions and how to combine these conditions for a powerful search facility. You'll move on to see how more advanced conditions and comparisons can give you even greater control over the rows returned, even in situations where you need to be vague in the conditions you set (that is, finding records based on small hints). Finally, you'll examine a topic that will come up time and time again: dealing with NULL data (where no value has been entered for that field).

Eliminating Duplicate Data Using DISTINCT

You'll often encounter situations where the same data value occurs multiple times in the same column, whether by design or accident. Sometimes, you may want to ensure that you retrieve only unique rows of data from a query prior to processing. For example, from a Customers table during a purchase, you wouldn't want to charge a customer twice for a single order!

To filter out duplicate rows of data, you use the DISTINCT keyword. Let's start with the simplest case, where you're returning rows from a single column.

If you only want to see unique row values for this column, the query would look as follows:

```
SELECT DISTINCT ColumnA FROM Table;
```

This can often be very useful. For example, single columns in a database may have a restricted set of values allowed. To find out all the different values in a column, you don't really want to have to read through every row in the table just to find the values that exist. To demonstrate this clearly, say that you wanted to query the Exam table in the InstantUniversity database to get a list of all the dates on which exams have been taken. You might try the following:

```
SELECT SustainedOn from Exam;
```

The result would look as follows:

```
SustainedOn

---------
3/12/2003
3/13/2003
3/11/2003
3/18/2003
3/19/2003
3/25/2003
3/26/2003
3/10/2003
3/21/2003
3/26/2003
3/24/2003
```

This is actually quite a simple case because there are only 11 rows and only one duplicate value, 3/26/2003, but in any event it's much more convenient to issue the following query:

```
SELECT DISTINCT SustainedOn FROM Exam;
```

The results are as follows:

```
SustainedOn
------------
3/10/2003
3/11/2003
3/12/2003
3/13/2003
3/18/2003
3/19/2003
3/21/2003
3/24/2003
3/25/2003
3/26/2003
```

This time the duplicate value has been removed and you have a simple list of unique exam dates—and as an added bonus you'll see that the dates have been automatically sorted into ascending order.

Let's move on to the case where you want to retrieve multiple columns. When you do this, you can guarantee that every row you obtain contains unique data for the specified set of columns with the following query:

```
SELECT DISTINCT ColumnA, ColumnB FROM Table;
```

For example, the following query will return only unique combinations of customer names and credit card details:

```
SELECT DISTINCT CustomerName, CreditCard FROM Customers;
```

Note that this doesn't mean you won't have duplicates in either column, only that each combination is unique. You could, for example, have several customers with the same name but with different credit card numbers. To illustrate this point, suppose you changed the query on InstantUniversity as follows:

```
SELECT DISTINCT ExamID, SustainedOn FROM Exam;
```

You would obtain the full 11 rows from the database. This is because there are 11 different combinations of these two fields, even though there's a duplicate in the SustainedOn column. Always remember that DISTINCT acts on the *combination* of columns you use in the query.

Using WHERE Conditions

The WHERE clause allows you to filter queries by demanding that the rows in your result set satisfy a particular condition:

```
SELECT ColumnA, ColumnB FROM Table
WHERE Condition;
```

Condition is very flexible, allowing you to test for equalities and inequalities in column data, ranges of values to look for, and much more. You achieve all this using a simple syntax that includes various operators and keywords that, when combined, allow you to search for pretty much anything.

Before you get to the more complex usages of this clause, though, you'll look at the simplest: equalities. These are particularly useful because they allow you to constrain the rows you obtain from queries in the tightest way. The syntax is as follows:

```
SELECT ColumnA, ColumnB FROM Table
WHERE ColumnC = Value;
```

The WHERE clause lets you apply a search condition to the rows of data gathered by your SELECT query. The search condition can take various forms, all of which can be evaluated to a Boolean value. In this case, you're only interested in rows for which the condition ColumnC = Value evaluates to TRUE; in other words, you're interested in those rows in which ColumnC has a value of Value. If this condition is TRUE, then the row is returned. If it evaluates to FALSE or UNKNOWN (because the presence of a NULL value), then it's ignored.

Note that there's no need for a WHERE clause of this type to use a column that's being returned by the query (here only ColumnA and ColumnB are returned for rows). However, in practice, because you know what's contained in ColumnC, there's no need to extract this data from the database.

For example, you might extract a single row from a Customers table based on the ID of the customer (assuming that customer IDs are unique):

```
SELECT FirstName, LastName, Address FROM Customers
WHERE CustomerID = 7;
```

Alternatively, you could extract all the customers with a certain last name:

```
SELECT FirstName, LastName, Address FROM Customers
WHERE LastName = 'Smith';
```

Of course, in many countries, searching for people called Smith in this way could land you with an awful lot of results!

You don't have to use literals in these comparisons. You could, for example, use equalities between columns:

```
SELECT FirstName, LastName, Address FROM Customers
WHERE LastName = FirstName;
```

Here all customers with identical first and last names will be found. For example, Major Major would be there.

Suppose you wanted to query the InstantUniversity database to find the name of the student whose ID is 3:

```
SELECT Name FROM Student
WHERE StudentID = 3;
```

This will yield you the following result:

```
Name

----------------
Emily Scarlett
```

This sort of query is extremely useful when you know the ID of a record and want to get other pertinent data about that record. Rather than extract a lot of potentially useless data in a single query, you can use this technique to home in on the data you actually want.

Using Other WHERE Clause Comparisons

As mentioned earlier, equalities are just one of the many things you can test for in a WHERE clause. You can use several other operators, which vary by RDBMS, as described in Table 2-1.

Table 2-1. Comparison Operators

Operator	RDBMSs	Meaning
=	All	Used to check if values are equal to one another
!=	All except Access	Used to check if values aren't equal to one another
^=	Oracle	Same meaning as !=
<>	All	Same meaning as !=
>	All	True if the first operand is greater than the second operand
>=	All	Used to check if the first operand is greater than or equal to the second
!<	SQL Server, DB2	Same as >= (Means "not less than," which is logically equivalent to "greater than or equal to")
<	All	True if the first operand is less than the second operand
<=	All	Used to check if the first operand is less than or equal to the second
!>	SQL Server, DB2	Same as <=

As you can see, there's some redundancy here, with the possibility of a choice of operator to use in some situations. The main reason for this is so you can use the operator that fits in best with your development experience—you're likely to have similar operators available in whatever programming language you're used to using.

An example SQL query that you could run on the `InstantUniversity` database is as follows:

```
SELECT ExamID, SustainedOn, Comments FROM Exam
WHERE SustainedOn > '2003-03-20';
```

In this example, you extract data from the `Exam` table, only getting data for exams that occur after March 20, 2003. The results from this query are as follows:

```
ExamID  SustainedOn  Comments

------  -----------  ----------------------------
6       3/25/2003
7       3/26/2003    They'll enjoy this one
9       3/21/2003    Two hours long. They might find it tricky
10      3/26/2003    2hr test
11      3/24/2003    Part two should be an hour and a half long
```

It's worth noting here that it's the RDBMS that's responsible for interpreting a date or time format string, and the specific string you need to use will depend on factors such as what the RDBMS can interpret and your operating system's locale settings. However, the format YYYY-MM-DD as used in this query works on all platforms. See Chapter 5, "Performing Calculations and Using Functions," for more details on working with date values.

Access expects dates to be enclosed, Visual Basic–style, within pound characters (#), so this query won't work with Access. Instead, you need to use the following:

```
SELECT ExamID, SustainedOn, Comments FROM Exam
WHERE SustainedOn > #2003-03-20#;
```

Combining WHERE Conditions

Often a single WHERE clause isn't enough to narrow down the data you require. You might want to get only those rows with specified data in one column *and* other specified data in another column. Alternatively, you might require rows that have certain data in one column *or* certain data in another column. Here you need to combine multiple WHERE clauses as follows:

```
SELECT ColumnA, ColumnB FROM Table
WHERE Condition LINK Condition;
```

Note that *LINK* in the previous query isn't a keyword. Instead, it refers to one of the keywords shown in Table 2-2.

Table 2-2. Basic Operators

Link Keyword	Meaning
AND	Both conditions must be met for the records found.
OR	Either condition must be met for the records found.

For example, suppose you wanted to specify particular conditions on the Occupation and FiscalStatus fields when querying the Customers table. You could ask that both of your conditions be met as follows:

```
SELECT CustomerID, CustomerName FROM Customers
WHERE Occupation = 'Carpenter' AND FiscalStatus = 'Loaded';
```

Alternatively, you could select rows where either one of the two conditions is met or both are met:

```
SELECT CustomerID, CustomerName FROM Customers
WHERE Occupation = 'Carpenter' OR FiscalStatus = 'Loaded';
```

Additionally, the NOT keyword can be applied to a condition, making the condition evaluate to true when it isn't met rather than when it is:

```
SELECT CustomerID, CustomerName FROM Customers
WHERE Occupation = 'Carpenter'
  AND NOT FiscalStatus = 'Bankrupt';
```

The following SQL statement queries the InstantUniversity database to select only those records from the StudentExam table where the ExamID field is equal to 1 and the IfPassed field is also 1:

```
SELECT StudentID, Mark, Comments FROM StudentExam
WHERE ExamID = 1 AND IfPassed = 1;
```

Here are the results:

```
StudentID    Mark         Comments

-----------  -----------  ------------------------
1            55           Satisfactory
8            71           Excellent, great work!
```

Performing Range Tests

It's possible to combine two comparison operators to select values that fall within a within a specified range. For example:

```
SELECT ExamID, SustainedOn, Comments FROM Exam
WHERE SustainedOn >= '2003-03-20'
AND SustainedOn <= '2003-03-24';
```

However, it's also possible to use another of the SQL keywords, BETWEEN, to make such range tests more readable:

```
SELECT ColumnA, ColumnB FROM Table
WHERE ColumnC BETWEEN LowerLimit AND UpperLimit;
```

Here the value of *ColumnC* is checked to see if it's greater than or equal to *LowerLimit* and less than or equal to *UpperLimit*. For example:

```
SELECT ExamID, SustainedOn, Comments FROM Exam
WHERE SustainedOn BETWEEN '2003-03-20' AND '2003-03-24';
```

You can also use NOT with BETWEEN to exclude a range:

```
SELECT ExamID, SustainedOn, Comments FROM Exam
WHERE SustainedOn NOT BETWEEN '2003-03-20' AND '2003-03-24';
```

Defining Set Membership

As well as checking to see if values fall inside (or outside) set ranges of values, it's also possible to check to see if values are one of a set number of possibilities.

Again, you can achieve this using operators and keywords that you've already met:

```
SELECT ColumnA, ColumnB FROM Table
WHERE ColumnC = Value1
OR ColumnC = Value2
OR ColumnC = Value3;
```

However, you can achieve this much more elegantly using the IN keyword in your WHERE clause, along with a set of possible values:

```
SELECT ColumnA, ColumnB FROM Table WHERE ColumnC IN (Set);
```

Here *Set* (enclosed in parentheses) is the set of values you're looking for in *ColumnC*. You can define sets in a number of ways. The simplest is probably to provide a set of literal values in the query:

```
SELECT ColumnA, ColumnB FROM Table
WHERE ColumnC IN ('Value1', 'Value2', 'Value3');
```

Alternatively, you can create your set by including by a completely separate SELECT query:

```
SELECT ColumnA, ColumnB FROM Table
WHERE ColumnC IN (SELECT ColumnD FROM Table2);
```

> **NOTE** *This is an example of a* subquery, *a topic you'll look at in more detail in Chapter 6, "Combining SQL Queries."*

As with the other keywords you've seen in this chapter, IN can be combined with NOT to search for values that don't occur in a set:

```
SELECT ColumnA, ColumnB FROM Table
WHERE ColumnC NOT IN ('Value1', 'Value2', 'Value3');
```

EXAMPLE: FINDING RECORDS IN A SET

As a more concrete example, you can try selecting information from the StudentExam table in the InstantUniversity database where the StudentID is one of three values:

```
SELECT StudentID, ExamID, Mark FROM StudentExam
WHERE StudentID IN (2, 7, 3);
```

This query produces the following results:

StudentID	ExamID	Mark
2	3	44
2	5	39
2	6	63
3	4	78
3	7	82
7	6	84
7	8	62
7	11	68

Using Pattern Matching

One of the most powerful ways of filtering rows is to search for text values in column data using patterns. You can, for example, look for rows with text columns that contain a certain word or for more complex patterns of characters. To do this, you use the LIKE keyword (you can also specify NOT LIKE) and supply a pattern to match:

```
SELECT ColumnA, ColumnB FROM Table
WHERE ColumnC LIKE Pattern;
```

Pattern is made up of literal characters plus certain wildcards that represent one or more characters. The wildcards shown in Table 2-3 are supported by all the database systems covered in this book.

Table 2-3. Wildcards

Wildcard	Meaning
%	Any string of characters, including strings of zero length
_	Any one character

 CAUTION *Patterns are case sensitive in Oracle and DB2 but not in SQL Server, MySQL, or Access.*

For example, to search for a string value that contains the text 'manager', you could use the following:

```
SELECT CustomerID, ContactName, ContactTitle FROM Customers
WHERE ContactTitle LIKE '%manager%';
```

You need to be aware of several issues when using patterns. Perhaps most important, you need to be very specific when you use them. Simply including one space too many could break the query, for example:

```
SELECT CustomerID, ContactName, ContactTitle FROM Customers
WHERE ContactTitle LIKE '%manager %';
```

This pattern searches for the string 'manager '—including a trailing space. If any columns contain the string 'manager' at the end of their value, there will be no trailing space, and the record won't be matched.

As another example, this query looks for four characters followed by a space at the start of the Name column in the Student table:

```
SELECT Name FROM Student WHERE Name LIKE '____ %';
```

This returns all the students whose first names are four characters long:

```
Name

-----------
John Jones
Gary Burton
Anna Wolff
```

Another issue to be aware of is that wildcards are reserved characters and must be escaped if you want to include them in a pattern without their wildcard meaning. To do this, you need to include more information when these characters occur in the data you're searching. Let's say you want to look for percentages. The following search isn't good enough:

```
SELECT CustomerName, CustomerRating FROM Customers
WHERE CustomerRating LIKE '%50%%';
```

Here the % character is interpreted as a wildcard as usual, and the match will actually be for the string '50' rather than '50%'. To get round this, you can use an escape character to force the first % of the %% part of the pattern to be interpreted as the character % rather than a string:

```
SELECT CustomerName, CustomerRating FROM Customers
WHERE CustomerRating LIKE '%50<Escape Char>%%';
```

There's no escape character defined in SQL, so instead you need to specify your own using the ESCAPE keyword. You can choose any character you like for this, but you should try to choose one that doesn't occur elsewhere in the string, for example:

```
SELECT CustomerName, CustomerRating FROM Customers
WHERE CustomerRating LIKE '%50p%%' ESCAPE 'p';
```

Here p is used as an escape character and causes the first % character to be interpreted as a character, not as an escape code.

Access doesn't support this syntax, but you can escape the wildcard character by enclosing it in square brackets:

```
SELECT CustomerName, CustomerRating FROM Customers
WHERE CustomerRating LIKE '%50[%]%';
```

SQL Server also supports this syntax.

EXAMPLE: PATTERN MATCHING

Let's look at an example from the InstantUniversity database. Suppose you wanted to search for exam results in the StudentExam table that had been described as "great." You could try something like this:

```
SELECT StudentID, ExamID, Mark, Comments FROM StudentExam
WHERE Comments LIKE '%great%';
```

This works for SQL Server, MySQL, and Access because pattern matching is case insensitive in these systems. However, it will find 'great' but not 'Great' in DB2 and Oracle. To get around this, you need to convert the column to upper case before applying the match. You can do this in both DB2 and Oracle using the UPPER() function:

```
SELECT StudentID, ExamID, Mark, Comments FROM StudentExam
WHERE UPPER(Comments) LIKE '%GREAT%';
```

This query produces the following results:

StudentID	ExamID	Mark	Comments
3	7	82	Great result!
8	1	71	Excellent, great work!

However, this will also match records with a comment such as 'So far from great I'm expelling this student.' Be careful when using patterns because it's easy to forget things such as this, and sometimes the logical process you use to create a pattern will have unexpected results!

Performing Complex Pattern Matching

SQL Server, Access, and MySQL allow a more complex form of pattern matching based more or less closely on regular expressions. In the case of SQL Server and Access, this consists merely of extensions to the standard LIKE syntax, but MySQL uses a completely different keyword (REGEXP or RLIKE) for regular expression pattern matching.

SQL Server and Access

As well as the wildcards % and _, SQL Server and Access patterns can contain characters enclosed in square brackets. A match will be made if the entire pattern matches using any one of these characters. For example, '%[abcde]%' will match any expression that contains any of the letters A, B, C, D, or E anywhere (matches aren't case sensitive).

You can also use a hyphen to indicate a range of values, so you could also write the previous expression as '%[a-e%]'. You can therefore use [a-z] to represent any alphabetic character, [0-9] to match any numeric character, and [a-z0-9] to match any alphanumeric character.

In addition, SQL Server allows you to prefix the sign ^ to a character or range of characters in order to match only characters that aren't in that range; for example, [^a-z0-9] will match nonalphanumeric characters.

EXAMPLE: COMPLEX PATTERN MATCHING (ACCESS AND SQL SERVER)

Execute the following query against the InstantUniversity database:

```
SELECT Name FROM Student
WHERE Name LIKE '% [a-dw-z]%';
```

This query looks for all student names that contain a space, followed by a character in the range A–D or W–Z. The effect (because this sample data contains only students with two names) is to return a list of all the students whose second names start with one of the first four or last four letters of the alphabet:

```
Name

--------------
Gary Burton
Anna Wolff
Vic Andrews
Steve Alaska
Mohammed Akbar
```

MySQL

The basic syntax for MySQL's regular expression matching is similar but provides more options. You can use square brackets to match one of a set of characters or a specific range of characters, as in SQL Server and Access, but there are some important differences. First, MySQL regular expression patterns are case sensitive, so to match all alphabetic characters, you need to use [a-zA-Z] instead of just [a-z]. Second, matches will be found anywhere in the string, regardless of whether anything comes before or after (unless you explicitly say otherwise), so you don't need (and in fact can't use) the % wildcard.

There are also some more character-matching patterns available, as shown in Table 2-4.

Table 2-4. Character-Matching Patterns

Character	Matches
^	The start of the string. For example, '^B' matches the first but not the second B in 'BOB'.
$	The end of the string. For example, 'B$' matches the second but not the first B in 'BOB'.
.	Any single character.
*	The previous character repeated zero or more times. For example, 'Ke*l' matches 'Kl', 'Kel', 'Keel', and so on.
{n}	The previous character repeated *n* times. For example, 'b{3}' matches 'bbb' but not 'bb'.

To use MySQL's regular expression matching, you use the REGEXP (or RLIKE) keyword instead of LIKE:

```
SELECT Name FROM Student WHERE Name REGEXP '^[Aa]';
```

This is equivalent to the following:

```
SELECT Name FROM Student WHERE Name LIKE 'A%';
```

EXAMPLE: REGULAR EXPRESSION MATCHING (MYSQL)

Execute the following query against the InstantUniversity database:

```
SELECT Name FROM Student
WHERE Name REGEXP '^[AM].*r$';
```

This query matches all student names that begin with either 'A' or 'M', followed by any number of characters and ending with the character 'r'. Two names in the sample data match these criteria:

```
Name

--------------
Andrew Foster
Mohammed Akbar
```

Dealing with NULL Data

The final topic you're going to look at in this chapter is how to deal with columns that contain NULL values—that is, columns that don't contain a value at all. This may occur by design but may also be the result of an error, such as a failure to enter the appropriate data into the database.

In general, RDBMSs allow you to specify whether columns allow NULL values, which can make your life easier. If you say that a column can't contain a NULL value, then an attempt to add a row without specifying a value for that column will result in an error. Furthermore, for tables that allow NULL values in one or more columns, then you can't always rely on values being present when you perform SELECT queries. Where NULL values are allowed, you must be prepared to deal with them in your code; otherwise, unpredicted errors could occur.

You can use the NULL SQL keyword to test for NULL values:

```
SELECT ColumnA, ColumnB FROM Table WHERE ColumnC IS NOT NULL;
```

Similarly, you could select only those rows with NULL values:

```
SELECT ColumnA, ColumnB FROM Table WHERE ColumnC IS NULL;
```

Enforcing a non-null condition can be useful. For example, in the Exam table in the InstantUniversity database, the Comments column contains a couple of NULL values. Suppose you wanted to extract a list of only rows with no comments. You could use the following query:

```
SELECT ExamID, CourseID, ProfessorID, SustainedOn FROM Exam WHERE Comments IS NULL;
```

This query produces the following results:

ExamID	CourseID	ProfessorID	SustainedOn
4	4	3	03/18/2003
6	6	3	03/25/2003

Summary

This chapter introduced the basic usage of SQL and examined how to use simple SELECT queries to extract data from tables in a relational database. Specifically, you learned about the following:

- Understanding basic SELECT syntax

- Providing aliases for columns and tables

- Calculating new rows based on existing content

- Sorting data

- Filtering data with the WHERE clause

- Combining multiple WHERE clauses

- Performing advanced WHERE clause filtering, including ranges

- Defining set membership

- Using pattern matching

- Filtering NULL values

In the next chapter you'll look at how you can use SQL to modify data in a database table. You'll see how to update existing data, add new data, and delete specific rows.

CHAPTER 3

Modifying Data

IN THE PREVIOUS CHAPTER, you saw how to extract data from databases using SQL. Now you'll look at another major use of SQL—modifying data in a database.

Data modification falls into three categories:

- Adding new data

- Modifying existing data

- Deleting data

You'll look at each of these subjects in turn.

Introducing SQL Data Modification

SQL modification of data uses three main keywords that correspond to the three categories of modification:

- INSERT: Adds rows to tables

- UPDATE: Modifies the column data in existing rows

- DELETE: Removes rows from tables

As with SELECT, there are plenty of options to look at concerning the use of these keywords in full statements.

Adding New Data

Obviously, SQL wouldn't be much use if all it allowed you to do were to extract data. In order for it to be useful, you need to be able to add data as well, which you do using the INSERT keyword.

Performing a Single Row INSERT

The basic use of INSERT uses the following syntax:

```
INSERT INTO Table (Columns) VALUES (Values);
```

The word INTO is an optional keyword in some Relational Database Management System (RDBMS) implementations, notably SQL Server and MySQL. It is, however, part of the SQL-99 specification and a required keyword for Access, DB2, and Oracle. Including INTO also makes what you're doing a bit more obvious, so we've included it in the SQL statements in this section. The following continues your examination of the syntax:

- *Table* is the table to add values to, and acceptable values for this part of the SQL statement are the same as for SELECT statements examined in the previous chapter.

- *Columns* is a comma-delimited list of the columns in the table into which to insert data. This can be a complete list of the columns in a table, but it doesn't necessarily have to be, depending on the database configuration.

- *Values* is a comma-delimited list of the values to insert into those columns, which must appear in the same order as the columns in *Columns*.

Let's look at a simple example:

```
INSERT INTO LineProducts (ProductName, ProductCost, ItemsInStock)
VALUES ('Plastic Asparagus Tips', 15.99, 10);
```

This example would add a single new row into the LineProducts table. Notice that the literal values to be inserted (one string, one float, and one int) are formatted in various ways. This formatting depends on the data type of the column and the RDBMS being used. In the previous chapter you saw several string literal values enclosed in ' characters, but other values such as integer and floating-point values don't have delimiters.

> **NOTE** *Chapter 5, "Performing Calculations and Using Functions," explores literal values in more depth.*

We discussed earlier that the list of columns provided doesn't necessarily have be a complete list of the columns in a table. For example, the LineProducts table may well contain a primary key column called ProductID, in which case you might expect to see an INSERT statement such as the following:

```
INSERT INTO LineProducts (ProductID, ProductName, ProductCost, ItemsInStock)
VALUES (8, 'Plastic Asparagus Tips', 15.99, 10);
```

However, you can omit ProductID from your INSERT statement if the RDBMS is configured to automatically insert a value into that column whenever a row is added to the table. Such columns are often referred to as *identity* columns. This is often the case for primary key columns because it's much easier and safer to let the RDBMS take responsibility for entering data into such columns (where each value entered into that column must be unique).

 NOTE *The technique you use to instruct your RDBMS to automatically insert values into a primary key column varies from one RDBMS to another. Chapter 12, "Working with Database Objects," discusses these techniques in detail.*

There are other reasons why you might be able to omit columns from your INSERT statements, so let's summarize them now:

- The column value *must* be automatically created by the RDBMS, which is usually the case for primary key columns.

- The column value *may* be automatically created by the RDBMS—that is, where a default column value exists and can be added by the RDBMS when no alternative is supplied.

- The column is set to be a timestamp type, in which case some RDBMSs will insert the current date and time for the column value.

- The column is set to allow NULL values, and none of the previous reasons apply, meaning that the column will simply not have any data in it for the inserted row.

The previous conditions are RDBMS dependent, and some simpler implementations may work slightly differently. For example, there may not be a timestamp data type. For the most part, though, the previous will hold true whichever RDBMS you use.

Let's look at a working example.

EXAMPLE: ADDING A SINGLE ROW TO A TABLE

Say you want to insert a single row into the Professor table of your InstantUniversity database. Table 3-1 shows the Professor table.

Table 3-1. The Professor *Table*

Column Name	Null?	Data Type
PROFESSORID	NOT NULL	NUMBER(38)
NAME	NOT NULL	VARCHAR2(50)

In this case, the ProfessorID column is the primary key column, but you haven't instructed the RDBMS to automatically insert values on this column because, as discussed, the way in which you do this varies from RDBMS to RDBMS and because you want the base database to work on each platform. So, in this case, you have to specify both the ProfessorID and Name columns in the INSERT statement.

Let's see what data is in the table:

```
SELECT ProfessorID, Name from Professor;
```

You'll get the following results:

```
ProfessorID  Name

-----------  ----------------
1            Prof. Dawson
2            Prof. Williams
3            Prof. Ashby
4            Prof. Patel
5            Prof. Jones
6            Prof. Hwa
```

Now that you know which values have already been used in the `ProfessorID` column, you can safely insert your new row:

```
INSERT INTO Professor (ProfessorID, Name)
VALUES (7, 'Snail at work');
```

If you now rerun your previous `SELECT` query, you'll see the following:

```
ProfessorID   Name

-----------   ----------------
1             Prof. Dawson
2             Prof. Williams
3             Prof. Ashby
4             Prof. Patel
5             Prof. Jones
6             Prof. Hwa
7             Snail at work
```

You've added a new row to the `Professor` table in the `InstantUniversity` database.

If the `ProfessorID` column were an identity column, then you would have to omit it in the `INSERT` statement because the RDMBS would be responsible for adding this data automatically. If you did attempt to insert a value into such a column in an RDBMS such as SQL Server that includes such functionality, you'd receive the following error:

Server: Msg 544, Level 16, State 1, Line 1

*Cannot insert explicit value for identity column in table '*ColumnName*' when IDENTITY_INSERT is set to OFF.*

This message implies that this behavior can be overridden, which is true although this book won't be covering how to do things such as this until later. Even then, it's difficult to think of a situation where supplying your own value to an automatically numbered column would be useful. One possible situation could be where data absolutely must have specific values for all columns, but of course then you run the risk of insert failure if duplicate identity values crop up.

> **NOTE**   *Incidentally, the sharp-eyed among you may notice that* `'Snail at work'` *is an anagram, but you'll have to figure it out for yourself.*

Before moving on, it's worth mentioning that it isn't strictly necessary to include *Columns* in your INSERT statements. If you know the names of each column in the table and the exact order in which they were entered into the database, then you can omit the list of columns. For example:

```
INSERT INTO Professors
VALUES (7, 'Snail at work');
```

However, this isn't practical for larger tables and, in any event, it's much clearer and safer to explicitly name the columns in your statements.

Note also that on certain RDBMSs, including SQL Server, you can create a new row based on default values that are defined in the table specification using the DEFAULT VALUES method in place of the VALUES section. Suppose you have a table like this:

```
CREATE TABLE Author (
    AuthorID int IDENTITY PRIMARY KEY,
    Name varchar(100) DEFAULT 'Anonymous',
    Dates varchar(20) DEFAULT 'Unknown'
);
```

and you want to insert a new row with just the default values for each column and the auto-generated ID field. You can't do it using the standard INSERT...VALUES syntax, so instead you'd use this:

```
INSERT INTO Author DEFAULT VALUES;
```

And that does the trick. Using DEFAULT VALUES instead of the standard VALUES clause inserts the default value for every column (or an auto-generated value for identity columns). If there isn't a default value for a non-identity column, the value is treated as NULL. If any column in the table is NOT NULL, isn't an identity column, and doesn't have a default value, then an error will be raised.

This could be useful for keeping an activity log (inserting date/time information whenever a transaction occurs) or for entering a placeholder record (for example, an "anonymous" user as the default entry for posts to a forum where registration isn't required).

Performing a Multi-Row INSERT

The first thing to point out in this section is that SQL doesn't allow you to add multiple rows using literal values as in the previous section. However, it's possible to add multiple rows using values obtained from the results of an embedded SELECT query. In effect, what this means is that you copy data from one database table into another although of course the names and number of columns needn't be the same for the source and destination tables.

When using an INSERT statement in this way, there are two changes from the syntax used in the previous section:

> You don't use the VALUES keyword; instead, you use SELECT to embed the query that obtains the data to insert.

> The list of columns to insert data to is optional. If it's supplied, then there must be an equal number of columns of the right types and in the right order returned by the SELECT query that makes up the values for the INSERT statement. If it isn't supplied, then the columns in the SELECT query must match the columns in the target table. As a rule, it's always worth including column names because it'll make debugging much easier.

> This makes the syntax for a multi-row INSERT statement as follows:

```
INSERT INTO Table (Columns) SELECT SelectStatement;
```

where Columns is optional.

This statement can be useful in moving large amounts of data around in a database without having to do much work, for example, in backing up data. For instance, you could create a backup table called StuffBackup and then execute the following:

```
INSERT INTO StuffBackup SELECT ThingName, ThingCost FROM Stuff;
```

Alternatively, you can easily reshape data and rename columns of rows using a statement such as this:

```
INSERT INTO StuffV2 (TheName, TheCost)
SELECT ThingName, ThingCost FROM Stuff;
```

EXAMPLE: ADDING MULTIPLE ROWS TO A TABLE

Execute the following SQL statement against the InstantUniversity database:

```
INSERT INTO Professor (ProfessorID, Name)
    SELECT StudentID + 7, Name
    FROM Student;
```

If you then query the table in the same way as before, you should see something like the following:

```
ProfessorID  Name

-----------  ---------------
...          ...
6            Prof. Hwa
7            Snail at work
8            John Jones
9            Gary Burton
...          ...
```

Here you've taken data from the StudentID and Name columns in the Student table and added the data to the similarly named columns in the Professor table. With one short SQL statement, you added 12 rows of data to the Shippers table.

Note that the data also underwent some modification on the way—you added seven to the StudentID value before assigning it to the ProfessorID column, simply to avoid overlapping non-unique values.

In addition to this method for inserting multiple rows into a database, in SQL Server it's also possible to call a stored procedure when performing an insert, which could result in multiple rows being inserted into a table. For example:

```
INSERT INTO Professor (ProfessorID, Name)
EXEC sp_RecruitProfessors;
```

In this case, the stored procedure you've used (`sp_RecruitProfessors`) could contain SQL to perform a similar operation to the inline `SELECT` you saw in the example, producing the same result.

Changing Existing Data

In most databases, you'll want to modify data at some point as it becomes out-of-date. This isn't always the case; for example, you wouldn't want to change data in a database containing a list of World Cup–winning snowboarders of recent years, but in many cases it's vital. Allowing customers to update their details in an e-commerce application is essential, for example, or else they would forever be getting orders delivered to houses at which they no longer lived. In SQL you use the `UPDATE` keyword to do this.

Updating Rows with UPDATE

The basic syntax for `UPDATE` is as follows:

```
UPDATE Table SET NewColumnValues WHERE RowFilter;
```

As before, *Table* selects the table containing the row (or rows) you want to modify. *NewColumnValues* is where you provide the new values you want to apply to row(s), and *RowFilter* allows you to select what row or rows to update, using the same `WHERE` syntax you saw in the previous chapter.

The main new thing here is *NewColumnValues*. This part of the statement involves providing a list of comma-separated column names and new values as follows:

```
UPDATE Table
SET ColumnA = NewValueA, ColumnB = NewValueB
WHERE RowFilter;
```

The values can be literal values, column names if you want to copy data from other columns, or the results of some calculation. Calculations are covered in detail in Chapter 5, "Performing Calculations and Using Functions," but for now it's worth noting that you can perform tasks such as incrementing column values, adding values based on values in other columns, and so on. As a quick example, the following query would be great if someone were feeling generous and wanted to increase their wife's bank account by a substantial amount to pay for hair-care products:

```
UPDATE BankAccounts
SET Balance = Balance * 10
WHERE AccountHolder = 'Donna Watson';
```

Unfortunately, we don't have access to the database we'd need to do this, but the idea is nice.

More typically, you'll change values with literal values obtained as part of some other application, for example:

```
UPDATE LineProducts
SET ProductName = 'New Improved Plastic Asparagus Tips', ItemsInStock = 1000
WHERE ProductID = 47;
```

Here a row is identified by its ID and values changed. Note that there's no need to provide values for all the columns in the table; where a new column value isn't specified, the old value will remain after the statement has executed.

EXAMPLE: MODIFYING ROW DATA

Execute the following code against the InstantUniversity database:

```
UPDATE Professor
SET Name = 'Prof. ' || Name
   WHERE ProfessorID > 6;
```

Note that for SQL Server and Access, the || concatenation symbol should be replaced with a +. Also, the syntax for concatenation for MySQL is quite different, and the previous SQL should appear as follows:

```
UPDATE Professor
SET Name = CONCAT('Prof. ', Name)
   WHERE ProfessorID > 6;
```

The rows should now have been altered as follows:

```
ProfessorID   Name

-----------   ---------------
...           ...
6             Prof. Hwa
7             Prof. Snail at work
8             Prof. John Jones
9             Prof. Gary Burton
...           ...
```

This example changes the value in the Name column in Professor to a concatenation of 'Prof. ' and the original value of this column. This modification is applied to the 13 new records added to the Professor table in the previous two examples. To filter these rows, we selected all records with a ProfessorID value of more than six.

NOTE *Care should be taken when using an* UPDATE *statement—omitting the* WHERE *clause will result in changes to every row of the table. If in doubt, replace the word* UPDATE *with* SELECT *while building your statement to test the results before applying them.*

Using UPDATE with Different RDBMSs

Again, different RDBMSs include their own additions to the UPDATE syntax:

SQL Server: Includes the option of having a FROM clause after the SET clause to make updating related tables much simpler. It can also include an OPTION clause that contains optimizer hints used to optimize the way the statement is executed by SQL Server. For example, specifying OPTION FAST *n* causes SQL Server to optimize the query so that the first *n* rows are returned as quickly as possible, before the rest of the result set is returned.

Oracle: Oracle allows you to include a RETURNING clause at the end of the UPDATE statement to return the amended rows into a variable.

MySQL: Includes a LIMIT clause to limit the number of rows that will be affected (see the next chapter for more information on this keyword).

DB2: Includes an ONLY clause that can be used to limit the scope of the update to just the table in question and not to any subtables. This clause is only used with typed tables and typed views. These are special DB2-specific constructs that allow you to store object instances and to define the hierarchical relationships between them.

There are also capabilities for dealing with cursors, which you'll look at a little later in the book (in Chapter 9, "Using Stored Procedures"), using the WHERE CURRENT OF *cursor* syntax in SQL Server, Oracle, and DB2.

Deleting Data

The other essential part of any language intended to access databases is the ability to delete rows. Again, not all tables will need this functionality, but more often than not they will—even if just to remove rows that have been added in error. SQL uses the DELETE keyword for this purpose.

Deleting Rows with DELETE

To use DELETE statements, you use the following syntax:

```
DELETE FROM Table WHERE RowFilter;
```

which makes DELETE statements the simplest ones you've seen so far. Here *Table* and *RowFilter* mean just what they did in the previous example. An appropriate choice of *RowFilter* can remove one or more rows from the chosen *Table*.

As with the INTO keyword from the INSERT statement, the FROM keyword is optional. Again, this chapter continues to use it because it makes SQL statements easier to read.

To remove a single row, you'd normally specify the ID (primary key) of the row as follows:

```
DELETE FROM Customers WHERE CustomerID = 23;
```

CAUTION *If you don't specify a* WHERE *clause, then* all *rows will be removed from the chosen table.*

Selecting based on an identity column is a little safer than selecting by other columns because the values are guaranteed to be unique. Selecting based on a customer name, for example, may result in more than one row being deleted.

EXAMPLE: DELETING ROW DATA

Execute the following statement against the InstantUniversity database:

```
DELETE FROM Professor WHERE ProfessorID > 6;
```

Executing this statement and then viewing the amended table will produce the following result:

```
ProfessorID  Name

-----------  ----------------
1            Prof. Dawson
2            Prof. Williams
3            Prof. Ashby
4            Prof. Patel
5            Prof. Jones
6            Prof. Hwa
```

The SQL statement in this example deletes all rows from the Professor table with a ProfessorID value of more than six. This removes all the records added in previous examples and takes the table back to its original state, before you started mucking around with it. We must say, we're a little sad to see them go. Wave goodbye for us.

Using DELETE with Different RDBMSs

In addition to the functionality shown previously, similar vendor-specific options are available to those discussed:

SQL Server: Includes facility for overriding the default optimizer behavior. SQL Server also includes the ability to specify a second FROM clause to apply a delete to a related row in a related table. For example, if you have a Books table and an Authors table, and you want to delete one author and all his books from your database, you could use a statement like this:

```
DELETE FROM Books FROM Authors
WHERE Books.AuthorID = Authors.AuthorID AND Books.AuthorID = 1;
```

Oracle: The RETURNING clause can be used to store deleted data in a variable.

MySQL: Includes the LIMIT keyword for limiting the scope of a deletion (which you'll look at in the next chapter).

DB2: Includes the ONLY keyword to limit the scope of the deletion for typed tables and typed views.

SQL Server, Oracle, and DB2 also have the facility for dealing with cursors, which you'll look at later in the book.

Using the TRUNCATE Statement

If you do want to delete all rows in a table, you might want to use the alternative command TRUNCATE TABLE *TableName*, which is supported by SQL Server and Oracle. The syntax of the TRUNCATE command is as follows:

```
TRUNCATE TABLE name;
```

TRUNCATE is optimized to work faster than DELETE because it doesn't log details of the deletion. This also means that rollback is impossible because the data is permanently deleted.

For example, you could execute the following statement against the InstantUniversity database to permanently delete all of the available rooms:

```
TRUNCATE TABLE Rooms;
```

This might be useful if the university moved premises.

Summary

In this chapter, you've looked at how you can use SQL to make modifications to the data stored in database tables. Specifically, you've seen the following:

- How to use INSERT statements to add one or more rows

- How to change row data using UPDATE

- How to use DELETE to remove rows from a table

In the next chapter you'll look at using SQL to deal with multiple rows of data simultaneously, grouping data, and summarizing data.

CHAPTER 4

Summarizing and Grouping Data

THE PREVIOUS TWO CHAPTERS introduced the basics of SQL usage, and in fact this is all you'll need for some applications. However, there's a lot more that becomes possible when you delve into the wealth of additional facilities contained in SQL. In this chapter, you'll look at ways of summarizing and grouping data. This enables you to perform many versatile data manipulation techniques. For example, you can find out the maximum value or the average value in a column (say, the highest mark scored by a student in any exam). Or, perhaps more usefully, you can look at maximum or average values for columns based on groupings defined by other columns (so you could group the rows in a table according to the exam taken and then find out the minimum/maximum/average scores for each exam).

Of course, you could create much of this functionality using your own application code. After using basic SQL to extract data from a database, you can summarize and manipulate what you've extracted to your heart's content—but aggregate functions really are best done in SQL. After all, if you're going to examine hundreds of rows to calculate a single row summary answer, then it's much better to perform the aggregate calculation in the database and then send only the single row result over the network.

Summarizing Data

SQL includes several ways of looking at multiple rows simultaneously and extracting summary data. Most of this involves using aggregate functions. In the following sections, you'll look at how to use aggregate functions to achieve the following:

- Count rows and columns

- Obtain the sum of values from a single column

- Calculate average values of columns

- Get maximum and minimum values from columns

- Limit the number of rows returned by a query and with which the previous calculations work

Performing Row and Column Counting

SQL includes a function called COUNT that you can use for counting the number of rows that meet a certain condition. You can use this function in several ways, but the basic syntax is the same in all cases. In general, you'll place this function inside a SELECT query as follows:

```
SELECT COUNT(CountSpecification) FROM Table;
```

As this is a SELECT statement, you can include a WHERE clause and anything else you might use in a SELECT statement. Without a filter, all rows will be processed by the COUNT function; otherwise, you'll only be applying it to the subset of the rows you've chosen.

CountSpecification can be one of the keywords described in Table 4-1.

Table 4-1. Count Specification Keywords

Count Specification	Meaning
*	Count all rows selected, including those with NULL values.
ALL *Column*	Count all rows with a non-NULL value for the specified column. This is the default operation if you simply specify *Column* without ALL or DISTINCT.
DISTINCT *Column*	Count all unique rows with a non-NULL value for the specified column.

NOTE   *Note that the* ALL *and* DISTINCT *keywords can't be used with Microsoft Access databases in this context. Only* * *or simply* Column *will work.*

One interesting feature is that you name the value returned in much the same way as you named calculated columns in Chapter 2, "Retrieving Data with SQL":

```
SELECT COUNT(CountSpecification) AS ColumnName FROM Table;
```

You can also use several COUNT functions at once, separated with commas just as if you were selecting several columns. However, you can't mix this function with column names as if it were a normal SELECT statement, at least not without considering groups, which you'll do later in this chapter. In other words, you can't do something like this:

```
SELECT COUNT(ReportsTo), FirstName, LastName
FROM Employees;
```

The previous variations are best learned with a few quick examples. The following is the simplest case:

```
SELECT COUNT(*) AS LegendCount FROM ArthurianLegends;
```

The previous expression returns the number of records in the table ArthurianLegends, returning it as a single entry in a column called LegendCount.
Here's another:

```
SELECT COUNT(ALL NameOfSwordInLegend) FROM ArthurianLegends;
```

This will return a single entry in an unnamed column, which indicates how many non-NULL values there are in the NameOfSwordInLegend column of the ArthurianLegends table.
Finally, the following:

```
SELECT COUNT(DISTINCT NameOfSwordInLegend)
FROM ArthurianLegends;
```

is practically the same as the previous, but this time you're only counting unique values. Should the text *Excalibur* appear several times in this column in different rows, it'll still only be counted once.

Execute the following query against the `InstantUniversity` database:

```
SELECT COUNT(*) AS NumberOfExams,
       COUNT(DISTINCT SustainedOn) AS UniqueDates,
       COUNT(Comments) AS ExamsWithComments
FROM Exam;
```

This query actually performs three separate counting calculations for all the records in the `Exam` table. Because you want to be able to tell the values apart, you name each calculation according to the calculation being performed.

The first calculation uses `COUNT(*)` to obtain the total number of rows in the table, storing it in a column called `NumberOfExams`.

The second calculation uses `COUNT(DISTINCT SustainedOn)` to determine the total number of unique entries in the `SustainedOn` column, storing the result in a column called `UniqueDates`.

The third calculation uses `COUNT(Comments)`—equivalent to `COUNT(ALL Comments)` because `ALL` is the default behavior—to count all the non-`NULL` entries in the `Comments` column, returning the result in a column called `ExamsWithComments`.

The output from this query is as follows:

NumberOfExams	UniqueDates	ExamsWithComments
11	10	9

Even with this simple example, it should already be apparent that aggregate functions such as `COUNT` can be extremely handy.

Retrieving Column Totals

The next function you'll look at is SUM, used to calculate the total value of a column. Because this function performs a mathematical summing operation, it can only be used where the data type of the column you want to examine is appropriate. It works fine with numerical types, but it won't work at all with string values.

The syntax is much the same as with COUNT:

```
SELECT SUM(SumSpecification) FROM Table;
```

The only difference between the SUM function and the COUNT function is that you can't use a wildcard (*) in a SUM function. However, you specify ALL or DISTINCT in the same way (although not in Access) to select between all values or just unique ones. For example:

```
SELECT SUM(ALL Age) FROM Students;
```

This query will return a single entry in an unnamed row that's the sum of all entries in the Age column of a table called Students.

EXAMPLE: SUMMING COLUMNS

Enter and execute the following query:

```
SELECT SUM(Credits) AS TotalCredits FROM Course;
```

This simple example just adds up the entries in the Credits column of the Course table. It should give the following output:

```
TotalCredits

-----------

55
```

Getting Column Averages

Column averages (arithmetic mean values) are easily calculated by dividing the sum of the column by the number of rows summed, but to make it even easier you can use the AVG function. This function works in the same way as those you've already examined:

```
SELECT AVG(AvgSpecification) FROM Table;
```

As with SUM, you can use ALL or DISTINCT in *AvgSpecification* (but, again, not in Microsoft Access). In both cases, NULL values are ignored.

 NOTE   *Note that only this function exists for average values—there are no equivalents for obtaining modal or median values. However, these are relatively easy to calculate with combinations of other techniques, so this isn't really a problem.*

For example, the following query obtains the average age of the students in a Students database by getting the average value of data in the Age column:

```
SELECT AVG(ALL Age) FROM Students;
```

EXAMPLE: GETTING COLUMN AVERAGES

Execute this query against the InstantUniversity database:

```
SELECT AVG(Mark) AS AverageMark
FROM StudentExam
WHERE StudentID = 10;
```

This simple example uses the AVG function to calculate the average exam mark achieved by the student with an ID of 10, from data in the StudentExam table. Note that the answer you receive may depend on the RDBMS you're using. In some cases, the result will be converted into the same data type as the column. In SQL Server and DB2, for example, this column is of type INT, giving the answer shown shortly. In Oracle and Access, the column data type is NUMBER, which can hold floating-point values, so the answer will be 73.5. It's important to be aware of this to avoid getting false or inaccurate results.

NOTE   *To get around this problem, you need to convert the column to a floating-point type before calculating the average. You'll look at data type conversion functions in Chapter 5, "Performing Calculations and Using Functions."*

The results (with rounding) are as follows:

```
AverageMark

-----------
73
```

Retrieving Maximum and Minimum Values

The last two aggregate functions you'll look at here are MAX and MIN, which return maximum and minimum values of columns. These work in the same way as most of the other functions you've looked at in this chapter:

```
SELECT MAX(MaxSpecification) FROM Table;
SELECT MIN(MinSpecification) FROM Table;
```

As before, you can use ALL or DISTINCT in the specifications of these functions; although with these functions, this is for compatibility reasons only. Looking at either all values or only unique ones won't make a blind bit difference to the functionality here because how many times a value occurs is irrelevant when you're looking for extreme values.

EXAMPLE: MAXIMUM AND MINIMUM COLUMN VALUES

Enter and execute this query:

```
SELECT MAX(Mark) AS TopMark, MIN(Mark) AS BottomMark
FROM StudentExam
WHERE ExamID = 6;
```

In this, the last simple example of aggregate functions, you use the MAX and MIN functions to obtain the maximum and minimum values in the Mark column of the StudentExam table. This returns the top and bottom marks scored by any student in the electronics exam:

```
TopMark     BottomMark

----------- -----------
84          63
```

Grouping Data

So far, you've only applied your aggregate functions to either all the records in a table or a filtered set. This means that if you want to get, say, summed values for subsets of data in a database, it could mean several separate queries. For example:

```
SELECT SUM(UnitCost) FROM Products WHERE SupplierID = 1;
SELECT SUM(UnitCost) FROM Products WHERE SupplierID = 2;
SELECT SUM(UnitCost) FROM Products WHERE SupplierID = 3;
```

And so on. Obviously, this isn't ideal. As an alternative, SQL provides a way to divide tables into groups of rows and apply aggregate functions to groups rather than all the records returned by a query. This is when using aggregate functions becomes most powerful.

Filtering Group Data

To group data in SQL, you use the GROUP BY clause, with typical syntax as follows (typical because SELECT queries themselves are so variable):

```
SELECT ColumnA, AggFunc(AggFuncSpec) FROM Table
WHERE WhereSpec
GROUP BY ColumnA;
```

Here the values in ColumnA are enumerated, and groups are created for rows with matching values in ColumnA. For example, if there are 40 records with 15 different possible values in ColumnA, then 15 groups will be created. This means that 15 rows are returned, each consisting of an entry for the ColumnA values they share and the result of the aggregate function applied to the rows in a group.

Note that there's actually no need to return *ColumnA* in the query, but it tends to make sense so that you can identify the group. As with other queries involving aggregate functions, you can't include other columns in the data returned because this wouldn't make logical sense. For example:

```
SELECT ColumnA, ColumnB, AggFunc(AggFuncSpec) FROM Table WHERE WhereSpec
GROUP BY ColumnA;
```

Each group might have several rows with *ColumnB* values, and because the returned rows can only show one, this query is simply too vague to be interpreted, so an error will be raised.

The best way to look at this grouping behavior is to see an example.

EXAMPLE: GROUPING DATA

Enter and execute the following query:

```
SELECT StudentID, COUNT(*) AS HighPasses
FROM StudentExam
WHERE Mark > 70
GROUP BY StudentID;
```

The way in which a database will generally execute this query is to group together rows with the same value in the StudentID column and then execute the COUNT function to find out the number of exams that each of the students in your database has passed with a mark of greater than 70. The result looks as follows (only the first four rows are shown in the output):

```
StudentID   HighPasses

----------- -----------
1           1
3           2
4           1
6           1
...         ...
```

You'll notice that, in this example, if a student hasn't achieved any high passes, then he or she isn't listed at all.

Including All Rows in a Group (SQL Server)

In SQL Server, you can also add the ALL keyword to the GROUP BY clause:

```
SELECT ColumnA, AggFunc(AggFuncSpec) FROM Table
WHERE WhereSpec
GROUP BY ALL ColumnA;
```

If you do this, then groups will be selected from values in all the rows in the table, not just those filtered by the WHERE clause. However, the values calculated for these groups by aggregate functions do take the WHERE clause into account, meaning that some groups will be shown with misleading (or NULL) values calculated by these functions.

Compare the previous example with the following query:

```
SELECT StudentID, COUNT(*) AS HighPasses
FROM StudentExam
WHERE Mark > 70
GROUP BY ALL StudentID;
```

You now add the ALL keyword, meaning that all students will be considered, even if they have no exam marks this high. The result of this is that the COUNT function has no records to count for some students, hence the zero entries in the HighPasses column in the results and the increased number of results returned (again, only the first four rows are shown):

```
StudentID   HighPasses

----------- -----------
1           1
2           0
3           2
4           1
...         ...
```

Using the HAVING Clause

Suppose you want to filter your result set not by any actual value in the database but by the results of an aggregate function. For example, perhaps you want to find out which students did particularly well or badly in their exams in general. You don't want to filter based on any particular mark but on the average mark for all exams they took. You might think this would be as simple as adding the condition to the WHERE clause:

```
SELECT StudentID, AVG(Mark) AS AverageMark
FROM StudentExam
WHERE AVG(Mark) < 50 OR AVG(Mark) > 70
GROUP BY StudentID;
```

Unfortunately, this won't work. The WHERE clause is used to filter data *before* the aggregate function is calculated, whereas you need to filter the data on the basis of the aggregate values. If you try to execute this query, you'll get an error.

The answer to the problem (as you've probably already guessed from the heading of this section) is the HAVING clause. This clause is placed after the GROUP BY clause and takes the following form:

```
HAVING FilterCondition
```

So, to find out which students scored on average more than 70 percent or less than 50 percent in their exams, you'd use this query:

```
SELECT StudentID, AVG(Mark) AS AverageMark
FROM StudentExam
GROUP BY StudentID
HAVING AVG(Mark) < 50 OR AVG(Mark) > 70;
```

This returns the results:

```
StudentID    AverageMark

-----------  ------------
2            48
3            80
7            71
10           73
```

You can also use HAVING in conjunction with WHERE if you want to filter the data both before and after the aggregate column is calculated. For example, let's suppose you want to restrict yourself to the results of the mathematics exams. There are three math exams, with ExamID values of 5, 8, and 11. So your new query will look like this:

```
SELECT StudentID, AVG(Mark) AS AverageMark
FROM StudentExam
WHERE ExamID IN ( 5, 8, 11 )
GROUP BY StudentID
HAVING AVG(Mark) < 50 OR AVG(Mark) > 70;
```

The WHERE filter is applied before the aggregate values are calculated, so any rows in the StudentExam table where the ExamID field doesn't contain one of the values 5, 8, or 11 will be ignored completely. Once the aggregate values have been calculated, you use the HAVING clause to restrict the rows returned to those students whose average over these three exams is either particularly good or particularly bad. The result of this query is as follows:

```
StudentID    AverageMark

-----------  -----------
2            39
10           71
```

Using Top-N Queries

Sometimes, for whatever reason, you won't want to return all the rows in a database that match the filter criteria. If you only want, say, the top 10 rows, then it makes little sense to get hundreds of rows from a database and only work with 10 of them because this means that more data is being exchanged between servers, which impairs performance. All of the database systems covered in this book support ways of doing this. Unfortunately, these are all different, so you'll look at each system in turn.

SQL Server and Access

SQL as implemented in Microsoft SQL Server and Access allows you to choose how many rows to return using the TOP keyword:

```
SELECT TOP RowCount ColumnA, ColumnB FROM Table;
```

The TOP *RowCount* section shown here can be added to any SELECT query. *RowCount* can be an absolute number, which will be how many rows to return, or it can be a number followed by the PERCENT keyword, meaning that a percentage of the total rows selected will be returned.

In its most basic usage, the TOP keyword simply returns the first matches found in a table:

```
SELECT TOP 5 CustomerID, CustomerName FROM Customers;
```

This query would return data from the first five rows in the Customers table.

However, one important point to note here is that the top rows are snipped off after any sorting is performed. This makes it possible to select, say, the rows with the highest or lowest values in a certain column:

```
SELECT TOP 10 PERCENT StudentID, Mark
FROM StudentExam
ORDER BY Mark;
```

The previous query returns the bottom 10 percent of marks in the StudentExam table—it's the bottom because ORDER BY Mark specifies an ascending order (the row with the lowest Mark value is the first one in the result set generated by the query).

EXAMPLE: RETRIEVING THE TOP FIVE STUDENTS (SQL SERVER/ACCESS)

Execute this query against the InstantUniversity database:

```
SELECT TOP 5 StudentID, AVG(Mark) AS AverageMark
FROM StudentExam
GROUP BY StudentID
ORDER BY AVG(Mark) DESC;
```

Here you've retrieved the average mark scored by each student in his or her exams and ordered the student IDs according to this average, with the top average first in the result set. You use the TOP keyword to extract only the top five records, showing the five rows with the highest average mark:

StudentID	AverageMark
3	80
10	73
7	71
6	68
9	68

Notice that you repeat AVG(Mark), rather than using the AverageMark alias, in the ORDER BY clause because Access doesn't allow computed aliases to be used in GROUP BY or ORDER BY clauses. This isn't a problem for SQL Server.

Also, notice that because SQL Server rounds the averages down to the nearest integer, the order isn't guaranteed to be accurate—in this case, the student with an ID of 9 (Andrew Forster, if you're asking) actually has a slightly higher average than Vic Andrews (with the ID of 6), but because they're both rounded down to 68, SQL Server treats them as equal.

This last point raises another issue—what if the cut-off point occurs in the middle of a sequence of several rows with the same value in the ORDER BY column? What if you asked for the top four values instead of the top five? SQL Server simply returns whatever rows it places at the top of the result set, so the record for Vic Andrews will be returned but not that for Andrew Foster.

To ensure that all rows with matching values are returned, you need to add WITH TIES to your query:

```
SELECT TOP 4 WITH TIES StudentID, AVG(Mark) AS AverageMark
FROM StudentExam
GROUP BY StudentID
ORDER BY AverageMark DESC;
```

This returns the rows for both Vic Andrews and Andrew Foster, so five rows rather than four are returned. This is the default behavior for Access, so the WITH TIES keywords aren't supported.

NOTE `WITH TIES` *can only be used if the query has an* `ORDER BY` *clause.*

MySQL

In MySQL, the `LIMIT` keyword is used in a similar way (although in a different place) as the `TOP` keyword:

```
SELECT ColumnA, ColumnB
FROM Table
LIMIT StartRecord, TotalRecords;
```

Here `TotalRecords` is the total number of rows to return, and `StartRecord` shows how many rows to omit. This is slightly more flexible than `TOP` (although no `PERCENT` equivalent exists) because you can get chunks of data at a time.

For example, you could use the following SQL query in MySQL:

```
SELECT CustomerID, CustomerName FROM Customers LIMIT 0, 5;
```

This would get data from the first five records in the `Customers` table. If only one number is supplied, this is taken as the number of rows to return, and a default of zero is assumed for the starting row. So, you could have written the previous query as this:

```
SELECT CustomerID, CustomerName FROM Customers LIMIT 5;
```

As with `TOP`, combining this keyword with `ORDER BY` can be a useful technique.

EXAMPLE: RETRIEVING THE TOP FIVE STUDENTS (MYSQL)

Execute this query against the `InstantUniversity` database:

```
SELECT StudentID, AVG(Mark) AS AverageMark
FROM StudentExam
GROUP BY StudentID
ORDER BY AverageMark DESC
LIMIT 0, 5;
```

Again, you retrieve the average mark scored by each student in his or her exams and order the records accordingly. You add the `LIMIT 0, 5` clause to specify that you want to retrieve only five records, starting with the first record (record number zero):

```
StudentID    AverageMark

------------ ------------
3            80
10           73.5
7            71.3333
9            68.6667
6            68.3333
```

DB2

DB2 uses a `FETCH FIRST` clause to limit the number of rows returned from a query. This has two basic forms; to retrieve just the top row, you can write the following:

```
SELECT CustomerID, CustomerName FROM Customers
FETCH FIRST ROW ONLY;
```

If you don't specify the number of rows to retrieve, only one row will be returned. To fetch more than one row, you must specify a positive integer value in the `FETCH FIRST` clause. For example, to fetch five rows, you can write this:

```
SELECT CustomerID, CustomerName FROM Customers
FETCH FIRST 5 ROWS ONLY;
```

Again, you can use this clause in conjunction with an `ORDER BY` clause to retrieve the highest or lowest values in the result set. The `FETCH FIRST` clause is placed at the end of the query, after the `ORDER BY` clause.

EXAMPLE: RETRIEVING THE TOP FIVE STUDENTS (DB2)

Enter and execute this query:

```
SELECT StudentID, AVG(Mark) AS AverageMark
FROM StudentExam
GROUP BY StudentID
ORDER BY AverageMark DESC
FETCH FIRST 5 ROWS ONLY;
```

Here again you retrieve the five students with the highest average marks from the StudentExam table by averaging the Mark value for each separate StudentID using the AVG function. You limit the result set to five rows by appending the clause FETCH FIRST 5 ROWS ONLY to the query:

```
StudentID    AverageMark

-----------  ------------
3            80
10           73
7            71
6            68
9            68
```

Note that, as with SQL Server, the order isn't guaranteed to be 100-percent accurate because the averages are rounded down to fit into the INT data type.

As with SQL Server, if the cut-off point comes in the middle of a group of records with the same value in the ORDER BY column, the values that are (arbitrarily) placed later won't be returned from the query.

To get around this, you need to use the RANK function, which assigns a rank to every row returned by a query. RANK has the following syntax:

```
RANK() OVER (ORDER BY ColumnName ASC | DESC)
```

You use RANK much like any other SQL function: to add a new column to the result set returned from the query. This column indicates what rank each row has when the results are ordered by the column named in the RANK() OVER clause. For example, to add a column indicating the rank for each of the students based on the average mark they scored in the exams they took, you'd use the following query:

```
SELECT RANK() OVER (ORDER BY AVG(Mark) DESC) AS Ranking,
       StudentID, AVG(Mark) AS AverageMark
FROM StudentExam
GROUP BY StudentID;
```

So, to retrieve the top four students, taking any ties into account, you just need this query with a WHERE Ranking <= 4 clause, right? Nearly. Unfortunately, though, you can't access the computed Ranking column in the same query. Instead, you need to define this query as a subquery and then query that subquery, adding the WHERE clause to the outer query. The syntax for creating a subquery in DB2 is as follows:

```
WITH SubQueryName (SubQueryColumnList)
AS (SubQueryStatement)
... Outer query ...
```

So, when you put all that together for your top students query, you end up with this monster of a SQL statement:

```
WITH RankedMarks (Ranking, StudentID, AverageMark)
AS (
    SELECT RANK() OVER (ORDER BY AVG(Mark) DESC) AS Ranking,
           StudentID, AVG(Mark) AS AverageMark
    FROM StudentExam
    GROUP BY StudentID)
SELECT Ranking, StudentID, AverageMark
FROM RankedMarks
WHERE Ranking <= 4;
```

Oracle

Finally, Oracle allows a similar query to be performed using the ROWNUM keyword, where every record in a table is assigned a row number according to its position, separate from the ID of the row or any other data. This keyword, however, must be specified in a WHERE clause with a comparison operator, and so it isn't as flexible (and won't work with ORDER BY because reordered rows maintain their original row number).

```
SELECT CustomerID, CustomerName FROM Customers
WHERE ROWNUM <= 5;
```

To get around this, you can embed your SELECT statement as a subquery into an outer query, querying that subquery for the top *n* rows. For example, to retrieve the first five rows sorted alphabetically by CustomerName, use the following:

```
SELECT CustomerID, CustomerName FROM (
    SELECT CustomerID, CustomerName
    FROM Customers
    ORDER BY CustomerName ASC)
WHERE ROWNUM <= 5;
```

EXAMPLE: RETRIEVING THE TOP FIVE STUDENTS (ORACLE)

Enter and execute this query:

```
SELECT StudentID, AverageMark FROM (
    SELECT StudentID, AVG(Mark) AS AverageMark
    FROM StudentExam
    GROUP BY StudentID
    ORDER BY AverageMark DESC
)
WHERE ROWNUM <= 5;
```

Here you define a subquery that retrieves the average mark for each student over all exams taken, sorted in descending order (so the student with the highest average comes first):

```
SELECT StudentID, AVG(Mark) AS AverageMark
FROM StudentExam
GROUP BY StudentID
ORDER BY AverageMark DESC
```

To retrieve the top five students, you embed this subquery into a SELECT statement and use the ROWNUM keyword to select just the top five rows:

StudentID	AverageMark
3	80
10	73.5
7	71.3333333
9	68.6666667
6	68.3333333

Although rounding down to integers doesn't occur in this example, you still have the problem that some rows may be arbitrarily discarded if the cut-off point occurs in the middle of a group of rows with the same average mark. The way around this is similar to the DB2 approach—you use the RANK() function. This has the same syntax and is used in the same way as in DB2:

```
RANK() OVER (ORDER BY ColumnName ASC | DESC)
```

You use this to add a new column to your subquery, containing a value for each row that indicates the rank of that row in the result set. The subquery that uses this function has the same form as the DB2 subquery:

```
SELECT RANK() OVER (ORDER BY AVG(Mark) DESC) AS Ranking,
       StudentID, AVG(Mark) AS AverageMark
FROM StudentExam
GROUP BY StudentID
```

To retrieve the top four placed students (taking any ties into account), the outer query just needs to retrieve all the rows from this subquery that are ranked four or less:

```
SELECT Ranking, StudentID, AverageMark FROM (
    SELECT RANK() OVER (ORDER BY AVG(Mark) DESC) AS Ranking,
           StudentID, AVG(Mark) AS AverageMark
    FROM StudentExam
    GROUP BY StudentID)
WHERE Ranking <= 4;
```

Using Analytic Functions

With the introduction of the RANK() function in the previous section, you actually strayed from the realm of basic aggregate functions into the more complex topic of *analytic* functions. Oracle and DB2 provide a range of analytic functions that allow you to perform complex computation that would otherwise need to be performed outside of the SQL standard.

Of the databases covered in this book, analytic functions are currently only supported in Oracle and DB2, so this section won't tackle the subject in much detail. You should consult your database documentation to see exactly which analytic functions are supported and how they work. However, if you do happen to be using Oracle or DB2, you can at least learn how aggregate functions such as SUM and AVG can be used as analytic functions.

The basic syntax for analytic functions is as follows:

```
Function (<argument>) OVER
(<Partition clause> <ORDER BY clause> <Windowing clause>)
```

It's the OVER keyword that identifies your function as an analytic function. The best way to get a feel for this is to see it in action. Let's start with the simplest example:

```
SELECT StudentID, Mark, AVG(Mark) OVER
() Average_Mark
FROM StudentExam
ORDER BY StudentID, Mark;
```

The output from this query is as follows (the output is cropped after six rows):

```
STUDENTID   MARK        AVERAGE_MARK

----------  ----------  ----------------
1           55          63.9310345
1           73          63.9310345
2           39          63.9310345
2           44          63.9310345
2           63          63.9310345
3           78          63.9310345
...
```

In the absence of any clauses, the average mark is computed over every row. The resulting value displayed for each row is the same as that which would have been obtained by a simple SELECT AVG(Mark) from StudentExam; query. Let's see what happens when you add an ORDER BY clause:

```
SELECT StudentID, Mark, AVG(Mark) OVER
(ORDER BY StudentID, Mark) Running_Average
FROM StudentExam
ORDER BY StudentID, Mark;
```

You now obtain the following:

```
STUDENTID   MARK    RUNNING_AVERAGE

----------  ------- ----------------
1           55      55
1           73      64
2           39      55.6666667
2           44      52.75
2           63      54.8
3           78      58.6666667
...<output cropped>...
10          79      63.9310345
```

As you can see, the calculation is performed differently when an ORDER BY clause is specified. It applies ordering to a group of data and essentially tells the database to calculate the average of the current row and all preceding rows (in effect, this applies a default windowing clause, but more about that in a moment). Thus, you get a running average over the group of data. In this case the "group" is every row of data, so by the time you get to the last row, you arrive at the average over all rows—the same value that the previous query supplied.

Finally, let's add a partitioning clause:

```
SELECT StudentID, Mark, AVG(Mark) OVER
(PARTITION BY StudentID
 ORDER BY StudentID, Mark) Running_Avg_by_Student
FROM StudentExam
ORDER BY StudentID, Mark;
```

The output should look as follows:

```
STUDENTID   MARK    RUNNING_AVG_BY_STUDENT

----------  ------- ----------------------
1           55      55
1           73      64
2           39      39
2           44      41.5
2           63      48.6666667
3           78      78
3           82      80
```

The partitioning clause logically breaks the data down into groups, and the function is applied independently to each group. Thus, you obtain a running average by student.

To finish off, let's briefly look at the windowing clause. The syntax gets a little complex here, and you should definitely refer to your database manual for full details. However, it basically allows you to supply a specific range of data against which you should execute the function. The previous query is actually equivalent to this:

```
SELECT StudentID, Mark, AVG(Mark) OVER
(PARTITION BY StudentID
 ORDER BY StudentID, Mark
 RANGE BETWEEN UNBOUNDED PRECEDING AND
 CURRENT ROW
 ) Running_Avg_by_Student
FROM StudentExam
ORDER BY StudentID, Mark;
```

The highlighted code specifies that the window of data is the current row and all rows preceding it (which is the default). However, you can change this. For example, the following code would take the average over only the current row and the preceding row:

```
SELECT StudentID, Mark, AVG(Mark) OVER
(PARTITION BY StudentID
 ORDER BY StudentID, Mark
 ROWS 1 preceding
 ) Running_Avg_by_Student
FROM StudentExam
ORDER BY StudentID, Mark;
```

This short section should have at least given you a feel for the potential power of analytic functions.

Summary

In this chapter, you saw how you can use SQL to summarize data from multiple rows. To start with, the rows that were summarized were selected simply by a WHERE clause. To make summarization techniques more powerful, you can also look at groups of data, which you did in the second half of the chapter.

To be specific, you learned about the following:

- Using the COUNT function

- Using the SUM function

- Using the AVG function

- Using the MAX and MIN functions

- Grouping data using the GROUP BY clause

- Using the HAVING clause with data groups

- Limiting the number of rows returned, using Top-N queries

You even took a sneaky look at the more advanced topic of analytic functions.

This chapter used calculations and functions in many of its examples. In the next chapter, you'll learn about this subject in more detail.

CHAPTER 5

Performing Calculations and Using Functions

A NUMBER OF TIMES over the past few chapters you found that selecting data based on the simple column name didn't meet your needs. Instead you needed to combine values or calculate new values based on the data in your database, such that the values you obtained in your results were ready for you to use. You have, for example, concatenated strings to create columns more suited to applications, and you've also performed simple calculations involving numerical data, such as multiplying the values of two columns together.

In this chapter, you're going to look at calculations in more detail, outlining what is and isn't possible, as well as the syntax required. You're also going to examine several of the important single row functions (which act on a single row, rather than a set of rows, and return a value) that SQL provides for you. These allow you to perform all sorts of operations. You can, for example, do the following:

- Perform various mathematical and trigonometric actions on data

- Reformat dates and times

- Manipulate string values

- Convert between different data types

Along the way, you'll see how you can use these functions in conjunction with some of the aggregate functions you explored in the previous chapter, which act on a set of rows and provide summary data to powerful effect.

You'll finish up by discussing how to create your own custom functions for when the built-in versions don't quite meet your specific needs.

Performing Calculations in SQL

SQL provides a rich set of functionality for performing calculations with the data stored in a database. Some of this is already apparent from the WHERE clauses you've been using in earlier chapters because you've seen how you can perform basic comparisons to filter data. You've also looked at calculated columns as a means of reshaping database data. As yet, though, you haven't explored the full range of options available or all the places that you can use calculations.

Consider the following SQL query:

```
SELECT ColumnA, Expression1 AS ColumnB FROM Table
WHERE Expression2;
```

Although `Expression1` can simply be a column name and `Expression2` can be just a comparison involving a column, you have more options at your disposal. `Expression1` evaluates to a value to be stored in `ColumnB`, but that evaluation can be a complex as you like, involving as many columns and literal values as you like (as well as functions, as you'll see later in the chapter). `Expression2` has to evaluate to Boolean `true` or `false` values for each row. If it's true, a row is filtered and included in the results, but this can involve much more than a simple comparison.

To build up the various expressions that can be placed into SQL statements (not just queries—the same applies to other SQL statements such as `UPDATE`), you combine column names with operators and/or literal values. There's even nothing stopping you from doing something as simple as using just a literal value for a calculated column; however, because the result will be just a set of rows with a set value for a certain column, this isn't particularly useful. In general, you will be performing calculations based on the data stored in a row while avoiding simply returning column values.

Using Operators

SQL includes many operators for use in expressions, some of which you've seen already, such as + and *. Several of the keywords you've seen earlier in the book are also technically operators—including `AND`, `LIKE`, and `BETWEEN`—although in practice some of these work in a more complex way than the simpler arithmetic or comparison ones.

The full list of arithmetic operators is +, -, *, /, and %. Of these, the first four are for addition (doubling as string concatenation in SQL Server and MySQL), subtraction, multiplication, and division, and the fifth is the slightly more complex modulus operator. This operator returns the integer remainder of a division operation. For example:

```
19 % 7 = 5
```

This is because seven fits into 19 twice, leaving a remainder of five.

You saw all the comparison operators in Chapter 2, "Retrieving Data with SQL," but to recap the full list is =, !=, <>, <, <=, !<, >, >=, and !>.

There are also several bitwise operators that perform bitwise operations on numeric values, where the binary equivalent of numbers are operated on. Table 5-1 shows these operators.

Table 5-1. Bitwise Operators

Bitwise Operator	Operation
&	Bitwise AND
|	Bitwise OR
^	Bitwise XOR (exclusive OR)
~	Bitwise NOT

Finally, you can use parentheses to specify the order that operators are executed. This is necessary in situations such as the following:

```
5 + 3 * 2
```

In this example, the * operator takes precedence over the + operator and executes first, so the result will be 11. However, using parentheses you could write the following:

```
(5 + 3) * 2
```

Here the calculation in parentheses executes first, making the result 16.

NOTE *For a full list of operators, precedence, and so on, see the documentation that accompanies the Relational Database Management System (RDBMS) you're using.*

Using Expressions

Now you've seen all the building blocks of expressions (apart from functions), so it's time to put them together and see the rules behind expression building.

In general, you'll be building either standard expressions that evaluate to a calculated value or Boolean expressions that evaluate to true or false.

For calculated values, you'll typically work with column values, literal values, and arithmetic operators to build values. For example:

```
ColumnA / ColumnB
```

Or, for example:

```
(ColumnA + 2) * ColumnB
```

For Boolean expressions, you build up Boolean calculations with comparison and logical operators:

```
(ColumnA < 2) OR NOT (ColumnB >= 5)
```

In all cases, the column values used are for whatever row is currently being processed.

As you can see, although there isn't a huge amount to cover here because there aren't that many operators, the possibilities are limitless, allowing complex expressions to be built with ease.

EXAMPLE: USING EXPRESSIONS

Connect to the InstantUniversity database and execute this query:

```
SELECT StudentID, Mark,
       (Mark * 100) / 80.0 AS ActualPercentage, IfPassed,
       Comments
FROM StudentExam
WHERE ExamID = 3;
```

In this example you're assuming that the Mark column in the StudentExam table gives an absolute mark rather than a percentage result and that the total marks available in the exam with an ExamID of 3 is 80. You use an expression to convert the value in the Mark column into a percentage based on this information as follows:

```
(Mark * 100) / 80.0
```

Note that the Mark column is of type int. For this reason, the total number of marks, 80, is expressed as a floating-point value (by appending .0), which forces the integer result of Mark * 100 to be converted into a floating-point value. The reason for this is that integers can always be expressed as floating-point values, but not vice versa. To guarantee a successful result, the RDBMS performs this conversion automatically for you. If you used the following, there would be a possibility that no conversion would be performed, and you would lose accuracy because the result would be expressed as an integer:

```
(Mark * 100) / 80
```

 NOTE *This is dependent on the RDBMS in use—SQL Server and DB2 treat the result as an integer, but Oracle, MySQL, and Access allow floating-point values.*

The output from this query is as follows:

```
StudentID   Mark  ActualPercentage    IfPassed  Comments

----------- ----- ------------------- --------- ----------------
2           44    55.000000           1         Scraped through
6           78    97.500000           1         Excellent work
8           46    57.500000           1         Poor result
```

Using Functions in SQL

As you saw in the past chapter, functions can be extremely useful in processing data stored in a database and can save you a lot of work when you deal with results returned by SQL queries. So far, most of the functions you've seen have been aggregate functions, but there are a lot more than that available to you.

The general syntax for calling a function is simply as follows:

```
FUNC(Parameters);
```

Here *FUNC* is the name of the function, and *Parameters* are the parameters of the function, which may be column names, literals, expressions, or even other functions. Where more than one parameter is required, they're separated by commas:

```
FUNC(Parameter1, Parameter2, ...);
```

Functions can be used pretty much anywhere in a SQL statement because they can evaluate to numeric values, strings, Boolean values, and so on.

Unfortunately, functions tend to be very RDBMS specific, where each of the major RDBMSs has its own suite of functions—far too many to list here. However, there's some overlap, and you can examine some of the more commonly used functions without too much worry concerning compatibility issues.

One area where many functions are shared is with mathematical functions. Whatever RDBMS you're using, you're likely to have access to functions that do the following:

- Return the absolute value of a value, typically called ABS or similar

- Perform trigonometric calculations, such as SIN, COS, and so on

- Calculate logarithms, such as LOG10 or LOG, to use base e

- Calculate square roots, SQRT

- Raise values to a given power, POWER

- Generate random numbers, RAND

RDBMSs usually include functions for dealing with date and time values, working with strings (obtaining substrings, replacing characters, reversing character order, and so on), and much more. Typically, access to all the functionality of a database is achieved via functions, including security functionality, general database statistics, configuration, and most other things you might imagine.

As an example, consider the situation where you want to obtain the square root of the numbers in a column, which means using a function such as SQRT, as noted previously. In SQL Server, Oracle, DB2, and MySQL, you could use simply the following:

```
SELECT SQRT(ColumnName) AS RootOfColumnName FROM TableName;
```

However, Access doesn't have a SQRT function, so you have to use SQR instead:

```
SELECT SQR(ColumnName) AS RootOfColumnName FROM TableName;
```

The result is the same, but the name of the function is different. Sadly, this is typical and can mean checking the function list of the RDBMS you're using to find the exact syntax you need to use.

Because there are so many functions available, and because they're so database-specific, there's really no point in attempting to cover everything here.

Instead you'll look at some of the main areas where you need functions—manipulating numbers, strings, and dates and times and converting between different data types—and you'll deal with other individual functions as you come across them in the remainder of the book. Later, at the end of the chapter, you'll also look at the CREATE FUNCTION statement that lets you define your own functions.

Working with Numbers

Previously, you saw integer values being used simply by inserting the numeric value, without any ' characters or other delimiting character:

```
2763
```

This holds for all numeric types, but there are also several other elements of notation you can use. First, you can include decimal points for floating-point numbers:

```
3.142
```

You can also include scientific notation to include the exponent of a number, for example:

```
7.34E3
```

You can use the - symbol to specify either a negative number or a negative exponent (or both):

```
-2.43E-15
```

You can also use the + symbol in a similar way although this isn't really necessary because numbers will be interpreted as positive by default.

SQL Server and Access have a specific money data type, which allows for constants including a currency symbol, with all the other options described previously:

```
-$300.50
```

Other RDBMSs include additional, more exotic string representations of numeric values, such as preceding a string literal with X in DB2 and MySQL to indicate a hexadecimal value.

Working with Hexadecimal Numbers

The following is a DB2/MySQL hexadecimal number:

```
X'5A0F'
```

SQL Server, however, uses the prefix 0x for hexadecimal values, which aren't enclosed in quotes (this is also supported by the latest versions of MySQL):

```
0x5A0F
```

 NOTE *By default, MySQL will treat hexadecimal values as ASCII character codes and return the corresponding character(s), but you can ensure that they're treated as numbers by adding zero to them. For example,* X'4A' *returns* 'J', *but* X'4A' + 0 *returns* 74.

DB2, MySQL, and Access have a HEX() function that allows you to convert a numeric value into a hexadecimal string. For example, HEX(74) returns '4A'. You can achieve the same thing with Oracle using the TO_CHAR() function. You'll look at this function in a bit more detail later, but it's used to convert different data types to strings. As well as the data to convert, it can take a string that indicates how the string is to be formatted. An 'X' character in this string represents a hexadecimal digit, so you can convert the number 74 to hexadecimal using TO_CHAR(74, 'XX').

Rounding Up and Down

As an example of using mathematical functions in SQL, let's look at the functions used to round numbers up or down to the nearest integer or to a specific precision. There are three basic functions involved:

FLOOR(*number*): Rounds *number* down to the highest integer less than *number*. For example, FLOOR(57.4) and FLOOR(57.8) will both return 57.

CEILING(*number*) or CEIL(*number*): Rounds *number* up to the lowest integer greater than *number*. For example, FLOOR(57.4) and FLOOR(57.8) will both return 58.

ROUND(*number, precision*): Rounds *number* to the nearest integer or floating-point number with the specified *precision*. For example, ROUND(57.4, 0) returns 57 and ROUND(57.8, 0) returns 58. If the number is negative, the number will be rounded on the left side of the decimal point, so ROUND(57.4, -1) returns 60 and ROUND(57.4, -2) returns 100.

NOTE   *Access doesn't support either* FLOOR() *or* CEILING(), *but you can achieve the same effect using* INT(), *which works in much the same way as* FLOOR() *for numeric values, and* ROUND(number + 0.5, 0) *to replace* CEILING(). *Also, Access doesn't support negative precision with* ROUND().

To see this in action, let's revisit the example from Chapter 4, "Summarizing and Grouping Data," where you calculated the average mark that a student scored in his or her exams. You'll show the same data (but for all students), but this time you'll present the average as a floating point, rounded up and rounded down and rounded to the nearest integer.

There are slight differences in the way you implement this in the various RDBMSs, so you'll look at these examples separately.

SQL Server and DB2

The same SQL query will run on both SQL Server and DB2, so you'll look at these together. The main issue here is that both SQL Server and DB2 will store the value of AVG(Mark) as an integer, so you need to convert the Mark to a float before calculating the average:

```
AVG(CAST(Mark AS FLOAT))
```

You'll look at data type conversion functions in more detail shortly. Also, notice that SQL Server supports only the CEILING() function, but DB2 has both CEIL() and CEILING().

EXAMPLE: ROUNDING UP AND DOWN (SQL SERVER AND DB2)

Enter this query and execute it against the InstantUniversity database:

```
SELECT StudentID, AVG(CAST(Mark AS FLOAT)) AS AverageMark,
       FLOOR(AVG(CAST(Mark AS FLOAT))) AS RoundDown,
       CEILING(AVG(CAST(Mark AS FLOAT))) AS RoundUp,
       ROUND(AVG(CAST(Mark AS FLOAT)), 0) AS ClosestInt
FROM StudentExam
GROUP BY StudentID;
```

This gives the following output:

StudentID	AverageMark	RoundDown	RoundUp	ClosestInt
1	64	64	64	64
2	48.6666666666667	48	49	49
3	80	80	80	80
4	63.3333333333333	63	64	63
5	52	52	52	52
6	68.3333333333333	68	69	68
7	71.3333333333333	71	72	71
8	51.6666666666667	51	52	52
9	68.6666666666667	68	69	69
10	73.5	73	74	74

Oracle

The query for Oracle is similar, but Oracle supports only CEIL(), not CEILING(). Also, you don't need to use the CAST() function (although it's supported, using the same syntax).

EXAMPLE: ROUNDING UP AND DOWN (ORACLE)

Enter this query into SQL*Plus:

```
SELECT StudentID, AVG(CAST(Mark AS FLOAT)) AS AverageMark,
       FLOOR(AVG(CAST(Mark AS FLOAT))) AS RoundDown,
       CEIL(AVG(CAST(Mark AS FLOAT))) AS RoundUp,
       ROUND(AVG(CAST(Mark AS FLOAT)), 0) AS ClosestInt
FROM StudentExam
GROUP BY StudentID;
```

This gives the same output as for the SQL Server/DB2 example:

```
StudentID  AverageMark  RoundDown   RoundUp    ClosestInt

---------- -----------  ----------  ---------- ----------

1          64           64          64         64
2          48.6666667   48          49         49
3          80           80          80         80
4          63.3333333   63          64         63
...        ...          ...         ...        ...
```

MySQL

MySQL doesn't support the CAST() function and uses CEILING() rather than
CEIL(). Otherwise, the query is the same as for Oracle.

EXAMPLE: ROUNDING UP AND DOWN (MYSQL)

Enter this query and execute it against the InstantUniversity database:

```
SELECT StudentID, AVG(Mark) AS AverageMark,
       FLOOR(AVG(Mark)) AS RoundDown,
       CEILING(AVG(Mark)) AS RoundUp,
       ROUND(AVG(Mark), 0) AS ClosestInt
FROM StudentExam
GROUP BY StudentID;
```

This gives the following output:

```
StudentID AverageMark RoundDown RoundUp ClosestInt

--------- ----------- --------- ------- ----------

1         64.0000     64        64      64
2         48.6667     48        49      49
3         80.0000     80        80      80
4         63.3333     63        64      63
...       ...         ...       ...     ...
```

NOTE *This example won't work against a MySQL server running in ANSI mode. Strict ANSI SQL demands that all columns not included in aggregate functions must be included in the* GROUP BY *clause. This doesn't make any sense (and isn't permitted) for your rounded columns, so this query will only work against MySQL running in standard mode.*

Access

The Access version of this query is significantly different because as you saw previously, Access doesn't support the FLOOR() or CEILING() function.

EXAMPLE: ROUNDING UP AND DOWN (ACCESS)

The Access version of your query looks like this:

```
SELECT StudentID, AVG(Mark) AS AverageMark,
       INT(AVG(Mark)) AS RoundDown,
       ROUND(AVG(Mark) + .5, 0) AS RoundUp,
       ROUND(AVG(Mark), 0) AS ClosestInt
FROM StudentExam
GROUP BY StudentID;
```

Here you use INT() to round down the mark. INT() converts a non-integer type to an integer. For floating-point values, this effectively means that INT() works in the same way as FLOOR(). The ROUND() function has the same syntax as in the other RDBMSs. You also use this function to simulate CEILING(): If you add 0.5 to a value and then round this to the nearest integer, this has the effect of rounding up to the next integer.

Here are the results:

StudentID	AverageMark	RoundDown	RoundUp	ClosestInt
1	64	64	64	64
2	48.6666666666667	48	49	49
3	80	80	80	80
4	63.3333333333333	63	64	63
...	...	...	...	...

Manipulating Strings

As you've seen in earlier chapters, string literal values are enclosed in ' characters as follows:

```
'This is a string. Honest.'
```

One thing you haven't looked at yet is how you embed ' characters themselves in strings, which is a reasonably common occurrence. All you have to do is to replace any single quotes in the string with '':

```
'It''s cold outside.'
```

All other characters can be contained in the string literal value as normal. It's also possible for a string literal to represent an empty string as follows:

```
''
```

This is simply two ' characters with nothing in between.

Although the ' character is the ANSI standard, some RDBMSs such as Access and MySQL (when not run in ANSI mode) allow the use of " characters instead. If you use this syntax, then ' characters can be used in the string without doubling up. However, if you want to use " characters, you must instead use "".

In addition, some RDBMSs use escape characters for certain characters such as tabs and carriage returns. MySQL uses syntax similar to that seen in many C++ (and C++ related) implementations, for example, \n for a new line character and \t for a tab. However, these escape codes are the exception rather than the norm.

Using String Manipulation Functions

Most RDBMSs provide a large number of functions that you can use to manipulate strings in various ways, for example, to extract substrings, determine the length of the string, find a character in the string, or convert the string to upper or lower case. Although the behavior of these functions is more or less standard, their names vary slightly from system to system, and in a few cases (such as SUBSTR), the parameter list can vary a little.

In general, these functions take the forms described in Table 5-2.

Table 5-2. String Manipulation Functions

Function	Description
LEFT(*string*, *n*)	Returns the *n* leftmost characters of *string*.
RIGHT(*string*, *n*)	Returns the *n* rightmost characters of *string*.
SUBSTRING(*string*, *x*, *y*)	Returns the substring of *string* of length *y* that starts at position *x*. Oracle, DB2, and MySQL permit you to omit the last argument, in which case the substring from *x* to the end of the string will be returned.
INSTR(*string*, *substr*)	Returns the position of the first instance of the character or substring *substr* within *string*.
LENGTH(*string*)	Returns the length of *string* (that is, the number of characters in *string*).
UPPER(*string*)	Returns *string* converted to upper case.
LOWER(*string*)	Returns *string* converted to lower case.

The names of these functions in the individual RDBMSs are as described in Table 5-3.

Table 5-3. Names of the Functions

SQL Server	DB2	Oracle	MySQL	Access
LEFT	LEFT	(Use SUBSTR)	LEFT	LEFT
RIGHT	RIGHT	(Use SUBSTR)	RIGHT	RIGHT
SUBSTRING	SUBSTR	SUBSTR	SUBSTRING	MID
CHARINDEX	POSSTR	INSTR	INSTR	INSTR
LEN	LENGTH	LENGTH	LENGTH	LEN
UPPER	UCASE/UPPER	UPPER	UCASE/UPPER	UCASE
LOWER	LCASE/LOWER	LOWER	LCASE/LOWER	LCASE

Note that SQL Server's CHARINDEX() function takes its parameters in the opposite order of the INSTR() functions. So, CHARINDEX(' ', 'Apress LP') will return 7, the position of the space in 'Apress LP'.

To see more clearly how these functions are used, let's look at an example. In this example, you'll reverse the first and last names of the students in the `InstantUniversity` database (for example, you'll format `'John Jones'` as `'Jones, John'`).

To do this, you'll find the first occurrence of the space in their name and retrieve the substring from the next character to the end of the name (this is the student's last name). Next, you'll concatenate a comma and a space to this using the concatenation techniques you learned in Chapter 2, "Retrieving Data with SQL." Finally, you'll add the first name, which you retrieve by extracting the substring from the start of the string to the character before the space.

Again, you'll examine the examples for each RDBMS separately.

SQL Server

Apart from the idiosyncratic `CHARINDEX()` function noted previously, the SQL Server version of the example is fairly straightforward.

EXAMPLE: MANIPULATING STRINGS (SQL SERVER)

This is the SQL Server version of your query:

```
SELECT
    RIGHT(Name, LEN(Name) - CHARINDEX(' ', Name) + 1) + ', ' +
    LEFT(Name, CHARINDEX(' ', Name) - 1) AS StudentName
FROM Student
ORDER BY StudentName;
```

Here you use the `RIGHT()` function to retrieve the last name for each student and `LEFT()` to get the first name (although you could have used `SUBSTRING()`). You also use the `LEN()` function to calculate the length of the name, and you use this value to calculate the length of the last name. The first four rows output from this query are as follows:

```
StudentName

---------------

Akbar, Mohammed
Alaska, Steve
Andrews, Vic
Burton, Gary
...
```

Oracle

Oracle doesn't support LEFT() or RIGHT(), so you'll use SUBSTR() to extract the first and last names from the student's full name as stored in the database.

EXAMPLE: MANIPULATING STRINGS (ORACLE)

The query looks like this in Oracle:

```
SELECT
    SUBSTR(Name, INSTR(Name, ' ') + 1) || ', ' ||
    SUBSTR(Name, 1, INSTR(Name, ' ') - 1) AS StudentName
FROM Student
ORDER BY StudentName;
```

Oracle allows you to use the version of SUBSTR() with only two parameters, retrieving the whole of the remainder of the string from the specified position onward, so you'll use this to extract the last name (the whole string after the space). You retrieve the first name by retrieving the substring from position one (the first character) to the character before the space. Here are the results:

```
StudentName

---------------
Akbar, Mohammed
Alaska, Steve
Andrews, Vic
Burton, Gary
...
```

DB2

DB2 does support LEFT() and RIGHT(), but because its version of SUBSTR() can take only two arguments, the query is actually no longer if you don't use them.

EXAMPLE: MANIPULATING STRINGS (DB2)

This is how the query looks in DB2:

```
SELECT
    SUBSTR(Name, POSSTR(Name, ' ') + 1) || ', ' ||
    SUBSTR(Name, 1, POSSTR(Name, ' ') - 1) AS StudentName
FROM Student
ORDER BY StudentName;
```

Apart from the fact that DB2 uses POSSTR() for the more usual INSTR(), this is the same as the Oracle version. The output from this query is the same as on SQL Server and Oracle:

```
StudentName

---------------
Akbar, Mohammed
Alaska, Steve
Andrews, Vic
Burton, Gary
...
```

One interesting side note is what happens if you try to perform the query using the LEFT() and RIGHT() functions:

```
SELECT
    RIGHT(Name, LENGTH(Name) - POSSTR(Name, ' ') + 1) ||
    ', ' || LEFT(Name, POSSTR(Name, ' ') - 1) AS StudentName
FROM Student
ORDER BY StudentName;
```

What you get is this error:

```
An expression resulting in a string data type with a maximum
length greater than 255 bytes is not permitted in:

A SELECT DISTINCT statement
A GROUP BY clause
An ORDER BY clause
A column function with DISTINCT
A SELECT or VALUES statement of a set operator other than
    UNION ALL.
```

This is because the LEFT() and RIGHT() functions return results as varchar(4000), so although your formatted StudentName will never approach a length of 255 bytes, it's treated by DB2 as potentially greater than that. To correct that, you can set the length of the column using the VARCHAR() function, which you'll look at shortly when you learn about data type conversions.

MySQL

Like DB2, MySQL supports both LEFT() and RIGHT() and the version of SUBSTRING() with just two parameters.

The query looks like this in MySQL:

```
SELECT
    CONCAT(RIGHT(Name, LENGTH(Name) - INSTR(Name, ' ') + 1),
           ', ', LEFT(Name, INSTR(Name, ' ') - 1))
    AS StudentName
FROM Student
ORDER BY StudentName;
```

This query, using the CONCAT() operator, will work in both standard and ANSI modes. In ANSI mode, you can also use the || operator to perform concatenation, but that won't work in standard mode. Here are the results:

```
StudentName

---------------
Akbar, Mohammed
Alaska, Steve
Andrews, Vic
Burton, Gary
...
```

Access

Access supports LEFT() and RIGHT() but uses MID() instead of SUBSTRING().

This is how the query looks in Access:

```
SELECT
    RIGHT(Name, LEN(Name) - INSTR(Name, ' ') + 1) & ', ' &
    LEFT(Name, INSTR(Name, ' ') - 1) AS StudentName
FROM Student
ORDER BY
    RIGHT(Name, LEN(Name) - INSTR(Name, ' ') + 1);
```

Remember that you can't use the alias column names of calculated columns in Access `ORDER BY` clauses. This means you have to repeat the formula used to calculate the column. To save space, here you've just sorted by the last name part; because no two of the sample students have the same last name, this won't affect the ordering:

```
StudentName

---------------
Akbar, Mohammed
Alaska, Steve
Andrews, Vic
Burton, Gary
...
```

Working with Dates and Times

In general, datetime literal values are a special case of string values where the specific string is formatted in a certain way. Most RDBMSs will accept a wide variety of datetime specifications, but you do have to be careful to write date-time literal values in a form that will work internationally. For example, the following literal value might be considered unacceptable:

```
'05/02/2003'
```

This is because the locale settings on a server might mean that this is inter-preted either as `'mm/dd/yyyy'` or `'dd/mm/yyyy'`.

However, reversing the values to `'yyyy/mm/dd'` works in every locale. Note that the separator here, /, can be replaced with - or in some formats can be omitted entirely or replaced with a dot (.), with the date expressed as an eight-digit number. The standard form is to use dashes; the following literal, then, is unambiguous:

```
'2003-05-02'
```

NOTE *Note that Access requires datetime literals to be enclosed in pound characters, so you'd write this as* #2003-05-02# *if you're using Access.*

In addition, you can be even clearer by using a more human readable format such as:

```
'May 2, 2003'
```

However, formatting a date in this way may take more fiddling around with strings in your code than you'd like.

Time constants are formatted as follows:

```
'hh:mm:ss.fff'
```

Here hh is hours, mm is minutes, ss is seconds, and fff is used to get even more precise with fractions of seconds, for example:

```
'14:59:02.129'
```

However, you needn't specify as much information as this. You can omit second data, for example:

```
'14:59'
```

You can also use a 12-hour clock:

```
'2:59 PM'
```

Finally, date and time values can be combined into a single string:

```
'2003-05-02 14:59:02.129'
```

Here a space separates the date and time values, and you can use any of the formats described previously for the date and time.

Note that there are certain restrictions placed on SQL date and time formats enforced by the various RDBMSs. For example, when using Oracle it may be necessary to include a DATE, TIME, or TIMESTAMP keyword before the string used to represent the date and time in order to specify how the string should be interpreted.

For example, you could represent a date using the following Oracle literal value:

```
DATE '2003-05-02'
```

Oracle also allows time intervals to be represented, using a similar syntax as the previous example with the addition of a requirement to specify what the first number in the interval string is (such as YEAR or DAY, with an optional single-digit precision specification saying how many digits are used for the value, for example, YEAR(4) for a four-digit amount of years) and, optionally, what the last number is (using similar nomenclature) using a suffix. There are two types of Oracle interval, known as YEAR TO MONTH and DAY TO SECOND, where the former has a precision of months or less and the latter seconds or less.

The following shows a DAY TO SECOND interval of five days and four hours:

```
INTERVAL '5:4' DAY TO HOUR
```

The following is a YEAR TO MONTH interval of 5,000 years:

```
INTERVAL '5000' YEAR(4)
```

For more details on this, consult your Oracle documentation.

Using Datetime Functions

The syntax and functionality of the date functions vary significantly from system to system, so we won't list them here. Instead, we'll present an example for each RDBMS where you calculate how long each student has been enrolled by working out the maximum difference between the current date and the date when they first enrolled.

You group the rows in the Enrollment table by StudentID and use the MAX aggregate function to get the amount of days since the first enrollment (because students may have enrolled in multiple classes, the MAX function finds the earliest). Finally, you order the resultant data by this calculated average to rank students.

In most cases, you can use some form of subtraction to work out the number of days since each student's first enrollment, but the exact syntax varies considerably.

SQL Server

To calculate the difference between two dates in SQL Server, you use the DATEDIFF() function. Subtracting one date from another is permitted in SQL Server, but the return value is itself a date and not very meaningful.

EXAMPLE: DIFFERENCES BETWEEN DATES (SQL SERVER)

Enter and execute this query against the InstantUniversity database:

```
SELECT StudentID, MAX(DATEDIFF(dd, EnrolledOn, GETDATE()))
                                    AS DaysEnrolled
FROM Enrollment
GROUP BY StudentID
ORDER BY DaysEnrolled DESC;
```

DATEDIFF() calculates the time difference between two dates; the first parameter of this function selects the units to work with, in this case, days. You look at
how many days have elapsed between the enrollment date stored in the EnrolledOn
column and the current date, obtained using the GETDATE() function. The output
is as follows:

```
StudentID    DaysEnrolled

-----------  ------------
4            152
7            152
10           152
9            149
8            149
5            149
6            149
1            149
3            142
2            -216
```

Note that the last value is negative because some of the enrollment dates are
in the future (at the time of writing). This wouldn't happen if you were using real
data, of course, but it does demonstrate that DATEDIFF() returns a signed rather
than an absolute value.

Oracle

With Oracle, you can perform a straightforward subtraction of two dates.

EXAMPLE: DIFFERENCES BETWEEN DATES (ORACLE)

The Oracle version of the query looks like this:

```
SELECT StudentID,
       FLOOR(MAX(CURRENT_DATE - EnrolledOn)) AS DaysEnrolled
FROM Enrollment
GROUP BY StudentID
ORDER BY DaysEnrolled DESC;
```

You retrieve the current date and time using CURRENT_DATE and subtract the value of the EnrolledOn column to find out how long each student has been enrolled for each class. This operation returns an INTERVAL value; because this can contain a time portion (expressed using decimals), you round this down to the nearest day using FLOOR() (you use FLOOR() rather than CEILING() to include only complete days). The output is the same as for the SQL Server version:

```
StudentID    DaysEnrolled

----------   ------------
4            152
7            152
10           152
...          ...
```

DB2

You again use subtraction to calculate the number of days each student has been enrolled with DB2, but you need first to convert the dates into a simple count of days by calling the DAYS() function.

EXAMPLE: DIFFERENCES BETWEEN DATES (DB2)

In DB2, the query looks like this:

```
SELECT StudentID,
       MAX(DAYS(CURRENT_DATE) - DAYS(EnrolledOn))
                                AS DaysEnrolled
FROM Enrollment
GROUP BY StudentID
ORDER BY DaysEnrolled DESC;
```

Again, you retrieve the present date using CURRENT_DATE. The DAYS() function allows you to represent a date as a simple integer by returning the number of days since December 31, 1 BC, so you just need to calculate the difference between the DAYS() values for the current date and for the EnrolledOn date:

```
StudentID   DaysEnrolled

----------- ------------
4           152
7           152
10          152
...         ...
```

MySQL

The MySQL version of the query is similar to the DB2 version except that you use the TO_DAYS() function.

EXAMPLE: DIFFERENCES BETWEEN DATES (MYSQL)

This is the MySQL version of the query:

```
SELECT StudentID,
       MAX(TO_DAYS(CURRENT_DATE) - TO_DAYS(EnrolledOn))
                                        AS DaysEnrolled
FROM Enrollment
GROUP BY StudentID
ORDER BY DaysEnrolled DESC;
```

As in Oracle and DB2, you use CURRENT_DATE to retrieve the present date. TO_DAYS() works in a similar way to DB2's DAYS() function, but it returns the number of days since the start of a mythical "Year Zero" (this figure is 365 days greater than the figure returned by DAYS()):

```
StudentID    DaysEnrolled

-----------  ------------
4            152
7            152
10           152
...          ...
```

Access

The Access version of the query is the simplest; all you need to do is perform a straightforward subtraction.

EXAMPLE: DIFFERENCES BETWEEN DATES (ACCESS)

The query looks like this in Access:

```
SELECT StudentID, MAX(DATE() - EnrolledOn) AS DaysEnrolled
FROM Enrollment
GROUP BY StudentID
ORDER BY MAX(DATE() - EnrolledOn) DESC;
```

Here you use the DATE() function to get the current date. Simply subtracting one date from another returns the difference in days between the two dates. As in other Access examples, you can't use the alias of the calculated column in the ORDER BY clause, so you need to repeat the formula. Here are the results:

```
StudentID    DaysEnrolled

-----------  ------------
4            152
7            152
10           152
...          ...
```

Performing Data Type Conversions

You've already seen a few examples where you need to convert a value into a different data type. It may be necessary, for example, when you want to perform string concatenation including a numeric value or when you want to round a floating-point value to an integer for display. Most RDBMSs provide both generic functions that you can use to cast to any type and functions for casting to specific types such as strings or integers.

Casting to Strings

Let's look first at the functions that exist specifically for converting non-string types to strings. In most cases, you can also use these functions to alter the length of a string field.

SQL Server

In general, casts on SQL Server are performed using the CAST() or CONVERT() functions, which you'll look at shortly. However, you can use the STR() function to convert floating-point values into strings. This takes the following form:

```
STR(float, [length], [precision])
```

where *float* is the number you want to convert to a string, *length* is the length of the string, and *precision* is the number of decimal places to retain. Both the *length* and *precision* parameters are optional. If they aren't specified, *length* has a default value of 10, and *precision* a default of zero.

As an example, STR(43.2461, 5, 2) returns '43.25'. If the data is corrupted because the *length* isn't long enough to hold all the digits before the decimal point, the returned string will be filled with asterisks. For example, STR(4326.12, 3) returns '***'. If the *length* isn't sufficient to hold all the decimal places, these will be discarded and the value rounded according the space available, so STR(43.184, 4, 2) returns '43.2'.

Oracle

Oracle allows you to convert character, numeric, and date types to strings using the TO_CHAR() and TO_NCHAR() functions. With dates and numeric types, you can also specify a format string. For example:

```
TO_CHAR(333, '0000.0')                      -- '0333.0'
TO_CHAR(333.15, '0000.0')                   -- '0333.2'
TO_CHAR(DATE '2003-05-23', 'DD MONTH YYYY') -- '23 MAY 2003'
```

DB2

DB2 is relatively strongly typed and has specific conversion functions for all its supported data types. These include the CHAR() and VARCHAR() functions, which you use for converting data to the CHAR and VARCHAR types, respectively. CHAR() can be used with most data types, but VARCHAR() is limited to character, date, and graphic types. If used with a character type, VARCHAR() can take a second parameter indicating the length of the string returned; otherwise, it takes only one parameter—the value to convert.

Depending on the type of data involved, CHAR() can also have a second parameter. If you're converting a date, you can specify one of the values ISO, USA, EUR, JIS, or LOCAL to indicate how to format the string. For example, CHAR(DATE('2003-02-24'), USA) returns '02/24/2003', but CHAR(DATE('2003-02-24'), EUR) returns '24.02.2003'.

You can also specify the length for character types or the decimal point character to use for floating-point types. For example, CHAR(32.47, ',') returns '32,47'.

MySQL

MySQL is weakly typed and will generally try to convert values as necessary. If you need to convert a value explicitly to a string, you can simply concatenate the value with an empty string:

```
CONCAT(23.52, '')  -- Returns '23.52'
```

Access

Access supports the STR() function for converting dates and numeric types to strings:

```
STR(#2003-01-01#) ' Returns '01/01/2003', depending on locale
STR(23.52)        ' Returns '23.52'
```

Unlike the SQL Server version of this function, STR() in Access doesn't allow you to specify the length of the returned string.

Casting to Numbers

Some RDBMSs also provide specific functions for casting non-numeric types to numeric types, but in many cases more flexibility is available with the generic conversion functions.

SQL Server

SQL Server doesn't have specific functions for converting to numeric types—use CAST()/CONVERT() instead.

Oracle

Oracle supports the TO_NUMBER() function, which allows you to convert character types into numbers. As well as the string to convert, you can specify a format string that the function can use to work out how to interpret the string. This allows the string to contain characters such as hexadecimal and currency symbols that might not otherwise be permitted in a numeric value:

```
TO_NUMBER('FFFF', 'XXXX')              -- Returns 655535
TO_NUMBER('$5,102.25', '$9,999.99')    -- Returns 5102.25
```

DB2

DB2 supports a range of functions for converting numeric and character values to different numeric types. Some of the more common are the following:

- `INTEGER()`/`INT()`: Converts numeric or character data to an integer.

- `DOUBLE()`/`FLOAT()`: Converts numeric or character data to a floating-point value.

- `DECIMAL()`/`DEC()`: Converts numeric or character data to a decimal. As well as the data to convert, this function lets you specify the total number of digits and the number of digits after the decimal place; for example, `DECIMAL(37.54, 3, 1)` returns `37.5`.

MySQL

Because of its weak typing, MySQL allows you to convert strings or dates to numbers just by adding zero to them. For example, `'23.5' + 0` returns `23.5` as a numeric type. If the string begins with a number but contains non-numeric characters, only that section that can be interpreted as a number will be returned; if the string begins with characters that can't be converted to a numeric value, zero will be returned. For example, `'4.5 strings'` returns `4.5`, but `'strings 4 u'` returns `0`.

Access

Access supports the `INT()` function, which allows you to convert non-numeric data types into integers (with rounding down). For example, `INT('4.8')` returns `4`, and `INT('5.23e3')` returns `5230`.

Using Generic Casting

Two generic casting functions have fairly widespread support: `CAST()`, which is the ANSI standard and is supported by SQL Server, Oracle, DB2, and MySQL, and `CONVERT()`, which is the Open Database Connectivity (ODBC) form and is supported by SQL Server and MySQL.

 NOTE *Support for* `CAST()` *and* `CONVERT()` *was added in MySQL 4.0.2; in previous versions, you'll need to use the implicit casting methods mentioned previously.*

The syntax for CAST() is as follows:

```
CAST(expression AS data_type)
```

In SQL Server, Oracle, and DB2, the *data_type* can optionally include details of the size of the target data type and (for decimal values) the number of places after the decimal point:

```
CAST('3.521' AS DECIMAL(3,2))   -- Returns 3.52
```

> **NOTE** *Note that MySQL doesn't allow this syntax and only permits you to specify the data type itself—not size or precision details. Also, MySQL will only allow casting to one of the following types:* BINARY, DATE, DATETIME, TIME, SIGNED [INTEGER], *or* UNSIGNED [INTEGER].

The syntax for CONVERT() in MySQL is as follows:

```
CONVERT(expression, data_type)
```

Again, *data_type* must be one of the types listed previously, and you aren't permitted to indicate the length of the type.

The SQL Server syntax for CONVERT() is as follows:

```
CONVERT(data_type [(length)], expression [, style])
```

The *style* parameter is a number that indicates how to format a datetime value if you're casting to a datetime or how a datetime is formatted if you're converting one to another type:

```
CONVERT(varchar, GETDATE(), 106)   -- Returns current date in
                                   -- the format '27 Feb 2003'
```

See the Microsoft MSDN Web site at http://msdn.microsoft.com/library/ en-us/tsqlref/ts_ca-co_2f30.asp?frame=true for full details of the possible values of this number.

Creating Functions

Now that you've seen how to use some of the most common built-in functions available in most RDBMSs, let's look at how you can define your own. ANSI SQL-99 defines a CREATE FUNCTION statement, which is implemented (with the inevitable differences) by most vendors and which allows you to create your own User-Defined Functions (UDFs). The basic syntax, common to most implementations, boils down to no more than this:

```
CREATE FUNCTION function_name [(parameter_list)]
RETURNS data_type
<SQL statement(s)>
```

To learn the actual syntax in the different RDBMSs, you'll look at an example. Notice that Access doesn't support UDFs, so there isn't an example for that system. For the sake of both clarity and conciseness, we won't present every option for each RDBMS, but we'll explain the main options. This example is based on the string manipulation example earlier in this chapter, where you reversed the order of the first and last names of each student.

Calling user-defined functions is the same as calling the built-in functions. Once you've created it, you can call your FormatName() function in the query:

```
SELECT FormatName(Name) AS StudentName
FROM Student
ORDER BY StudentName;
```

However, you may need to specify the schema where the function is stored in SQL Server (for example, dbo.FormatName(Name)).

This will return a list of the students, sorted according to their last names:

```
StudentName

------------------
Akbar, Mohammed
Alaska, Steve
Andrews, Vic
Burton, Gary
Fernandez, Maria
Foster, Andrew
Jones, John
Jonsson, Isabelle
Lee, Bruce
Picard, Julia
Scarlett, Emily
Wolff, Anna
```

SQL Server

The basic syntax for creating a function in SQL Server is as follows:

```
CREATE FUNCTION function_name [(parameter_list)]
RETURNS data_type
AS
BEGIN
   [<SQL statements>]
   RETURN expression
END
```

The function can contain multiple SQL statements but mustn't perform any permanent changes to the data in the database.

EXAMPLE: CREATING A FUNCTION (SQL SERVER)

Here's the SQL Server version of the FormatName() UDF:

```
CREATE FUNCTION FormatName (@FullName varchar(50))
RETURNS varchar(50)
AS
BEGIN
   RETURN RIGHT(@FullName, LEN(@FullName) -
              CHARINDEX(' ', @FullName) + 1) + ', ' +
          LEFT(@FullName, CHARINDEX(' ', @FullName) - 1)
END
```

The parameter list defined after the function name takes the following form:

```
(@FullName varchar(50))
```

As with the parameters and variables of stored procedures (which you'll look at in Chapter 9, "Using Stored Procedures"), the parameters and variables in UDFs in SQL Server are prefixed with an @ character, both when they're defined in the parameter list and when they're referenced in the body of the function.

Although you could have multiple SQL statements in the function, in this case you just return the formatted name; this expression returned from the function is exactly the same expression as you used in the early example.

Oracle

In general, the basic syntax for defining Oracle functions is similar to that for stored procedures, which you'll look at in Chapter 9, "Using Stored Procedures":

```
CREATE [OR REPLACE] FUNCTION function_name
(parameter_list)
RETURN data_type
IS
variable_list
BEGIN
    [<SQL statements>]
    RETURN expression;
END;
/
```

There are a couple of differences to the standard syntax. First, as with many Oracle objects, you can indicate that you want to replace any existing object of the same name using the OR REPLACE option. Note that the return type is declared using the RETURN keyword rather than the standard RETURNS. Parameters can be marked as input (IN) or output (OUT) parameters, just as they can for stored procedures.

Second, you need to declare any variables used in the function before the BEGIN...END block. The final / is simply a device to let SQL*Plus know that you've reached the end of a block that includes a number of SQL statements (as the semicolon that usually marks the end of a statement is used within CREATE FUNCTION).

EXAMPLE: CREATING A FUNCTION (ORACLE)

The Oracle version of the FormatName() function is as follows:

```
CREATE OR REPLACE FUNCTION FormatName(FullName IN varchar)
RETURN varchar
IS
FormattedName varchar(50);
BEGIN
    FormattedName :=
        SUBSTR(FullName, INSTR(FullName, ' ') + 1) || ', ' ||
        SUBSTR(FullName, 1, INSTR(FullName, ' ') - 1);
    RETURN(FormattedName);
END;
/
```

Here you define just one input parameter—the name that you want to format—and no output parameters. You also declare a variable, FormattedName, just to show the syntax although you could actually manage without it for this function.

Within the body of the function, you set your FormattedName variable to the expression you want to return (using the special PL/SQL := operator) and then return this variable from the function using the RETURN keyword. You'll look at using variables in SQL in more detail in Chapter 9, "Using Stored Procedures."

DB2

The basic syntax for creating a function in DB2 follows the ANSI standard quite closely and looks like this:

```
CREATE FUNCTION function_name(parameter_list)
    RETURNS data_type
    [LANGUAGE SQL]
    [DETERMINISTIC | NON DETERMINISTIC]
    [CONTAINS SQL | READS SQL DATA]
[BEGIN ATOMIC]
    [<SQL statements>]
    RETURN expression;
[END]
```

There are a number of options you can specify for the function. First, you can tell DB2 that your function is in SQL (rather than a programming language such as C++ or Java) using the LANGUAGE SQL option. Second, you can use the DETERMINISTIC keyword to indicate that the function will always return the same result for a given parameter (or you can specify NOT DETERMINISTIC if this isn't the case); knowing this allows DB2 to optimize the function. Finally, you can specify READS SQL DATA to indicate that your function reads data from a database or CONTAINS SQL to indicate that your function uses SQL keywords and functions to manipulate the data passed in, without retrieving further data from the database.

The function body can consist merely of a RETURN statement followed by an expression, or it can contain a block of SQL statements surrounded by the BEGIN ATOMIC...END keywords.

EXAMPLE: CREATING A FUNCTION (DB2)

In DB2, the `FormatName()` UDF looks like this:

```
CREATE FUNCTION FormatName(FullName varchar(50))
    RETURNS varchar(50)
    LANGUAGE SQL
    DETERMINISTIC
    CONTAINS SQL
BEGIN ATOMIC
    DECLARE FormattedName VARCHAR(50);
    SET FormattedName =
        SUBSTR(FullName, POSSTR(FullName, ' ') + 1) || ', ' ||
        SUBSTR(FullName, 1, POSSTR(FullName, ' ') - 1);
    RETURN FormattedName;
END
```

This function will always return the same value for a given parameter, so you declare it as DETERMINISTIC. You don't read any data from the database—you just work with the string passed into the function—so you also include the CONTAINS SQL clause (rather than READS SQL DATA).

For this example, you could write the body of the function as a single RETURN statement, but you want to show the syntax using a block of SQL statements, so you haven't. Instead, as in the Oracle example, you've defined a variable to store the formatted name and then returned that. Before you use the variable, you must explicitly declare it:

```
DECLARE FormattedName VARCHAR(50);
```

You'll look at using DB2 variables in more detail in Chapter 9, "Using Stored Procedures."

MySQL

This last example is by far the most complicated because MySQL doesn't support UDFs written in SQL. Instead, you need to write the function in C or C++ and then register it with MySQL using the CREATE FUNCTION statement. The CREATE FUNCTION syntax for MySQL is as follows:

```
CREATE [AGGREGATE] FUNCTION function_name
RETURNS {STRING | REAL | INTEGER}
SONAME shared_library_name;
```

The AGGREGATE keyword must be specified if your function aggregates rows like SQL aggregate functions such as COUNT. This has an impact on the way the function is coded. The SONAME clause indicates the shared library (SO or DLL) where the function is defined.

Because this isn't a SQL example and because the example will differ depending on what platform you're using, we'll go through it quickly. For full details, check the MySQL documentation and the udf_example example functions, which are available as part of the source distribution of MySQL.

EXAMPLE: CREATING A FUNCTION (MYSQL)

First, then, you need to write the C/C++ code for the function. This code must be compiled into a shared object (Linux) or dynamic-link library (Windows). The following is the code for the FormatName() example:

```
#include <string>

#include <my_global.h>
#include <my_sys.h>
#include <mysql.h>

using namespace std;

char* FormatName(UDF_INIT *initid, UDF_ARGS *args,
                 char *result, unsigned long *length,
                 char *is_null, char *error)
{
   // Retrieve the Name parameter from the args parameter
   char* fullName = new char[args->lengths[0]];
   fullName = args->args[0];

   // Convert from char* to string
   string strName = fullName;

   // Trim whitespace from end of string
   int i = strName.length();
   while (strName[i] == ' ' || strName[i] == '\0') i--;
   string trimName = strName.substr(0, i + 1);
```

```
    // Arrange in 'LastName, FirstName' format
    int spaceIndex = trimName.find_first_of(" ");
    string firstName = trimName.substr(0, spaceIndex);
    string lastName = trimName.substr(spaceIndex + 1);
    string formattedName = lastName + ", " + firstName;

    // Convert back to char* and set the length argument
    char* fmtName = new char[];
    formattedName.copy(result, string::npos);
    *length = static_cast<unsigned long>(i + 2);

    return result;
}
```

Note that MySQL prescribes the signature for the function. There are three versions, depending on whether the function returns a string (as previously), a floating-point value, or an integer.

Before compiling the DLL/SO, you need to indicate to the linker that your function is to be exported so that MySQL can see it within the library. To do this, you can use a linker definition file (in this case called MySQLFunction.def):

```
LIBRARY "MySQLFunction"
EXPORTS
    FormatName
```

Once you've compiled the library, you need to register the function with MySQL. To do this, you just need to execute this CREATE FUNCTION statement:

```
CREATE FUNCTION FormatName
RETURNS STRING
SONAME 'C:\\MySQL\\lib\\MySQLFunction.dll';
```

In this case, you've specified the exact path to the DLL on a Windows machine. On a Linux machine, you would instead copy the SO to a location where the ld program can find it or configure ld to look in the directory where the SO is stored. How to do this varies depending on the exact platform.

Summary

This chapter cleared up some outstanding issues from previous chapters concerning literal values and calculations, and it covered the basic syntax behind using and creating functions in SQL. Specifically, you've learned about the following:

- Different types of literal values in SQL and how to express them

- SQL operators

- Building SQL expressions involving calculations

- Basic function syntax

- The variation in functions between RDBMSs and some of the most common functions that vary relatively little between platforms

- How to create your own user-defined functions using SQL statements.

This leaves you in a much better position to continue with the SQL tutorial.

CHAPTER 6

Combining SQL Queries

IN THIS CHAPTER, YOU'LL look for the first time at ways that you can combine several SELECT statements in a single query. The first topic discussed is the use of *subqueries*. Put simply, a subquery is a query that's embedded in some way inside another query.

For example, in Chapter 2, "Retrieving Data with SQL," you saw how you can check whether a value is in a certain set using the IN keyword. You can use the same syntax but extract the values from a SQL query rather than hard-coding them:

```
SELECT Name FROM Student
WHERE StudentID IN (
    SELECT StudentID FROM StudentExam
    WHERE ExamID = 1);
```

This returns the names of all the students who took a particular exam and is just one of many examples of using subqueries that you'll investigate in this chapter.

The latter half of the chapter discusses how to combine SQL queries using a variety of *set operators*, such as the UNION operator. You use these operators when you want to compare data from different tables that are similar in structure but that contain different data.

Using Subqueries

Any query embedded inside another in any way is termed a *subquery*. The subquery itself may include a subquery and so on, which is where you really start to see how the *Structured* part of SQL's name fits in! This is also the first time you start to see multitable queries creeping in because there's no reason why a subquery has to query the same table as any of its "parents" or "children." In the next chapter, you'll see how you can include multiple tables in a single query by using table joins; both techniques have their benefits, so we'll present them separately.

All subqueries can be divided into one of two categories: *non-correlated* or *correlated*. The true meaning of each of these terms will become clearer as you work through some examples, but basically the following is true:

- A non-correlated subquery is one where the subquery is "independent" of the outer query. The subquery will execute once in total and simply pass on any value (or values) to the outer query.

- A correlated subquery relies on data from the outer query in order to execute. The subquery will execute once *for every row* returned by the outer query.

It can be important to note this distinction in large databases because correlated queries typically take a lot longer to execute, and the time taken will increase dramatically as the volume of data increases. Let's look at some examples of how you can use subqueries. You'll see examples of each category along the way.

Subqueries As Calculated Columns

One simple form of a subquery is where the inner query returns a single result for each row returned by the outer query, usually as a result inserted into a calculated column:

```
SELECT ColumnA, (SubQuery) AS ColumnB FROM Table;
```

This type of subquery is useful when you have relationships between one table and another. For example, let's say you have a Customers table and a CreditCards table, and records in the CreditCards table are linked to individual customers via a foreign key. The following query enables you to see how many credit cards are on record for every customer in the database:

```
SELECT CustomerID, CustomerName, (
    SELECT COUNT(*) FROM CreditCards
    WHERE CreditCards.CustomerID = Customers.CustomerID)
    AS NumberOfCreditCards
FROM Customers
```

Here the subquery (highlighted in bold type) is one that wouldn't work on its own because it requires data (the CustomerID values) from the Customers table in the outer query but nestles into the outer query without problems. This is an example of a correlated subquery. The subquery executes once *for each row* acted on by the outer query. Let's look at a quick example showing a similar query in action.

EXAMPLE: SIMPLE SUBQUERIES

You're going to construct a query that will allow you to find out the number of exams taken by each student. Enter and execute the following against the InstantUniversity database:

```
SELECT StudentID, Name,
    (SELECT COUNT(*) FROM StudentExam
    WHERE StudentExam.StudentID = Student.StudentID)
    AS ExamsTaken
FROM Student
ORDER BY ExamsTaken DESC;
```

This query works in the same way as the one detailed previously, counting records in one table (StudentExam) with an aggregate function based on a value taken from a row in another table (Student). Note that you need to qualify names used in the subquery so you're unambiguous when referring to records in a different table.

Here the data used in the subquery is the StudentID column in the Student table, referred to using full syntax as Student.StudentID. This is compared with the StudentID column in the StudentExam table, referred to as StudentExam.StudentID, such that the number of records in the StudentExam table having the same StudentID value as that in the current record in the Student table is counted (using COUNT(*)).

The same qualification of names is necessary when the subquery works with the same table as the outer query, but here it's essential to use aliases for clarity.

The output from this query is as follows:

```
StudentID  Name              ExamsTaken

---------  ----------------  ----------
1          John Jones        2
2          Gary Burton       3
3          Emily Scarlett    2
4          Bruce Lee         3
...        ...               ...
```

As always, you can use aliases for the columns and tables in the query. The advantages of table aliases become obvious when you're querying multiple tables. If there are relationships between the tables, then it's quite likely that there will be column names that occur in more than one table. In this case, you need to prefix the table name to the column name to make it clear about which column you're talking. Because this can involve a lot of typing, it's useful to be able to replace the table name with an abridged name (usually with one or two letters).

EXAMPLE: USING ALIASES WITH SIMPLE SUBQUERIES

Execute the following query against the InstantUniversity database:

```
SELECT e1.StudentID, e1.ClassID, (
    SELECT COUNT(*) FROM Enrollment e2
    WHERE e1.ClassID = e2.ClassID)-1
    AS OtherStudentsInClass
FROM Enrollment e1
WHERE StudentID = 6;
```

Here you use aliases, even though you're only querying one table. Each time the outer query returns a row from Enrollment in this example, the inner query looks for records that have an identical entry in the ClassID column. In order to compare the ClassID values from the inner and outer queries, you must distinguish between them. Because the table name is the same, the only way to do this is using aliases, which is why e1 and e2 are used in the example.

Oracle 9i doesn't support the use of the AS keyword in this type of alias, even though it supports it elsewhere. This query will run on SQL Server, DB2, and Access with or without AS.

Note that the subquery also counts the row that's currently being examined by the outer query, so if you want to get the number of other students enrolled in the same class, you must subtract one from the value returned.

There are three rows returned from this query:

StudentID	ClassID	OtherStudentsInClass
6	3	2
6	6	3
6	10	1

Subqueries in the WHERE Clause

There are a number of ways to use subqueries in your SELECT statements. Another option is to use them in a WHERE clause. In its simplest form, you have a query embedded in the WHERE clause of another query:

```
SELECT ColumnA FROM TableA
WHERE ColumnB = (SubQuery);
```

One extremely helpful way to use this is to utilize data from one record in the table as part of the search criteria to find other records, all in a single query. For example, the following query will return all exams sustained on the same date as, or before, the exam with an ExamID of 5:

```
SELECT ExamID, SustainedOn FROM Exam
WHERE SustainedOn <= (
    SELECT SustainedOn FROM Exam WHERE ExamID = 5)
ORDER BY SustainedOn DESC;
```

Note that you don't need semicolons at the end of subqueries because these are in fact part of the outer statement.

Here the inner query obtains a single value that's the SustainedOn value of the exam with an ExamID of 5:

```
SELECT SustainedOn FROM Exam WHERE ExamID = 5
```

This value is used by the outer query, which finds all exams with an equal or earlier SustainedOn value. The results are ordered according to a descending value for SustainedOn, so you can expect the exam with an ExamID of 5 to be at the top of the results, with subsequent records being earlier exams and the earliest appearing last in the list.

Note that MySQL doesn't support subqueries in this way. Instead, you need to use two queries (getting the date when that exam was taken and then passing this date into a second query). For correlated subqueries, you can generally use the JOIN syntax presented in the next chapter.

In this example, both queries work independently on the same data. The subquery does not rely on data from the outer query in order to execute (an easy way to tell this is that the subquery will execute perfectly well as a stand-alone query). This is an example of a non-correlated subquery. The subquery executes once in total and simply passes the resulting value to the outer query.

In the previous example, you worked on a single table, but there's nothing stopping you from using multiple tables. Say, for example, you know that an exam was sustained on March 10, but you're not sure for which course and you need to know. The following query would do the trick:

```
SELECT Name FROM Course
WHERE CourseID =
(
SELECT CourseID from EXAM
WHERE SustainedOn='10-MAR-03'
);
```

In the inner query, you find out the `CourseID` for the exam sustained on March 10. That value is passed to the outer query, which then returns the name of the course. The output should look like this:

```
NAME
----------------
Core Mathematics
```

However, the previous query is only suitable if you know for a fact that the query will return only a *single row*. If, in fact, it returns multiple rows, then the query will fail:

```
SELECT Name FROM Course
WHERE CourseID =
(
SELECT CourseID from EXAM
WHERE SustainedOn='10-MAR-03'
);
select courseid from exam
*
ERROR at line 4:
ORA-01427: single-row subquery returns more than one row
```

Fortunately, it's quite easy to get around this problem.

Subqueries That Return Multiple Results

When you have a subquery that returns multiple rows, you simply use the `IN` keyword to check for set membership. For example:

```
SELECT ColumnA, ColumnB FROM Table
WHERE ColumnC IN (SELECT ColumnD FROM Table2);
```

Thus, you can easily rewrite the previous query so that it works for both single row and multiple row cases:

```
SELECT Name FROM Course
WHERE CourseID IN
(
SELECT CourseID from EXAM
WHERE SustainedOn='26-MAR-03'
);
```

Let's see a full example that uses this syntax; to add a bit of excitement, you'll use three nested subqueries.

EXAMPLE: USING SET MEMBERSHIP WITH SUBQUERIES

Say you want to obtain a list of the students who are taught by Professor Williams. Let's build the query up in stages. First, you find out the ID of Professor Williams:

```
SELECT ProfessorID FROM Professor
WHERE Name LIKE '%Williams%';
```

You use this value (in this case, the `ProfessorID` is 2) to find out the classes that Professor Williams teaches:

```
SELECT ClassID FROM Class WHERE ProfessorID IN
  (SELECT ProfessorID FROM Professor
  WHERE Name LIKE '%Williams%');
```

This query gets the `ClassID` values from the `Class` table that match your criteria. The set of values returned is passed to the next query:

```
SELECT StudentID FROM Enrollment WHERE ClassID IN
  (SELECT ClassID FROM Class WHERE ProfessorID IN
    (SELECT ProfessorID FROM Professor
    WHERE Name LIKE '%Williams%'));
```

This query uses that set of `ClassID` values to obtain from the `Enrollment` table the IDs of the students who take these classes. Finally, these IDs are passed to the outermost query:

```
SELECT StudentID, Name FROM Student WHERE StudentID IN
  (SELECT StudentID FROM Enrollment WHERE ClassID IN
```

```
(SELECT ClassID FROM Class WHERE ProfessorID IN
  (SELECT ProfessorID FROM Professor
  WHERE Name LIKE '%Williams%')));
```

If you execute the whole query against InstantUniversity, you should obtain the following results:

```
StudentID    Name

-----------  -----------------
2            Gary Burton
4            Bruce Lee
6            Vic Andrews
8            Julia Picard
10           Maria Fernandez
```

This may seem quite a complicated way to go about things, but it works. In fact, you can achieve the same results using simpler syntax with a multiple table JOIN query. You'll be looking at this subject in the next chapter.

Again, the previous example illustrates the use of non-correlated subqueries. No component query relies on its outer query in order to execute. Each query that makes up your subquery executes only once, and each in turn simply passes a value, or a set of values, to an outer query.

Before moving on, it's worth noting that the use of subqueries isn't restricted to the SELECT statement. You can include subqueries in any other SQL statement, such as an INSERT or DELETE statement, if appropriate.

Using Operators with Subqueries

You saw previously how you can use subqueries in conjunction with the IN operator to find rows where a field value belongs to a certain set of values. However, this isn't the only operator you can use with subqueries. In fact, there are four more: EXISTS, ALL, ANY, and SOME (although SOME is merely a synonym for ANY).

Using the EXISTS Operator

The EXISTS operator allows you to find rows that match a particular criterion. EXISTS is always followed by a subquery and evaluates to true if the subquery returns any rows at all.

This query returns the names and IDs of all the students who scored less than 40 in any one of their exams:

```
SELECT StudentID, Name FROM Student s
WHERE EXISTS (
   SELECT StudentID FROM StudentExam e
   WHERE Mark < 40 AND e.StudentID = s.StudentID);
```

The basic subquery here returns the IDs of all the students who scored less than 40 in an exam:

```
SELECT StudentID FROM StudentExam e
WHERE Mark < 40
```

However, this is a correlated subquery, so you want this query to run once for every row in the outer query. You do this by using table aliases and matching the value of the StudentID in the Student and StudentExam tables:

```
AND e.StudentID = s.StudentID
```

This query will execute once for every row in the Student table, so if a particular student scored less than 40 in one or more exam, the EXISTS condition for this query will be true, and the row for that student will be returned for the outer query. In total, you've got three of these underperforming students:

StudentID	Name
2	Gary Burton
5	Anna Wolff
8	Julia Picard

Using the ALL Operator

You're now quite well equipped if you want to find rows where the value in a particular column matches the values in a certain set. But what if you want to find rows where a column value is greater than or less than any or all of the values in a particular set? This is where the remaining operators come in—ALL and ANY.

The ALL operator is used with a subquery and a comparison operator such as =, >, or >= (and so on) and evaluates to true if the value being checked is greater than (or whatever) *all* the rows returned by the subquery. For example:

```
SELECT ColumnA FROM TableA
WHERE ColumnA > ALL (SELECT ColumnB FROM TableB);
```

This query will return all the rows from *TableA* where the value in *ColumnA* is greater than every single value in *ColumnB* of *TableB*.

EXAMPLE: USING THE ALL OPERATOR

Enter and execute the following query:

```
SELECT StudentID, Grade FROM Enrollment e
WHERE Grade > ALL (
    SELECT Mark FROM StudentExam s
    WHERE s.StudentID = e.StudentID);
```

Here you're looking for discrepancies between the overall performance of students and their marks in particular exams. In particular, you're looking to find the students whose overall grade for any class is greater than the top mark they received in all their exams.

Again, you use a correlated subquery with table aliases to achieve this. The subquery returns all the exam marks for each student in the outer query:

```
SELECT Mark FROM StudentExam s
WHERE s.StudentID = e.StudentID
```

You use this subquery with the ALL operator to find any rows in the Enrollment table where the Grade is greater than the highest exam mark received by the same student. This finds just one student in the sample data:

StudentID	Grade
2	68

Using the ANY Operator

ANY works in the same way as ALL but evaluates to true if the condition is true of *any* single value returned by the subquery. For example, the query:

```
SELECT ColumnA FROM TableA
WHERE ColumnA > ANY (SELECT ColumnB FROM TableB);
```

will return all the rows from *TableA* where the value in *ColumnA* is greater than any one of the individual values in *ColumnB* of *TableB*.

EXAMPLE: USING THE ANY OPERATOR

Type in this query and execute it against the InstantUniversity database:

```
SELECT StudentID, Grade FROM Enrollment e
WHERE Grade < ANY (
    SELECT Mark/2 FROM StudentExam s
    WHERE s.StudentID = e.StudentID);
```

Again, you're looking for discrepancies between students' exam marks and their overall grades. In this example, you retrieve the ID and grade of any student where that grade is less than half of the mark they got for any one exam.

The example works in a similar way to the previous example: The subquery returns the set of marks that each student in the outer query scored in their exams, divided by two:

```
SELECT Mark/2 FROM StudentExam s
WHERE s.StudentID = e.StudentID
```

You use the ANY operator to find out whether a student's grade is less than any single value in this set and, if so, return the student's ID and the grade:

```
StudentID    Grade

-----------  -----------
5            33
```

Combining Data from Queries

You may have noticed that, although you used data from various different tables in your subqueries, you only actually returned either a calculated column or column data from a single table. Sometimes it's useful to be able to retrieve data from multiple tables and to return all of that data, or a subset of that data, as a single set of rows.

SQL provides you with several *set operators* that allow you to combine SQL queries for this purpose—namely, UNION, UNION ALL, INTERSECT, and DIFFERENCE.

ANSI SQL refers to the DIFFERENCE operator, but it's referred to by other terms, depending on the database. Oracle calls this operator MINUS, and DB2 calls it EXCEPT.

The basic syntax for queries using these operators is as follows:

```
SELECT ColumnA, ColumnB FROM TableA
<Operator>
SELECT ColumnC, ColumnD FROM TableB;
```

The result will be two columns of data (generally called *ColumnA* and *ColumnB*) that contain data from all four columns. The actual set of data returned when you combine queries in this manner will vary depending on which operator you use.

The general rule for using these operators is that the data you extract from one table must have the same number of columns, and those columns must have the same data types, as the data extracted from other tables (or, at least, must be converted into the correct data types). So, as you can see, these operators were designed for use when you want to combine the contents of tables that have similar structure but different data. This means that in general, except of course where fortune (or indeed design) dictates, you have several tables with the same column data types.

The general technique for combining data from dissimilar tables is to use table joins, which you'll learn about in the next chapter.

A classic example of where you can use the UNION clause to great effect is when comparing an archived version of a table with the current version. Say, for example, that you archived the data in your InstantUniversity database on a yearly basis; you could then extract data from a table in the archived Class of 2002 database and compare it with data from the equivalent table in the current Class of 2003 database.

In general, however, you'll only extract a subset of the columns in each table. For example, if you were assembling a comparison between your products and those sold by a competitor, you might find that you could extract and combine the "similar" columns (product name, cost, and so on) from the tables carrying your own and your competitor's product information.

Let's start by examining the UNION operator.

Using the UNION Operator

The general syntax required to use UNION is simple:

```
SELECT ColumnA, ColumnB FROM TableA
UNION
SELECT ColumnC, ColumnD FROM TableB;
```

In general, whenever you use the UNION keyword, the column names are taken from the first SELECT query, but DB2 will assign arbitrary names if the column names aren't identical.

The UNION operator is supported in MySQL only from version 4.0 onward.

Suppose you have one table called Products with ProductID, ProductName, and ProductCost columns and one table called CompetitorProducts with ID, Name, and Cost columns, where the data types match. You could combine data from both these tables as follows:

```
SELECT ProductID, ProductName, ProductCost FROM Products
UNION
SELECT ID, Name, Cost FROM CompetitorProducts;
```

This would result in three columns of data—ProductID, ProductName, and ProductCost—containing data from both tables.

When you use UNION, you'll often need to include calculated columns or data type conversion to get column data to match. If, in the previous example, ProductID were a string value and ID were numeric, you would need to convert ID into a string. A handy way to do this would be to use the string conversion functions you looked at in the previous chapter. For example, you could use this on SQL Server:

```
SELECT ProductID, ProductName, ProductCost FROM Products
UNION
SELECT STR(ID), Name, Cost FROM CompetitorProducts;
```

Let's look at a working example.

EXAMPLE: COMBINING DATA WITH UNION

Enter and execute the following query:

```
SELECT Name, 'Professor' As Role FROM Professor
    WHERE ProfessorID = (
        SELECT ProfessorID FROM Class WHERE ClassID = 1)
UNION
SELECT Name, 'Student' FROM Student
    WHERE StudentID IN (
        SELECT StudentID FROM Enrollment WHERE ClassID = 1);
```

Note that this code won't work with MySQL 4.0 because it contains subqueries. A version of this query using table joins instead, which will work with MySQL, is available in the code download.

The query in this example extracts names from the Professor and Student tables that are involved in a specific class (subqueries are used here to match IDs with values in the Class and Enrollment tables, respectively). As well as extracting data, you provide a fixed value for a new calculated column, Role, which shows which table the name has come from:

```
Name            Role

-------------   ---------
Anna Wolff      Student
John Jones      Student
Julia Picard    Student
Prof. Dawson    Professor
...             ...
```

It's well worth noting here that the resultant data is sorted together rather than having two sorted lists on top of one another. You can use ORDER BY and filter on the result set just as you do with other data returned by queries.

NOTE   *It's normal for names to be sorted by last name rather than by first name. You could do this using the* FormatName() *function created in Chapter 5, "Performing Calculations and Using Functions."*

The previous example is pretty straightforward, but it doesn't quite fully illustrate how the UNION operator works. In set theoretical terms, a union of two sets of data will contain every member of each data set, *but with each member only being counted once.* So, the following:

```
{1, 2, 3, 4} UNION {3, 4, 5, 6}
```

produces this:

```
{1, 2, 3, 4, 5, 6}
```

In order to demonstrate this, let's use another query, which is designed to extract the underperforming students:

```
SELECT StudentID
    FROM StudentExam
    WHERE Mark < 40
UNION
SELECT StudentID
    FROM Enrollment
    WHERE GRADE < 40
ORDER BY StudentID;
```

This query returns the StudentID for every student who received one or more exam mark under 40, and every student who received one or more class grade under 40. The results are as follows:

```
StudentID

-----------
2
5
8
```

If you run each of the two queries involved in this UNION operation separately, you'll see that there's one student (with an ID of 5) who has received an exam mark under 10 and a class grade under 40. However, this student is only listed once in the result set. What in effect you have in this case is this:

```
{2, 5, 8} UNION {5},
```

which produces this:

```
{2, 5, 8}
```

Keeping Duplicate Rows

SQL allows you to override the usual rules of set theory and return all members of each set of data regardless of duplicates. You do this by simply using the UNION ALL operator:

```
SELECT ColumnA, ColumnB FROM TableA
UNION ALL
SELECT ColumnC, ColumnD FROM TableB;
```

By simply adding the ALL keyword to your UNION operator, your result set will include duplicate data.

This is in contrast to other SELECT queries, which as you've seen have required you to use the DISTINCT keyword to remove duplicate data.

This means that the following:

```
{1, 2, 3, 4} UNION ALL {3, 4, 5, 6}
```

produces this:

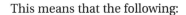

```
{1, 2, 3, 3, 4, 4, 5, 6}
```

This can be useful if you want to know the number of occurrences of a particular value in more than one table. Let's return to the underperforming students and perform the same query but using UNION ALL:

```
SELECT StudentID
    FROM StudentExam
    WHERE Mark < 40
UNION ALL
SELECT StudentID
    FROM Enrollment
    WHERE GRADE < 40
ORDER BY StudentID;
```

The results are as follows:

```
StudentID

-----------
2
5
5
8
```

Now, student 5, who was returned by both queries, is counted twice. This is quite useful because now you know that, although students 2 and 8 have suffered the odd bad exam grade, only student 5 is consistently underperforming in class.

Understanding Intersections and Differences

The last two operators are supported only by DB2 and Oracle, so we'll just present them briefly. The INTERSECT operator allows you to retrieve only the rows that occur in both queries. The following:

```
{1, 2, 3, 4} INTERSECT {3, 4, 5, 6}
```

produces this:

```
{3, 4}
```

The EXCEPT (called MINUS in Oracle) operator allows you to retrieve the rows that occur in the first but not the second query. For example, the following:

```
{1, 2, 3, 4} EXCEPT (or MINUS) {3, 4, 5, 6}
```

produces this:

```
{1, 2, 5, 6}
```

Let's demonstrate these by shaming the underachievers even more. The following query retrieves the IDs of all those students who scored less than 40 in at least one of their exams *and* were given at least one overall grade of less than 40:

```
SELECT StudentID
    FROM StudentExam
    WHERE Mark < 40
INTERSECT
SELECT StudentID
    FROM Enrollment
    WHERE GRADE < 40
ORDER BY StudentID;
```

The only row returned is, as you know, that for student 5:

```
StudentID

-----------
5
```

Let's alter the query a bit to find only those students who have done very badly in one or more exam but who haven't also received at least one very good grade. You can do this using the EXCEPT operator (DB2):

```
-- DB2 only
SELECT StudentID
    FROM StudentExam
    WHERE Mark < 40
EXCEPT
SELECT StudentID
    FROM Enrollment
    WHERE GRADE > 69
ORDER BY StudentID;
```

In Oracle, you use the MINUS operator in the same way:

```
-- Oracle only
SELECT StudentID
    FROM StudentExam
    WHERE Mark < 40
MINUS
SELECT StudentID
    FROM Enrollment
    WHERE GRADE > 69
ORDER BY StudentID;
```

This query returns the IDs of all the students who scored less than 40 in an exam, minus the set of students who achieved a grade of 70 or more. Two of the usual suspects show up:

```
StudentID

-----------
2
5
```

Summary

In this chapter, you examined subqueries and saw how to combine data from multiple queries into a single result set. To be specific, you've looked at the following:

- Formulating simple subqueries

- Using subqueries that return multiple values

- Understanding the difference between correlated and non-correlated subqueries

- Using the UNION keyword

- Using ALL with UNION to retain duplicate rows

- Extracting matching/nonmatching data from queries with INTERSECT and EXCEPT/MINUS

This chapter has been the first in which you've combined data from several tables together. In the next chapter, you'll look at other ways of doing this that have their own advantages.

CHAPTER 7

Querying Multiple Tables

QUERYING DATA FROM MULTIPLE tables using subqueries is a great capability, but it doesn't always give you everything you need, and the syntax can become a bit messy and confusing. Also, as discussed in the previous chapter, when a subquery executes for each match of an outer query, performance can be affected. For this reason, SQL allows you to query multiple tables simultaneously with a simpler syntax. This capability doesn't completely replace some of the techniques you saw in the previous chapter involving subqueries across multiple tables, but it's extremely powerful when you simply want a result set that contains information from more than one table. Because relational databases are designed to hold data in more than one table, where records in one table are usually associated with records in other tables, this functionality is essential.

In this chapter, you'll look at the various ways that multitable queries can be performed using what's known in SQL parlance as *joins*. You'll start, as usual, with the basics before building up to more complex situations. The simpler material concerns situations where you get a result set consisting of matches between rows in different tables based on certain criteria, either by looking at equality between column values or by using some other comparison. The more complex techniques involve forcing unmatched rows from one or more tables to be included in the results you receive, even if there's no match with a row in another table.

Understanding Simple Joins

Let's consider a simple example. Imagine that someone at the example university wants to know when rooms are occupied and when they're free. You could find out this information by querying the Class and Room tables from the sample InstantUniversity database:

```
SELECT Class.ClassID, Class.Time, Room.RoomID
FROM Room, Class;
```

Unfortunately, this won't yield the results you're after. You might think that you'd simply get a set of rows that consists of all the columns for both tables, with each row containing data from a row in the first table and a row from the second. Well, you'd be right. However, what you may not imagine is quite how many rows you'd get (try it out for yourself and see what happens!).

Basically, the result of the join is the Cartesian product of the elements in each set. For example, the Cartesian product of the two sets {a, b, c} and {a, b} is the following set of pairs:

```
{(a, a), (a, b), (b, a), (b, b), (c, a), (c, b)}
```

What happens in this example is that each row in Room is combined with each row in Class to give a row in the result set. So, the first row of Room is combined with the first row of Class for the first row in the result set. Next, the first row of Room is combined with the second row of Class, then the third row, the fourth row, and so on. The number of elements in the Cartesian product is the product of the number of elements in each set. In the example, you have nine rooms and 10 classes, so you have 90 results. Taking this further, if you had 100 rooms in your university and 100 classes scheduled, you'd end up with 10,000 rows of results!

In generic terms, imagine the following pseudoquery:

```
SELECT Table1.Column1, Table2.Column2, Table2.Column3 FROM Table1, Table2
```

Consider the situation where the previous query is executed, with the column *Table1.Column1* having the values T1C1V1, T1C1V2, and so on, with *Table1.Column2* having T1C2V1, T1C2V2, and with the same naming scheme for *Table2.Column1*. The first few rows returned will be as follows:

Table1.Column1	Table1.Column2	Table2.Column1
T1C1V1	T1C2V1	T2C1V1
T1C1V1	T1C2V1	T2C1V2
T1C1V1	T1C2V1	T2C1V3
T1C1V1	T1C2V1	T2C1V4

and so on for the rest of the rows in *Table2.Column1*. Next, you move on to the second row in *Table1*:

Table1.Column1	Table1.Column2	Table2.Column1
T1C1V2	T1C2V2	T2C1V1
T1C1V2	T1C2V2	T2C1V2
T1C1V2	T1C2V2	T2C1V3
T1C1V2	T1C2V2	T2C1V4

As before, you'll get one result for each row in *Table2*.

This type of join is known as a *cross join*, or Cartesian product. In fact, in all the RDBMSs covered in this book, except DB2, you can write the previous as follows:

```
SELECT Table1.Column1, Table1.Column2, Table2.Column3 FROM Table1 CROSS JOIN Table2
```

This CROSS JOIN operator is the SQL-92 standard.

In some circumstances, you might want this to happen but not many. What you need to do is to specify which rows in *Table1* should be joined with which rows in *Table2*. The way you tend to do this is to use table relationships. For example, you might stipulate that a row with a primary key value of *x* in *Table1* is joined to a row with the same foreign key value in *Table2*.

That way you might end up with 100 rows if there was a one-to-one correlation, or perhaps even less, if for example you were only joining a filtered group of rows in *Table1* to a filtered group of rows in *Table2*.

Using Two Table Equi-Joins

The most common way of associating rows from one table to another is via an *equi-join*. This is where you link rows based on an equality (hence "equi") between the values contained in a column of each row:

```
SELECT Table1.Column1, Table1.Column2, Table2.Column3 FROM Table1, Table2
   WHERE Table1.Column1 = Table2.Column2
```

As with cross joins, you can also express this using a more explicit keyword form, which is the SQL-92 standard and works for all current versions of the RDBMSs covered in this book:

```
SELECT Table1.Column1, Table1.Column2, Table2.Column3FROM Table1 JOIN Table2
   ON Table1.Column1 = Table2.Column2
```

Here, the difference is that you use the JOIN keyword rather than a comma and ON rather than WHERE. Because this is the standard form, you'll be using it in subsequent example code.

 NOTE   *For this example syntax to work on all database platforms and produce the same results,* JOIN *may have to be replaced by* INNER JOIN. *You'll see this in action in the upcoming example.*

Returning to the rooms and classes example, if you use the following SQL code, you'll see a much smaller result set:

```
SELECT Class.ClassID, Class.Time, Room.RoomID
FROM Room
    JOIN Class ON Room.RoomID = Class.RoomID;
```

You now see just 10 rows, one for each class, indicating what time and in which room each class is held.

You should note that versions of Oracle up to 8.1.7 don't support the JOIN keyword. Instead, simply use the following syntax:

```
SELECT Room.RoomID, Class.Time, Class.ClassID
FROM Room, Class
WHERE Room.RoomID = Class.RoomID;
```

As another example, if you had a table called Customers with a CustomerID column and a table called CreditCards that also had a CustomerID column (going back to an earlier example where you had multiple credit cards per customer), you might write the following:

```
SELECT Customers.CustomerID,
       Customers.CustomerName,
       CreditCards.CardNumber
FROM Customers
    JOIN CreditCards
    ON Customers.CustomerID = CreditCards.CustomerID;
```

Assuming there's a one-to-many relationship between these tables (one customer can have multiple credit cards), you'd get one row returned for each credit card in CreditCards. Note that some of these rows would have identical customer information because this is how you've asked for the data.

EXAMPLE: TWO TABLE EQUI-JOINS

Say you want to report the marks that have been achieved for every exam taken by every student. The following query will do the trick. Execute it against the InstantUniversity database:

```
SELECT StudentExam.ExamID,
       StudentExam.Mark,
       Student.Name AS StudentName
```

```
FROM StudentExam
    JOIN Student
    ON StudentExam.StudentID = Student.StudentID
ORDER BY ExamID;
```

Note that to run this example with MySQL and Access, you need to use `INNER JOIN` instead of `JOIN`:

```
...
FROM StudentExam
    INNER JOIN Student
...
```

(We'll explain what this extra clause means in just a moment.)
You should see the following results:

```
ExamID   Mark   StudentName

-------  -----  -------------
1        55     John Jones
1        26     Anna Wolff
1        71     Julia Picard
2        62     Anna Wolff
...      ...    ...
```

In this example, you've joined data from `StudentExam` directly to data from the `Student` table and presented it in a single result set. Rather than getting the `StudentID` value and having to then extract student names, joining the tables with the equi-join specification of `ON StudentExam.StudentID = Student.StudentID` gives you direct access to this information. This is much more efficient because you get the information you want without having to run a separate query or, as might be the case, several separate queries for each student.

Again, instead of using the JOIN clause in this example, you could have constructed the same query using WHERE clauses as follows:

```
SELECT StudentExam.ExamID,
       StudentExam.Mark,
       Student.Name AS StudentName
FROM StudentExam, Student
WHERE StudentExam.StudentID = Student.StudentID
ORDER BY ExamID;
```

Another point to note is that this type of join, and in fact any other type of join, can include additional clauses as examined in other chapters. A WHERE clause, for example, is just as valid in a join as in any other query. The following modification to the previous example gives just those students with a mark of 80 or more:

```
SELECT StudentExam.ExamID,
       StudentExam.Mark,
       Student.Name AS StudentName
FROM StudentExam JOIN Student
ON StudentExam.StudentID = Student.StudentID
WHERE StudentExam.Mark >= 80
ORDER BY ExamID;
```

It's important to bear this in mind in later examples, where you won't concentrate on anything other than the joining of tables because there's a whole world of flexibility available.

Using Multitable Equi-Joins

When it comes to equi-joins, there's no need to stop at two tables. You can include as many tables as you like, taking care to match rows to one another to avoid obtaining thousands of rows. To do this, you simply add another JOIN and ON clause after the first one:

```
SELECT * FROM Table1 JOIN Table2
   ON Table1.Column1 = Table2.Column2
   JOIN Table3
   ON Table1.Column3 = Table3.Column4
```

To go back to the customers and credit cards example, imagine that you have another table called Addresses, where each customer has one or more addresses stored. You could expand on the query to get columns from this new table with simple additions:

```
SELECT Customers.CustomerID,
       Customers.CustomerName,
       CreditCards.CardNumber,
       Addresses.Country
FROM Customers
   JOIN CreditCards
   ON Customers.CustomerID = CreditCards.CustomerID
   JOIN Addresses
   ON Customers.CustomerID = Addresses.CustomerID
```

Let's look at an example of this using the InstantUniversity database.

NOTE *Access doesn't seem to support multitable equi-joins like the other database platforms do. Instead, you need to use a nested join to achieve the same results, as you'll see in a moment.*

EXAMPLE: MULTI-TABLE EQUI-JOINS (NOT ACCESS)

The following example displays, for every exam taken by every student, what mark they achieved and the date on which the exam was given. This combines data from the Student and Exam tables via the StudentExam junction table (displaying data from both sides of the many-to-many relationship).

Execute the following statement (again, change JOIN to INNER JOIN for MySQL):

```
SELECT StudentExam.ExamID,
       StudentExam.Mark,
       Exam.SustainedOn,
       Student.Name AS StudentName
FROM StudentExam
   JOIN Student
   ON StudentExam.StudentID = Student.StudentID
   JOIN Exam
   ON StudentExam.ExamID = Exam.ExamID
ORDER BY StudentExam.ExamID;
```

This should produce the following results:

ExamID	Mark	SustainedOn	StudentName
1	55	2003-03-12 00:00:00.000	John Jones
1	26	2003-03-12 00:00:00.000	Anna Wolff
1	71	2003-03-12 00:00:00.000	Julia Picard
2	62	2003-03-13 00:00:00.000	Anna Wolff
...	...	...	...

Here you've extended the previous example by getting the SustainedOn field from Exam and using the ExamID field to join the tables. All you had to do to get this information was to include an extra JOIN ON clause for the new table, and then you could extract the data using Exam.SustainedOn. Note that one more change was necessary: The ORDER BY clause changed from ExamID to StudentExam.ExamID, which was needed because now there are two ExamID columns, one in StudentExam and one in Exam. You have to be explicit when referencing columns in such a situation.

So, let's see how you can achieve similar results in Microsoft Access, as well as the other platforms by altering how you nest joins.

EXAMPLE: NESTED MULTI-TABLE EQUI-JOINS (ALL PLATFORMS)

Access seems to prefer to start from one end of the relationship and use nested joins to display the same results that you saw previously, for example:

```
SELECT StudentExam.ExamID,
       StudentExam.Mark,
       Exam.SustainedOn,
       student.Name
FROM Exam
   INNER JOIN (student
       INNER JOIN StudentExam ON student.StudentID = StudentExam.StudentID)
   ON Exam.ExamID = StudentExam.ExamID
ORDER BY StudentExam.ExamID;
```

This syntax will work on all platforms. Again, you see the same results:

```
ExamID   Mark   SustainedOn               StudentName

-------  -----  ------------------------  -----------
1        55     2003-03-12 00:00:00.000   John Jones
1        26     2003-03-12 00:00:00.000   Anna Wolff
1        71     2003-03-12 00:00:00.000   Julia Picard
2        62     2003-03-13 00:00:00.000   Anna Wolff
...      ...    ...                       ...
```

In this example, you first perform a join between the Student and StudentExam tables, then you join the resulting table to the Exam table to produce the results. Access requires that you use INNER JOIN instead of JOIN, and it also requires brackets around the first join.

Using Non-Equi Joins

All equi-joins use the equality operator (=) in their WHERE clause. However, this is by no means essential. You can use any comparison operator you like, for example:

```
SELECT * FROM Table1, Table2
WHERE Table1.Column1 < Table2.Column2
```

This is likely to result in more results than an equi-join because there are likely to be more matches in the WHERE clause.

Let's look at an example:

EXAMPLE: NON-EQUI JOINS

First, let's see which classes are being held in which rooms at a certain time, as you saw earlier.

Execute the following against the InstantUniversity database:

```
SELECT Room.RoomID, Class.Time, Class.ClassID
FROM Room JOIN Class ON Room.RoomID = Class.RoomID;
```

You should see the following list:

RoomID	Time	ClassID
6	Mon 09:00-11:00	1
5	Mon 11:00-12:00, Thu 09:00-11:00	2
3	Mon 14:00-16:00	3
2	Tue 10:00-12:00, Thu 14:00-15:00	4
9	Tue 14:00-16:00	5
2	Tue 16:00-17:00 Thu 15:00-17:00	6
3	Wed 09:00-11:00	7
8	Wed 11:00-13:00 Fri 09:00-11:00	8
5	Fri 11:00-13:00	9
9	Fri 14:00-16:00	10

Notice that room 2 is busy on Tuesday morning from 10 A.M. to 12 P.M., and room 3 is busy on Monday afternoon from 2 A.M. to 4 P.M.

Second, what if you wanted to have a list of when rooms are free? Alter the query, dropping the ClassID column, as follows:

```
SELECT Room.RoomID, Class.Time
FROM Room JOIN Class ON Room.RoomID <> Class.RoomID;
```

You should now see the following:

```
RoomID  Time

-------  ----------------------------------
...      ...
2        Mon 11:00-12:00, Thu 09:00-11:00
2        Mon 14:00-16:00
2        Tue 14:00-16:00
2        Wed 09:00-11:00
2        Wed 11:00-13:00 Fri 09:00-11:00
2        Fri 11:00-13:00
2        Fri 14:00-16:00
3        Mon 09:00-11:00
3        Mon 11:00-12:00, Thu 09:00-11:00
3        Tue 10:00-12:00, Thu 14:00-15:00
3        Tue 14:00-16:00
3        Tue 16:00-17:00 Thu 15:00-17:00
...      ...
```

Notice that room 2 doesn't have an available 10 A.M. to 12 P.M. slot, and room 3 is also booked on Monday afternoons from 2 A.M. to 4 P.M. (these times don't appear in this list). This is a bit of a crude way to identify if a room is actually free (the only times that appear are times when there are classes). However, it does at least demonstrate, in this database, how using an inequality operator instead of an equality operator produces many more results because the search is broader in this case.

Using Aliasing in Equi-Joins

The example queries you've seen so far have had one thing in common—they all tend to be rather long. However, the aliasing technique you've used previously in this book really comes into its own here. For example, you can rewrite the query used earlier:

```
SELECT StudentExam.ExamID,
       StudentExam.Mark,
       Student.Name AS StudentName
FROM StudentExam
   JOIN Student
   ON StudentExam.StudentID = Student.StudentID
ORDER BY ExamID
```

using aliases as so:

```
SELECT SE.ExamID,
       SE.Mark,
       S.Name AS StudentName
FROM StudentExam AS SE
   JOIN Student AS S
   ON SE.StudentID = S.StudentID
ORDER BY ExamID
```

The query operates in the same way, but you save a fair bit of space, making the important bits easier to read along the way.

Inner vs. Outer Joins

When you join tables together, you're associating rows from one table with rows from another and extracting data from the combinations. Depending on the join condition you use, you may end up with every row from both tables being matched with a row from the other table, but you might not.

In an inner join, the data returned from a query consists of data from each matched combination—no unmatched rows are considered. This is the type of join you've been using in the examples in this chapter so far, and as you know, it was necessary to explicitly mark some of these joins as inner joins for MySQL and Access. Using JOIN on those platforms that support it implicitly performs an INNER JOIN.

Let's look at how inner joins work in a bit more detail: In order to illustrate the various types of join and how they work, consider two simple tables, each with four rows comprising one column and as follows:

Table1.Column1	Table2.Column2
1	2
2	4
3	5
4	4

Using Inner Joins

Let's perform an inner join between the two tables, as follows:

```
SELECT Table1.Column1, Table2.Column2
FROM Table1
INNER JOIN Table2
ON Table1.Column1 = Table2.Column2;
```

Figure 7-1 shows the rows that are returned.

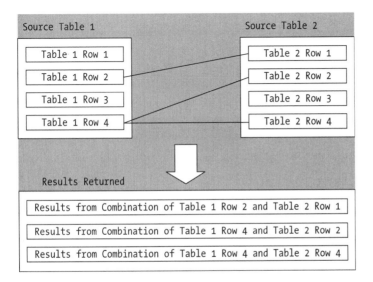

Figure 7-1. Inner join behavior

A row is only returned if a particular column value appears in both *Table1* and *Table2*. In this case, the results will be as follows:

```
COLUMN1   COLUMN2

-----     ------------------
2         2
4         4
4         4
```

To perform an INNER JOIN on the Room and Class tables, you use code similar to the following:

```
SELECT Room.RoomID, Class.Time
FROM Room
    INNER JOIN Class
    ON Room.RoomID = Class.RoomID
ORDER BY Room.RoomID;
```

This will yield the following results (presented ordered by RoomID):

RoomID	Time
2	Tue 10:00-12:00, Thu 14:00-15:00
2	Tue 16:00-17:00 Thu 15:00-17:00
3	Wed 09:00-11:00
3	Mon 14:00-16:00
5	Mon 11:00-12:00, Thu 09:00-11:00
5	Fri 11:00-13:00
6	Mon 09:00-11:00
8	Wed 11:00-13:00 Fri 09:00-11:00
9	Tue 14:00-16:00
9	Fri 14:00-16:00

Because no classes are scheduled for room 1, you don't see any entries for room 1 in this list.

Using Outer Joins

Outer joins, on the other hand, consider some of the table rows from source tables that aren't matched up. There are three types of outer join: left, right, and full, where all rows are included from the left table, the right table, and both tables, respectively.

You perform outer joins using a similar syntax to inner joins, using LEFT OUTER JOIN, RIGHT OUTER JOIN, or FULL OUTER JOIN clauses. All of these require an ON clause for joining:

```
SELECT *
FROM Table1
    LEFT OUTER JOIN Table2
    ON Table1.Column1 = Table2.Column2

SELECT *
FROM Table1
    RIGHT OUTER JOIN Table2
    ON Table1.Column1 = Table2.Column2

SELECT *
FROM Table1
    FULL OUTER JOIN Table2
    ON Table1.Column1 = Table2.Column2
```

Let's see these in action.

Left Outer Join

Using the small test tables, you can perform a left outer join as described previously. Figure 7-2 shows the rows returned for this join.

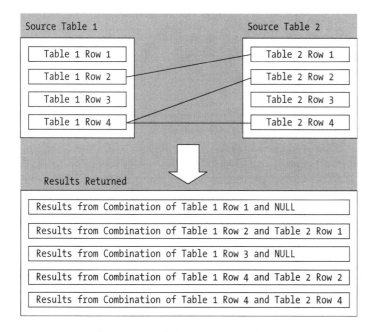

Figure 7-2. Left outer join behavior

Notice that in this case a row is returned from *Table1*, even if no corresponding value exists in *Table2*. So, the results would be as follows:

COLUMN1	COLUMN2
1	
2	2
3	
4	4
4	4

You can perform a left outer join on the classes and room example using the following:

```
SELECT Room.RoomID, Class.Time
FROM Room
    LEFT OUTER JOIN Class
    ON Room.RoomID = Class.RoomID
ORDER BY Room.RoomID;
```

This yields the following results:

RoomID	Time
1	
2	Tue 10:00-12:00, Thu 14:00-15:00
2	Tue 16:00-17:00 Thu 15:00-17:00
3	Mon 14:00-16:00
3	Wed 09:00-11:00
4	
5	Mon 11:00-12:00, Thu 09:00-11:00

```
5          Fri 11:00-13:00
6          Mon 09:00-11:00
7
8          Wed 11:00-13:00 Fri 09:00-11:00
9          Tue 14:00-16:00
9          Fri 14:00-16:00
```

Notice that rooms 1, 4, and 7, currently unused in the database, now appear in the list of rooms.

Right Outer Join

Figure 7-3 shows a right outer join.

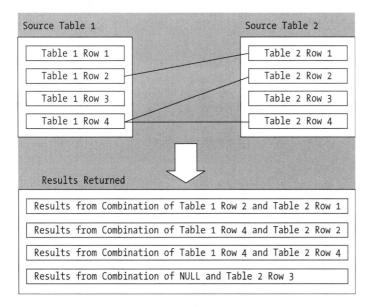

Figure 7-3. Right outer join behavior

This is basically the opposite of a right outer join. A row is returned from *Table2*, even if no corresponding value exists in *Table1*. So, the results would be as follows:

COLUMN1	COLUMN2
2	2
4	4
4	4
	5

Performing this join on the room and class example will yield the same results as an inner join because you don't have any null fields in the Class table, but the syntax you'd use is as follows:

```
SELECT Room.RoomID, Class.Time
FROM Room
    RIGHT OUTER JOIN Class
    ON Room.RoomID = Class.RoomID
ORDER BY Room.RoomID;
```

However, switching the SQL around (effectively inverting the example), you can produce the same results as the left inner join:

```
SELECT Room.RoomID, Class.Time
FROM Class
    RIGHT OUTER JOIN Room
    ON Class.RoomID = Room.RoomID
ORDER BY Room.RoomID;
```

Full Outer Join

Finally, Figure 7-4 shows the result of a full outer join.

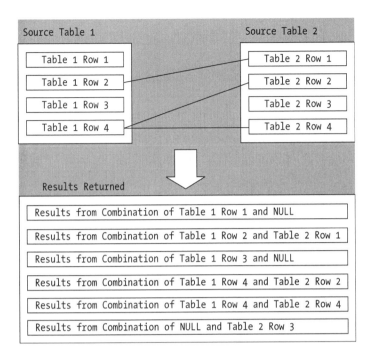

Figure 7-4. Full outer join behavior

In the test case, the results are as follows:

```
COLUMN1    COLUMN2

-----      ------------------
1
2          2
3
4          4
4          4
           5
```

Using the room and class example, you see the same set of results as produced when using a LEFT OUTER JOIN:

```
SELECT Room.RoomID, Class.Time
FROM Room
    FULL OUTER JOIN Class
    ON Room.RoomID = Class.RoomID
ORDER BY Room.RoomID;
```

Note that MySQL and Access don't support the FULL OUTER JOIN syntax.

Alternative Outer Join Syntax

Some RDBMSs still use an older method for performing outer joins, where operators such as + were used to specify the different types of join. However, this is a most confusing way of doing things when compared to this more explicit specification using keywords. Although in most cases RDBMSs have been upgraded to use the new syntax, it's worth looking at the operators here because you may well come across them.

You might see the operators *=, =*, or *=* being used in a WHERE clause as follows:

```
SELECT *
FROM Table1, Table2
WHERE Table1.Column1 *= Table2.Column2
```

```
SELECT *
FROM Table1, Table2
WHERE Table1.Column1 =* Table2.Column2
```

```
SELECT *
FROM Table1, Table2
WHERE Table1.Column1 *=* Table2.Column2
```

These stand for left outer join, right outer join, and full outer join, respectively. Alternatively, when using Oracle, you might see a + operator being used in a similar way:

```
SELECT *
FROM Table1, Table2
WHERE Table1.Column1(+) = Table2.Column2
```

This syntax was used for Oracle versions prior to 9i. In the previous case, a null value would be returned for *Table1* if there isn't any value in *Column1* that corresponds to a value in *Column2* of *Table2*. So, this is equivalent to a right outer join. You achieve a left outer join as follows:

```
SELECT *
FROM Table1, Table2
WHERE Table1.Column1 = Table2.Column2(+)
```

As a final note before you move on to a proper example, note that you can include multiple tables in outer joins just as with inner joins. As you saw earlier with inner joins, you simply add more JOIN and ON clauses after specifying the first join. You can even mix types of join in a single query—although things quickly become complicated if you do!

Seeing Inner and Outer Joins in Practice

Let's investigate the use of each join type in a full working example.

EXAMPLE: INNER AND OUTER JOINS

In this example, you're extending the classes and rooms example, looking at matches between rows in the Class table and rows in the Room table where values in the RoomID columns match. This would be useful because just knowing the ID of a room isn't quite as useful as knowing the name of a room; unless you have a list to match the IDs against, you'll end up with the professor teaching himself.

Execute the following against the InstantUniversity database:

```
SELECT Class.ClassID,
       Class.CourseID,
       Class.Time,
       Room.Comments AS RoomName
FROM Class INNER JOIN Room
ON Class.RoomID = Room.RoomID
ORDER BY ClassID;
```

This is the inner join example, and it produces the following:

```
ClassID  CourseID  Time                                  RoomName

-------  --------  ----------------------------------    ------------------
1        1         Mon 09:00-11:00                       Languages Room 2
2        2         Mon 11:00-12:00, Thu 09:00-11:00      Languages Room 1
3        3         Mon 14:00-16:00                       Science Room 1
4        4         Tue 10:00-12:00, Thu 14:00-15:00      Science Department
5        5         Tue 14:00-16:00                       Engineering Room 2
6        6         Tue 16:00-17:00, Thu 15:00-17:00      Science Department
7        7         Wed 09:00-11:00                       Science Room 1
8        8         Wed 11:00-13:00, Fri 09:00-11:00      Engineering Room 1
9        9         Fri 11:00-13:00                       Languages Room 1
10       10        Fri 14:00-16:00                       Engineering Room 2
```

Running this example results in a set of data that only includes those row combinations where matches are found. This gives you the name of the room for each class in the Class table.

Now enter and execute the following:

```
SELECT Class.ClassID,
       Class.CourseID,
       Class.Time,
       Room.Comments AS RoomName
FROM Class RIGHT OUTER JOIN Room
ON Class.RoomID = Room.RoomID
ORDER BY ClassID;
```

The results are as follows:

```
ClassID  CourseID  Time                                  RoomName

-------  --------  ----------------------------------    ------------------
NULL     NULL      NULL                                  Main hall
NULL     NULL      NULL                                  Languages Block
NULL     NULL      NULL                                  Engineering Center
1        1         Mon 09:00-11:00                       Languages Room 2
2        2         Mon 11:00-12:00, Thu 09:00-11:00      Languages Room 1
```

3	3	Mon 14:00-16:00	Science Room 1
4	4	Tue 10:00-12:00, Thu 14:00-15:00	Science Department
5	5	Tue 14:00-16:00	Engineering Room 2
6	6	Tue 16:00-17:00, Thu 15:00-17:00	Science Department
7	7	Wed 09:00-11:00	Science Room 1
8	8	Wed 11:00-13:00, Fri 09:00-11:00	Engineering Room 1
9	9	Fri 11:00-13:00	Languages Room 1
10	10	Fri 14:00-16:00	Engineering Room 2

This time around, you're including all rows in the second table, which is Room. This shows you explicitly which rooms aren't used for classes because you can see NULL values in the first three columns of the results for those rooms. At the same time, the results are including information that you wouldn't otherwise have obtained, namely a complete list of rooms available, not just those where classes are taking place.

You could also perform a left outer join as follows:

```
SELECT Class.ClassID,
       Class.CourseID,
       Class.Time,
       Room.Comments AS RoomName
FROM Class LEFT OUTER JOIN Room
ON Class.RoomID = Room.RoomID
ORDER BY ClassID
```

However, this would give you the same result as the inner join because *all* RoomID values in the Class table have corresponding values in the Room table. If you were to add a record to the Class table that had a different RoomID value—10, for example—then as well as the results that are the same as those for an inner join, you would see a result as follows:

ClassID	CourseID	Time	RoomName
11	3	Wed 14:00-16:00	NULL

You'd see all the data from the Class table columns, but because there's no corresponding row in the Room table, you get a NULL value for RoomName.

You could also have performed a full outer join, but with the default data this would give the same result as the right outer joins example. If you add a record as shown previously for a left outer join, though, then it too would be included. This would make the result for a full outer join as follows:

ClassID	CourseID	Time	RoomName
NULL	NULL	NULL	Main hall
NULL	NULL	NULL	Languages Block
NULL	NULL	NULL	Engineering Center
1	1	Mon 09:00-11:00	Languages Room 2
2	2	Mon 11:00-12:00, Thu 09:00-11:00	Languages Room 1
3	3	Mon 14:00-16:00	Science Room 1
4	4	Tue 10:00-12:00, Thu 14:00-15:00	Science Department
5	5	Tue 14:00-16:00	Engineering Room 2
6	6	Tue 16:00-17:00, Thu 15:00-17:00	Science Department
7	7	Wed 09:00-11:00	Science Room 1
8	8	Wed 11:00-13:00, Fri 09:00-11:00	Engineering Room 1
9	9	Fri 11:00-13:00	Languages Room 1
10	10	Fri 14:00-16:00	Engineering Room 2
11	3	Wed 14:00-16:00	NULL

As you can see, although outer joins can be a little difficult to understand at first, they provide interesting possibilities.

Exploring Additional Joins in Oracle

In addition to the joins you've just been looking at, Oracle 9i offers a few additional options, which you'll take a quick look at now.

Using Natural Joins

A natural join performs a join for all columns with matching values in two tables. To put this in context, you could rewrite an earlier example from this:

```
SELECT Class.ClassID,
       Class.CourseID,
       Class.Time,
       Room.Comments AS RoomName
FROM Class INNER JOIN Room
ON Class.RoomID = Room.RoomID
ORDER BY ClassID;
```

to this:

```
SELECT Class.ClassID,
       Class.CourseID,
       Class.Time,
       Room.Comments AS RoomName
FROM Class NATURAL JOIN Room
ORDER BY ClassID;
```

Working with the Using Clause

This clause is used if several columns share the same name. Again, you can modify a previous example to demonstrate this:

```
SELECT Room.Comments, Class.Time
FROM Room
    INNER JOIN Class
    ON Room.RoomID = Class.RoomID;
```

This query lists the name of each room and the times when it's in use:

```
Comments                      Time

--------------------------    ----------------------------------
Science Department            Tue 16:00-17:00 Thu 15:00-17:00
Science Department            Tue 10:00-12:00, Thu 14:00-15:00
Science Room 1                Wed 09:00-11:00
Science Room 1                Mon 14:00-16:00
Languages Room 1              Fri 11:00-13:00
Languages Room 1              Mon 11:00-12:00, Thu 09:00-11:00
Languages Room 2              Mon 09:00-11:00
Engineering Room 1            Wed 11:00-13:00 Fri 09:00-11:00
Engineering Room 2            Fri 14:00-16:00
Engineering Room 2            Tue 14:00-16:00
```

Using the USING clause, you could write this as follows:

```
SELECT Room.Comments, Class.Time
FROM Class
    JOIN Room
    USING (RoomID);
```

This would produce the same results. Note that you can't use any further qualifiers, including WHERE or GROUP BY in this statement.

Summary

In this chapter, you've seen how you can use SQL to query multiple tables at the same time. You've looked at the following:

- The basic syntax for multitable queries

- Cross joins, where every row from one table is matched with every row from another

- Equi-joins, where an equality is used to match table rows

- Non-equi joins, where a different comparison is used to match rows

- The use of aliases to ease comprehension of joins

- The difference between inner and outer joins

Next, you'll look at how you can create different arrangements of your data by using views.

CHAPTER 8

Hiding Complex SQL with Views

SO FAR, WHEN YOU'VE WANTED to restructure data with calculated columns or extract data from multiple tables based on comparisons between column values, you've had to resort to relatively complex SQL statements. Typically, though, you'll want to obtain data in this modified form more than once. Certain tasks, such as getting the name of the customer associated with an order, will be performed so often that it can seem awkward to have to query multiple tables all the time.

To get around this, SQL allows you to create *views* in a database, which provide (semi)permanent reshaping of data from tables in a database that you can access with queries as an alternative to accessing tables directly. This has the advantage of providing an additional layer of abstraction to the user, which can mean that you can format data in a more consistent way and even enhance security by providing access only to views, not to the underlying data. Views are sometimes referred to as *virtual tables*.

Overview of SQL Views

A view is basically the set of rows you'd receive should you execute a given query. This set of rows looks exactly like any other table to a user of the database although all the data it contains is in fact stored in other tables.

This can be extremely useful for restricting access to certain data. Instead of giving users access to the actual tables in the database, you can instead give them access to a view of the table, which might not contain all of the available data. In addition, modifying data through a view is usually not possible, so you can provide a simple, read-only version of the data that's accessible to low-privilege users.

Another great thing about views is that they're updated whenever their underlying data changes, without you having to do anything!

 NOTE *At the time of writing, views have not yet been implemented in MySQL or Microsoft Access, but they're available in SQL Server, Oracle, and DB2.*

Creating a View

To create a view, you use the following syntax:

```
CREATE VIEW ViewName AS Query [WITH CHECK OPTION]
```

Here, *Query* can be any query you like, which could involve any of the techniques you've seen in previous chapters.

For example:

```
CREATE VIEW StudentSummary
AS
SELECT Student.StudentID, Student.Name,
    COUNT(*) AS ExamsTaken
FROM Student
INNER JOIN StudentExam
ON Student.StudentID = StudentExam.StudentID
GROUP BY Student.StudentID, Student.Name
```

Here you create a view called `StudentSummary`, which consists of a `StudentID` column, a `Name` column, and an `ExamsTaken` column, which is a count of how many exams that student has taken. After doing this, it's possible to use the following query:

```
SELECT StudentID, Name, ExamsTaken FROM StudentSummary
```

This will return the desired order count information without having to use the clumsy syntax required to calculate this information.

You can use views wherever you might otherwise use tables in SQL statements, so you can query them, perform joins with them, and so on.

 NOTE *You'll look at the* WITH CHECK OPTION *clause in just a moment when you learn about modifying data using views.*

EXAMPLE: CREATING A VIEW (SQL SERVER)

For SQL Server, you should execute the following statement against the
InstantUniversity database:

```
CREATE VIEW ClassAttendees AS
SELECT Class.ClassID, SUBSTRING(Professor.Name,
   LEN(Professor.Name) - CHARINDEX(' ', REVERSE(Professor.Name)) + 2, 100)
   + ', '
   + LEFT(Professor.Name, LEN(Professor.Name)
   - CHARINDEX(' ', REVERSE(Professor.Name)))
   AS Name, 'Professor' AS Role
FROM Professor
   INNER JOIN Class ON Professor.ProfessorID =
      Class.ProfessorID
UNION
SELECT Enrollment.ClassID, SUBSTRING(Student.Name,
      LEN(Student.Name) - CHARINDEX(' ', REVERSE(Student.Name)) + 2, 100)
      + ', '
      + LEFT(Student.Name,
            LEN(Student.Name) - CHARINDEX(' ', REVERSE(Student.Name)))
      AS Name, 'Student'
FROM Student
   INNER JOIN Enrollment ON Student.StudentID =
      Enrollment.StudentID
```

Oracle and DB2 will use a slightly different syntax for this example, as you'll
see in a moment.
   Then, execute the following statement:

```
SELECT ClassID, Name, Role FROM ClassAttendees
```

You should see the following output (the first six rows are shown):

ClassID	Name	Role
1	Dawson, Prof.	Professor
1	Jones, John	Student
1	Picard, Julia	Student
1	Wolff, Anna	Student
2	Dawson, Prof.	Professor
2	Jones, John	Student
...	...	...

In this example, you've used a modified version of the complicated string manipulation query from Chapter 6, "Combining SQL Queries," to build a view called ClassAttendees. This view shows who takes part in each class in the university, both students and professors.

This is an ideal use of a view because you wouldn't want to use the whole lengthy query every time you wanted such information. You could refine the results by adding clauses into the SELECT statement to filter the results, for example:

```
SELECT ClassID, Name, Role
FROM ClassAttendees
WHERE ClassID = 1;
```

This statement would return only the attendees of the first class on Monday morning.

EXAMPLE: CREATING A VIEW (ORACLE)

The main difference between the SQL Server implementation of this example and the Oracle implementation is that the code that modifies the names of the students and professors will be constructed differently, as you can see in the following code equivalent:

```
CREATE VIEW ClassAttendees AS
SELECT Class.ClassID,
    SUBSTR(Professor.Name, INSTR(Professor.Name, ' ') + 1)
            || ', '
            || SUBSTR(Professor.Name, 1,
                INSTR(Professor.Name, ' ') - 1)
    AS Name, 'Professor' AS Role
FROM Professor
    INNER JOIN Class ON Professor.ProfessorID =
        Class.ProfessorID
UNION
SELECT Enrollment.ClassID,
    SUBSTR(Student.Name, INSTR(Student.Name, ' ') + 1)
            || ', '
            || SUBSTR(Student.Name, 1,
                INSTR(Student.Name, ' ') - 1)
    AS Name, 'Student'
FROM Student
    INNER JOIN Enrollment ON Student.StudentID = Enrollment.StudentID;
```

This code will produce the same results as the SQL Server equivalent.

Finally, let's quickly look at the change in syntax to implement the same view in DB2.

EXAMPLE: CREATING A VIEW (DB2)

Note that when using DB2, in addition to the string manipulation code being slightly different, each column must be explicitly named using the AS *Name* syntax:

```
CREATE VIEW ClassAttendees AS
SELECT Class.ClassID AS ClassID,
    SUBSTR(Professor.Name, POSSTR(Professor.Name, ' ') + 1)
            || ', '
            || SUBSTR(Professor.Name, 1,
                    POSSTR(Professor.Name, ' ') - 1)
    AS Name, 'Professor' AS Role
FROM Professor
    INNER JOIN Class ON Professor.ProfessorID =
        Class.ProfessorID
```

```
UNION
SELECT Enrollment.ClassID AS ClassID,
    SUBSTR(Student.Name, POSSTR(Student.Name, ' ') + 1) || ', ' ||
    SUBSTR(Student.Name, 1, POSSTR(Student.Name, ' ') - 1)
    AS Name, 'Student' AS Role FROM Student INNER JOIN Enrollment
ON Student.StudentID = Enrollment.StudentID;
```

Again, this code will produce the same results as the implementations shown previously.

Modifying Data Through a View

Depending on the view specification, it may be possible to modify data through a view. However, this isn't always possible. In order for a view to be modifiable via INSERT, UPDATE, or DELETE (which will actually result in modification of the underlying data), certain conditions must be met:

- The view can't contain any aggregate functions, such as COUNT or MAX, or use a GROUP BY clause. One exception is that subqueries can use aggregate functions although the values calculated here can't be modified.

- The view doesn't contain a TOP clause (SQL Server only).

- The view doesn't use DISTINCT.

- The view doesn't use calculated columns.

- The view must obtain data from one or more tables rather than simply providing explicit values.

This basically restricts view data modification to simple cases but can nonetheless be useful in some circumstances.

You can also utilize something more advanced to make views modifiable, notably triggers and partitioned views, but these are advanced topics that we won't cover here.

The WITH CHECK OPTION clause at the end of a CREATE VIEW statement is used on views that allow data modification to the data visible to the view. For example, if there's a filter on a column such as WHERE ClassID = 4, then you couldn't change the value of this column to any value other than for any record, and you couldn't add a new record with a different value of `ClassID`. However, you could alter any visible columns that adhere to that condition.

Updating a View

Once you've defined a view, you might at some point want to modify its definition. To do this, you use the following statement in SQL Server:

```
ALTER VIEW ViewName AS NewQuery
```

In Oracle you use slightly different syntax to alter the definition of a view:

```
CREATE OR REPLACE VIEW ViewName AS NewQuery
```

The `ALTER VIEW` statement in Oracle performs a different action to the one used in SQL Server. You can use the `ALTER VIEW` statement to recompile a view or alter its constraints. For more information, you should check the Oracle documentation.

In DB2 there's also an `ALTER VIEW` statement; however, its meaning is quite different. This statement allows you to modify individual columns in a view, making them refer to additional data. The simplest way to *change* a view in DB2 is to delete it and add it again.

EXAMPLE: CHANGING A VIEW

In SQL Server, execute the following statement:

```
ALTER VIEW ClassAttendees AS
SELECT Class.ClassID, NULL AS StudentID, SUBSTRING(Professor.Name,
      LEN(Professor.Name) - CHARINDEX(' ', REVERSE(Professor.Name)) + 2, 100)
      + ', '
      + LEFT(Professor.Name,
             LEN(Professor.Name) - CHARINDEX(' ', REVERSE(Professor.Name)))
      AS Name, 'Professor' AS Role
FROM Professor INNER JOIN Class ON Professor.ProfessorID = Class.ProfessorID
UNION
```

```
SELECT Enrollment.ClassID, Student.StudentID, SUBSTRING(Student.Name,
       LEN(Student.Name) - CHARINDEX(' ', REVERSE(Student.Name)) + 2, 100)
       + ', '
       + LEFT(Student.Name,
              LEN(Student.Name) - CHARINDEX(' ', REVERSE(Student.Name)))
       AS Name, 'Student' FROM Student
       INNER JOIN Enrollment ON Student.StudentID = Enrollment.StudentID;
```

For Oracle, change the first line to the following:

```
CREATE OR REPLACE VIEW ClassAttendees AS
```

Then execute the following statement:

```
SELECT ClassID, StudentID, Name, Role FROM ClassAttendees;
```

to display the amended view:

ClassID	StudentID	Name	Role
1	NULL	Dawson, Prof.	Professor
1	1	Jones, John	Student
1	5	Wolff, Anna	Student
1	8	Picard, Julia	Student
2	NULL	Dawson, Prof.	Professor
2	1	Jones, John	Student
...	...	...	...

Here you've modified the view created in the last example, adding a new StudentID column. For contacts in the Student table, you have a column called StudentID that you can look at via this view, but no such information exists for the Professor table, so you simply insert a NULL value.

Deleting a View

Finally, you can remove views from the database using the following:

```
DROP VIEW ViewName
```

Execute the following statement against the `InstantUniversity` database:

```
DROP VIEW ClassAttendees;
```

Then, try to execute the following statement:

```
SELECT * FROM ClassAttendees;
```

You'll receive an error message:

```
Server: Msg 208, Level 16, State 1, Line 1

Invalid object name 'Rolodex'.
```

The query in this example simply deletes the view used in the previous examples, restoring the database to its virgin state. The error shown might not match the one you get because this is a SQL Server error, but you'll definitely get an error of some sort!

Summary

In this chapter, you saw how to use SQL views to save you from having to execute complicated queries when you want to get at shaped data. You've learned the following:

- How to create a view

- How to modify an existing view

- How to delete a view

In the next chapter, you'll look at a similar but more powerful way of abstracting SQL statements—stored procedures.

CHAPTER 9

Using Stored
Procedures

IN THE PREVIOUS CHAPTER, you saw how you can store a SQL query in a Relational Database Management System (RDBMS) as a view, making it easy to access complex, shaped data without having to use a lengthy query. Stored procedures fulfill a similar role but do so in a much more powerful way. With stored procedures, you're not limited to queries or even single statements. A single stored procedure could add a record, modify some data, perform some calculation or other, and return some data—all with a single command from the user. Unfortunately, they can't make you dinner and record *Buffy* while you're out shopping, but they're pretty useful nevertheless.

Effectively, what you're doing when you create a stored procedure is creating a function, complete with input and output parameters, that you can call in the same way as you execute a standard SQL statement, simply by telling the RDBMS to execute it and sitting back while it gets on with it. A stored procedure itself contains one or more SQL statements that are processed as part of the stored procedure execution. However, when a stored procedure is processed, you have access to additional functionality, such as controlling the flow of execution with loops and conditional execution, which can provide enormous benefits.

There is, however, one problem when it comes to stored procedures. Unfortunately, pretty much every RDBMS does things its own way. Although the basic ideas are the same across systems, the way they're implemented isn't. You'll examine these differences as you work through this chapter.

 NOTE   *At the time of this writing, stored procedures aren't supported in the latest version of MySQL. However, support for stored procedures is planned for a future version.*

Stored Procedure Overview

You can execute a stored procedure using the CALL keyword in Oracle and DB2 (which is actually the SQL standard) or using the EXECUTE (or the short form EXEC) keyword in SQL Server or Access.

Oracle also supports the EXECUTE *sp_name (param)* syntax as a shorthand form for the following:

```
BEGIN
    sp_name(param);
END;
```

Older versions of Oracle support only this syntax and don't support CALL.

To illustrate this, imagine you have a stored procedure called DeleteRow in each of these databases, which takes as a parameter a numerical ID value corresponding to the row to be deleted. In Oracle or DB2, you could do the following to delete the row with an ID of 5:

```
CALL DeleteRow(5);
```

In SQL Server or Access, you can use the following:

```
EXECUTE DeleteRow 5;
```

Note that when calling SQL Server or Access stored procedures, you don't enclose the parameters in parentheses.

As you can see, although the syntax does vary, the basic idea is the same—you provide the name of the stored procedure and the parameter(s) it requires. These parameters may also be output parameters; that is, the value will be set by the stored procedure and returned to the caller. In all cases, the meaning of a parameter is determined by its position in the list of parameters of a stored procedure, where multiple parameters are separated by commas. Which parameter goes in which position is determined by the definition of a stored procedure.

Creating a Stored Procedure

You create stored procedures using the SQL keyword combination CREATE PROCEDURE (with the abbreviation or CREATE PROC available in some RDBMSs). Again, the exact usage varies. In the following sections, you'll look at the various RDBMS syntaxes and see them in action with a simple InsertStudent stored procedure that inserts a new student into the Student table.

The syntax for creating a stored procedure (supported by SQL Server, Oracle, DB2, and Access) is as follows:

```
CREATE PROCEDURE sp_name (parameter_list)
AS
    sp_body;
```

Although this much is standard, the individual RDBMSs each provide their own extensions to this and in particular their own keywords for programming code within a stored procedure. To show the basic syntax for creating stored procedures in the different RDBMSs, we'll run through a simple example that inserts a new row into the Student table.

 NOTE   *Oracle supports using the keyword* IS *instead of* AS.

SQL Server

The basic format for creating a SQL Server stored procedure is identical to the ANSI standard. The most important point to note is that the names of parameters in SQL Server must begin with the @ character. In fact (as you'll see shortly), this is true of variables in SQL Server generally.

EXAMPLE: CREATING A SIMPLE STORED PROCEDURE (SQL SERVER)

Enter this query and execute it against the InstantUniversity database:

```
CREATE PROCEDURE InsertStudent(@i_StudentID   INT,
                               @i_StudentName VARCHAR(50))
AS
BEGIN
    INSERT INTO Student(StudentID, Name)
    VALUES (@i_StudentID, @i_StudentName);
END;
```

This creates a stored procedure called InsertStudent with two input parameters, @i_StudentID and @i_StudentName. These parameters appear in the parameter list after the procedure name in the form *param_name data_type*. They allow you to pass values into the stored procedure, which you can then access in your SQL statements. In this case, you just insert these values straight into the Student table.

The body of the procedure can consist of a single statement, but you can also include it in a BEGIN...END block, which allows you to create stored procedures consisting of multiple statements. You use this syntax here, even though it's not necessary because there's only one statement in the body of the procedure.

Once you've created the procedure, you can execute it using this statement:

```
EXECUTE InsertStudent 500, 'Víteslav Novák';
```

This will enter a row with the name 'Víteslav Novák' and a StudentID of 500 into the Student table.

Oracle

The fundamental syntax for stored procedures in Oracle is similar to SQL Server and the ANSI standard:

```
CREATE [OR REPLACE] PROCEDURE sp_name (parameter_list)
AS
BEGIN
    sp_body;
END;
/
```

The first thing to notice here is the OR REPLACE option, available when you're creating most types of database objects in Oracle. If this is specified, an existing stored procedure with the same name will be replaced when you create the new procedure. If this isn't specified and a procedure with the same name exists, an error will be thrown, and the new procedure won't be created.

As with SQL Server, you include the SQL statements for the procedure in a BEGIN...END block (although in the case of Oracle, this is mandatory, even if there's only one statement). The biggest difference in the basic syntax is in the way you use parameters. First, Oracle parameters don't start with an @ character; second, you need to explicitly declare the "direction" of your parameters—that is, whether they're input parameters that you simply pass into the procedure, output parameters that you use to return values to the application that called the procedure, or input/output parameters that both pass data into and out of the procedure.

When you create a stored procedure, Oracle typically attempts to compile the procedure, even if it contains PL/SQL errors. A faulty procedure can't be executed, but it will still be created, so you'll need either to drop it before recompiling or to use the REPLACE option. Also, notice that Oracle won't tell you what's wrong with the procedure unless you specifically ask it to do so. To do this, just enter SHOW ERRORS at the SQL*Plus command prompt.

EXAMPLE: CREATING A SIMPLE STORED PROCEDURE (ORACLE)

Enter this query into SQL*Plus:

```
CREATE OR REPLACE PROCEDURE InsertStudent(
                            i_StudentID   IN INT,
                            i_StudentName IN VARCHAR)
AS
BEGIN
   INSERT INTO Student (StudentID, Name)
   VALUES (i_StudentID, i_StudentName);
END;
/
```

Again, you create a stored procedure called InsertStudent with two input parameters, i_StudentID, and i_StudentName. You mark the fact that these are input parameters by placing the IN keyword between the parameter's name and its data type.

You can execute your new procedure from SQL*Plus as follows:

```
CALL InsertStudent(500, 'Víteslav Novák');
```

DB2

And now for something completely different.... Although you use a SQL statement to create stored procedures in DB2, you can't just execute this statement in Command Center or a similar tool: You need to create and compile using the DB2 Development Center.

Development Center can only compile stored procedures if a C++ compiler is installed on the machine on which it's running. On Windows, this means Microsoft Visual C++ must be installed; you'll also need to alter the Path, Include, and Lib system environment variables. Please consult the DB2 documentation for further details.

To create a DB2 stored procedure, start by opening Development Center. You'll be invited to create a new project, as shown in Figure 9-1.

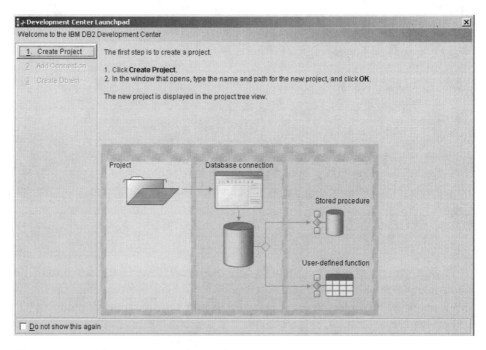

Figure 9-1. Development Center's opening screen

Click the Create Project button, and you'll be asked to give a name for the new project. Call it *InstantUniversitySprocs*, as shown in Figure 9-2.

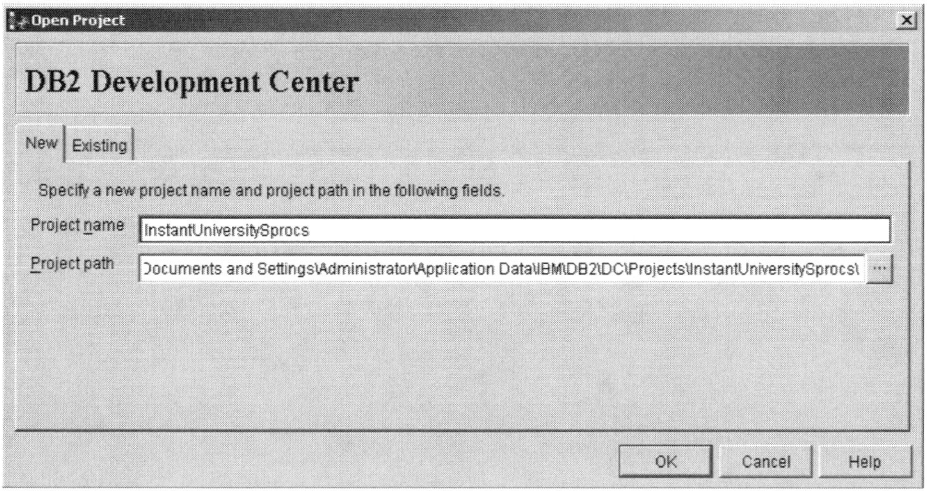

Figure 9-2. Naming the project

The next task is to connect to the InstantUniversity database. First, you have to specify whether you want to work offline or you want to connect to the DB2 server. Ensure that Online is selected and click Next, as shown in Figure 9-3.

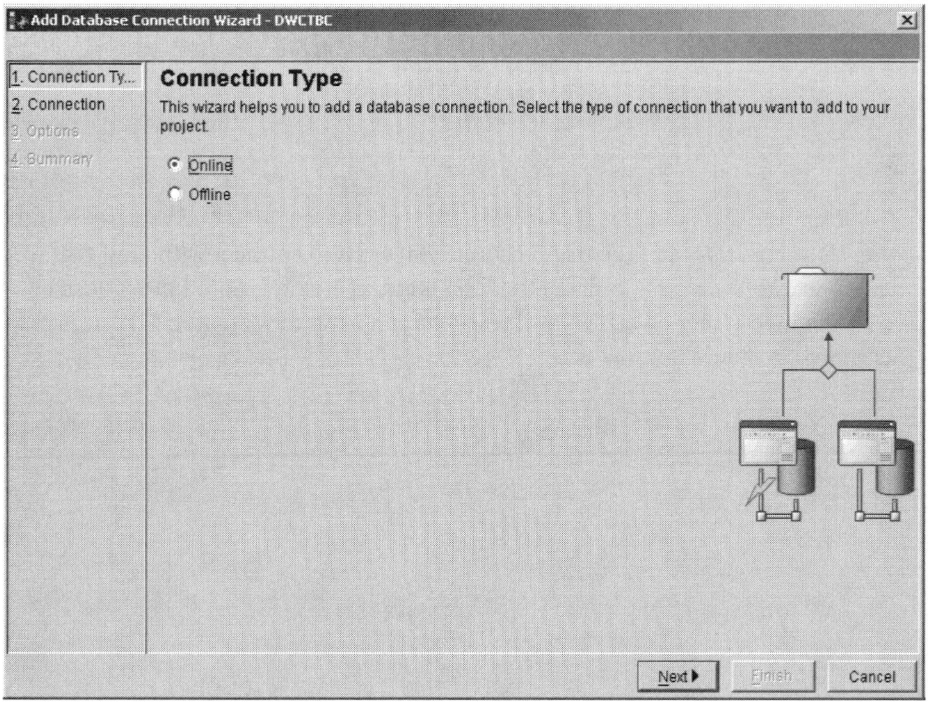

Figure 9-3. Specifying whether you want to work online

You're now asked to supply details of the database you want to connect to, as shown in Figure 9-4.

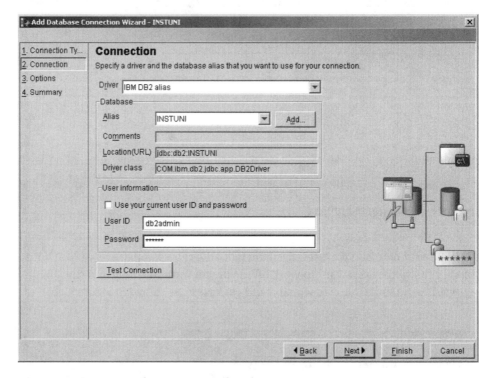

Figure 9-4. Setting up the connection details

Enter the alias for the InstantUniversity database (INSTUNI in this case) and the ID and password of the user account you want to connect with, and then click Next. You're now asked whether you want to create a stored procedure or User-Defined Function (UDF) and whether you want to write it in SQL or Java, as shown in Figure 9-5.

Figure 9-5. Choosing the type of object to create

Java stored procedures are beyond the scope of the book, so make sure that both Stored Procedure and SQL are selected, and click OK. You're now requested to give a name to the procedure, as shown in Figure 9-6.

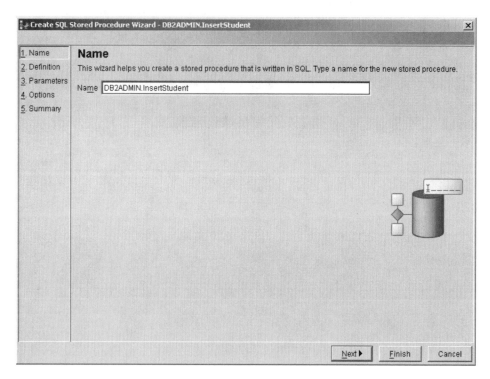

Figure 9-6. Naming the stored procedure

Replace the default name with *InsertStudent*, and click the Next button (you've left the name of the schema where it's stored as the prefix of the procedure name).

DB2 provides a wizard that creates the SQL statements for the stored procedure, but this is a SQL book, so you're going to do this manually. DB2 allows stored procedures to return none, one, or more result sets; this first example doesn't return a result set, so select None for the Result Set field and then click Finish, as shown in Figure 9-7.

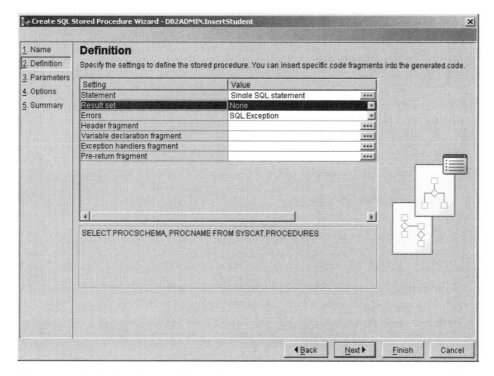

Figure 9-7. Defining the stored procedure

Back in the main Development Center window, open the stored procedure by double-clicking it. DB2 has added some default SQL code to create the procedure, as shown in Figure 9-8.

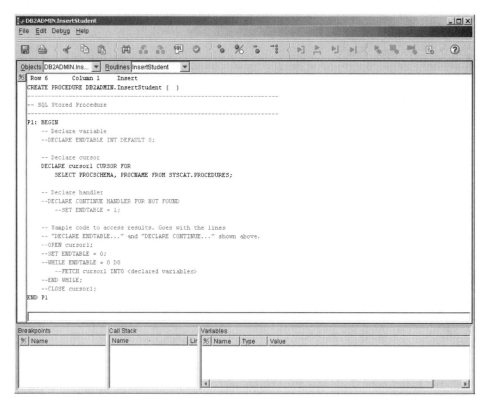

Figure 9-8. The InsertStudent *stored procedure*

You're going to create the procedure manually, so delete this code and replace it with the code for the stored procedure:

```
CREATE PROCEDURE DB2ADMIN.InsertStudent (
        i_StudentID    INT,
        i_StudentName VARCHAR(50))
P1: BEGIN
    INSERT INTO Student (StudentID, Name)
    VALUES (i_StudentID, i_StudentName);
END P1
```

Now that you've got this far, the SQL syntax for creating the procedure isn't too different from the standard:

```
CREATE PROCEDURE sp_name (parameter_list)
block_name: BEGIN
    sp_body;
END block_name;
```

DB2 can optionally use labels for BEGIN...END blocks, so it's clear which block the END keyword finishes.

Save the procedure in the editor and return to the main Development Center window. Before you can use this stored procedure, you need to compile it. Do this by right-clicking the procedure name and selecting Build. Once the procedure has compiled, you can call it from Command Center using this statement:

```
CALL InsertStudent(500, 'Víteslav Novák');
```

This will enter a row with the specified values into the Student table.

Access

Access doesn't support stored procedures as such, but it does allow you to create *stored queries* using the CREATE PROCEDURE syntax. You can use stored queries like stored procedures or (if they return a result set) like views, so if you have a query named GetStudents that returns a result set of all the students in the database, you call it just as you call a view:

```
SELECT StudentID, Name FROM GetStudents;
```

Or you could call it as you would a stored procedure in SQL Server:

```
EXECUTE GetStudents;
```

You should be aware of a couple more restrictions with Access queries. First, queries can only contain one SQL statement, so you can't perform two actions with a query. Second, you can't enter the CREATE PROCEDURE statement directly into the SQL window in Access. When you create an Access query, you're effectively executing a CREATE PROCEDURE statement behind the scenes, so you'll get an error if you type the statement manually into the SQL window. Because you want to show the full syntax, you'll print the whole CREATE PROCEDURE statement. You can run this against the InstantUniversity database from an application via a data-access technology such as ADO.

EXAMPLE: CREATING A SIMPLE STORED QUERY (ACCESS)

Execute this query against InstantUniversity:

```
CREATE PROCEDURE InsertStudent(@i_StudentID   INT,
                              @i_StudentName VARCHAR(50))
AS
INSERT INTO Student (StudentID, Name)
VALUES (@i_StudentID, @i_StudentName);
```

If you want to type this directly into the SQL window in Access, the syntax is as follows:

```
PARAMETERS @i_StudentID INT, @i_StudentName VARCHAR(50);
INSERT INTO Student (StudentID, Name)
VALUES (@i_StudentID, @i_StudentName);
```

Otherwise, the syntax is identical to that for SQL Server stored procedures. As in SQL Server, Access parameter names are all preceded by the @ character. You can execute this query using the EXECUTE keyword:

```
EXECUTE InsertStudent 500, 'Víteslav Novák';
```

Note that you don't use parentheses for the arguments passed into an Access query.

Dropping and Modifying Stored Procedures

As with all database objects, you can delete an existing stored procedure using the DROP command:

```
DROP PROCEDURE ProcName;
```

This is supported by all platforms that support stored procedures.

You can also modify a stored procedure using the ALTER PROCEDURE statement in SQL Server and Oracle. In SQL Server, the ALTER PROCEDURE statement has the same syntax as the CREATE PROCEDURE statement and simply re-creates the stored procedure with the new specification. As with views, the ALTER PROCEDURE statement in Oracle is used to recompile the view rather than to redefine it.

Creating and Using Variables and Parameters

We mentioned earlier that the parameters to stored procedures can be of three types: input, output, or input/output. As you've seen in the previous examples, input parameters are used solely to pass information to the procedure, for example, to determine which rows to retrieve, update, and so on. On some systems, stored procedures can also return values, in the same way that functions in programming languages (or indeed, SQL UDFs) return values. However, before you look at output parameters and return values in detail, you need to understand how to create and use variables in SQL code.

SQL Variables

Variables in SQL are similar to variables in other languages. That's to say that they're basically a means of storing a value in memory, referenced by a unique name. For example, you could have a variable called MyVar that you assign a value to and then use it to send data to a stored procedure via a parameter. Alternatively, you might get a value from a stored procedure into a variable, either via an output parameter or a return value.

As you've seen, you can use literal values as parameters when calling a stored procedure. However, you'll often need to use variables to store and retrieve data values from parameters, and even if you don't you may have to use variables inside a stored procedure.

Note that Access doesn't support variables (apart from input parameters).

SQL variables are simply defined names for a specific item of data. Like parameters, variables must have an @ symbol prefix in SQL Server and MySQL, but not in Oracle or DB2.

Declaring Variables

Variables are declared using the DECLARE keyword:

```
DECLARE var_name var_type(length);
```

You can also declare several variables of the same type simultaneously:

```
DECLARE var1_name, var2_name, var3_name var_type(length);
```

The *var_type* can be any of the data types defined in your RDBMS, such as int or nvarchar; *length* is an optional integer value saying how much storage to allocate (that is, the width of the column). You can also specify a scale (the number of decimal places) to use for floating-point values. Typically, you'll be declaring variable types that match column data types in tables that are manipulated by the stored procedure you're calling, so you'll often have to take this into account in both *var_type* and *length*. Also, some values won't be meaningful for the data type in use, and some variable types don't require a value for this parameter (including int), so you need to be careful here.

In DB2, variables can only be declared within a BEGIN...END block. When these blocks are used in dynamic SQL (that is, not in a stored procedure or function), you need to specify the ATOMIC keyword:

```
BEGIN ATOMIC
    DECLARE myvar VARCHAR(50);
    -- Assign and use variable
END;
```

We'll discuss the atomic properties when you look at transactions in Chapter 10, "Transactions."

If you're entering a compound statement such as this via DB2's Command Center, you need to change the character that marks the end of the statement from the default semicolon, or Command Center won't pass the complete statement to DB2 (it will only reach the first semicolon in the embedded statements). You can change the statement termination character on the General tab of the Tools ➤ Tools Settings menu, as shown in Figure 9-9.

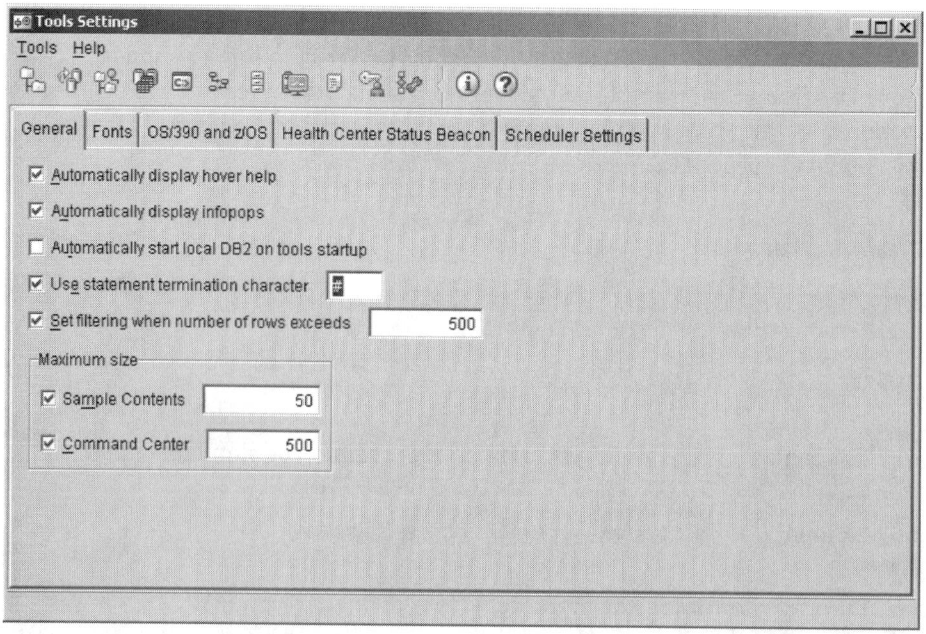

Figure 9-9. The Tools Settings dialog box

In Oracle, the DECLARE statement is placed before the BEGIN block. Any variables you want to use in the compound statement must be declared in this DECLARE statement:

```
DECLARE
    myvar       VARCHAR(50);
    myothervar  INT;
BEGIN
    -- Assign and use variables
END;
/
```

As well as RDBMS-specific types, you can also use the special type of CURSOR:

```
DECLARE cursor_name CURSOR FOR cursor_spec;
```

This is a special case of variable, used to loop through rows returned from a query. Cursors are used by Oracle and DB2 to return result sets from a stored procedure, and you'll learn about them in more depth a little later.

Assigning Variables

Once you've declared a variable, you may need to assign a value to it prior to a procedure call. The syntax for this varies between RDBMSs. In SQL Server you assign values with the SET or SELECT keywords:

```
SET @VarName = Value;
SELECT @VarName = Value;
```

Here *VarName* is the name of the variable, and *Value* is a literal value of the appropriate type or some expression that evaluates to a value of the appropriate type. This could include a SELECT statement used as a subquery.

Variables can also have values assigned to them in other ways, such as via functions or subqueries.

In MySQL and DB2, you can also use SET in the same way as previously described (though DB2 doesn't use the @ character for variable names). However, MySQL also allows values to be assigned to variables in any SQL statement although this requires using the := assignment operator rather than = because = is used as a comparison operator outside of SET statements. For example:

```
@VarName := Value;
```

Oracle also uses this syntax (although you don't need @):

```
VarName := Value;
```

Oracle and DB2 have a special syntax for storing values from a SELECT query into variables:

```
SELECT Name FROM Professor INTO ProfessorName
WHERE ProfessorID = 1;
```

This will store the name of the professor with an ID of 1 into the ProfessorName variable.

Once you have a value in a variable, you can then go ahead and use the value in subsequent SQL statements in the same batch of commands. This is important in the body of stored procedures. Effectively, what happens with parameters is that the parameter is a variable declared and assigned when the stored procedure executes. For example, if you had a DeleteStudent stored procedure that deleted a single row from the Student table according to an ID parameter, you could define the stored procedure as follows (with minor variations for the different platforms):

```
CREATE PROCEDURE DeleteStudent(i_StudentID INT)
AS
BEGIN
    DELETE FROM Student
    WHERE StudentID = i_StudentID;
END;
```

Here the parameter i_StudentID is in fact a variable, which is subsequently used in the WHERE clause to select the correct name. This applies to all RDBMSs with stored procedures.

Default Parameter Values

If you want, you can provide a default value for a parameter. If a value isn't provided for that parameter, the default value will be used. You do this in SQL Server and Access by adding the default value after the parameter's data type, separated by an equals sign. For example, to create an InsertProfessor procedure that uses a default value of 'Prof. A.N. Other' for the professor's name if one isn't supplied, use this:

```
CREATE PROCEDURE InsertProfessor (
    @i_ProfID INT,
    @i_ProfName VARCHAR(50) = 'Prof. A.N. Other')
AS
    INSERT INTO Professor (ProfessorID, Name)
    VALUES (@i_ProfID, @i_ProfName);
```

In Oracle, you use the keyword DEFAULT instead of an equals sign:

```
CREATE OR REPLACE PROCEDURE InsertProfessor (i_ProfID IN INT,
    i_ProfName IN VARCHAR DEFAULT 'Prof. A.N. Other')
AS
BEGIN
    INSERT INTO Professor (ProfessorID, Name)
    VALUES (i_ProfID, i_ProfName);
END;
/
```

You can then call this procedure as usual.

 NOTE *DB2 doesn't support default parameter values.*

Using Output Parameters

Now that you know how to use variables, you can look in more detail at output parameters. Output parameters are used to pass data back from the procedure to the calling application. The parameter is assigned a value within the body of the procedure, and this value is returned to the application.

Return values for procedures do exist on some platforms (although not Oracle or Access) as well as output parameters, but they can only be integers and are used for returning the error status of the operation.

For example, suppose you have a stored procedure that returns the name of a student given an ID. You would pass the ID in as an input parameter and return the name as an output parameter. To show how output parameters work, let's see how you implement this in the various RDBMSs.

SQL Server

Output parameters in SQL Server are marked by adding the keyword OUT or OUTPUT after the parameter's data type. For example:

```
(@OutputParamName INT OUTPUT)
```

EXAMPLE: USING OUTPUT PARAMETERS (SQL SERVER)

Create the following stored procedure:

```
CREATE PROCEDURE GetStudentName(
                        @i_StudentID    INT,
                        @o_StudentName VARCHAR(50) OUTPUT)
AS
BEGIN
    SET @o_StudentName = (SELECT Name FROM Student
                            WHERE StudentID = @i_StudentID);
END;
```

Here you retrieve the name of a student given the student's ID number. This ID is passed into the stored procedure as an input parameter. You return the name from the procedure as an output parameter called @o_StudentName. You set the value of this parameter using a subquery in the SET statement, selecting the name of the appropriate student.

Once this procedure has been compiled, you can execute it by entering the following statements into Query Analyzer:

```
DECLARE @StudentName varchar(50);
EXEC GetStudentName 4, @StudentName OUTPUT;
PRINT @StudentName;
```

Here you declare the variable that you'll use to store the output parameter and then use the EXEC keyword to execute the parameter. Notice that you have to specify the OUTPUT keyword when you call the procedure, as well as when you define it. Finally, you print the value of the @StudentName variable using Query Analyzer's PRINT function:

```
Bruce Lee
```

Oracle

For output parameters in Oracle, you just replace the IN keyword with OUT:

```
(OutputParamName OUT INT)
```

EXAMPLE: USING OUTPUT PARAMETERS (ORACLE)

Create the GetStudentName procedure by entering this code into SQL*Plus:

```
CREATE OR REPLACE PROCEDURE GetStudentName(
                            i_StudentID    IN   INT,
                            o_StudentName OUT VARCHAR)
AS
BEGIN
   SELECT Name INTO o_StudentName FROM Student
   WHERE StudentID = i_StudentID;
END;
/
```

Here you use Oracle's SELECT INTO syntax to store the name of the student with the specified ID into your output parameter, o_StudentName. When the procedure is executed, this value will be available to the application. You can execute the stored procedure and print the value of o_StudentName in SQL*Plus using the following lines:

```
SET SERVEROUT ON
DECLARE
   StudentName VARCHAR(50);
BEGIN
   GetStudentName(3, StudentName);
   dbms_output.put_line(StudentName);
END;
/
```

The first line here, SET SERVEROUT ON, is a SQL*Plus command that allows you to print output to SQL*Plus; if you don't set SERVEROUT to on, you won't be able to display the value of your output parameter after the procedure has executed.

Next, you declare a variable called StudentName to hold the output value and pass this into the stored procedure. Notice that you don't use the CALL keyword when calling a stored procedure from inside a BEGIN block. Finally, you display the value by calling SQL*Plus's dbms_output.put_line() function:

```
Emily Scarlett
```

DB2

In DB2, you place the OUT keyword before the parameter name:

```
(OUT OutputParamName INT)
```

EXAMPLE: USING OUTPUT PARAMETERS (DB2)

The DB2 code for creating your GetStudentName procedure looks like this:

```
CREATE PROCEDURE GetStudentName(i_StudentID INT,
                               OUT o_StudentName VARCHAR(50))
P1: BEGIN
   SET o_StudentName = (SELECT Name FROM Student
                           WHERE StudentID = i_StudentID);
END P1
```

Create a new stored procedure in the InstantUniversitySprocs project in Development Center, enter this code, and build the procedure.

In DB2, you can set a variable to a value retrieved from a query using the normal SET syntax, assigning the result of the SELECT query to the variable:

```
SET o_StudentName = (SELECT Name FROM Student
                        WHERE StudentID = i_StudentID);
```

To execute the procedure in DB2 Command Center, you just need to enter one line:

```
CALL GetStudentName(2, ?);
```

You use a question mark (?) to represent the output parameter. After the procedure has been executed, Command Center displays the values of any output parameters:

```
Value of output parameters

-------------------------
Parameter Name  : O_STUDENTNAME
Parameter Value : Gary Burton

Return Status = 0
```

Input/Output Parameters

As well as input and output parameters, DB2 and Oracle both support input/output parameters. These are parameters that you use both to feed data into the stored procedure and to return data from it. Input/output parameters are defined using the INOUT keyword:

```
(INOUT SomeParamName INT)    -- DB2
(SomeParamName INOUT INT)    -- Oracle
```

To use an input/output parameter, you need to declare and initialize a variable and then pass it into the stored procedure. The value of the parameter will then be modified within the stored procedure, and you can read the value of the variable again once the procedure has been executed.

Coding in Stored Procedures

As mentioned earlier, stored procedures consist mainly of SQL statements. However, you also have access to certain structured language functionality, including conditional execution of statements and looping. The keywords and structures vary a little between platforms, but the basic operation is the same in all cases. In general, the keywords and structures introduced here are available for use in batches of SQL statements, but they're more commonly found in stored procedures and UDFs.

NOTE   *This section applies only to SQL Server, Oracle, and DB2; Access supports only single-statement stored queries, and MySQL doesn't support stored procedures.*

Conditional Execution

In some cases, you might only want a stored procedure to execute a query if certain conditions are met, such as valid parameters being supplied. Alternatively, you might execute one query and then only move on to execute another if the result of the first query meets your approval. Also, you might have several statements that you could execute and choose one of them based on a parameter or query result.

Two types of conditional statements are available in most RDBMSs:

- `IF...ELSE` statements, where one of two blocks of code is executed depending on a condition

- `CASE...WHEN` statements, where a value is used to choose the result of the structure, which may take one of several values

The SQL Server structure for `IF...ELSE` is as follows:

```
IF Condition
BEGIN
    ...Statements executed if Condition evaluates to true
END
ELSE
BEGIN
    ...Statements executed if Condition evaluates to false
END
```

The `BEGIN` and `END` keywords can be omitted if only a single statement is required in a block, and the whole ELSE block can be omitted if desired.

Oracle and DB2 require a `THEN` keyword after each condition and also allow the use of `ELSIF/ELSEIF` clauses so that you can evaluate more than one condition (in SQL Server, you just use a nested `IF` statement instead). The syntax for Oracle is as follows:

```
IF Condition THEN
    ...Statements if Condition evaluates to true ...
ELSIF Condition2 THEN
    ...Statements if Condition evaluates to false
        and Condition2 evaluates to true...
ELSE
    ...Statements if Condition and Condition2
        both evaluate to false...
END IF;
```

Here, `ELSIF` and `ELSE` blocks are optional. DB2 is identical except that it uses two Es in `ELSEIF`.

In all cases, the conditions are simply Boolean expressions of the type you've used many times before.

You can also use `CASE...WHEN` statements to test a single expression for multiple values:

```
CASE Expression
    WHEN Value1 THEN Result1
    WHEN Value2 THEN Result2
    ...
    WHEN ValueN THEN ResultN
    ELSE ResultElse
END;
```

Here, `Expression` is evaluated, and if it matches any of the values listed, then the result of the structure is the result associated with the first matching value. Any subsequent matches are ignored. If no match is made, then the result is `ResultElse` (if this appears because the `ELSE` section is optional). In SQL Server, `CASE` can only be used within a `SELECT` or variable assignment statement:

```
SET @somevar = CASE @someothervar
                   WHEN 1 THEN 'one'
                   WHEN 2 THEN 'two'
                   ELSE 'can''t count that high'
               END;
```

In Oracle and DB2, `CASE` can also be used as in procedural programming languages—the result for each `WHEN` case can be a complete statement. Used in this way, you need to provide semicolons at the end of each statement, and the `CASE` statement is terminated by `END CASE` rather than just `END`. For example, in DB2:

```
CASE somevar
    WHEN 1 THEN SET someothervar = 'one';
    WHEN 2 THEN SET someothervar = 'two';
    ELSE SET someothervar = 'can''t count that high';
END CASE;
```

The Oracle syntax is identical (except, of course, that the syntax for the variable assignations uses `:=` rather than `SET`).

You can also look at several conditions in a `CASE` statement:

```
CASE
    WHEN Comparison1 THEN Result1
    WHEN Comparison2 THEN Result2
    ...
    WHEN ComparisonN THEN ResultN
    ELSE ResultElse
END;
```

If any of the comparisons evaluate to true, then the result is determined by the THEN clause for the first match (subsequent matches will be ignored). As before, if none is true, then the result is *ResultElse*.

Conditional Execution Example

Let's look at an example of using conditions in stored procedures. You'll create a stored procedure that calculates the average mark that a particular student scored in his or her exams and then returns a comment about how that student is doing based on this average. The ID will be passed in as an input parameter, and the comment will be returned as an output parameter. The code is similar for all three systems, but you'll look at each one individually because the syntax for assigning variables and so on is different.

SQL Server

The chief point to notice about the SQL Server version of this procedure is the slightly divergent syntax for the IF and CASE constructions.

EXAMPLE: CONDITIONAL EXPRESSIONS (SQL SERVER)

Enter this code into Query Analyzer and execute it:

```
CREATE PROCEDURE GetStudentComments (
        @i_StudentID INT, @o_Comments VARCHAR(100) OUTPUT)
AS
BEGIN
DECLARE @exams_sat    INT;
DECLARE @avg_mark     INT;
DECLARE @tmp_comments VARCHAR(100);
SET @exams_sat = (SELECT COUNT(ExamID) FROM StudentExam
                    WHERE StudentID = @i_StudentID);
```

```
IF @exams_sat = 0
    SET @avg_mark = -1;
ELSE
    SET @avg_mark = (SELECT AVG(Mark) FROM StudentExam
                        WHERE StudentID = @i_StudentID);
    SET @tmp_comments = CASE
        WHEN @avg_mark < 0 THEN
            'n/a - this student sat no exams'
        WHEN @avg_mark < 50 THEN
            'Very poor. Needs to spend less time in the bar.'
        WHEN @avg_mark < 60 THEN
            'Adequate, but could work harder.'
        WHEN @avg_mark < 70 THEN
            'Very satisfactory. Should pass easily.'
        ELSE 'Excellent! Will pass with flying colors.'
    END;
SET @o_Comments = @tmp_comments;
END;
```

You start by declaring three variables: a variable to hold the number of the exams sat by the student, a variable to hold the average mark in the exams, and a variable to hold the comments to which you'll eventually assign the output parameter. Next, you retrieve the number of exams taken by the student into a variable called `@exams_sat`. If this is zero, you set the `@avg_mark` variable to `-1`. Otherwise, you set this variable to the average mark for the student.

Once you've set `@avg_mark`, you use a CASE statement to set the `@tmp_comments` variable. If `@avg_mark` is less than zero, you return a message indicating that you have no comments because the student hasn't taken any exams. Otherwise, you set the message to reflect the marks scored by the student. Finally, you set the output parameter to the value of `@tmp_comments`.

Once you've created the procedure, you can run it from Query Analyzer as follows:

```
DECLARE @comments VARCHAR(100);
EXEC GetStudentComments 12, @comments OUTPUT;
PRINT @comments;
```

The result of this is as follows:

```
n/a - this student sat no exams
```

Oracle

The Oracle code for this procedure is similar to the SQL Server version, but there are some differences in the way the conditional statements are implemented.

EXAMPLE: CONDITIONAL EXPRESSIONS (ORACLE)

Enter this code into SQL*Plus:

```
CREATE OR REPLACE PROCEDURE GetStudentComments(
                               i_StudentID IN  INT,
                               o_Comments  OUT VARCHAR)
AS
    exams_sat    INT;
    avg_mark     INT;
    tmp_comments VARCHAR(100);
BEGIN
SELECT COUNT(ExamID) INTO exams_sat FROM StudentExam
    WHERE StudentID = i_StudentID;
IF exams_sat = 0 THEN
    tmp_comments := 'n/a - this student sat no exams';
ELSE
    SELECT AVG(Mark) INTO avg_mark FROM StudentExam
    WHERE StudentID = i_StudentID;
    CASE
        WHEN avg_mark < 50 THEN tmp_comments :=
            'Very poor. Needs to spend less time in the bar.';
        WHEN avg_mark < 60 THEN tmp_comments :=
            'Adequate, but could work harder.';
        WHEN avg_mark < 70 THEN tmp_comments :=
            'Very satisfactory. Should pass easily.';
        ELSE tmp_comments :=
            'Excellent! Will pass with flying colors.';
    END CASE;
END IF;
o_Comments := tmp_comments;
END;
/
```

The first thing to notice is that you place the variable declarations between the AS keyword and the BEGIN keyword that marks the start of the procedure body. When you declare local variables within a procedure, notice that you don't include the DECLARE keyword.

Within the procedure body, you store the number of exams taken by the student in the exams_sat variable using Oracle's SELECT INTO syntax. If this is zero, you set the message in the tmp_comments variable to indicate that comments aren't applicable. Otherwise, you retrieve the average exam mark for the student and use a CASE statement to set tmp_comments. Notice that you use the alternative syntax for CASE here, whereby the result for each case is a complete statement, rather than a value that you store in a variable. Finally, you set the output parameter to return the value stored in tmp_comments.

You can run this procedure from SQL*Plus using the following code:

```
SET SERVEROUT ON
DECLARE
    comments VARCHAR(100);
BEGIN
    GetStudentComments(2, comments);
    dbms_output.put_line(comments);
END;
/
```

The output from this is as follows:

```
Very poor. Needs to spend less time in the bar.
```

DB2

The DB2 code for this procedure is fundamentally similar to that for Oracle. Apart from the spelling of ELSEIF, the syntax for IF and CASE statements is identical in DB2 and Oracle.

EXAMPLE: CONDITIONAL EXPRESSIONS (DB2)

Create and build the following stored procedure using Development Center:

```
CREATE PROCEDURE DB2ADMIN.GetStudentComments (
          IN i_StudentID INT, OUT o_Comments VARCHAR(100))
P1: BEGIN
DECLARE exams_sat    INT;
DECLARE avg_mark     INT;
DECLARE tmp_comments VARCHAR(100);
SET exams_sat = (SELECT COUNT(ExamID) FROM StudentExam
                 WHERE StudentID = i_StudentID);
IF exams_sat = 0 THEN
    SET tmp_comments = 'n/a - this student sat no exams';
ELSE
    SET avg_mark = (SELECT AVG(Mark) FROM StudentExam
                    WHERE StudentID = i_StudentID);
    CASE
       WHEN avg_mark < 50 THEN SET tmp_comments =
           'Very poor. Needs to spend less time in the bar.';
       WHEN avg_mark < 60 THEN SET tmp_comments =
           'Adequate, but could work harder.';
       WHEN avg_mark < 70 THEN SET tmp_comments =
           'Very satisfactory. Should pass easily.';
       ELSE SET tmp_comments =
           'Excellent! Will pass with flying colors';
    END CASE;
END IF;
SET o_Comments = tmp_comments;
END P1
```

Again, you start by declaring the variables you'll be using in the procedure. You then check whether the student took any exams and if so store the average mark; otherwise, you set tmp_comments to indicate that comments aren't applicable. If exams were set, you use the average mark value in a CASE statement to set the tmp_comments variable to the message that indicates how the student is performing. Finally, you return this message from the procedure by assigning the value of the output parameter to tmp_comments.

You can run this procedure from Command Center as follows:

```
CALL GetStudentComments(3, ?)
```

This gives the following output:

```
Value of output parameters

--------------------------
Parameter Name  : O_COMMENTS
Parameter Value : Excellent! Will pass with flying colors.

Return Status = 0
```

Loops

The various dialects of SQL each have their own ways of performing loops, that is, repeatedly executing blocks of SQL statements. SQL Server, DB2, and Oracle all support the WHILE loop. Unfortunately, the syntax is slightly different in each case.

In SQL Server, WHILE is followed by either a single statement or a BEGIN...END block of SQL statements:

```
WHILE Condition
BEGIN
    ...statements to execute if Condition is true...
END;
```

With Oracle, you mark the start of the loop using the LOOP keyword placed after the condition and mark the end of the block using END LOOP:

```
WHILE Condition
LOOP
    ...statements to execute if Condition is true...
END LOOP;
```

DB2 uses DO to mark the start of the loop and END WHILE to mark the end:

```
WHILE Condition
DO
    ...statements to execute if Condition is true...
END WHILE;
```

In each case, the block of statements (or a single statement) executes if *Condition* is true and again if *Condition* is still true and so on. If, at the end of the block of statements, *Condition* evaluates to false, then the loop ends and processing continues. If *Condition* is false to start off with, then the block never executes.

This is the most basic type of loop, but some RDBMSs support variations of this. Oracle and DB2 also support FOR loops, which are used to iterate through every row in a cursor. Because loops are particularly important with cursors, you'll look at examples of looping shortly.

Using Cursors

Cursors are a way of representing a result set within SQL code, and they allow you to loop through a set of rows, one row at a time. In general, if it's possible to avoid using cursors, then you should use the alternative because the performance of cursors is generally poor. However, situations do arise where you need to be able to loop through every row of a result set individually. More important, though, you need to use cursors in Oracle and DB2 if you want to create a stored procedure that returns a result set.

You'll look quickly at the syntax for declaring and using cursors before you move on to look at an actual example, which should make everything much clearer!

Declaring Cursors

As mentioned previously, you can declare cursor variables using this syntax:

```
DECLARE CursorName CURSOR FOR CursorSpec;
```

Here the *CursorSpec* section is the SQL query with which the cursor will be used. For example:

```
DECLARE cur_students CURSOR FOR
    SELECT StudentID, Name FROM Student;
```

Oracle

Oracle uses IS instead of FOR:

```
DECLARE cur_students CURSOR IS
    SELECT StudentID, Name FROM Student;
```

If you want to update the data in the database through the cursor, you need to add the FOR UPDATE clause:

```
DECLARE cur_students CURSOR IS
    SELECT StudentID, Name FROM Student
    FOR UPDATE;
```

This locks any tables queried so that no other user can update the data in the table; if the query affects more than one table, you can lock only a specific table using FOR UPDATE OF *ColumnList*, where *ColumnList* is a comma-delimited list of column names. In this case, a table will only be locked if one or more of its columns appears in the list of column names.

You'll look at locking in Chapter 10, "Transactions."

SQL Server

SQL Server also allows you to specify a FOR UPDATE [OF *ColumnList*] clause to indicate which columns you want to be updateable (alternatively, you can specify FOR READ ONLY if you don't want the cursor to be updateable). You can also specify that you want the cursor to be insensitive to changes made by other uses by placing the word INSENSITIVE after the cursor name; and you can specify whether you want the cursor to be scrollable (rather than forward only) by inserting the keyword SCROLL before CURSOR:

```
DECLARE cur_students INSENSITIVE SCROLL CURSOR
FOR
    SELECT StudentID, Name FROM Student
    FOR UPDATE OF Student;
```

Notice that, unlike other variables, SQL Server cursor names don't begin with the @ character.

As well as this SQL-92 syntax, Transact-SQL has an extended syntax:

```
DECLARE CursorName CURSOR
    [Scope]
    [Scrollability]
    [CursorType]
    [LockType]
    [TYPE_WARNING]
    FOR CursorSpec
    [FOR UPDATE [OF ColumnList]]
```

Table 9-1 describes the options available using this syntax.

Table 9-1. Transact-SQL Options for Cursors

Option	Description
Scope	This can be LOCAL or GLOBAL. Local cursors can only be accessed from within the current stored procedure or batch of SQL statements; global cursors are available to any procedures using the same connection.
Scrollability	FORWARD_ONLY or SCROLL. Indicates whether the cursor is scrollable, so you can move backward and forward through it or forward only (in which case you can only move forwards, one row at a time).
CursorType	One of STATIC, KEYSET, DYNAMIC, or FAST_FORWARD. Static cursors make a local copy of the data, so they don't reflect changes made by other users or allow modifications to the underlying data. Keyset cursors fix the order and number of the rows when the cursor is opened; changes to nonkey values by other users will be visible, but rows inserted by other users won't be accessible. If another user deletes a row, then it won't be possible to fetch that row. If a key value for a row is changed, the keyset cursor will treat that as the deletion of the existing row and an insertion of a new row. Dynamic cursors reflect any changes made by other users. Fast-forward cursors are a special type of forward-only, read-only cursor, which is optimized for performance.
LockType	This can be READ_ONLY, SCROLL_LOCKS, or OPTIMISTIC. Read-only cursors aren't updateable at all, optimistic cursors allow rows to be updated only if the underlying data hasn't changed since the cursor was opened, and cursors with scroll locks lock each row as it's fed into the cursor, so updates are always possible.
TYPE_WARNING	If this option is specified, a warning will be generated if the cursor is implicitly converted to another type because the *CursorSpec* is incompatible with the requested options.

DB2

DB2 has two extra options in the DECLARE CURSOR statement (Table 9-2 describes these options):

```
DECLARE CURSOR CursorName
    [WITH HOLD]
    [WITH RETURN [TO CALLER | TO CLIENT]]
FOR CursorSpec;
```

Table 9-2. DB2 Options for Cursors

Option	Description
WITH HOLD	If the WITH HOLD option is specified, the cursor can be kept open over multiple transactions. If the transaction is aborted, the cursor will be closed.
WITH RETURN [TO CALLER | TO CLIENT]	Indicates whether the cursor can be returned to a client application from a stored procedure. If WITH RETURN TO CALLER is specified, an open cursor will return a result set to any caller, such as a client application or another stored procedure. The WITH RETURN TO CLIENT option only allows the procedure to return a result set directly to the client application—the result set will be invisible to any intermediate stored procedure or UDF.

Using Cursors

Before you can use a cursor, you need to open it:

```
OPEN CursorName;
```

You can now retrieve rows from this cursor into local variables. To do this, you use the FETCH keyword (but the syntax varies somewhat for the different RDBMSs). The simplest is DB2:

```
FETCH CursorName INTO var1, var2, ...varn;
```

The variables that you're storing the row values in must obviously match the data types of the columns. For example, to fetch the values from the cur_students cursor into variables called StudID and StudName, you use this statement:

```
FETCH cur_students INTO StudID, StudName;
```

SQL Server uses the following syntax:

```
FETCH [NEXT] FROM CursorName INTO @var1, @var2, ...@varn;
```

So, the previous statement appears in SQL Server as follows:

```
FETCH NEXT FROM cur_students INTO @StudID, @StudName;
```

Depending on the cursor type, you can also fetch the first, previous, or last row from the cursor by specifying FETCH FIRST, FETCH PRIOR, or FETCH LAST, instead of FETCH NEXT. Alternatively, you can specify a particular row to retrieve using FETCH ABSOLUTE n, which retrieves the nth row in the cursor, or FETCH RELATIVE n, which retrieves the row n rows after the current row (for a positive number) or before it (if n is negative).

The syntax for Oracle is a bit different, in that you read the row from the cursor into a single variable. This variable must, of course, be of the same type as a row in the cursor or CursorName%ROWTYPE. You can retrieve a row into this variable using the syntax:

```
FETCH CursorName INTO RowTypeVariable;
```

You can then access an individual column value using RowTypeVariable.ColumnName.

Each system provides its own mechanism for looping through the rows in the cursor, so you'll examine these using an example. Once you've finished with the cursor, you need to close it:

```
CLOSE CursorName;
```

Finally, if you're using SQL Server, you also need to release the resources used by the cursor with the DEALLOCATE keyword:

```
DEALLOCATE CursorName;
```

This step isn't necessary in Oracle and DB2, and they don't support DEALLOCATE.

Using Implicit Cursors

Before you look at a concrete example of cursors in action, you need to look briefly at implicit cursors in Oracle and DB2. Implicit cursors provide a shortcut syntax for creating, opening, looping through, and finally closing a cursor. This syntax uses a FOR loop and resembles somewhat the foreach construct available in some programming languages.

The syntax for Oracle is as follows:

```
FOR CursorName IN (CursorSpec)
LOOP
    ...statements that use the cursor...
END LOOP;
```

And for DB2:

```
FOR CursorName AS CursorSpec
DO
    ...statements that use the cursor...
END FOR;
```

This opens a cursor, loops through each row in turn, and then closes the cursor. As you can see, this approach is much easier to code and also more readable. The following DB2 and Oracle examples use both the implicit and explicit syntaxes.

Cursor Example

For this example, you'll print a list of each professor in the database and all the students in each class they take. Although there are some significant differences between the SQL Server, Oracle, and DB2 versions of this procedure, the overall structure is similar. You start by opening a cursor containing the ProfessorID and Name columns of the Professor table and looping through each row in this cursor, printing the name of the professor. For each row, you open a nested cursor containing the names of all the students taught by that professor and loop through this, printing each name.

SQL Server

To loop through the rows in a cursor in SQL Server, you use the WHILE loop you saw previously. SQL Server has a system variable called @@FETCH_STATUS, which returns zero as long as the last attempt to fetch a row from the cursor was successful.

EXAMPLE: USING CURSORS (SQL SERVER)

Enter the following code into Query Analyzer and execute it:

```
DECLARE @ProfName VARCHAR(50);
DECLARE @StudentName VARCHAR(50);
DECLARE @ProfID INT;
DECLARE cur_profs CURSOR FOR
    SELECT ProfessorID, Name FROM Professor;
OPEN cur_profs;
FETCH NEXT FROM cur_profs INTO @ProfID, @ProfName;
WHILE @@FETCH_STATUS = 0
BEGIN
    PRINT @ProfName;
    DECLARE cur_students CURSOR FOR
        SELECT DISTINCT Name FROM Student s
        INNER JOIN Enrollment e
        ON s.StudentID = e.StudentID
            INNER JOIN Class c
            ON e.ClassID = c.ClassID
        WHERE c.ProfessorID = @ProfID;
    OPEN cur_students;
    FETCH NEXT FROM cur_students INTO @StudentName;
    WHILE @@FETCH_STATUS = 0
    BEGIN
        PRINT @StudentName;
        FETCH NEXT FROM cur_students INTO @StudentName;
    END
    CLOSE cur_students;
    DEALLOCATE cur_students;
    PRINT '---------------';
    FETCH NEXT FROM cur_profs INTO @ProfID, @ProfName;
END
CLOSE cur_profs;
DEALLOCATE cur_profs;
```

To see what's going on here more clearly, let's look at the outer loop separated from the inner loop:

```
DECLARE cur_profs CURSOR FOR
    SELECT ProfessorID, Name FROM Professor;
OPEN cur_profs;
FETCH NEXT FROM cur_profs INTO @ProfID, @ProfName;
```

```
WHILE @@FETCH_STATUS = 0
BEGIN
    PRINT @ProfName;
    -- Use cursor
    PRINT '---------------';
    FETCH NEXT FROM cur_profs INTO @ProfID, @ProfName;
END
CLOSE cur_profs;
DEALLOCATE cur_profs;
```

You declare and open the cursor as normal and fetch the first row into two variables, @ProfID and @ProfName. You then loop for as long as the @@FETCH_STATUS variable remains at zero, printing out the professor's name at the start of the loop and fetching the next row at the end (after you've finished using the current row). When the end of the cursor is reached, @@FETCH_STATUS will be set to -1, so the loop will end. You then close and deallocate the cursor.

Now let's look at the inner loop:

```
DECLARE cur_students CURSOR FOR
    SELECT DISTINCT Name FROM Student s
    INNER JOIN Enrollment e
    ON s.StudentID = e.StudentID
        INNER JOIN Class c
        ON e.ClassID = c.ClassID
    WHERE c.ProfessorID = @ProfID;
OPEN cur_students;
FETCH NEXT FROM cur_students INTO @StudentName;
WHILE @@FETCH_STATUS = 0
BEGIN
    PRINT @StudentName;
    FETCH NEXT FROM cur_students INTO @StudentName;
END
CLOSE cur_students;
DEALLOCATE cur_students;
```

The structure of this loop is basically the same as that for the outer one: You declare and open the cursor containing the students' names and fetch the first row into a variable. You then loop through each row, printing out the student's name and fetching the next row from the cursor. When @@FETCH_STATUS is set to zero, the loop ends, and you close and deallocate the cursor. At this point, you fetch the next row for the professor cursor, so @@FETCH_STATUS will be reset, and the outer loop will continue.

The output from this example is as follows:

```
Prof. Dawson

Anna Wolff
John Jones
Julia Picard
---------------
Prof. Williams
Bruce Lee
...
```

Oracle

The chief difference between the examples for SQL Server and Oracle is that you're using an implicit cursor for the inner loop. The way that you loop through the rows of the explicit cursor is similar. The cursor has a FOUND attribute (*CursorName*%FOUND), which evaluates to true if the last FETCH returned a row or false otherwise. You therefore just need to loop while this remains true.

EXAMPLE: USING CURSORS (ORACLE)

Enter the following code into SQL*Plus:

```
SET SERVEROUT ON
DECLARE
    CURSOR cur_profs IS
        SELECT ProfessorID, Name FROM Professor;
    prof cur_profs%ROWTYPE;
BEGIN
    OPEN cur_profs;
    FETCH cur_profs INTO prof;
    WHILE cur_profs%FOUND
```

```
    LOOP
        dbms_output.put_line(prof.Name);
        FOR c1 IN (SELECT DISTINCT Name FROM Student s
                        INNER JOIN Enrollment e
                    ON s.StudentID = e.StudentID
                        INNER JOIN Class c
                        ON e.ClassID = c.ClassID
                    WHERE c.ProfessorID = prof.ProfessorID)
        LOOP
            dbms_output.put_line(c1.Name);
        END LOOP;
        FETCH cur_profs INTO prof;
        dbms_output.put_line('----------------');
    END LOOP;
    CLOSE cur_profs;
END;
/
```

Again, let's look at the outer loop separated from the inner loop to see more clearly what's happening:

```
    OPEN cur_profs;
    FETCH cur_profs INTO prof;
    WHILE cur_profs%FOUND
    LOOP
        dbms_output.put_line(prof.Name);
        ... Use cursor
        FETCH cur_profs INTO prof;
        dbms_output.put_line('----------------');
    END LOOP;
    CLOSE cur_profs;
```

You start by opening the professor cursor and reading the first row into the prof variable, which you've declared as cur_profs%ROWTYPE. You then loop while cur_profs%FOUND remains true. For each row, you print the professor's name using dbms_output.put_line(), and (after you've looped through the inner cursor) fetch the next row. When the end of the cursor is reached, cur_profs%FOUND will evaluate to false, the loop will end, and you close the cursor.

The inner loop is much simpler because it uses an implicit cursor:

```
FOR c1 IN (SELECT DISTINCT Name FROM Student s
              INNER JOIN Enrollment e
           ON s.StudentID = e.StudentID
              INNER JOIN Class c
              ON e.ClassID = c.ClassID
           WHERE c.ProfessorID = prof.ProfessorID)
LOOP
   dbms_output.put_line(c1.Name);
END LOOP;
```

Notice that you access the `ProfessorID` column of the current row in the cur_profs cursor through the prof rowtype variable as `prof.ProfessorID`. You can access the columns in the implicit cursor using the same syntax (but without the need for a rowtype variable):

```
c1.Name
```

The output from this example is as follows:

```
Prof. Dawson

Anna Wolff
John Jones
Julia Picard
----------------
Prof. Williams
Bruce Lee
...
```

DB2

This example is a little trickier in DB2 for a number of reasons. The first is purely practical—DB2 doesn't provide an easy way of writing directly to the Command Center output. In DB2, `DECLARE CURSOR` isn't valid outside stored procedures, so you need to define a stored procedure for the example. So, what you'll do is construct a long string that contains the names of the professors and students and then pass this as an output parameter. True, this does seem a bit contrived, but it demonstrates the cursor syntax just as well as if you were printing to Command Center directly!

The next problem is that DB2 doesn't provide a convenient attribute of the cursor that tells you when the end of the cursor has been reached. To get around this, you need to define a "continue handler" that will execute when a particular SQL state occurs (in this case, the SQL state 02000):

```
DECLARE CONTINUE HANDLER FOR SQLSTATE '02000'
    SET eof = 1;
```

When the end of the cursor is reached, SQL state 02000 will be signaled, your continue handler will execute, and the stored procedure will continue to execute. Within the continue handler, you just set the value of a flag to 1.

You'll look at SQL states in more detail shortly, when you learn about error handling in stored procedures.

EXAMPLE: USING CURSORS (DB2)

Create and build this procedure using Development Center:

```
CREATE PROCEDURE GetClassAttendees (
                    OUT AllClassAttendees VARCHAR(1000))
P1: BEGIN
DECLARE ProfID    INT;
DECLARE ProfName VARCHAR(50);
DECLARE tmp_msg  VARCHAR(1000) DEFAULT '';
DECLARE eof       SMALLINT      DEFAULT 0;
DECLARE cur_profs CURSOR FOR
    SELECT ProfessorID, Name FROM Professor;
DECLARE CONTINUE HANDLER FOR SQLSTATE '02000'
    SET eof = 1;
OPEN cur_profs;
WHILE eof = 0
DO
    FETCH cur_profs INTO ProfID, ProfName;
    SET tmp_msg = tmp_msg || ProfName || ': ';
    FOR cur_students AS SELECT DISTINCT Name FROM Student s
                    INNER JOIN Enrollment e
                    ON s.StudentID = e.StudentID
```

```
                          INNER JOIN Class c
                          ON e.ClassID = c.ClassID
                        WHERE c.ProfessorID = ProfID
    DO
        SET tmp_msg = tmp_msg || Name || ', ';
    END FOR;
END WHILE;
CLOSE cur_profs;
SET AllClassAttendees = LEFT(tmp_msg, LENGTH(tmp_msg) - 2);
END P1
```

Again, let's look at the outer loop first:

```
DECLARE cur_profs CURSOR FOR
    SELECT ProfessorID, Name FROM Professor;
DECLARE CONTINUE HANDLER FOR SQLSTATE '02000'
    SET eof = 1;
OPEN cur_profs;
WHILE eof = 0
DO
    FETCH cur_profs INTO ProfID, ProfName;
    SET tmp_msg = tmp_msg || ProfName || ': ';
END WHILE;
CLOSE cur_profs;
```

Here you declare the cursor and the continue handler. You then open the cursor and continue fetching rows into it and adding the professor names to a string variable that you use to build the output message until no more rows are found. At this point, the SQL state 02000 is signaled, the continue handler runs and sets the eof flag to 1, and the WHILE loop terminates.

The inner loop uses an implicit cursor and looks like this:

```
FOR cur_students AS SELECT DISTINCT Name FROM Student s
                    INNER JOIN Enrollment e
                    ON s.StudentID = e.StudentID
                      INNER JOIN Class c
                       ON e.ClassID = c.ClassID
                     WHERE c.ProfessorID = ProfID
DO
    SET tmp_msg = tmp_msg || Name || ', ';
END FOR;
```

This simply loops through each row in the Student table and adds the Name for any students taught by the current professor to your tmp_msg variable.

You can run the procedure in Command Center using this statement:

```
CALL GetClassAttendees(?);
```

The output from this is as follows:

```
Value of output parameters

-------------------------
Parameter Name  : ALLCLASSATTENDEES
Parameter Value : Prof. Dawson: Anna Wolff, John Jones,
Julia Picard, Prof. Williams: Bruce Lee ...
Return Status = 0
```

Returning Result Sets from a Procedure

So far, you've only seen how to retrieve individual values from stored procedures using output parameters. It's also possible to return a whole result set from a procedure (or even, in the case of DB2, multiple result sets). In the case of SQL Server and Access, this involves nothing new—you just include a SELECT statement in the body of the procedure. However, for Oracle and DB2, you need to use cursors to do this, so now that you understand cursors, you're in a position to see how to return a result set from a stored procedure.

In DB2, you need to open a cursor WITH RETURN and leave it open at the end of the procedure. Things are trickier in Oracle, though: You need to create a special object called a *package*, which is used to associate multiple objects into a single object. You can place a cursor and your procedure into a single package and return the cursor as an output parameter from your procedure.

Let's start by looking quickly at the SQL Server and Access code.

SQL Server and Access

This is probably the simplest example in the chapter!

Execute the following CREATE PROCEDURE statement against the InstantUniversity database:

```
CREATE PROCEDURE GetStudents
AS
SELECT StudentID, Name FROM Student;
```

You can execute this using the EXEC or EXECUTE keyword:

```
EXEC GetStudents;
```

The output from this query is as follows:

```
StudentID   Name

----------  --------------
1           John Jones
2           Gary Burton
3           Emily Scarlett
...         ...
```

DB2

One feature of DB2 is that it allows you to return more than one result set from a stored procedure, simply by leaving more than one cursor open at the end of the procedure. Because of this, it also allows you to specify how many result sets are returned from a procedure using the RESULT SETS clause, which is placed before the LANGUAGE SQL clause.

EXAMPLE: RETURNING ROWS (DB2)

Build the following procedure in Development Center:

```
CREATE PROCEDURE GetStudents()
RESULT SETS 1
LANGUAGE SQL
P1: BEGIN
    DECLARE cur_Students CURSOR WITH RETURN FOR
        SELECT StudentID, Name FROM Student;
    OPEN cur_Students;
END P1
```

You're just returning one cursor, so you add the clause RESULT SETS 1 to your CREATE PROCEDURE statement. Within the body of the procedure, you simply declare and open the cursor for the appropriate SELECT statement. Notice that you declare the cursor WITH RETURN because you want to return the result set from the procedure.

You can execute this using the standard CALL keyword:

```
CALL GetStudents;
```

The output from this query is as follows:

```
StudentID   Name

----------  --------------
1           John Jones
2           Gary Burton
3           Emily Scarlett
...         ...
```

Oracle

As mentioned previously, you have to do a bit more work with Oracle. First, you need to create a package that will hold your cursor and the stored procedure. To create a package, you need to use the CREATE PACKAGE statement:

```
CREATE [OR REPLACE] PACKAGE PackageName
AS
-- Types, procedures, etc., in the package
END PackageName;
```

Next, you have to define the body for the package. The package body is where the actual code for any functions, procedures, and so on in the package is defined. As expected, you create this using the CREATE PACKAGE BODY statement:

```
CREATE [OR REPLACE] PACKAGE BODY PackageName
AS
-- Definitions of procedures and functions
END PackageName;
```

Note that the package body must be given the same name as the package with which it is associated.

It's also possible for the stored procedure to be defined outside the package; you'll see examples of this in the first case study.

Let's see how this works in practice by implementing the GetStudents procedure in Oracle.

EXAMPLE: RETURNING ROWS (ORACLE)

First, you have to define the package:

```
CREATE OR REPLACE PACKAGE student_pkg
AS
TYPE studCur IS REF CURSOR;
PROCEDURE GetStudents(o_StudCur OUT studCur);
END student_pkg;
/
```

As well as the signature of the GetStudents procedure, the package defines a cursor type called studCur. This is a special type of cursor, called a REF CURSOR. Whereas the implicit and explicit cursors you used in the previous example needed to be defined when the procedure was written, REF CURSORs can be used even if the cursor spec isn't known until runtime.

Second, you create the package body:

```
CREATE OR REPLACE PACKAGE BODY student_pkg
AS
    PROCEDURE GetStudents(o_StudCur OUT studCur)
    IS
    BEGIN
        OPEN o_StudCur FOR
            SELECT StudentID, Name FROM Student;
    END GetStudents;
END student_pkg;
/
```

In this case, the package body contains just one item—the definition of the GetStudents stored procedure. This has one output parameter, o_StudCur, which is an instance of your REF CURSOR type, studCur. Within the body of the procedure, you open this cursor, specifying the cursor spec in the OPEN statement. Notice that you can't declare the cursor because it's a parameter—this is why you need to use a REF CURSOR rather than a standard explicit cursor.

Now you can test the procedure. Because this procedure is intended to return a result set to a client application, rather than being accessed from SQL code, you need to retrieve the cursor from the output parameter and loop through the rows manually:

```
SET SERVEROUT ON
DECLARE
    TYPE studCurType IS REF CURSOR;
    mycur studCurType;
    studrow Student%ROWTYPE;
BEGIN
    student_pkg.GetStudents(mycur);
    FETCH mycur INTO studrow;
    WHILE mycur%FOUND
    LOOP
        dbms_output.put_line(studrow.StudentID || '    ' ||
                                studrow.Name);
        FETCH mycur INTO studrow;
    END LOOP;
END;
/
```

The output from this query is as follows:

```
1    John Jones
2    Gary Burton
3    Emily Scarlett
... ...
```

Error Handling

Because the coding in stored procedures goes beyond standard SELECT statements, INSERT statements, and so on into the realms of procedural programming, it's inevitable that errors will occur. This may be because of a faulty query or other SQL statement, but it's just as likely to be a result of bad data being passed to a stored procedure or even an error raised on purpose. Unlike errors in other languages, SQL errors don't necessarily result in exiting of code (although other code may not work as planned—see the next chapter concerning transactions). Instead, you may have to check to see if an error has occurred or leave it to the user of the procedure to deal with it.

SQL Server, Oracle, and DB2 all provide mechanisms for handling errors that occur in stored procedure code. Unfortunately, as you've probably guessed, these are all completely different. A full coverage of error handling in these systems is beyond the scope of this book, but we'll cover the basics.

Providing Return Values

In DB2 and SQL Server, you can provide a return value for a stored procedure using the RETURN keyword:

```
RETURN value;
```

However, you can only return scalar values in this way, and you can only return integers.

When a RETURN statement is encountered in a stored procedure, the procedure terminates immediately, and no further lines of code execute. Bear in mind that this may mean that some output parameters aren't assigned values.

Return values are used to indicate whether the stored procedure executed successfully. Normally, you'd return zero for successful execution or an error code if something went wrong.

SQL Server Error Handling

In SQL Server, you can use the @@ERROR global to check if an error occurred (*globals* are special variables that are accessible to all code accessing a database, and in general they start with @@). If no error has occurred, then @@ERROR will have a value of 0; otherwise, it'll have an integer value reflecting the error that has occurred. You can check for this as follows:

```
IF (@@ERROR <> 0)
    ...Do something, because an error has occurred...
```

You might choose to exit the procedure, for example, or save the error value to an output parameter for later inspection.

In addition, you can raise your own errors if, for example, you only allow certain values for a parameter and the procedure call uses a value that isn't allowed. You can do this using the RAISERROR statement:

```
RAISERROR { msg_id | msg_str }, severity, state [, argument]]
```

If a *msg_id* is specified, rather than a string error message, it must be between 13,000 and 2,147,483,647, and the message must be defined in the sysmessages system table. The *severity* is a value from 0 to 25 that indicates how serious the error is—values from 20 onward are fatal errors and will cause the connection to be lost. Values from 19 onward are reserved for users in the sysadmin role. The next parameter, *state*, is an arbitrary integer value between 1 and 127 that allows you to return information about the state of the error. Finally, you can also specify arguments that are passed into the message string. This can be used to return information about the specific values that caused the error. If any arguments are added, the message string needs to contain markers to indicate where the arguments are to be placed. These markers consist of a percent sign and a character indicating the type of the argument; for example, %d represents a signed integer, %u an unsigned integer, and %s a string.

Let's look at a quick example. You'll create a simple stored procedure that inserts a row into the Students table and call this twice, passing in the same details.

Create the following stored procedure:

```
CREATE PROCEDURE ErrorTest(@i_StudID INT,
                          @i_StudName VARCHAR(10))
AS
BEGIN
    DECLARE @errno INT;
    INSERT INTO Student VALUES (@i_StudID, @i_StudName);
    SET @errno = @@ERROR;
    IF @errno <> 0
    BEGIN
        RAISERROR (
            'Can''t insert row with ID %d into database', 10,
            1, @i_StudID);
        RETURN @errno;
    END;
    ELSE
        RETURN 0;
END;
```

This procedure simply inserts a new row into the Student table, based on the parameters passed in. Once you've executed the INSERT statement, you store the @@ERROR value because this will change if further statements are executed. You then check the value of this variable; if it's not zero, you raise an error, giving the ID of the row that caused the problem. You then return the error number as the return value of the procedure. If everything went well, you just return zero.

Test this procedure by executing these two lines in Query Analyzer:

```
EXEC ErrorTest 99, 'John Fields';
EXEC ErrorTest 99, 'Charles Ives';
```

The first statement will execute without problems, but the second will generate an error because there's already a row with the ID 99:

```
(1 row(s) affected)

Server: Msg 2627, Level 14, State 1, Procedure ErrorTest, Line 7
Violation of PRIMARY KEY constraint 'PK_Student_1920BF5C'.
Cannot insert duplicate key in object 'Student'.
The statement has been terminated.
Can't insert row with ID 99 into database
```

An error is raised before you check the error number, but execution continues (this won't always happen but depends on the severity of the original error). The custom error is then raised, so your own error message appears as the last line of the output.

Oracle Error Handling

In Oracle, you handle errors by placing an EXCEPTION block at the end of a BEGIN block (immediately before the END keyword). Within this EXCEPTION block, you can write code that will execute whenever a certain error occurs.

```
BEGIN
    -- SQL code here
EXCEPTION
    WHEN Exception1 THEN
        -- Handle Exception1
    WHEN Exception2 THEN
        -- Handle Exception2
    -- Handle other exceptions
END;
```

You can define your own exceptions and handle them here, but there are also a number of predefined exceptions. The most common are the following:

- CURSOR_ALREADY_OPEN: This exception is raised if you try to open a cursor that's already open.

- DUP_VAL_ON_INDEX: This is raised if you try to insert a row with a duplicate value in a primary key column or a column with a unique index.

- INVALID_NUMBER: This is raised when you try to convert a string into a number if the string doesn't contain a valid numerical value.

- NO_DATA_FOUND: This exception is raised if you use a SELECT INTO statement to store a value in a variable, but no row is returned by the SELECT query.

- TOO_MANY_ROWS: If you try to use a SELECT INTO statement to populate a variable but the SELECT statement returns more than one row, a TOO_MANY_ROWS exception will be thrown.

- OTHERS: Handles any exceptions not handled by any of the previous exception handlers.

To define your own exception, you simply declare a variable of type EXCEPTION and then RAISE that exception when a particular condition is met. You handle custom exceptions in exactly the same way as predefined exceptions.

Let's look at an example of this in action.

EXAMPLE: ERROR HANDLING (ORACLE)

Create the following stored procedure:

```
CREATE OR REPLACE PROCEDURE ErrorTest(
                                i_StudID    IN INT,
                                i_StudName IN VARCHAR)
AS
    UnluckyNumber EXCEPTION;
BEGIN
    IF i_StudID = 13 THEN
        RAISE UnluckyNumber;
    END IF;
    INSERT INTO Student VALUES (i_StudID, i_StudName);
EXCEPTION
    WHEN DUP_VAL_ON_INDEX THEN
        dbms_output.put_line(
            'A student already exists with ID ' || i_StudID);
```

```
    WHEN UnluckyNumber THEN
        dbms_output.put_line(
            'Can''t insert a student with an unlucky ID');
END;
/
```

In this procedure, you insert a new row into the Student table. You check for two exceptions—the predefined DUP_VAL_ON_INDEX exception, which will be thrown if you try to insert a row with a StudentID that already exists in the table, and a custom exception called UnluckyNumber, which is thrown if you try to insert a row with a StudentID of 13 (just to protect the feelings of any superstitious students).

You implement this by declaring UnluckyNumber as an EXCEPTION in your procedure's declarations section and then checking the value of the i_StudID input parameter before you make the INSERT. If this is 13, you raise the following error:

```
IF i_StudID = 13 THEN
    RAISE UnluckyNumber;
END IF;
```

Within the exception handlers, you just write an error message to the output. Test this procedure by executing this line in SQL*Plus:

```
CALL ErrorTest(10, 'John Fields');
```

A student with an ID of 10 already exists, so the DUP_VAL_ON_INDEX exception will be raised:

```
A student already exists with ID 10
```

Now enter the following statement:

```
CALL ErrorTest(13, 'Charles Ives');
```

This will cause the UnluckyNumber exception to be raised:

```
Can't insert a student with an unlucky ID
```

DB2 Error Handling

DB2 uses two variables to handle errors in stored procedures—SQLSTATE, which contains a five-character string representing the standard SQL state code for the current error status, and SQLCODE, which is an integer. You can only use one of these because accessing either will cause the other to be reset.

See the DB2 Message Reference at http://www-3.ibm.com/cgi-bin/ db2www/data/db2/udb/winos2unix/support/document.d2w/ report?fn=db2v7m0frm3toc.htm for a complete list of the SQL state codes supported by DB2.

Before you use either of these variables, you need to declare them in the procedure. Usually you would initialize them with default values that indicate all is well:

```
DECLARE SQLCODE   INT     DEFAULT 0;
DECLARE SQLSTATE CHAR(5) DEFAULT '00000';
```

By default, any exception thrown will cause the stored procedure to stop executing, so you have to handle errors if you want execution to continue. To do this, you need to set up a handler for that exception. You do this using the DECLARE...HANDLER statement:

```
DECLARE handler_type HANDLER FOR error_type
BEGIN
    -- handler code
END;
```

There are three types of handler you can use:

- CONTINUE: Continue handlers execute the code in the handler and then continue execution after the line that caused the error. You used a continue handler in the example previously where you looped through a cursor.

- EXIT: If you define an exit handler for an error, then execution will continue after the current BEGIN block once the code in the handler has run. If the current block is nested within another BEGIN block, the stored procedure will continue the execution of the outer block.

- UNDO: This can only be used within a transaction (see the next chapter for a discussion of transactions). If an error handled by an undo handler occurs, any changes made by the current transaction will be rolled back, and execution will continue at the end of the current BEGIN block.

The error_type specifies the type of error associated with this handler. You can handle a specific SQL state, or you can handle one of the following general conditions:

- SQLEXCEPTION: The handler will be invoked whenever a SQL exception is raised.

- SQLWARNING: The handler will be invoked whenever a SQL warning is raised.

- NOT FOUND: This is raised when a WHERE clause matches no rows in the database.

For example, if you want to handle SQL state '23505', which occurs if you try to insert a duplicate value into a primary key or unique column, and you want to continue execution at the next statement, you use the following:

```
DECLARE CONTINUE HANDLER FOR SQLSTATE '23505'
   -- Do something here to handle the error
```

You can raise custom errors using the SIGNAL statement:

```
SIGNAL SQLSTATE SqlStateCode
   SET MESSAGE_TEXT = ErrorDescription;
```

This raises an error with the specified SQL state and error message, which will be returned to the client application if it isn't handled by an exception handler. Note that you can only use SQL state codes beginning with characters in the range '7' to '9' or 'T' to 'Z' for custom exceptions.

Let's see an example to see how this works in practice.

EXAMPLE: ERROR HANDLING (DB2)

Build the following stored procedure:

```
CREATE PROCEDURE DB2ADMIN.ErrorTest (
                          i_StudID    INT,
                          i_StudName VARCHAR(50),
                  OUT o_Status    CHAR(5))
P1: BEGIN
   DECLARE SQLSTATE CHAR(5) DEFAULT '00000';
   DECLARE EXIT HANDLER FOR SQLEXCEPTION
      SET o_Status = SQLSTATE;
   IF i_StudID = 13 THEN
      SIGNAL SQLSTATE '75000'
         SET MESSAGE_TEXT =
            'Can''t insert a student with an unlucky ID';
   END IF;
   INSERT INTO Student VALUES (i_StudID, i_StudName);
   SET o_Status = SQLSTATE;
END P1
```

Here you define just one error handler—an exit handler for all SQL exceptions. In it, you just set the value of the o_Status output parameter to the SQL state associated with the error:

```
DECLARE EXIT HANDLER FOR SQLEXCEPTION
   SET o_Status = SQLSTATE;
```

You then check to make sure that no unfortunate student has been assigned the unlucky ID number 13, and if they have, you raise a custom error:

```
IF i_StudID = 13 THEN
    SIGNAL SQLSTATE '75000'
       SET MESSAGE_TEXT =
          'Can''t insert a student with an unlucky ID';
```

Finally, you execute the INSERT statement and return the resulting SQL state as an output parameter.

After building this procedure, test it by entering the following statement into Command Center:

```
CALL ErrorTest(10, 'Zdenek Fibich', ?)
```

A SQL exception is raised here because a student with the ID of 10 already exists. However, because it's handled by your exit handler, the error isn't passed directly back to the user. Instead, you see the relevant SQL state in your output parameter:

```
Value of output parameters

--------------------------
Parameter Name  : O_STATUS
Parameter Value : 23505

Return Status = 0
```

Now try entering a student with an ID of 13:

```
CALL ErrorTest(13, 'Rasmus Rask', ?)
```

This will cause your custom error to be raised, but because all SQL exceptions are handled by the exit handler, this error isn't passed on to the client. Instead, you can see the SQL state for your error in the output parameter:

```
Value of output parameters

--------------------------
Parameter Name  : O_STATUS
Parameter Value : 75000

Return Status = 0
```

If you hadn't handled the error, the exception would have been raised back to the client, as shown in Figure 9-10.

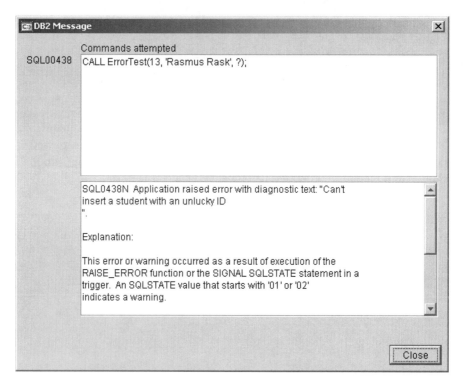

Figure 9-10. Raising the exception back to the client

A Final Note on Stored Procedures

There's a school of thought that says *all* database access should be carried out through stored procedures. The reason for this is that this enhances security and allows the RDBMS you're using to optimize itself for the use of the stored procedures it contains, without having to interpret new SQL statements. Also, because stored procedures are usually precompiled inside the RDBMS, this is another reason for enhanced performance.

One major advantage is that using stored procedures avoids the risk of so-called SQL insertion attacks. Suppose you have a standard SELECT query where a parameter is taken straight from user input. It's possible for that user input to perform operations you really don't want it to perform. Rather than inserting a literal value, you might find that a malicious user inserts an entire SQL statement, perhaps one that would delete all the tables in your database. As you've seen, multiple statements can be executed in a single batch, so this is possible. If you accidentally assign too many security privileges to users, they may just destroy your data. Using stored procedures, on the other hand, avoids this possibility because parameters won't be interpreted as entire SQL statements.

Summary

In this chapter, you've explored using SQL stored procedures. You've learned about the following:

- Creating and executing stored procedures

- Using input and output parameters

- Coding in procedures with loops, conditional statements, and variables

- Working with cursors

- Returning result sets from a stored procedure

- Error handling in stored procedures

You'll be using stored procedures a lot in the rest of the book, and you'll build on these techniques. In the next chapter, you'll look at SQL transactions, which allow you to treat multiple statements as a single unit.

CHAPTER 10

Transactions

ALTHOUGH IT'S GENERALLY CONSIDERED to be an advanced topic, the concept of transactions is easy to understand because it models natural processes that happen in our everyday lives.

Transactions aren't necessarily related to financial operations, but this is the simplest way to look at them. For example, every time you buy something, a transaction happens—you pay an amount of money and then receive in return the product for which you paid. The two operations (paying the money and receiving the product) form the transaction.

Imagine that a customer called Sally wants to transfer $1,000 from her checking account to her savings account. From Sally's point of view, this operation is a single operation (*one* money transfer operation), but in fact inside the database something like this happens:

```
UPDATE Checking
    SET Balance = Balance - 1000
    WHERE Account = 'Sally';
UPDATE Savings
    SET Balance = Balance + 1000
    WHERE Account = 'Sally';
```

Of course, this piece of SQL code is a simplified version of what really happens inside a production database, but it demonstrates how a set of simple operations can form a single larger operation. In this example you have only two operations, but in reality there are likely to be many more. When you perform such a complex operation, you need to be assured it really executes as a single, atomic operation.

This isn't as easy as it sounds because you need to make sure all the constituent operations execute successfully—if any of them don't (and this can happen because of a wide area of reasons such as operating system or database software crashes, computer viruses, or hardware crashes), the larger operation fails.

In the bank scenario, two database operations need to happen in order to correctly transfer the money—if one of the two operations fails (say, a hardware failure happens after the first UPDATE), Sally would lose $1,000. You need to find a way to ensure the two UPDATE statements both either execute successfully or don't execute at all.

Fortunately, modern databases have the technology to protect transactions for you—you just need to tell the database about the statements that form a transaction, and the database will do everything for you.

In this chapter, you'll learn what transactions are and how they're implemented in databases. More specifically, this chapter answers the following questions:

- What are transactions? Why do you need them?

- What are the rules that transactions must follow?

- How can you implement database transactions?

- What are the performance problems associated with database transactions, and what are the best practices to avoid them?

This chapter also looks at the differences between the database platforms that you've been working with when it comes to implementing transactions. Let's start with the basics....

What Is a Transaction?

Transactions are all about data being transformed from one state to another. Before giving an accurate definition for transactions, let's look at yet another scenario involving transactions—this time, an example that's not necessarily related to databases. Imagine what happens when a user who is visiting an e-commerce shop decides to buy the items in his or her shopping cart. From the user's perspective, all that's required is a simple action such as clicking the Order Items button. However, the actual processes that happen behind the scenes could be something like the following:

1. Create a new order in the database by assigning an identifier, storing a customer ID and storing the current date.

2. Clear the customer's shopping cart.

3. Charge the customer's credit card.

4. Send a request to the supplier (or the warehouse) that the ordered items be shipped to the customer.

5. Update database statistics and perform various other operations depending on the way the e-shop is designed to work.

6. Finally, send the customer a confirmation e-mail containing details about his or her order.

Of course, this list of individual tasks is purely hypothetical, but it gives you an idea about the work that needs to be done after the customer clicks a single button. This is another example of a complex operation that's composed of many smaller ones.

You need to be sure that the specified operations execute either in their entirety or not at all. The process outcome should be black or white, success or failure, nothing in between.

So, in more formal terms, a transaction is a logical unit of work consisting of a sequence of separate operations that brings a system from one consistent state to another. The data should be, at any moment, in a consistent state. The transaction is successful if all of its constituent operations are successful. If any of the operations fail (because of any kind of software or hardware problem), all the changes made by the successful operations are reversed, and the system is brought back to its original state. A transaction can either succeed or fail, but nothing in between. In both cases, the system is brought to a consistent state.

If a problem occurs, all the successful operations are reversed, and everything goes back to the way it was before starting the transaction. This process of reversing the successful operations is called a *transaction rollback*.

If, instead, everything goes just fine and all operations complete successfully, the changes are declared to be permanent, and you say that the transaction has been *committed*. After a transaction is committed, it can't be rolled back.

Transactions (not only the database ones) must conform to a set of properties, collectively known as the *ACID properties*.

The ACID Properties

ACID is an acronym used to describe the four properties of a transaction:

Atomicity refers to the all-or-nothing nature of a transaction: The transaction executes completely, or it doesn't execute at all. In the case of a failed transaction, all the successful individual actions need to be reverted, and the transaction is rolled back to the original state. Atomicity is perhaps the most representative property of transactions and it's typically used when describing and defining transactions. Nevertheless, the other three properties are just as important as this one.

Consistency refers to the fact that a transaction must take the system from one consistent state to another consistent state. That is, the transaction as a whole must not break any business rules specified for the environment. Contrary to the atomicity property, consistency isn't a rule that the database system can take care of: You, the programmer, must make sure the system gets to a consistent state (in respect to the rules that you define) after the transaction successfully completes.

Isolation specifies that each transaction should perform independently of the other transactions and operations that happen at the same time. In practice, this means that the outside world shouldn't see individual changes to the database while the transaction is happening. In other words, changes made by the active transaction aren't visible to other concurrently running transactions—this is essential, especially because you can't know ahead of time if the transaction will be successful. The changes made by a transaction are declared permanent and become visible to the other transactions and processes only *after* the transaction is committed.

Durability ensures that after the transaction is completed, its outcome is persisted and resists even in the event of a system failure. So, after a transaction is committed, you can be sure its results are persisted even if the power goes down one second later.

Understanding Database Transactions

In the case of database transactions, the group of actions that you attempt to execute (a process that either succeeds or fails—the all-or-nothing proposition) are SQL statements, and the system that needs to be kept in a consistent state is the database itself.

Luckily enough, SQL-99 has support for transactions, as do the major database systems. Otherwise, you would need to manually enforce the ACID rules, which would be a tough job!

In order to implement transactions, databases keep log files with everything that happens inside the transaction. When rolling back the transaction, all the successful operations are reversed based on the data in the log files, and the affected data is brought back to its previous state.

 NOTE *The way log files work is considered an advanced topic and will not be covered in this book. Moreover, because each database system has its own particularities regarding this subject, you would be best off consulting the documentation for your database platform.*

SQL Server, Oracle, DB2, and MySQL do support transactions and the ACID rules. Access doesn't support transactions.

The Typical Database Transaction

Transactions work differently with each Relational Database Management System (RDBMS), but there are some concepts and steps common to all transactions. We'll describe how transactions work and then give specific examples for each RDBMS, discussing the particularities of each database platform.

Beginning the Transaction

Transactions must have a clearly defined start and end point. The point the transaction starts is very important—it's the point you can roll back to in case some failure or problem occurs in any of its constituent SQL statements. In respect to the consistency rule, at the moment a new transaction is created, the data must be in a consistent state.

The SQL-99 standard specifies the START TRANSACTION statement, which should mark the point at which a new transaction starts, but this command isn't implemented in the database platforms covered in this book.

Oracle and DB2 start transactions automatically. In other words, a transaction automatically begins as soon as you execute the first SQL statement. With SQL Server, you use the BEGIN TRANSACTION statement, which can also accept a transaction name, and with MySQL you simply use BEGIN. You'll see more details in the examples later in this chapter.

Executing the SQL Statements

Whether the statements execute correctly will determine whether the transaction is committed or rolled back. You'll usually need a mechanism that can test whether all the SQL statements ran without problems so that you can decide how to end the transaction (to commit it if everything went okay or to roll back if it didn't go okay).

Implementing a testing mechanism is important because, by default, the transaction is not rolled back if a noncritical error occurs. Let's take another look at the checking/savings accounts example:

```
UPDATE Checking
    SET Balance = Balance - 1000
    WHERE Account = 'Sally';
UPDATE Savings
    SET Balance = Balance + 1000
    WHERE Account = 'Sally';
```

If these two statements are part of a transaction, and one of them generates an error because it can't be executed successfully, the transaction will most likely not be rolled back by default. Instead, you need to manually test whether each statement performed successfully; if either of them didn't, you can roll back the transaction. Also, if everything runs okay, you need to manually to commit the transaction.

In this chapter's examples, you'll see how to test if any of the statements generated errors and how to react to them.

Rolling Back the Transaction

As you saw earlier, when problems occur inside the transaction, you can roll it back to its starting point or to a *savepoint* if the database system supports savepoints (we'll cover these in more detail a little later).

The SQL-99 syntax for rolling back transactions is as follows:

```
ROLLBACK [WORK] [TO SAVEPOINT savepoint_name]
```

This structure is fully supported by Oracle, DB2, and partially by MySQL, which doesn't support savepoints.

The SQL Server syntax is a bit different, but it serves the same purpose:

```
ROLLBACK TRANSACTION [<transaction name>|<savepoint name>]
```

What's important to keep in mind is that rolling back a transaction brings the data it has affected to its previous state and closes the transaction, but the execution of the batch continues normally. For example, if you have a ROLLBACK statement in the middle of a stored procedure, the execution doesn't stop at ROLLBACK (so ROLLBACK isn't like a RETURN or a GOTO command, and it doesn't move the execution pointer). If you want the stored procedure to stop executing when you do a ROLLBACK, you need to manually handle this—you'll see how to accomplish this in the upcoming examples.

Committing the Transaction

If all of the SQL commands in the transaction execute successfully (or in a way you consider to be okay), you issue a COMMIT command. This tells the database to persist the changes made by the transaction in the database. From this moment, the changes can't be undone using a ROLLBACK command.

The SQL-99 syntax for committing transactions is as follows:

```
COMMIT [WORK]
```

This syntax is supported by all major database vendors, but some of them also accept additional parameters. SQL Server supports COMMIT WORK but also has a COMMIT TRANSACTION command that accepts as a parameter the name of the transaction to be committed (SQL Server supports having transaction names).

Particulars of Database Transactions

You'll now look at some features that aren't supported by all database systems covered in this book or that are supported differently. First, we cover the concepts, and then we'll show how to apply them in a few examples.

Autocommit

A database that runs in autocommit mode will treat every SQL query as a separate transaction, without needing any additional SQL commands such as BEGIN, COMMIT, or ROLLBACK. After a SQL data modification statement is executed, the changes are automatically committed (so the results are considered final) by the database system.

 NOTE *SQL Server and MySQL work by default in autocommit mode.*

With a database that works in autocommit mode, these two statements will be considered as two separate transactions:

```
UPDATE Checking
    SET Balance = Balance - 1000
    WHERE Account = 'Sally';
UPDATE Savings
    SET Balance = Balance + 1000
    WHERE Account = 'Sally';
```

While in autocommit mode, if you want to start a transaction formed by more than one SQL command, you must use a BEGIN command and then manually finish the transaction with either ROLLBACK or COMMIT. So if you want to have a single transaction containing the previous two SQL statements, you need to do something like this:

```
BEGIN WORK
UPDATE Checking
    SET Balance = Balance - 1000
    WHERE Account = 'Sally';
UPDATE Savings
    SET Balance = Balance + 1000
    WHERE Account = 'Sally';
COMMIT WORK
```

However, note that here you didn't do any checking to see whether either of the two UPDATE statements executed successfully. In a real-world example, you'd need to implement some error handling mechanism and ROLLBACK the transaction in case an error happens.

If the database *isn't* in autocommit mode, it's said to be in *automatic-transactions* mode.

> **NOTE** *Oracle and DB2 work by default in automatic-transactions mode.*

In this mode, a new transaction starts automatically with the first SQL query you type, but it's not automatically committed. In other words, the database system works as if you had already typed a BEGIN command and then waits for you to call COMMIT or ROLLBACK to finish the transaction. With a database working in automatic-transactions mode, you can integrate the previous two UPDATE commands in a transaction like this:

```
UPDATE Checking
    SET Balance = Balance - 1000
    WHERE Account = 'Sally';
UPDATE Savings
    SET Balance = Balance + 1000
    WHERE Account = 'Sally';
COMMIT WORK
```

SQL Server and MySQL work by default in autocommit mode while Oracle and DB2 work by default in automatic-transactions mode, but in all cases the default mode can be changed (although most developers prefer to keep the default mode of the database system).

For Oracle, you change the default mode with SET AUTOCOMMIT ON/OFF. With SQL Server you use SET IMPLICIT_TRANSACTIONS ON/OFF, and with MySQL you use SET AUTOCOMMIT=0/1. When working with DB2, you can handle this by selecting Command Center ➤ Options from the main menu of the Command Center tool and then checking or unchecking the Automatically Commit SQL Statements box in the Execution tab as appropriate (see Figure 10-1).

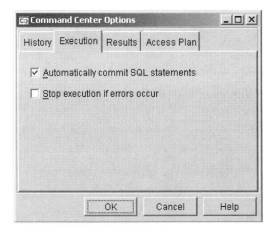

Figure 10-1. Choosing to automatically commit SQL statements

 CAUTION   *It's possible that your data access provider (for example, JDBC or OLEDB) will be working in autocommit mode. If you want to issue SQL statements in automatic-transactions mode, then you may have to alter the default behavior of your provider as well.*

In general, because of the *isolation* property of transactions, other users will not be able to see your changes if you forget to send a COMMIT command. Be sure to always issue COMMIT statements after an update, insert, or delete when working in automatic-transactions mode.

Savepoints

A *savepoint* acts as a bookmark inside a transaction. You can roll back any actions that have been performed by a transaction to a certain savepoint, without actually closing the transaction. Rolling back to a certain savepoint brings the database to the status it was when the savepoint was created, but it doesn't end the transaction. A final ROLLBACK or COMMIT is still required.

NOTE *Savepoints are supported by Oracle, DB2, and SQL Server. MySQL supports transactions but doesn't support savepoints.*

SQL-99 specifies the SAVEPOINT command to create savepoints, and this command is implemented in Oracle and DB2. Because you can have multiple savepoints in a single transaction, you always need to supply a savepoint name:

```
SAVEPOINT <savepoint name>
```

SQL Server uses SAVE TRANSACTION instead of SAVEPOINT:

```
SAVE TRANSACTION <savepoint name>
```

This is how you would add a savepoint to the bank transactions example using the SQL Server syntax:

```
BEGIN TRANSACTION

SAVE TRANSACTION BeforeChangingBalance
UPDATE Checking
    SET Balance = Balance - 1000
    WHERE Account = 'Sally';
ROLLBACK TRANSACTION BeforeChangingBalance

UPDATE Savings
    SET Balance = Balance + 1000
    WHERE Account = 'Sally';

COMMIT TRANSACTION
```

After executing this batch, Sally will have $1,000 more in her account. The first UPDATE statement is rolled back (but the transaction still remains active!), and finally the transaction is committed.

We'll see examples with SQL Server, Oracle, and DB2 savepoints in the following sections.

Transactions at Work

Here, we'll provide a closer look at how transactions are supported by the database products you've been investigating so far.

SQL Server

SQL Server works by default in autocommit mode, with each SQL command treated as a separate transaction, unless you use BEGIN TRANSACTION to start a multistatement transaction.

TIP *You can set SQL Server to work with implicit transactions (by turning off autocommit mode) by using* SET IMPLICIT_TRANSACTIONS ON. *When working in implicit transactions mode, SQL Server assumes the* BEGIN TRANSACTION *command before the first SQL query is issued. In the following examples, we assume you'll work with the default transactions mode of SQL Server, which requires you to manually start multistatement transactions with* BEGIN TRANSACTION.

The statements that deal with transactions in SQL Server are as follows:

```
BEGIN TRANSACTION [<transaction name>]
COMMIT TRANSACTION [<transaction name>]
ROLLBACK TRANSACTION [<transaction name>|<savepoint name>]
SAVE TRANSACTION <savepoint name>
```

The TRANSACTION keyword can be optionally replaced by its shorter form, TRAN.

BEGIN, COMMIT, and ROLLBACK receive an optional transaction name. Using names for transactions doesn't bring any new functionality, but it can help for readability if you use suggestive names, especially in stored procedures or batches, that have more transactions.

If ROLLBACK doesn't have a parameter or if the parameter specifies a transaction name, the whole transaction is rolled back. If a savepoint name is received instead, the transaction is rolled back to the specified savepoint.

Note that after rolling back to a savepoint, the transaction is still active. It still needs a final ROLLBACK or COMMIT, with either no parameter or with the transaction's name as a parameter to finalize the transaction.

EXAMPLE: SQL SERVER TRANSACTIONS AND SAVEPOINTS

In this example, you'll see a simple SQL Server transaction. In this transaction, you'll add two new students to the Student table from the InstantUniversity database. However, the second INSERT operation is rolled back using a savepoint. Finally, the transaction is committed:

```
BEGIN TRANSACTION MyTransaction;
INSERT INTO Student (StudentID, Name) VALUES (98, 'Good Student');
SAVE TRANSACTION BeforeAddingBadStudent;
INSERT INTO Student (StudentID, Name) VALUES (99, 'Bad Student');
ROLLBACK TRANSACTION BeforeAddingBadStudent;
COMMIT TRANSACTION MyTransaction;
SELECT * FROM Student;
```

The example starts by declaring the new transaction with this well-known command:

```
BEGIN TRANSACTION MyTransaction
```

Then you add Good Student to the Student table:

```
INSERT INTO Student (StudentID, Name) VALUES (98, 'Good Student')
```

Then you add yet another student to the table. However, the operation is rolled back using the BeforeAddingBadStudent savepoint:

```
SAVE TRANSACTION BeforeAddingBadStudent
INSERT INTO Student (StudentID, Name) VALUES (99, 'Bad Student')
ROLLBACK TRANSACTION BeforeAddingBadStudent
```

Practically, this piece of code actually does nothing because the changes are annulled. Also, after rolling back to a savepoint, the transaction is still active, so you still have the power to commit it or roll it back completely. In the end, you commit the transaction and display the contents of the Employee table:

```
COMMIT TRANSACTION MyTransaction
SELECT * FROM Student
```

If you had rolled back the transaction instead of committing it, the changes done by both INSERT statements would have been void, and the Student table would have ended up being just as it was before starting the transaction.

SQL Server Transactions and Error Handling

The first example was interesting enough, but it didn't show how to roll back the whole transaction in case something bad happens in any of the queries (that was the whole point after all, right?).

Let's see how to do that in another example.

EXAMPLE: SQL SERVER TRANSACTIONS WITH ERROR HANDLING

In this example, you'll insert a number of rows into the Student table as part of a transaction, and after each insert, you'll check whether an error occurred. If it did, you'll roll back the transaction. If all the inserts succeed, you commit the transaction. In both cases, you display a message saying whether the transaction was committed or rolled back:

```
BEGIN TRANSACTION MyTransaction

INSERT INTO Student (StudentID, Name) VALUES (101, 'Dave')
IF @@ERROR != 0
BEGIN
    ROLLBACK TRANSACTION MyTransaction
    PRINT 'Cannot insert Dave! Transaction rolled back.'
    RETURN
END
```

```
INSERT INTO Student (StudentID, Name) VALUES (102, 'Claire')
IF @@ERROR != 0
BEGIN
    ROLLBACK TRANSACTION MyTransaction
    PRINT 'Cannot insert Claire! Transaction rolled back.'
    RETURN
END


INSERT INTO Student (StudentID, Name) VALUES (103, 'Anne')
IF @@ERROR != 0
BEGIN
    ROLLBACK TRANSACTION MyTransaction
    PRINT 'Cannot insert Anne! Transaction rolled back.'
    RETURN
END


COMMIT TRANSACTION MyTransaction
IF @@ERROR != 0
    PRINT 'Could not COMMIT transaction'
ELSE
    PRINT 'Transaction committed.'
```

This example looks a bit different from the previous one. The batch of statements tries to insert three records to the Student table. If any of the INSERT statements fail, you roll back the transaction, display a message on the screen, and stop the execution.

You achieve this by verifying the @@ERROR system variable after each statement that could generate an error:

```
INSERT INTO Student (StudentID, Name) VALUES (101, 'Dave')
IF @@ERROR != 0
BEGIN
    ROLLBACK TRANSACTION MyTransaction
    PRINT 'Cannot insert Dave! Transaction rolled back.'
    RETURN
END
```

The @@ERROR system variable is automatically updated after each SQL query, so it is necessary to test it each time you do something to the database. Another important thing to note is that you call RETURN after rolling back the transaction. This wouldn't be necessary if you had rolled back to a savepoint, but if you roll back the entire transaction, the execution should stop; otherwise, the following SQL statements would mistakenly assume that they're part of a transaction and call ROLLBACK or COMMIT at certain points.

You can also test the outcome of the COMMIT command. This way you deal with the case where there's a problem and the transaction can't be committed. The most likely reason for this is if you already finalized the transaction (say, rolled back the transaction when an INSERT failed without calling RETURN after ROLLBACK). This is a great debugging technique because it provides feedback about the transaction's output, but once you're confident that the SQL script is well constructed, you can omit this:

```
COMMIT TRANSACTION MyTransaction
IF @@ERROR != 0
    PRINT 'Could not COMMIT transaction'
ELSE
    PRINT 'Transaction committed.'
```

The first time the batch is executed, the output should read as follows:

```
Transaction committed.
```

However, if you now execute the batch again, the transaction will be rolled back because you can't insert two rows with the same primary key value into a table:

```
Violation of PRIMARY KEY constraint PK__Student__59063A47'.

Cannot insert duplicate key in object 'Student'.
The statement has been terminated.
Cannot insert Dave! Transaction rolled back.
```

Oracle

Oracle transactions work by default in automatic-transactions mode. In other words, it starts a new multistatement transaction with the first SQL query you type. This mode is used by default in DB2 as well, and it's the mode used in these examples.

COMMIT and ROLLBACK are still your best friends when working in automatic-transactions mode. You create savepoints using the SAVEPOINT command, and if you want to roll back to a savepoint, you must use ROLLBACK TO <savepoint name>.

EXAMPLE: ORACLE TRANSACTIONS AND SAVEPOINTS

To start a new transaction, you just need to start executing SQL queries. In this example, you'll add two new students to the Student table. However, the second INSERT operation is rolled back using a savepoint. Finally, you commit the transaction:

```
INSERT INTO Student (StudentID, Name) VALUES (98, 'Good Student');
SAVEPOINT BeforeAddingBadStudent;
INSERT INTO Student (StudentID, Name) VALUES (99, 'Bad Student');
ROLLBACK TO BeforeAddingBadStudent;
COMMIT;
```

You added two new students to the Student table. However, before adding the second one, you created a savepoint—which was then used as a point to which you rolled back the transaction. Right now, if you type SELECT * FROM Student, in addition to the original rows, you'll see a single new row, containing Good Student.

Oracle Transactions and Exception Handling

Oracle has a robust and powerful exception handling system, which proves to be helpful when dealing with real-world transactions. When an error occurs in your code, the transaction needs to be rolled back, and the other SQL statements shouldn't execute anymore.

You saw in the SQL Server example that one way to deal with this is to check the outcome of each SQL statement and deal with them separately. Oracle has another way of dealing with this.

EXAMPLE: ORACLE TRANSACTIONS AND EXCEPTION HANDLING

In this example, you'll try to insert three rows into the Student table. One of the inserts will be rolled back using a savepoint. If any exceptions are raised in the process, you roll back the whole transaction and bring the Student table back to its original state.

Here's the piece of code that does this:

```
BEGIN

    INSERT INTO Student (StudentID, Name) VALUES (101, 'Dave');
    INSERT INTO Student (StudentID, Name) VALUES (102, 'Claire');

    SAVEPOINT BeforeAddingAnne;
    INSERT INTO Student (StudentID, Name) VALUES (103, 'Anne');
    ROLLBACK TO BeforeAddingAnne;

    COMMIT;

EXCEPTION
    WHEN OTHERS
        THEN ROLLBACK;
END;
/
```

After typing the batch, you can save it using SAVE:

```
SAVE exception
```

Once the procedure is saved to a file, you can call it like this:

```
@exception
```

If any of the SQL queries in the BEGIN block generates an error, the execution is passed to the EXCEPTION block:

```
EXCEPTION
    WHEN OTHERS
        THEN ROLLBACK;
```

You can handle separately many different kinds of predefined exceptions, and you can also define and raise your own exceptions. Also, if you have nested BEGIN blocks or stored procedures, the unhandled exceptions propagate vertically. In this case, you have used the WHEN OTHERS option, which handles all exceptions. There you use ROLLBACK to roll back the transaction. You can learn more about Oracle exception handling in Chapter 9.

The procedure you wrote would end up adding two rows into the Student table, as long as no errors are generated inside the script. If an error does occur, everything is brought back to the original state. If, for example, you already have a student with a StudentID of 102 before executing the script, an error will be generated when trying to add Claire, and the transaction is rolled back (so not even Dave will end up being in the Student table).

After you've run this code once, each subsequent time you execute @exception, the transaction will be rolled back.

DB2

DB2 supports the COMMIT, ROLLBACK, and SAVEPOINT commands. Like Oracle, DB2 works in automatic-transactions mode by default.

To switch between automatic-transactions mode and autocommit mode, you need to alter the Command Center options, as shown earlier in this chapter. For the purpose of this example, clear the Automatically Commit SQL Statements checkbox. So, let's look at an example.

EXAMPLE: DB2 TRANSACTIONS

In this example, you'll add two new students to the Student table—a good student and a bad student. You reverse the addition of the bad student by using a savepoint:

```
INSERT INTO Student (StudentID, Name) VALUES (98, 'Good Student');
SAVEPOINT BeforeAddingBadStudent ON ROLLBACK RETAIN CURSORS;
INSERT INTO Student (StudentID, Name) VALUES (99, 'Bad Student');
ROLLBACK TO SAVEPOINT BeforeAddingBadStudent;
COMMIT;
```

Notice the way you create the savepoint:

```
SAVEPOINT BeforeAddingBadStudent ON ROLLBACK RETAIN CURSORS;
```

The ON ROLLBACK RETAIN CURSORS statement ensures that your code will continue to execute from the point where the rollback was called after the rollback has been performed.

MySQL

MySQL does have support for transactions, but only if you know how to create your data tables. Yes, this sounds a bit weird, but it's true.

The MySQL engine supports more internal data storage formats for its data tables. When creating a new data table with CREATE TABLE, the default table type is used, which is MyISAM. This table type is pretty basic and doesn't support features such as transactions or the capability to enforce referential integrity through foreign keys, but it's the fastest one available for MySQL.

In total, MySQL supports at least five table types: MyISAM, HEAP, ISAM, BDB, and InnoDB. For detailed information about each table type supported by MySQL, please visit http://www.mysql.com/doc/en/Table_types.html.

 TIP *MySQL documentation recommends using the default table type,* MyISAM, *if transactions aren't required because it works much faster without the overhead of keeping a transaction log.*

The important fact to understand, for the purposes of this chapter, is that BDB and InnoDB are the only types that support transactions. InnoDB fully supports the ACID properties, and as such, we'll be using this table type here. You can learn more about this table type at http://www.mysql.com/doc/en/InnoDB.html.

By default, MySQL works in autocommit mode (like SQL Server does). Each update on the database is committed immediately, without the need to call COMMIT. To explicitly start a multistatement transaction, you use BEGIN, and you finish the transaction with either COMMIT or ROLLBACK. MySQL doesn't support savepoints.

For transaction-safe tables (BDB and InnoDB), you can also instruct MySQL to work in non-autocommit mode (just like Oracle works by default) using SET AUTOCOMMIT=0.

EXAMPLE: MYSQL TRANSACTIONS

Let's look at a simple example with MySQL transactions. Start a new transaction with BEGIN, add two new students to the Student table, and then roll back the transaction. Open a new MySQL console, open the InstantUniversity database, and type the following:

```
BEGIN;

INSERT INTO Student (StudentID, Name) VALUES (98, 'Anne');
INSERT INTO Student (StudentID, Name) VALUES (99, 'Julian');

ROLLBACK;
```

Now, read the Student table, and you'll see that it has no new rows—the transaction was successfully rolled back.

Access

This is really simple: Microsoft Access doesn't support transactions, so there's not a lot to discuss here!

Moving onto Advanced Topics

Having experimented with some simple transactions, we're now going to present further issues involved in writing advanced transaction code. The basics of transactions that you've looked at so far form the foundation for what you'll be looking at here as you consider the wider implications of executing transactions in the real world.

We'll discuss the different *transaction isolation levels* that you can use. These define certain rules that govern the degree of "interaction" between multiple transactions acting on the same data. We'll also discuss the use of database *locks*—one of the mechanisms by which you can control concurrent access to shared resources in the database.

There are several different isolation levels and many different types of lock that can be applied, depending on your specific RDBMS. It's way beyond the scope of this chapter to provide a definitive guide to transactions and locking for each RDBMS. Instead, we aim to provide a good general understanding of the requirements that apply to each level, how you often have to use locks to meet those requirements, and the potential performance consequences of locking database resources.

Concurrency and Transaction Isolation Levels

It's a fact that, most of the time, you can't guarantee that transactions will execute one at a time—on the contrary, in complex databases it's likely that many transactions will run concurrently. This leads to potential *concurrency problems*, which occur when many transactions try to interact with the same database object (access the same data) at the same time. The nature of the interaction depends on the actions each transaction performs: from simply reading data to inserting, updating, or deleting data.

You need to consider these issues because they're directly related to the isolation property of transactions, which dictates that changes made by a transaction shouldn't be visible to other concurrently running transactions. If a transaction modifies information in a data table, should other transactions be able to access that data table? If yes, in what way? What if the transaction only reads from the data table without modifying it?

The answer to these questions depends on the *transaction isolation level*. You can manually set the isolation level for each transaction, and this establishes the way transactions behave when they're trying to access the same piece of data.

Transactions ask for ownership of a particular piece of data by placing *locks* on it. There are many different types of locks, and they differ in the way they limit access to database resources. For example, a row can be locked in such a way that other transactions can't access it in any way or can read it but not modify it. Also, depending on the lock granularity, the resource they apply to can be an entire database, a data table, a row or a number of rows, and so on.

It's important to understand the difference between locks and the transaction isolation level. Locks limit access to database objects, and the transaction isolation level specifies how the active transaction places locks on the resources with which it works.

SQL-99 specifies four transaction isolation levels. With each level, a different balance is struck between the level of data integrity protection offered and the performance penalties imposed.

The four transaction isolation levels, listed from the one that offers the best performance to the one that offers the best protection, are as follows:

- READ UNCOMMITTED

- READ COMMITTED

- REPEATABLE READ

- SERIALIZABLE

The SQL-99 standard also categorizes transactions into *read-only* transactions and *read-write* transactions. Read-only transactions are a special kind of transaction, and you'll learn about them in a moment.

NOTE *The isolation levels mentioned previously can only be applied to read-write transactions.*

The SQL-99 command for setting the transaction type is SET TRANSACTION. The complete syntax is as follows:

```
SET [LOCAL] TRANSACTION { { READ ONLY | READ WRITE } [,...]
| ISOLATION LEVEL
    { READ COMMITTED
    | READ UNCOMMITTED
    | REPEATABLE READ
    | SERIALIZABLE } [,...]
| DIAGNOSTIC SIZE INT };
```

Therefore, to choose between read-only and read-write transactions, the syntax is as follows:

```
SET TRANSACTION [READ ONLY|READ WRITE]
```

To set a transaction level, you can use a command such as the following. Note that setting the transaction isolation level automatically assumes a read-write transaction:

```
SET TRANSACTION ISOLATION LEVEL <isolation level name>
```

The default transactional mode in all databases covered in this book is READ COMMITTED.

Read-Only Transactions

Read-only transactions are so named because they can't contain any data modification statements—only plain SELECT statements are allowed.

The default state for read-write transactions is *statement-level consistency*. In other words, if, within the scope of a transaction, the same record is read twice, different values may be retrieved each time if the record was modified between readings.

Read-only transaction mode solves this problem by establishing *transaction-level read consistency*. In a read-only transaction, all queries can only see the changes committed before the transaction began.

To set a transaction as being read-only, you type the following command:

```
SET TRANSACTION READ ONLY;
```

Read-only transactions aren't supported by SQL Server, DB2, or MySQL. They are supported, however, by Oracle.

READ UNCOMMITTED Isolation Level

This is the first and most dangerous isolation level, but it's also the one that offers the best performance. The following command sets the READ UNCOMMITTED isolation level for the next transaction:

```
SET TRANSACTION ISOLATION LEVEL READ UNCOMMITTED;
```

The READ UNCOMMITTED isolation level isn't supported by Oracle but is supported by SQL Server, DB2, and MySQL.

When the transaction is in READ UNCOMMITTED mode, its isolation property isn't enforced in any way, and the transaction is able to read uncommitted changes from other concurrently running transactions (effectively breaking the isolation property of the ACID rules).

With READ UNCOMMITTED mode, the transaction is susceptible to *dirty reads* and many other existing kinds of consistency problems.

Data Consistency Problem: Dirty Reads

Dirty reads happen when a transaction reads data that was modified by another transaction but that hasn't yet been committed. If the other transaction rolls back, the first transaction ends up reading values that, theoretically, never existed in the database.

To understand dirty reads, imagine two concurrent transactions that work with the Student table. One transaction calculates the total number of students from that table, and the second removes or adds students to the table, as shown in Table 10-1.

Table 10-1. Sequence of Actions That Demonstrate Dirty Reads

Time	Transaction 1	Transaction 2
T1	The transaction starts.	
T2	Removes or adds records from/to the Student table.	Transaction starts.
T3		Calculates the total number of students based on the uncommitted results of Transaction 1.
T4	Transaction rolls back.	

If Transaction 2 works with the READ UNCOMMITTED isolation level, it can read the uncommitted changes from Transaction 1. In this example, because Transaction 1 finally rolls back, Transaction 2 ends up calculating an erroneous number of students. This is a dirty read.

Another scenario of a dirty read would be if Transaction 1 changed the data of a student (say, the name), then Transaction 2 read that uncommitted data, and finally Transaction 1 rolled back.

NOTE *Oracle doesn't support the* READ UNCOMMITTED *isolation level. Oracle always reads the last-committed values, even if the data is being changed by other ongoing transactions.*

You can avoid dirty reads by forbidding data that's being modified by other transactions from being read.

However, there are certain situations in which you might want to allow dirty reads, the most common of which is when you want to get quick reports or statistics from your database, where it isn't critical to get very accurate data. In such situations, setting an isolation mode of READ UNCOMMITTED can help you because it locks fewer resources and results in better performance than the other isolation levels.

The default transaction isolation level, READ COMMITTED, doesn't permit dirty reads, so you explicitly need to set the isolation level to READ UNCOMMITTED in situations where you want to allow dirty reads. The other isolation levels (REPEATABLE

READ and SERIALIZABLE) are even more stringent about enforcing data consistency, and they don't permit dirty reads either.

READ COMMITTED Isolation Level

The second isolation level in terms of enforcing transaction isolation is READ COMMITTED, which is the default mode for most database systems.

When in READ COMMITTED mode, all resources modified by the transaction are locked until the transaction is completed—in other words, any updated, inserted, or deleted records won't be visible to other transactions (or will be only visible to their last-committed values), until (and unless) you commit the transaction. Transactions that run in READ UNCOMMITTED mode are the exception to this rule because they can uncommitted changes from other transactions.

Also, other transactions aren't allowed to modify the rows that are being modified by your transaction but are able to modify the rows that are simply read by your transaction.

When in READ COMMITTED mode, no dirty reads will happen in your current transaction because you can't see or modify data that is being updated by other transactions. However, the READ COMMITTED mode doesn't guard against *unrepeatable reads*.

Data Consistency Problem: Unrepeatable Reads

An unrepeatable read happens when you read some data twice in a transaction and you get different values because it has been modified in the meantime by another transaction.

When in READ COMMITTED mode, other transactions are allowed to modify data that has only been accessed for reading by your transaction. So, if you start a transaction, read a record, do some other things, and then read the same record again, you might read a different value.

If this is acceptable and no serious problems can occur because of unrepeatable reads, it's best to stick with the READ COMMITTED isolation mode. Additionally, in some cases, you can avoid unrepeatable reads by saving pieces of information in variables or temporary tables and using the saved data instead of querying the database again.

Before moving on to the next transaction isolation level (which prevents unrepeatable reads), you'll see an example demonstrating unrepeatable reads (see Table 10-2). In this example, Transaction 1 tries to calculate the average mark for all students by summing up all their marks and then dividing by the number of students.

For the purposes of this example, assume the mark of each student is stored in the Student table (so working with marks implies working with Student).

Table 10-2. Sequence of Actions That Demonstrate Unrepeatable Reads

Time	Transaction 1	Transaction 2
T1	The transaction starts. (READ COMMITTED)	
T2	Sums up the students' marks.	Transaction starts.
T3	(Waits for Transaction 2 to release locks.)	Deletes one student, locking the Student table.
T4	(Waits for Transaction 2 to release locks.)	Transaction commits, releases locks.
T5	Retrieves number of students.	
T6	Calculates average mark by dividing the two numbers calculated earlier.	

Transaction 1 ends up calculating a wrong average mark because the students' data changes while the transaction is running. The students' data can be modified by other transactions because Transaction 1 is only reading it and doesn't place any locks on it.

In fact, after Transaction 2 updates the Student table (placing locks on it), Transaction 1 needs to wait until Transaction 2 finishes in order to calculate the number of students.

NOTE *Oracle would behave as before, reading the last-committed values from the Student table without blocking Transaction 1 until Transaction 2 finishes executing.*

If you don't find any solutions to avoid unrepeatable reads, SQL-99 has an isolation level that does the work for you, guarding against unrepeatable reads and dirty reads: the REPEATABLE READ isolation level.

REPEATABLE READ Isolation Level

This transaction isolation mode provides an extra level of concurrency protection by preventing not only dirty reads but also unrepeatable reads.

The way most databases (again, not Oracle) enforce repeatable reads is to place *shared read locks* on rows that are being read by the transaction, not just on the ones that are being updated (as the READ COMMITTED isolation mode does). This way, as soon as one record is read, you can guarantee you'll get the same value if you read it again during the same transaction.

Having a shared lock on a record permits other transactions to read the record but not to modify it. In the previous example, setting the first transaction to REPEATABLE READ would prevent the second transaction from removing the student, ensuring the calculated average mark is correct. Table 10-3 shows the same transactions running, but this time the first transaction runs in REPEATABLE READ mode.

Table 10-3. Sequence of Actions That Explain the REPEATABLE READ *Isolation Mode*

Time	Transaction 1	Transaction 2
T1	The transaction starts in REPEATABLE READ mode.	
T2	Sums up the students' marks (placing shared locks on the rows in the Student table).	Transaction starts.
T3	Retrieves number of students.	Tries to delete one student but finds the table locked.
T4	Calculates average mark by dividing the two numbers calculated earlier.	(Waits.)
T5	Transaction completes executing, releases locks.	(Waits.)
T6		Deletes student.

You get the right answer this time, but because other transactions need to wait for your transaction to finish processing before getting to the requested data, this can result in important performance penalties for your applications. The longer your transaction lasts, the longer the locks will be held, practically not allowing other transactions to perform any modifications on them.

With the REPEATABLE READ isolation level, you can be sure unrepeatable reads will be avoided. However, there's still one more concurrency-related problem that can happen: *phantoms*.

Data Consistency Problem: Phantoms

Phantoms are similar to repeatable reads, except they also take into account the case where new records are being introduced to a data table by another transaction while the current transaction is working with the table.

Let's imagine another scenario, similar to the previous example, but this time Transaction 2 inserts a new student rather than removing an existing one. Table 10-4 shows the actions performed by the two transactions.

Table 10-4. Sequence of Actions That Demonstrate Phantoms

Time	Transaction 1	Transaction 2
T1	Transaction starts in REPEATABLE READ mode.	
T2	Sums up the students' marks (placing shared locks on the rows in the Student table).	Transaction starts.
T3	Tries to count the number of students, but Transaction 2 has a lock on the newly created student.	Inserts one student (placing a lock on the new created record).
T4	(Waits.)	Transaction commits, releases locks.
T5	Calculates the total number of students.	
T6	Calculates average mark by dividing the two numbers calculated earlier.	

Transaction 2 is allowed to insert new records to the Student table because it doesn't affect any of the existing rows in Student (on which Transaction 1 has set shared locks). Phantoms refer to the situation when other transactions insert new records that meet one of the WHERE clauses of any previous statement in the current transaction. The SERIALIZABLE isolation level guards your transaction against phantoms, as well as the previously presented concurrency-related problems.

SERIALIZABLE Isolation Level

The SERIALIZABLE isolation level guarantees the transactions will run as if they were serialized—with other words, they're guaranteed not to interfere, and they execute as if they were run in sequence.

When you set the transaction isolation level to SERIALIZABLE, you're guaranteed that other transactions cannot modify (with UPDATE, INSERT, or DELETE) any data that meets the WHERE clause of any statement in your transaction.

The SERIALIZABLE transaction isolation level is a dangerous one when it comes to performance. It does provide the highest level of consistency—indeed, transactions works the same as if they were executed one at a time.

However, while increasing consistency, you get much lower concurrency because other transactions are restricted in the actions they can do with database objects already used in other transactions—they need to wait one after the other to get access to shared data.

If Transaction 1 was set to SERIALIZABLE in the example presented in Table 10-4, Transaction 2 couldn't have inserted a new record to the Student table before Transaction 1 finished executing.

RDBMS-Specific Transaction Support

So far we've presented the SQL-99 features regarding a transaction's isolation level. Now you'll take a closer look at how they're supported by SQL Server, Oracle, MySQL, and DB2.

SQL Server

SQL Server supports the four specified isolation levels, but it doesn't support read-only transactions. After setting the transaction isolation level, it remains set as such for that connection, unless explicitly changed. The default isolation level is READ COMMITTED.

Here's the syntax:

```
SET TRANSACTION ISOLATION LEVEL
    { READ COMMITTED
    | READ UNCOMMITTED
    | REPEATABLE READ
    | SERIALIZABLE
    }
```

Oracle

Oracle supports read-only transactions, but it doesn't support the READ UNCOMMITTED and REPEATABLE READ isolation levels. The default isolation level is READ COMMITTED.

With Oracle, SET TRANSACTION affects only the current transaction—not other users, connections or other transactions. Here's its syntax:

```
SET TRANSACTION
{ { READ ONLY | READ WRITE }
  | ISOLATION LEVEL
      { READ COMMITTED
      | SERIALIZABLE } };
```

To change the default transaction isolation level for all the transactions on the current session, you use the ALTER SESSION command. Here's an example:

```
ALTER SESSION SET ISOLATION_LEVEL SERIALIZABLE;
```

MySQL

MySQL supports transaction isolation levels with InnoDB tables. Here's the syntax for setting the transaction isolation level:

```
SET [GLOBAL | SESSION]
TRANSACTION ISOLATION LEVEL
{ READ UNCOMMITTED | READ COMMITTED |
  REPEATABLE READ | SERIALIZABLE }
```

By default, in MySQL, SET TRANSACTION affects only the next (not yet started) transaction.

The SESSION optional parameter changes the default transaction level for all the transactions on the current session.

The GLOBAL optional parameter changes the default transaction isolation level for all new connections created from that point on.

DB2

DB2 supports transaction isolation levels, but the way that the isolation levels are implemented is quite different in DB2 compared to the other RDBMS implementations. In DB2, you can set the isolation level for a transaction on each statement that you use, for example:

```
UPDATE table name
SET assignment clause
WHERE search condition
WITH isolation level
```

where *isolation level* can be one of the following:

- RR: REPEATABLE READ

- RS: Read Stability (similar to REPEATABLE READ—locks all rows being read and modified but doesn't completely isolate the application process, leaving it vulnerable to phantoms)

- CS: Cursor Stability (similar to READ COMMITTED)

- UR: Uncommitted Read

The default isolation level of any statement relates to the isolation level of the package containing the statement.

For example, referring back to an example you saw in Chapter 3, "Modifying Data" (where you added some new professors to the university but without titles), you could use the following:

```
UPDATE Professor
SET Name = 'Prof. ' || Name
   WHERE ProfessorID > 6;
   WITH RS
```

This method of applying an isolation level also applies to other SQL statements, for example, SELECT INTO, INSERT INTO. For more information, please refer to the DB2 documentation.

Playing Concurrency

Let's do a short exercise now and test how the database enforces consistency, depending on how you set the transaction isolation level.

For this you'll need to open two connections to the same database. If you're running DB2, please first uncheck the Automatically Commit SQL Statements checkbox in the Command Center ➤ Options ➤ Execution window of Command Center. This way you'll start multistatement transactions just like with Oracle (which works in automatic-transactions mode).

For the purpose of this exercise you'll use the default isolation level, READ COMMITTED, for both transactions. This means that you don't need SET TRANSACTION statements to explicitly set the transaction isolation level.

First, you need to start new transactions on the two connections. If you're using Oracle or DB2, no additional statements are required. Use BEGIN TRANSACTION for SQL Server or BEGIN for MySQL.

Then, add a new record to the Student table on the first connection:

```
INSERT INTO Student (StudentID, Name) VALUES (115, 'Cristian');
```

After executing this command, while still in the first connection, test that the row was indeed successfully added:

```
SELECT * FROM Student
```

The results show the newly added student:

```
StudentID    Name

-----------  ----------------------------------------
1            John Jones
2            Gary Burton
3            Emily Scarlett
...          ...
12           Isabelle Jonsson
115          Cristian
```

Now, while the first transaction is still active, switch to the second connection and read the Student table:

```
SELECT * FROM Student
```

Because the first transaction is in READ COMMITTED mode, it doesn't allow other transactions to READ UNCOMMITTED changes in order to prevent dirty reads. However, the databases implement this protection differently.

With Oracle and MySQL, the second transaction simply ignores the changes made by the first one (which is still running because it wasn't committed or rolled back yet). The list of students will be returned:

```
StudentID    Name

-----------  ----------------------------------------
1            John Jones
2            Gary Burton
3            Emily Scarlett
...          ...
12           Isabelle Jonsson
```

DB2 and SQL Server, on the other hand, have a different approach: They don't allow the second transaction to read the entire Student table until the first one decides to commit or roll back. The SELECT in the second transaction will be blocked until the first transaction (which keeps the Student table locked) finishes.

Note that a SELECT statement in the second transaction that refers strictly to rows that weren't added, modified, or deleted by the first transaction isn't affected in any way by that transaction (for example, it isn't blocked until the first transaction finishes, in SQL Server and DB2). An example of such a statement is as follows:

```
SELECT * FROM Student WHERE StudentID=10
```

Or even:

```
SELECT * FROM Student WHERE StudentID<100
```

Note that with SQL Server and MySQL, on the second connection you can set the transaction isolation level to READ UNCOMMITTED. This way, when you read the Student table, you'll see even the row that was inserted by the first transaction, even though that transaction hasn't been committed:

```
SET TRANSACTION ISOLATION LEVEL READ UNCOMMITTED;
SELECT StudentID, Name FROM Student WHERE StudentID>1200;
```

Now let's roll back the first transaction to get the database to its original form:

```
ROLLBACK;
```

Transaction Best Practices and Avoiding Deadlocks

Transactions are, in a way, a necessary evil in database programming. They provide the functionality you need to ensure data consistency, but they reduce concurrency. The more consistency a transaction isolation level provides, the less concurrency you have and hence the greater performance penalties for concurrently running transactions.

The higher the isolation level you set, the more the users accessing the database at the same time are affected. For this reason, it's important to always use the lowest possible transaction isolation level:

- The lowest isolation level, READ UNCOMMITTED, doesn't provide any concurrency protection, and it should be avoided except for the times when you don't require the data you read to be very accurate.

- The default isolation level, READ COMMITTED, is usually the best choice, because it protects you from dirty reads, which are the most common concurrency problem.

- The higher isolation protection levels, REPEATABLE READ and SERIALIZABLE, can and should usually be avoided. Apart from hurting performance, they also increase the probability of *deadlocks.*

A deadlock is a situation when two or more transactions started processing, locked some resources, and they both end up waiting for each other to release the locks in order to complete execution. When this happens, there can be only one that can win the battle and finish processing. The database server you use will choose one of the transactions (named a *deadlock victim*) and roll it back, so the other one can finish execution.

Deadlocks can rarely be entirely eliminated from a complex database system, but there are certain steps you can make to lower the probability of their happening. Of course, most of the times the rules depend on your particular system, but here are a few general rules to keep in mind:

- Use the lowest possible transaction isolation level.

- Keep the transactions as short as possible.

- Inside transactions, access database objects in the same order.

- Don't keep transactions open while waiting for user input (okay, this is common sense, but it had to be mentioned).

Distributed Transactions and the Two-Phase Commit

It's not unusual these days for companies to have, say, SQL Server, Oracle, and MySQL installations on their servers. This leads to the need of conducting transactions that spread over more databases (say, a transaction that needs to update information on three different database servers).

This situation is a bit problematic because all you've studied so far is about transactions that apply to a single database server only. Distributed transactions are possible through specific protocols (depending on the platform) that use a two-phase commit protocol system. The database originating the distributed transaction is called a *Commit Coordinator*, and it coordinates the transaction.

The first phase in the two phase-commit is when the Commit Coordinator instructs all participating databases to perform the required actions. The participating databases start individual transactions, and when they're ready to commit, they send a "ready to commit" signal to the Commit Coordinator.

After all participating databases send a "ready to commit" signal, the Commit Coordinator instructs all of them to commit the operations, and the distributed transaction is committed. If any of the participating databases report a failure, the Commit Coordinator instructs all the other databases to roll back and cancels the transaction.

Summary

We've covered some many new concepts in this chapter. You learned what transactions are, what the ACID properties are, and how they're enforced by the databases.

You could see that, unfortunately, each database product has its own view about how transactions should be implemented, and you learned about the most important features provided by some of the database systems. You then experimented with a few transaction examples that demonstrated transactions.

The chapter ended by previewing a few advanced topics that enhanced your understanding about how database transactions work. In the next chapter, you'll learn about users and security.

CHAPTER 11

Users and Security

IT'S A FACT OF LIFE THAT although storing and managing information is vital to the success of any business, having it fall into the wrong hands can bring a business down. As a result of this, database administrators have to be familiar with some complex security systems in order to protect a company's data.

The purpose of a database security system is to protect the stored information. There are various factors that you want to protect your data from; not only do you need to guard your database against attacks from outside the organization, but most of the time it's also vital to fine-tune access to sensitive database areas for employees inside the company (an obvious example would be locking access to personnel information so that only certain people can access salary details).

Security is a broad and complex subject. This chapter doesn't teach security theory; instead, you'll quickly look at the SQL commands and some database-specific commands that allow database administrators to configure their server's security. We'll present just enough so that you, the SQL programmer, will understand the basics of implementing security on database servers. If you're serious about learning more about security, you'll need to read a specialized book that's relevant to the database system with which you're working.

When implementing a security system, there are two fundamental concepts you need to understand:

- **Authentication** is the part that deals with uniquely identifying users. This is usually done via checking for user ID and password combinations, but other methods such as fingerprint scanning are becoming increasingly popular.

- **Authorization** takes care of the permissions an authenticated user has inside the database (what the user is allowed to do with his or her account). So, even if you log in to the database (you *authenticate* yourself), you may not be *authorized* to view or modify certain tables or other database objects.

With a modern Relational Database Management System (RDBMS), the administrator has a wide range of tools that help to fine-tune the security process and procedures. Although many of these features are beyond the scope of this book because they tend to be specific to particular database implementations, you'll learn how to deal with the basic security needs that are implemented in similar ways by all database software products.

In this chapter, you'll learn, with examples for SQL Server, Oracle, DB2, and MySQL, how to do the following:

- Create and remove database users and assign passwords to them (this has to do with the authentication part of security)

- Grant and revoke permissions to database users on the database resources (this has to do with authorization)

You'll also look quickly at the security provided by Microsoft Access.

Let's Talk About Security

Before moving on to the SQL security details, you need to understand some basic concepts regarding the way security is implemented in databases. It's important to understand the concepts of user, user permissions, and roles.

Users and Permissions

At the base of the authentication process is the concept of a *user account*. When installing database software, one or more administrative accounts are created by default, and nobody else has access to the system. However, it's likely you'll need to give database access to other people.

To give database access to someone, you need to take two steps:

1. Create a user account for that person (if he or she doesn't already have one). Using that account, the database system will be able to *authenticate* that person. Typically, the user is protected by a password that's requested during the login process.

2. When a user is created, by default the user doesn't have access (permissions) to any database objects. So, you need to grant the necessary permissions to the person's account; by doing this, you *authorize* the person to access the necessary database resources.

You can grant users various kinds of permissions, such as the rights to access various databases; create new data tables; update, select, insert, or delete records from data tables; execute stored procedures; add or modify other user accounts; and so on. The permissions can be generic (such as the user can create data tables or read any of the data tables), or they can be specific to existing database objects (such as the user can read or modify the Friend data table).

Each database supports a large number of possible permissions that a user can have. Users can be granted one or any combination of permissions; by setting permissions, a database administrator has the power to control who can do what to the database.

Along with the flexibility to provide each user with any combination of permissions, there comes the complexity of administering these permissions. When having a large number of users, each with its own combination of permissions, it can be become a nightmare to be in charge of security. What are the implications of an employee leaving the company or being transferred to another department? What about the permissions that the employee gave to other people while having the account?

SQL has answers for some of these problems. Additionally, most databases have started to offer additional tools to improve the database administrator's life. One of them is the support for *roles*.

Roles

A *role* is a named set of database permissions. In other words, a role contains permissions. Roles can be granted to or revoked from users; granting a role to a user has the same effect as granting the user all the permissions in that role.

Roles are important because they're extremely helpful for administering database security; they allow the database administrator to manage user privileges in a much more convenient way than setting individual permissions.

From the databases we've presented so far, SQL Server, Oracle, and DB2 support roles. MySQL doesn't support roles. Access supports the notion of "user groups," which is similar to the notion of roles.

Each database that supports roles ships with a number of predefined database roles. For example, the system administrator (sa) account in SQL Server is associated with the sysadmin role. After creating a new SQL Server user, if you want to give it full access to the server's resources, you just need to assign it to the sysadmin role, and the job is done; the user will have all permissions associated with the system administrator role. This is much easier than if you had to manually assign permissions (and believe us, a system administrator has *a lot* of individual permissions on the database).

Views

Views aren't directly related to security, but database administrators often use them to control the security of a database.

If you want to grant a user access to a portion of a table (such as a limited number of columns or only to certain rows), you can create a view based on that table (or even on multiple tables) and grant permissions on that view. Working with views sometimes offers more flexibility than assigning privileges on database tables.

For more information about views, please refer to Chapter 8, "Hiding Complex SQL with Views."

Understanding Database Security and SQL

For the authentication part, the SQL-99 standard doesn't provide you with any commands for managing user accounts. As a result, once again you're facing difficult territory, where each database has its own approach to the subject, even though the features they provide are quite similar. You'll see, for each database, how to create and remove users, assign passwords to them, and so on.

As for the authorization part, SQL-99 specifies two commands for managing permissions: GRANT and REVOKE. Most database systems support these two commands, but the syntax differs slightly between the implementations. You'll take a quick look at each of them before moving on to database specifics.

SQL-99 also specifies the CREATE ROLE, SET ROLE, and DROP ROLE commands, which are about managing roles and associating them with users. However, out of the RDBMS platforms covered in this book, only Oracle implements these commands; the other databases have different commands for dealing with roles. For this reason, we'll discuss roles separately for each database.

 TIP *Most databases ship with visual tools that allow administering security with mouse clicks instead of lengthy commands. MySQL doesn't ship with such tools, but you'll find many free ones provided by third parties. We'll leave these features for you to explore. The following sections cover how you can manage user accounts for each database system using command-line instructions.*

Using GRANT

You use GRANT to grant privileges to existing users. There are two main kinds of permissions: statement-level permissions and object-level permissions.

Statement-level permissions are about permitting users to perform certain actions that aren't related to a specific database object. Examples of statement-level permissions are CREATE DATABASE, CREATE TABLE, CREATE PROCEDURE, and CREATE VIEW. A user with the CREATE TABLE permission has the right to create data tables. For granting statement-level permissions, you use a command similar to the following:

```
GRANT <privilege type> TO <username>
```

Object-level permissions control access to specific, existing database objects. The most obvious database object type you might want to limit access to is the data table. The typical rights that can be granted for data tables are INSERT, UPDATE, DELETE, SELECT, or a combination of all of these. As an example, a user can be allowed to read a data table but will not be allowed to modify it. Some databases permit restricting access on a column-level basis inside the table. For stored procedures, the typical privilege type that can be granted is EXECUTE. When granting object-level permissions, you must also specify the object (resource):

```
GRANT <privilege type> ON <resource> TO <username>
```

By default, users have full access to the objects they create, but they don't have access to other users' objects. A user who creates a data table will have all possible rights on that table, including permissions to read, modify, and even drop it, and a user who creates a stored procedure will have the right to execute that stored procedure. However, if you want to access some other user's data, that user will have to grant you access to his or her objects.

With SQL Server, Oracle, and DB2, you can also use GRANT to assign roles to existing users. You'll see examples of this later in the chapter.

The exact GRANT options, privilege types, and supported resource types are database specific; you'll need to consult the documentation for your database for more details.

Here is the SQL-99 syntax for GRANT:

```
GRANT { [ALL PRIVILEGES] }
| SELECT
| INSERT [(column_name [,...n])]
| DELETE
| UPDATE [(column_name [,...n])]
| REFERENCES [(column_name [,...n])]
| USAGE }[,...n]
ON { [TABLE] table_name
| DOMAIN domain_name
| COLLATION collation_name
```

```
| CHARACTER SET charset_name
| TRANSLATION translation_name }
TO (granteee_name | PUBLIC}
[WITH GRANT OPTION]
```

Using REVOKE

You use REVOKE to remove privileges that had previously been granted with GRANT or deny permissions that users have by default (such as the rights users have over their own data).

REVOKE also works supports a statement-level syntax and an object-level syntax. For dealing with statement-level permissions, you use it like this:

```
REVOKE <privilege type> FROM <username>
```

For object-level permissions, you also need to specify the resources you're revoking privileges from:

```
REVOKE <privilege type> ON <resource> FROM <username>
```

When all rights are revoked from a given user, the user and its objects (such as data tables) aren't deleted from the database. Instead, the user is simply forbidden to access them.

SQL-99 specifies the following REVOKE syntax:

```
REVOKE [GRANT OPTION FOR]
{ ALL PRIVILEGES }
| SELECT
| INSERT
| DELETE
| UPDATE
| REFERENCES
| USAGE }[,...n]
ON { [TABLE] table_name
| DOMAIN domain_name
| COLLATION collation_name
| CHARACTER SET charset_name
| TRANSLATION translation_name }
FROM (granteee_name | PUBLIC} [,...n]
{CASCADE | RESTRICT}
```

Working with Access Security

Access isn't a real database server, and its security systems are something of a joke when compared with the features provided by its bigger brother and cousins. We'll have just a quick look at them before moving on. . . .

Access 2002 supports the GRANT and REVOKE commands, but with Access the visual wizards have always had much more success. You can access all security-related Access features by visiting the Tools ➤ Security menu.

The most basic way to secure an Access database (an .mdb file) is to set a database password on it. Once a password has been set on the database, it's requested each time the database is opened. You can set a database password by opening the database and selecting Tools ➤ Security ➤ Set Database Password. This option becomes more powerful when combined with database file encryption (Tools ➤ Security ➤ Encrypt/Decrypt Database). An encrypted data file is much harder to break than a nonencrypted, password-protected one.

Access also supports user-level security, which can be combined with the database password. User-level security allows you to fine-tune the access permissions for the users you define. To manage the database users, select Tools ➤ Security ➤ User and Group Accounts. This will allow you to add, remove, or modify existing user information (see Figure 11-1).

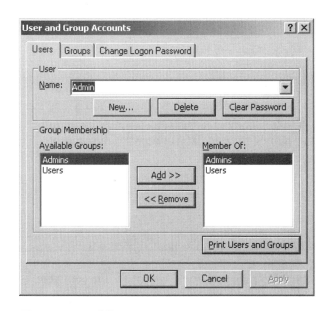

Figure 11-1. Adding users

Once you have added the users to the database, you can control their permissions by accessing Tools ➤ Security ➤ User and Group Permissions (see Figure 11-2).

Figure 11-2. Controlling permisssions

If you prefer a wizard to do some of the work for you, try calling the User-Level Security Wizard from Tools ➤ Security ➤ User-Level Security Wizard.

Working with SQL Server Security

In the following sections, you'll learn how you can use SQL Server's built-in stored procedures to add new users and change their passwords. You'll then see how you can use stored procedures and SQL statements to change the permissions of a particular user—that is, how you can determine what they can and can't do within a particular database.

Working with Users

With SQL Server, you can create a new user with the sp_addlogin stored procedure. You need to provide a username and optionally a password. There are more optional parameters; please consult SQL Server Books Online for the complete syntax:

```
EXEC sp_addlogin 'Alice', 'simplepassword'
```

TIP *For aesthetic purposes, we use proper casing for usernames, but database usernames are case insensitive. This is true for all databases covered in this book.*

You can change the user's password with the sp_password stored procedure. It takes as parameters the old password, the new password, and the username. If no username is supplied, the logged-in user is assumed by default. The following example illustrates how you can change Alice's simple password to a more complicated one:

```
EXEC sp_password 'simplepassword', 'complicatedpassword', 'Alice'
```

You can remove a user by using the sp_droplogin stored procedure, which takes as a parameter the username you want to delete. You can remove the Alice account using the following command:

```
EXEC sp_droplogin 'Alice'
```

This statement will drop the Alice account.

NOTE *In order to test the following statements, you'll need to keep the Alice account around.*

Integrated Security and Windows Authentication

Note that SQL Server also supports an alternative mode of authentication, known as *Integrated Security*, where access to the database is linked to Windows authentication (local user accounts or domain user accounts). If you're using Windows authentication, you can refer to domain accounts or local accounts in SQL statements in the same way as database user accounts except that you can't create a new user account in this manner.

To refer to domain users, you can use the syntax DOMAIN\UserName. Local accounts are referred to using the name of the machine you're using, for example, MyMachine\Administrator. If you're using Windows authentication, you'll need to have access to a user called Alice for these examples. You can create a local system user called Alice using the Computer Management console. For the following examples, you can use MachineName/Alice as your username.

TIP *SQL Server also supports mixed mode authentication, where both Windows authentication and SQL Server authentication are used.*

Granting Database Access

Once you've added a new database account, you can start playing with its rights and permissions. By default, the new account doesn't have any permissions.

For a start, you can grant the new user permission to access a particular database. You can do this with the sp_grantdbaccess stored procedure. Giving users access to a database allows them to connect to the database, but it doesn't give any specific permissions to individual objects.

If you're logged in with the sa account (or an account that has the rights to create databases), you can do this little experiment using Query Analyzer:

```
CREATE DATABASE TestDatabase
GO
USE TestDatabase
GO
CREATE TABLE TestTable (TestRow INT);
GO
EXEC sp_grantdbaccess 'Alice'
```

Note that the sp_grantdbaccess stored procedure always works with the current database. In this example, you first create a new database named TestDatabase. When you connect to the database, you create a new data table and then you grant Alice access to the database.

Now, if you log in using the Alice account you'll be able to connect to TestDatabase (by calling USE TestDatabase), but you won't be able to read any rows from TestTable. An attempt to read TestTable generates a SELECT permission denied error.

You can easily reverse this action and revoke Alice's access to TestDatabase using the sp_revokedbaccess stored procedure (you need to be logged on as a user with administrative privileges again):

```
USE TestDatabase
GO
EXEC sp_revokedbaccess 'Alice'
```

If you execute this command and then log in with Alice's account, TestDatabase will not be visible to you. An attempt to call USE TestDatabase would generate an error: `Server user 'Alice' is not a valid user in database 'TestDatabase'.`

> **NOTE** *For now, just make sure Alice does have access to* TestDatabase *so you'll be able to experiment further.*

After you've given the user access to the database itself, you'll most likely want to give the user access to objects *inside* the database—as you've seen, users can't access anything unless they are explicitly given the right to do so.

Setting Object-Level Permissions

For fine-tuning user permissions, SQL Server provides you with the SQL-99 commands GRANT and REVOKE. You also have an additional command named DENY. Here you'll see how to use these commands to control object-level access.

The basic syntax for GRANT when setting object-level permissions is as follows:

```
GRANT <privilege type> ON <resource> TO <username>
```

You can assign six privileges to SQL Server objects:

SELECT, INSERT, UPDATE, and DELETE are the four rights that apply to data tables and views. Users having the SELECT permission on a data table will be able to read information from that table by using the SELECT statement. Users can have a mix of these permissions—for example, a user can be allowed to insert new rows into a table but can be forbidden to read data from the table.

REFERENCES allow a user to insert rows into a table that has a FOREIGN KEY constraint to another table where the user doesn't have SELECT permissions. This permission was implemented because inserting rows into a table having FOREIGN KEY constraints can give you tips about the data in other tables on which you may not have SELECT rights.

EXECUTE allows the user to run the specified stored procedure.

If you want to give Alice SELECT access to a table named TestTable, you type the following:

```
GRANT SELECT ON TestTable TO Alice
```

If you want to give Alice the right to pass along the permissions she receives (using GRANT), you can use the WITH GRANT OPTION parameter of GRANT. This allows her to grant SELECT access to TestTable to other users:

```
GRANT SELECT ON TestTable TO Alice WITH GRANT OPTION
```

DENY is the opposite of GRANT: It prevents the user from accessing the targeted object. DENY overrides any previously issued GRANT statements and overrides any permissions the user may have because of role memberships.

REVOKE eliminates the effect of previously issued GRANT or DENY statements. After revoking all individual permissions, the user will revert to having the default set of permissions specified by any roles of which they're a member.

To remove the SELECT permission on TestTable from Alice, you can call either DENY or REVOKE. REVOKE nullifies the effect of the GRANT statement, which was initially issued because Alice couldn't access TestTable. DENY is even tougher and explicitly denies Alice from accessing TestTable. Let's use REVOKE now:

```
REVOKE SELECT ON TestTable FROM Alice
```

If you granted access using WITH GRANT OPTION, you must use CASCADE when revoking the permission. This will remove the SELECT permission from all the accounts Alice granted this permission to:

```
REVOKE SELECT ON TestTable FROM Alice CASCADE
```

TIP *Keep in mind that* GRANT, REVOKE, *and* DENY *allow you to control access down to column level.*

Using Roles

SQL Server has a number of predefined roles (for a full list, you should consult the SQL Server Books Online). Here you'll focus on the commands that create new roles and assign them to database users.

To create a new SQL Server role, you use the sp_addrole stored procedure, which takes as a parameter the name of the new role. While logged in with a system administrator account, create a new role named TestRole:

```
EXEC sp_addrole 'TestRole'
```

After adding the role, let's assign the permission to perform SELECT on TestTable to it. You do this using the GRANT command, where instead of a username to assign the permission, you specify the name of a role:

```
GRANT SELECT ON TestTable TO TestRole
```

Okay, so you have a role that has an associated permission. In this example, you're testing a role with a single permission, but remember that you can add any number of permissions to TestRole. You can also assign DENY permissions to a role—so you can have roles that are allowed to perform some actions but that are prevented from performing other tasks.

After creating a role, it's time to assign the role to the Alice account. The sp_addrolemember stored procedure take care of that:

```
EXEC sp_addrolemember TestRole, Alice
```

Now it's time to see if Alice has gotten her rights to access TestTable again. Log in using the Alice account, select TestDatabase to make it your current database, and make a query on TestTable. It should run without problems:

```
SELECT * FROM TestTable
```

NOTE DENY *is always more powerful than* GRANT. *If you explicitly deny* SELECT *access on* TestTable *to Alice, she won't be able to read* TestTable, *even if she's a member of* TestRole. *Also, if you explicitly granted to Alice* SELECT *access on* TestTable *but assigned her a role that denies the same privilege, Alice couldn't access* TestTable.

You can use the sp_droprolemember stored procedure to remove a role from a user account. Type the following command when logged in using an administrator account on TestDatabase:

```
EXEC sp_droprolemember TestRole, Alice
```

After executing this command, Alice can't access TestTable anymore.
You can drop roles from the database using sp_droprole:

```
EXEC sp_droprole TestRole
```

Setting Statement-Level Permissions

GRANT, DENY, and REVOKE also deal with the statement-level permissions. With two exceptions, these rights allow the user to create new database objects. The statement-level permissions supported by SQL Server are as follows:

- CREATE DATABASE

- CREATE DEFAULT

- CREATE FUNCTION

- CREATE PROCEDURE

- CREATE RULE

- CREATE TABLE

- CREATE VIEW

- BACKUP DATABASE

- BACKUP LOG

As an example, the following command gives Alice the right to create databases:

```
GRANT CREATE DATABASE TO Alice
```

Note that when you issue this command you need to have the master database currently selected, and Alice needs to be granted login permission to the master database before the administrator can run this command. As with object-level permissions, you use WITH GRANT OPTION if you want the grantee to be able to give the received permissions to other users as well.

It's also possible to grant a user the right to create tables within the current database. Make sure the database you want to give access to is your currently selected database and execute a GRANT CREATE TABLE statement, just like in the following example:

```
USE TestDatabase
GRANT CREATE TABLE TO Alice
```

Now you can log in with the Alice account and attempt to create a new table in TestDatabase—you'll see; it works.

Working with Oracle Security

In the following sections, you'll look at some of the same tricks you learned in the SQL Server section. You'll create a new user called Alice, see how you can change passwords, and then examine how you work with permissions in Oracle.

Working with Users

Oracle comes with two users that are created by default: SYSTEM and SYS. In order to create new users, you log in using the SYSTEM user because SYSTEM has the required privileges.

To create a new Oracle user, you use the CREATE USER command, which needs to be supplied with the username and its password. Here's how you create the Alice account in Oracle, with a default password of simplepassword:

```
CREATE USER Alice IDENTIFIED BY simplepassword;
```

If you want to change the simple password of Alice to a complicated one, you need to use the ALTER USER command. For example:

```
ALTER USER Alice IDENTIFIED BY complicatedpassword;
```

Alternatively, you can use the password command in SQL*Plus, which doesn't display the passwords as you type them. When logged in as Alice, simply type password and press Enter. When logged in as SYSTEM, type password Alice to change Alice's password.

You can remove users with the DROP USER command. If you want to give Alice a nasty surprise, try this:

```
DROP USER Alice;
```

NOTE *With Oracle, you can assign profiles to user accounts via the* CREATE PROFILE *command. Using this command, you can set the lifetime of a password, the number of consecutive failed attempts allowed before the account is automatically locked and for how much time it will remain locked, and other similar parameters regarding passwords. Please look up the* CREATE PROFILE *command in the Oracle Alphabetical Reference for more information about this command.*

Assigning User Permissions

Right now, although Alice does have a new account, she can't do many things with it. By default, a new user isn't even allowed to log in—all access rights must be explicitly defined. You'll use GRANT and REVOKE commands to adjust the permissions for each user.

The Predefined System Roles

To let Alice connect to Oracle, you need to assign her the CONNECT role. The CONNECT role allows a user to connect to the database, but this right only becomes meaningful when combined with other permissions (such as permissions to access or modify existing data tables).

 NOTE   CONNECT, RESOURCE, *and* DBA *are the three standard roles in Oracle. The* CONNECT *role permits users to connect to the database. Users with the* RESOURCE *role are allowed to create their own tables, procedures, triggers, and other types of database objects, and the* DBA *role allows for unlimited access.*

To assign Alice the CONNECT and RESOURCE roles, log in using a database administrator account (such as SYSTEM) and execute the following command:

```
GRANT CONNECT, RESOURCE to Alice;
```

Note that the RESOURCE role doesn't include the privileges supplied by CONNECT. You can test this by providing Alice only with the RESOURCE role (without CONNECT) and then trying to connect to the database using the Alice account—the database won't let you in!

Be aware that a user who is granted the RESOURCE role obtains many system-level privileges, including UNLIMITED TABLESPACE, which allows the user to consume any amount of space in any tablespace. Don't haphazardly grant the RESOURCE role to any user, and if you do use it, it's a good idea to revoke the UNLIMITED TABLESPACE privilege.

REVOKE has a similar format, except you use FROM instead of TO. Here's an example:

```
REVOKE RESOURCE FROM Alice;
```

After revoking the RESOURCE role from Alice, she won't be able to do anything with her account, except log in to the database. Give her the RESOURCE role again so you can do some more tests.

Granting and Revoking Object-Level Permissions

To grant object-level permissions, you use the usual syntax:

```
GRANT <privilege type> ON <resource> TO <username>
```

The object-level permissions supported by Oracle are as follows:

- ALTER allows the grantee to change the table definition using the ALTER TABLE command.

- DELETE, INSERT, SELECT, and UPDATE are the permissions that apply to data tables and views.

- INDEX allows the grantee to create indexes on the mentioned data table.

- REFERENCES allows a user to insert rows into a table that has a FOREIGN KEY constraint to another table where the user doesn't have SELECT permissions.

- EXECUTE allows the user to run the specified function or stored procedure or to access any program object declared in the specification of a package.

Let's look at a quick example to see how these work. First, connect to Oracle as Alice using a command similar to the following:

```
CONNECT Alice/complicatedpassword@service name;
```

where @*service name* is sometimes required by Oracle to connect to the database server.

 CAUTION   *Note how you can use the* CONNECT *command to change the logged-in user; don't confuse the* CONNECT *command (which changes the current user) with the* CONNECT *role.*

Second, when logged in as Alice, try to read data from the Student table in the InstantUniversity database. Note that when accessing some other user's objects you need to specify the owner username along with the object name:

 NOTE   *In these examples we assume you created the* InstantUniversity *database while logged on with the* INSTSQL *account. If you created it using another account (for example,* SYSTEM), *please use that account instead.*

```
SELECT * FROM INSTSQL.Student;
```

When executing this command using Alice's account, you'll be told that INSTSQL.Student doesn't exist. This is because Alice doesn't have SELECT permissions on Students.

To grant her access on Student, you need to log in again as the administrator of the InstantUniversity database:

```
CONNECT INSTSQL/password@service name;
```

> **NOTE** *You could run this command while logged on as* SYSTEM, *but as a general rule, you should always work with the least privileges necessary to perform a task; because you only need administrative privileges on the* InstantUniversity *database, you'll use the account that just has privileges for that database.*

When logged in as INSTSQL, execute the following GRANT command, which grants Alice access to SELECT and INSERT data on the Student table:

```
GRANT SELECT, INSERT ON Student TO Alice;
```

Now connect again as Alice and perform two operations on the Student table as follows:

```
INSERT INTO INSTSQL.Student (StudentID, Name)
VALUES (13, 'George Bush');
SELECT * FROM INSTSQL.Student;
```

The results will show the rows inserted with both the INSTSQL account that you've been using and the row added using the Alice account:

StudentID	Name
1	John Jones
2	Gary Burton
3	Emily Scarlett
4	Bruce Lee
5	Anna Wolff
6	Vic Andrews
7	Steve Alaska

8	Julia Picard
9	Andrew Foster
10	Maria Fernandez
11	Mohammed Akbar
12	Isabelle Jonsson
13	George Bush

Now, try to do an update (while still connected as Alice):

```
UPDATE INSTSQL.Student
SET StudentID = 555
WHERE StudentID = 13;
```

If you try this, you'll be told you don't have enough privileges. This is true because Alice only has INSERT and SELECT privileges.

You can use GRANT with the WITH GRANT OPTION that gives the user the right to pass along the received privileges to other users. If you wanted Alice to have the rights to give INSERT and SELECT permissions on SomeTable to other users, you need to execute something similar to this:

```
GRANT SELECT, INSERT ON Student TO Alice WITH GRANT OPTION;
```

To revoke the INSERT permission on Student from Alice, you use REVOKE:

```
REVOKE INSERT ON Student FROM Alice;
```

If you want to revoke the INSERT permission on Student from Alice and from all the other users who received this permission from Alice, you use the CASCADE keyword. This only applies if Alice was provided the permission using WITH GRANT OPTION:

```
REVOKE INSERT ON Student FROM Alice CASCADE;
```

Assigning Roles

In Oracle, in addition to the three system roles mentioned earlier, you can create new roles using the CREATE ROLE command. Oracle even supports associating passwords to roles.

While logged in with the SYSTEM account, create a new role named TestRole:

```
CREATE ROLE TestRole;
```

While you're still logged in as SYSTEM, assign it to Alice:

```
GRANT TestRole TO Alice;
```

When created, the role doesn't have any privileges. So, log back in as INSTSQL and add the UPDATE privilege on Student to TestRole:

```
GRANT UPDATE ON Student TO TestRole;
```

Now log in once again as Alice. While logged in as Alice, try to update Student. Remember that before having the role, this was impossible. Now, the following command executes successfully:

```
UPDATE INSTSQL.Student
SET StudentID = 555
WHERE StudentID = 13;
```

To remove the granted role from Alice, you use REVOKE while being logged in as SYSTEM:

```
REVOKE TestRole FROM Alice;
```

To finally drop the role, do the following:

```
DROP ROLE TestRole;
```

Don't forget to delete George Bush from the Student table when you're done.

Setting Statement-Level Permissions

GRANT and REVOKE also deal with statement-level permissions. With two exceptions, these rights allow the user to create new database objects. The list of statement-level permissions supported by Oracle is very long; please consult the GRANT section (under "System Privileges and Roles") in the Oracle SQL Reference for complete details.

Typical statement-level permissions are CREATE DATABASE, CREATE TABLE, ALTER TABLE, DROP TABLE, and so on. Statement-level permissions also can be granted using WITH GRANT OPTION, in which case the grantee can grant the received privileges to other users.

Note that many of these permissions are included with the RESOURCE role. For example, users having the RESOURCE role have permissions to create their own data tables. However, if you want to be restrictive about the permissions you grant to a user, you'll prefer to grant individual rights instead of assigning the RESOURCE role.

Working with DB2 Security

DB2 handles user accounts differently from the other database systems. DB2 user accounts are linked to local system users, relying on the authentication protocols of the underlying operating system rather than having self-contained users. To add a new user to DB2, you first need to create a new local system user using the standard tools available as part of the operating system. Once you have a local user account set up, you can then start granting and revoking permissions, which you'll learn about in the following sections.

For this example, let's assume you've created an account for Alice with a password of SimplePassword.

Granting and Revoking Object-Level Permissions

To grant object-level permissions, you use the usual syntax:

```
GRANT <privilege type> ON <resource> TO <username>
```

The object-level permissions supported by DB2 are as follows:

- ALTER allows the grantee to change the table definition using the ALTER TABLE command.

- DELETE, INSERT, SELECT, UPDATE are the permissions that apply to data tables and views.

- INDEX allows the grantee to create indexes on the mentioned data table.

- REFERENCES allows a user to insert rows into a table that has a FOREIGN KEY constraint to another table where the user doesn't have SELECT permissions.

- EXECUTE allows the user to run the specified function or stored procedure or to access any program object declared in the specification of a package.

- CONTROL grants all of the previous permissions to the user and also gives them the ability to grant any of the previous permissions, excluding CONTROL, to other users. The CONTROL permission can only ever be granted by users with database administrator or system administrator status.

So, let's start by granting some permissions to Alice. Open DB2 Command Center and enter the following code:

```
GRANT CONNECT ON DATABASE TO USER Alice;
```

So, Alice can now connect to the database. But if you try to connect to the InstantUniversity database as Alice and then view some data, you'll find that permission is denied. So, while you're logged on as the DB2Admin administrator, enter the following command:

```
GRANT SELECT, INSERT ON Student TO Alice;
```

Again, you could have specified WITH GRANT OPTION in this statement to allow Alice to grant these permissions to others.

Now, if you log on as Alice, you'll be able to run the following commands:

```
INSERT INTO DB2Admin.Student (StudentID, Name)
VALUES (13, 'George Bush');

SELECT StudentID, Name FROM DB2Admin.Student;
```

However, to be able to delete George Bush from the database, you need to give Alice DELETE privileges. Instead of granting this permission to Alice, let's revoke the INSERT permission on Alice and then experiment with adding her to a group (the equivalent of a role on DB2):

```
REVOKE INSERT ON Student FROM Alice;
```

Working with Groups

Alice is now limited to being able to select data from the table, but because DB2 doesn't have traditional users and roles, to give Alice more permissions more easily, you need to use a mixture of SQL and tools available to the operating system.

If you create a new group account on your system, called MyGroup, you can assign permissions on this group just as you did with Alice:

```
GRANT CONNECT ON DATABASE TO GROUP MyGroup;
GRANT SELECT, INSERT, DELETE ON Student TO MyGroup;
```

Because Alice isn't a member of the group yet, she still can't insert or delete students. However, if you add the Alice user to the MyGroup group on your system, you'll find that Alice now has much more power when it comes to creating and deleting students.

An interesting point to note is that if an individual member of a group has more permissions than the group itself, that user will still be able to perform all the appropriate tasks, even if other members of the group are unable to do so. To test this, create another system user called Joe and make him a member of MyGroup. Joe can now log on and select, insert, and delete students.

Now, log back in as the administrator and run the following commands:

```
REVOKE DELETE, INSERT On Student FROM MyGroup;
GRANT UPDATE on Student TO Alice;
GRANT CONTROL ON Student TO Joe;
```

Joe can now have much more fun with the Student table, creating, altering, or deleting information as much as he wants. Alice can view and update data, for example:

```
UPDATE DB2Admin.Student SET Name = 'George W. Bush'
WHERE StudentID=13;
```

Any other members in the group are limited to simply viewing data in the table.

To finish, you can revoke all privileges from the users:

```
REVOKE ALL PRIVILEGES ON Student FROM Alice;
```

Note that you must first revoke CONTROL from Joe and then revoke all the individual privileges that are added when the CONTROL privilege is added:

```
REVOKE CONTROL ON Student FROM Joe;
REVOKE ALL PRIVILEGES ON Student FROM Joe;
```

Note that, at this point, Alice and Joe can still view data in the Student table because the MyGroup group still has SELECT permission. This final command will prevent both users from viewing data in the Student table:

```
REVOKE ALL PRIVILEGES ON Student FROM MyGroup;
```

But note that the users are still able to log on until you revoke the CONNECT permission for the group (which revokes connect permission from Joe because you never explicitly granted him CONNECT permission), then from Alice, who had her own explicit CONNECT permission, which was the first thing you granted:

```
REVOKE CONNECT ON DATABASE FROM MyGroup;
REVOKE CONNECT ON DATABASE FROM Alice;
```

Setting Statement-Level Permissions

DB2 also has the ability to grant or revoke permissions for creating tables and databases. The full list of grantable permissions is quite lengthy, so you should consult the documentation.

If you want to allow a user to create tables, you could use the following command:

```
GRANT CREATETAB ON DATABASE TO Alice;
```

Note that to create a view, all you need is SELECT permission on each of the tables involved in the view.

If you want to make Alice a full administrator of the database, in case she wanted to do a lot of work on manipulating the database, you could make her a full administrator of that database:

```
GRANT DBADM ON DATABASE TO Alice;
```

Note that when you enable this permission, all of the other permissions available are added. Removing just this permission won't remove all the other permissions that were added, so you'll need to first remove DBADM and then do a REVOKE ALL PRIVILEGES, as you saw with Joe.

Working with MySQL Security

MySQL security isn't as involved as SQL Server, Oracle, or DB2 security. MySQL doesn't support roles, and it has a limited range of security options that can be set. You'll take a brief look at them here—please consult the MySQL online documentation for complete and more recent information.

MySQL user rights are stored in a series of security data tables known as *grant tables*, which are automatically created when MySQL is installed.

 TIP *The grant tables are kept in a database called* mysql. *When MySQL is installed, the* mysql *and* test *tables are created automatically.*

There are a total of six grant tables: user, tables_priv, columns_priv, db, func, and host. Each table serves a different purpose and can be manually updated in order to grant user privileges or add and remove users. You should consult the MySQL documentation for a description of each grant table.

It's unlikely that somebody would want to modify these tables by hand. If you don't believe me, here's an INSERT command that adds a new user named Alice@localhost with the password simplepass:

```
USE mysql
INSERT INTO user VALUES('localhost','Alice',PASSWORD('simplepass'),'Y','Y',
        'Y','Y','Y','Y','Y','Y','Y','Y','Y','Y','Y','Y');
FLUSH PRIVILEGES;
```

This adds a new user named Alice@localhost to the database system.

NOTE *MySQL stores security information for user/host combinations, but the* localhost *is allowed to be void. To this regard,* Alice@localhost *will be regarded as a different user than Alice.*

The 'Y' fields in this statement relate to the available privileges, but rather than learn what each one stands for, in just a moment you'll learn how to set the same privileges with a simpler method: using the GRANT command. Before you move on, if you look at this INSERT command, you can clearly see that passwords aren't stored in clear text. Instead, the password is encrypted with the PASSWORD function and stored in an encrypted form. Each time the user attempts to log in, the entered password is encrypted again using the same algorithm, and the result is compared to the value in the database. This way, somebody gaining access to the database (or even database administrators) can't obtain the password by reading the user table (the encryption process used by PASSWORD isn't reversible).

Note that the FLUSH PRIVILEGES command is required after any change to the grant tables because although these are loaded when MySQL starts, they aren't reloaded automatically when security information changes.

Okay, so it's pretty obvious that you won't be adding users by inserting records into the user table. The alternative to this is, as we said before, the GRANT command, which is much simpler. GRANT is primarily used to accord privileges to users, but if the user getting the privileges doesn't exist, the user is automatically created.

TIP *Unlike SQL Server, Oracle, and DB2, MySQL doesn't ship with a visual administrative interface. However, there are plenty of third-party visual interfaces that allow you to administer MySQL security, for example, the MySQL Control Center, available from* http://www.mysql.com/products/mysqlcc/.

The syntax of GRANT is similar to what you've seen with SQL Server or Oracle. One interesting feature is that it also allows you to set the user's password:

```
GRANT <privilege type> ON <resource> TO <username> [IDENTIFIED BY <passwd>];
```

A FLUSH PRIVILEGES call is still required, even when granting privileges using GRANT or revoking privileges with REVOKE. This tells MySQL to read again security information from its data tables.

In order to accord SELECT permissions for all the tables in the InstantUniversity database to Alice@localhost, you would type the following:

```
GRANT SELECT ON InstantUniversity.*
TO Alice@localhost IDENTIFIED BY 'simplepassword';
FLUSH PRIVILEGES;
```

MySQL also supports the WITH GRANT option, which allows the grantees to pass along the rights they receive:

```
GRANT SELECT ON InstantUniversity.*
TO Alice@localhost IDENTIFIED BY 'simplepassword' WITH GRANT OPTION;
```

Note the notation used to express all the tables in the test database: InstantUniversity.*. You can also grant privileges on all databases and all their tables using the *.* wildcard. To grant all possible privileges (including to grant privileges to other users) to Alice@localhost, you use the following command:

```
GRANT ALL ON *.* TO Alice@localhost;
```

The following command gives INSERT privileges to the Friend table of the Test database:

```
GRANT INSERT ON InstantUniversity.Student TO Alice@localhost;
```

To revoke user rights, you use—as you've probably guessed already—the REVOKE command. REVOKE works just like GRANT and has a similar syntax, except you use FROM instead of TO. The following example revokes from Alice@localhost the rights to drop the Friend table in Test database:

```
REVOKE DROP ON InstantUniversity.Student FROM Alice@localhost;
```

To revoke from Alice@localhost the rights to drop any objects from InstantUniversity, you use this command:

```
REVOKE DROP ON InstantUniversity.* FROM Alice@localhost;
```

If you want to revoke the rights to drop any database and any object from any database, you use the following command:

```
REVOKE DROP ON *.* FROM Alice@localhost;
```

Although GRANT can be used to create user accounts, REVOKE doesn't delete user accounts. The only way to remove MySQL accounts is manually delete the user from the user table. Here's an example:

```
DELETE FROM mysql.user WHERE user='Alice' AND host='localhost';
```

Notice that you prefixed the user table with the database in which it resides. This is required only if mysql isn't the currently selected database.

Finally, if you want to see which privileges a particular user has in the system, you use the SHOW GRANTS FOR command. Here's an example:

```
SHOW GRANTS FOR Alice@localhost;
```

Summary

Although most of the time security isn't the favorite field of a SQL programmer, it's important to have a basic knowledge of how it works.

In this chapter, you analyzed the basic security options available with SQL Server, Oracle, DB2, MySQL, and Access. You saw how to create, modify, and remove database user accounts and how to set the appropriate level of permissions to them. For more information on securing your database, you should consult an RDBMS-specific book or the appropriate documentation.

CHAPTER 12

Working with Database Objects

IN THIS CHAPTER, YOU'LL LEARN how to create, alter, and drop databases and other kinds of objects that live inside databases, such as tables, sequences, and so on.

Each of these objects has well-delimited purposes, and you'll examine them one at a time. The topics covered in this chapter include the following:

- How to create and drop entire databases

- How to create and drop data tables

- How to modify existing data tables

- Temporary tables

- Sequences

- Indexes

- Declarative Referential Integrity (DRI) and the FOREIGN KEY constraint

Most databases ship with visual tools that help design tables and relationships between them. MySQL is an exception, but you can download third-party tools at http://www.mysql.com/downloads/contrib.html. One of the utilities you can try is MySQL Control Center, available from http://www.mysql.com/products/mysqlcc. These programs work by generating SQL for you and executing the SQL against the database without you even seeing it. You might find these tools do the job, but they won't always. It's certainly worthwhile knowing the SQL required to create these yourself.

Creating and Dropping Databases

Creating and dropping database objects is the first subject you'll examine in this chapter. Databases are complex animals, and each database product has its own way of managing and storing internal data. We'll touch on the most common features and some specific product particularities, but for a closer look at them, you'll need an advanced, specialized book about your database product.

Creating Databases

SQL Server, Oracle, MySQL, and DB2 enable you to create whole databases using a SQL statement. The following syntax will work on all of these database systems:

```
CREATE DATABASE MyDatabase;
```

Each database system provides different options for CREATE DATABASE, which gives you extra control over certain properties of the database. However, for most purposes, you simply need to specify a name, and then the server will make all the other decisions for you.

Having said this, creating a database is a sensitive task that shouldn't be done hastily. The database is a complex object, and when you create a database, you have many options to fine-tune its performance and behavior, depending on for what purpose you'll use it. In most cases, it's much easier to use the tools that ship with the database system because they can do many of the tasks for you.

For example, if you're using Oracle, the easiest way to create a new database is via the Oracle Installer utility (when installing Oracle). When installing Oracle, you have the option to create a new database. The installer creates a *create-database script*, which can be then used as a starting point for your own scripts. You can typically find the scripts created by the Installer utility in the dbs subdirectory of the Oracle home directory.

If you're using Oracle, be careful because CREATE DATABASE can easily delete an existing database if this isn't used with caution. It's common for Oracle instances to contain only one database (or for a single database to be spread over several instances) and to use schemas rather than databases to group related tables and other objects.

With SQL Server, you can use Enterprise Manager, which offers both a New Database command and a Create Database Wizard. These handy tools allow for the quick creation of databases.

You can create databases in DB2 either with the Control Center application or via SQL commands using Command Center. If you use Command Center, it's not possible to create a new database if you're already connected to an existing database.

Using an open connection to the database server, you connect to an existing database using the USE command for SQL Server and MySQL like this:

```
USE MyDatabase;
```

On the other systems, you can reissue a CONNECT command to connect to the new database.

> **NOTE** *Appendix A, "Executing SQL Statements," covers the* CONNECT *command.*

Dropping Databases

Removing databases in SQL Server, MySQL, and DB2 is equally easy:

```
DROP DATABASE MyDatabase;
```

Oracle doesn't support the DROP DATABASE command. If you want to drop a database in Oracle, use CREATE DATABASE, specifying the name of the database you want to delete. You can also use the Oracle Database Assistant to drop databases.

Access doesn't support either of these commands. To create an Access database, use File ➤ New in the Access application window. To delete an Access database, just delete the database's .mdb file.

Creating and Dropping Data Tables

Fortunately, SQL Server, Oracle, DB2, and MySQL have similar ways to create data tables. As for dropping tables, they're identical.

Let's start with the basics. . . .

Understanding the Basic Syntax

The basic syntax for creating tables is simple:

```
CREATE TABLE <table name>
   (<column name> <column data type> [<column constraints>]);
```

Deleting database tables is even simpler:

```
DROP TABLE <table name>;
```

Tables being linked by FOREIGN KEY constraints can't be dropped. The constraints need to be dropped before dropping the table. You'll learn more about

FOREIGN KEY constraints later in this chapter, but for now it's enough to know they're the means to enforce table relationships. You need to be the owner of the table or have administrative rights in order to be allowed to drop the table.

In MySQL, dropping a table can't be undone. However, if a table is dropped inside a SQL Server, Oracle, or DB2 transaction, the table will be re-created if you roll back the transaction.

Using SQL Server, Oracle, or MySQL, you can also truncate a table instead of dropping it. This means that all the records in the table are deleted (the table itself isn't dropped), but the operation isn't logged in the transaction log. In other words, truncation works just like a fast DELETE that clears the entire table but can't be rolled back.

Because it isn't a logged operation, truncating a table also doesn't fire any triggers that would normally be executed when deleting rows from the table (you'll learn about triggers in the next chapter). When a table is truncated, the identity values used for auto-increment are also reset to their default values.

With MySQL, TRUNCATE drops the table and re-creates it again, thus deleting all its rows much faster than a DELETE command. Even though the internal procedure might be different for the other databases systems, truncating works just like dropping the table and creating it again.

The syntax of TRUNCATE is simple:

```
TRUNCATE TABLE <table name>;
```

Creating Simple Tables

If you connect to your favorite database, you can create a table called Friend using this syntax:

```
CREATE TABLE Friend (Name VARCHAR(50), PhoneNo VARCHAR(15));
```

By default, there are no constraints defined when a new table is created, and the columns accept NULL values. So, all of the following commands will execute successfully:

```
INSERT INTO Friend (Name, PhoneNo) VALUES ('John Doe', '555 2323');
INSERT INTO Friend (Name) VALUES ('John Doe');
INSERT INTO Friend (Name, PhoneNo) VALUES ('John Doe', NULL);
```

Executing these commands will populate the Friend table as shown in Table 12-1.

Table 12-1. The Friend *Table*

Name	PhoneNo
'John Doe'	'555 2323'
'John Doe'	NULL
'John Doe'	NULL

The second two INSERT statements are only allowed because NULLs are accepted by default, so NULLs are allowed for PhoneNo. They would also be allowed for Name, so you could have a statement like this:

```
INSERT INTO Friend (PhoneNo) VALUES ('123 4567');
```

and end up with a record like that shown in Table 12-2.

Table 12-2. The New Record

Name	PhoneNo
NULL	'123 4567'

 NOTE *If you try a* SELECT * FROM Friend *statement, SQL Server Query Analyzer and the MySQL command prompt will display* NULL *for the second and third entries of the* PhoneNo *column. The DB2 Command Center displays a dash (-). Oracle SQL*Plus and Access, on the other hand, will leave the spaces blank, and this might get you thinking that you have empty strings for that column. This is a bit confusing because* NULL *isn't the same as an empty string—it means something closer to "unknown."*

Disallowing NULLs

If you don't want to accept NULL values in a column, you should append NOT NULL to the definition. To test this, let's first drop the Friend table:

```
DROP TABLE Friend;
```

Now let's re-create the Friend table, but this time you won't allow NULL values for Name or PhoneNo:

```
CREATE TABLE Friend (Name VARCHAR(50) NOT NULL,
                        PhoneNo VARCHAR(15) NOT NULL);
```

After creating the new table, let's do the little test again:

```
INSERT INTO Friend (Name, PhoneNo)
        VALUES ('John Doe', '555 2323');
INSERT INTO Friend (Name) VALUES ('John Doe');
INSERT INTO Friend (Name, PhoneNo) VALUES ('John Doe', NULL);
```

If you execute these three statements, you'll probably be surprised to find out that your databases behave differently:

The first statement executes just fine on all database systems.

The second statement doesn't specify a value for PhoneNo. SQL Server, DB2, Access, and Oracle generate an error because a value must be specified for NOT NULL columns. MySQL, on the other hand, breaks the rules a little bit (even when running in ANSI mode) and executes the statement by adding an empty string for PhoneNo. In other words, MySQL tries to second-guess what you mean.

The third statement is rejected by all databases because you specifically try to insert NULL for PhoneNo.

Specifying Default Values

Let's suppose the following: If no phone number is specified when adding new rows, you want the database to add the value 'Unknown phone' for that column. How can you do that? First, once again, drop the Friend table:

```
DROP TABLE Friend;
```

Second, re-create it with the following statement:

```
CREATE TABLE Friend (
    Name    VARCHAR(50) NOT NULL,
    PhoneNo VARCHAR(15) DEFAULT 'Unknown Phone' NOT NULL);
```

TIP   *With SQL Server, DB2, Access, and MySQL, you can switch the order of the* DEFAULT *and* NOT NULL *clauses, but Oracle requires the* DEFAULT *clause to appear first.*

Now let's test again with your three friends:

```
INSERT INTO Friend (Name, PhoneNo) VALUES ('John Doe', '555 2323');
INSERT INTO Friend (Name) VALUES ('John Doe');
INSERT INTO Friend (Name, PhoneNo) VALUES ('John Doe', NULL);
```

The first statement succeeds, and the specified values are inserted in the table. The second also succeeds, and 'Unknown Phone' is supplied by default for PhoneNo because no value was explicitly provided. The third statement will fail because you tried to insert NULL into a column that doesn't support NULLs.

In SQL Server, Oracle, and DB2, you can use functions or system variables instead of fixed values to provide the default value for a column. The typical example is to use a function or variable that returns the current date and time, such as GETDATE() for SQL Server, CURRENT_DATE for DB2, or SYSDATE for Oracle. Newer versions of Oracle also support CURRENT_DATE, which performs the same as SYSDATE. For example:

```
-- Oracle
CREATE TABLE LibraryLoans (
    BookID       INT  NOT NULL,
    CustomerID   INT  NOT NULL,
    DateBorrowed DATE DEFAULT SYSDATE NOT NULL);
-- DB2
CREATE TABLE LibraryLoans (
    BookID       INT  NOT NULL,
    CustomerID   INT  NOT NULL,
    DateBorrowed DATE DEFAULT CURRENT_DATE NOT NULL);
-- SQL Server
CREATE TABLE LibraryLoans (
    BookID       INT      NOT NULL,
    CustomerID   INT      NOT NULL,
    DateBorrowed DATETIME DEFAULT GETDATE() NOT NULL);
```

 TIP *You learned about working with dates and times in Chapter 5, "Performing Calculations and Using Functions."*

Setting the Primary Key

So far, the Friend table has a significant disadvantage: It doesn't have a primary key. As you saw in Chapter 1, "Understanding SQL and Relational Databases," every table in a relational database should have a primary key so that each record can be uniquely identified by the value in one (or a group) of its columns. There are no exceptions to this rule in a relational database.

For the purposes of this exercise, you won't add an additional column (such as FriendID) as the primary key. Instead, you want each friend of yours to have unique names, so set Name as the primary key.

Remember that the primary key is a *constraint* that applies to table columns. The following command creates the Friend table and associates a PRIMARY KEY constraint named MyPrimaryKey to the Name field (remember to drop the Friend table before re-creating it):

```
CREATE TABLE Friend (
    Name     VARCHAR(50) NOT NULL,
    PhoneNo VARCHAR(15) DEFAULT 'Unknown Phone' NOT NULL,
    CONSTRAINT MyPrimaryKey PRIMARY KEY (Name));
```

NOTE   *For multi-column primary keys, you just list the constituent columns separated by commas. You'll look at working with multi-valued primary keys in Chapter 14, "Case Study: Building a Product Catalog."*

If you aren't interested in supplying a name for the PRIMARY KEY constraint, you can use this syntax:

```
CREATE TABLE Friend (
    Name     VARCHAR(50) NOT NULL,
    PhoneNo VARCHAR(15) DEFAULT 'Unknown Phone' NOT NULL,
    PRIMARY KEY (Name));
```

Also, you can use this shorter form, which has the same effect:

```
CREATE TABLE Friend (
    Name     VARCHAR(50) PRIMARY KEY NOT NULL,
    PhoneNo VARCHAR(15) DEFAULT 'Unknown Phone' NOT NULL);
```

NOTE   *Remember that primary key columns aren't allowed to store* NULL *values. For this reason, SQL Server, Oracle, MySQL, and Access don't require you to include the* NOT NULL *clause on primary key columns. However, for DB2 you must specify* NOT NULL *when creating primary key columns.*

To test your newly created table, try to add a NULL for the name and then two identical names:

```
INSERT INTO Friend (PhoneNo) VALUES ('555 2323');
INSERT INTO Friend (Name, PhoneNo) VALUES ('John Doe', '12345678');
INSERT INTO Friend (Name, PhoneNo) VALUES ('John Doe', '87654321');
```

The first command fails on SQL Server, DB2, Access, and Oracle because you tried to insert NULL for the name; however, it works with MySQL, which breaks the rules (remember the earlier exercise) and automatically inserts an empty string instead of NULL.

The second statement works just fine, but the last one throws an error because you tried to insert a duplicate value on the primary key column. So, the database takes care of its integrity, just like you expected.

When a PRIMARY KEY constraint is defined, a unique index is automatically created for it. We'll discuss indexes later in this chapter.

Setting the UNIQUE Constraint

Apart from the primary key, you can have one or more unique columns. In this scenario, this can apply to the PhoneNo column; this, of course, isn't representative enough to be used as a primary key (and anyway you couldn't use it as a primary key because you can have only one primary key in the table, and that primary key is set on the Name column). However, you can mark it as unique to ensure you don't have more than one friend with the same phone number. Maybe this rule wouldn't be very good in a real-world example, but still it's an example of a rule that you can enforce within the database.

 NOTE *We briefly discussed unique columns in Chapter 1, "Understanding SQL and Relational Databases."*

After dropping the current Friend table, create it like this:

```
CREATE TABLE Friend (
    Name    VARCHAR(50) PRIMARY KEY NOT NULL,
    PhoneNo VARCHAR(15) UNIQUE);
```

Now duplicate phone numbers will be rejected by the database because they violate the UNIQUE constraint. The UNIQUE constraint works fine when combined with DEFAULT values, but the default value can be added only once.

There's a difference in the way that NULL values are accepted by the different databases on columns having the UNIQUE constraint—a detail that may affect how you use it in real-world scenarios.

Oracle, MySQL, and Access allow you to have as many NULL values as you like in a unique column, as long as the column isn't set with NOT NULL. DB2 doesn't permit NULL values in a unique column at all.

SQL Server, on the other hand, permits only a single NULL value in a unique column. Although in SELECT queries a NULL value doesn't equal another NULL (as you learned in Chapter 1, "Understanding SQL and Relational Databases"), SQL Server regards two NULL values as identical with regard to the UNIQUE constraint.

Setting CHECK Constraints

CHECK constraints are the most flexible kind of constraints. They allow you to pose a wide range of restrictions on the rows you modify or insert into the database.

 CAUTION CHECK *constraints aren't yet enforced in MySQL.*

The main points to keep in mind about CHECK constraints are the following:

- The way you define a CHECK constraint is similar to the conditions you place in the WHERE clause, and they're evaluated at the time a new row is added to the table or an existing row is modified.

- CHECK constraints can contain in their definition a logical expression or a number of logical expressions combined with AND or OR, parentheses, and so on; the condition expressed by CHECK must evaluate to true or to false.

- A CHECK constraint can refer only to columns of the row being introduced or modified in a table—other tables can't be referenced in a CHECK constraint.

- You can place multiple CHECK constraints on a single column.

- You can place table-level CHECK constraints that can then be associated with more than one column.

- The CHECK constraint isn't enforced for columns that don't receive a value (in other words, for columns that are NULL).

The following command creates the Friend table with a field named Age and a constraint called AgeConstraint, which prevents the Age column having a value of less than 10 or more than 100:

```
CREATE TABLE Friend (
    Name      VARCHAR(50) PRIMARY KEY NOT NULL,
    PhoneNo VARCHAR(15) DEFAULT 'Unknown Phone',
    Age       INT,
    CONSTRAINT CheckAge CHECK (Age BETWEEN 10 and 100));
```

If you don't want to provide a name for the constraint, you can remove the CONSTRAINT keyword from CREATE TABLE and optionally remove the comma between the column definition and the CHECK keyword:

```
CREATE TABLE Friend (
    Name      VARCHAR(50) PRIMARY KEY NOT NULL,
    PhoneNo VARCHAR(15) DEFAULT 'Unknown Phone',
    Age       INT CHECK (Age BETWEEN 10 and 100));
```

The following CREATE TABLE statement specifies an SSN field with a CHECK constraint that ensures proper Social Security number formatting:

```
CREATE TABLE Friend (
    Name      VARCHAR(50) PRIMARY KEY NOT NULL,
    PhoneNo VARCHAR(15) DEFAULT 'Unknown Phone',
    SSN       VARCHAR(15) NOT NULL,
    CHECK (SSN LIKE '[0-9][0-9][0-9]-[0-9][0-9]-[0-9][0-9][0-9][0-9]'));
```

You can use CHECK constraints with any expression that returns true or false. For example, you can use them to restrict the possible values of a column, with a condition such as CHECK (SEX IN ('Male', 'Female')), or compare the values of two columns such as in CHECK (ShipDate <= OrderDate).

You can use the CHECK constraint with both NULL and NOT NULL columns. However, if you insert NULL for a field that has a CHECK constraint on it, it really means that you're not inserting any value—so the CHECK constraint doesn't do anything in this case.

Copying Tables

Another useful way to create a new table in a database is to simply copy the structure of an existing table. The way you do this varies from relational database to relational database.

In Oracle, the following statement would create a new table called My_Friends, which would be an exact copy (with data) of the structure (columns and data types) of the Friend table:

```
CREATE TABLE My_Friends AS SELECT * FROM Friend;
```

Note, however, that this doesn't copy any constraint definitions (primary keys and so on). This is one of the reasons why it's often recommended that you create only your basic columns and data types using the CREATE TABLE statement and then add all other constraints using the ALTER TABLE command. You can then simply apply your ALTER TABLE scripts to any tables copied in this manner, rather than having to go back through and add all the constraints again manually. If you want to copy only the table structure, with no data, then simply specify a WHERE clause that can never evaluate to true:

```
CREATE TABLE My_Friends AS SELECT * FROM Friend
WHERE 1=0;
```

In DB2, the syntax is similar:

```
CREATE TABLE My_Friends AS
 (SELECT * FROM Friend) DEFINITION ONLY;
```

Here, you use the DEFINITION ONLY keywords to ensure that you copy only the table structure.

Again, in MySQL, the syntax is similar:

```
CREATE TABLE My_Friends SELECT * FROM Friend
WHERE 1=0;
```

You should note that, for some reason, MySQL converts VARCHAR data types to CHAR during this process.

Finally, in SQL Server, you do things somewhat differently:

```
SELECT * INTO My_Friends FROM Friend
WHERE 1=0;
```

Altering Database Tables

Once a data table has been created, you can change it by adding, deleting, or modifying columns, constraints, and so on. The actual syntax for doing this differs slightly from database to database, so we won't cover all the details here.

The ALTER TABLE command, along with its many options, allows you to make structural changes to existing data tables. If you want to add a new column named Address to the Friend table, this query does the trick:

```
ALTER TABLE Friend ADD Address VARCHAR(50);
```

NOTE *The table must be empty if you want to add* NOT NULL *columns!*

You can also add more columns with a single ALTER TABLE statement, which looks like this in Oracle and MySQL:

```
ALTER TABLE Friend ADD (EMail VARCHAR(25), ICQ VARCHAR(15));
```

For SQL Server and Access, you don't enclose the new columns in parentheses:

```
ALTER TABLE Friend ADD EMail varchar(25), ICQ varchar(15);
```

NOTE *DB2 doesn't support adding more than one column to a table in a single* ALTER TABLE *statement.*

If you want to remove the PhoneNo column, use the following:

```
ALTER TABLE Friend DROP COLUMN PhoneNo;
```

You can use ALTER TABLE to add or remove not only columns but also primary keys, foreign keys, or other kinds of constraints.

The following code snippet demonstrates how you can drop a UNIQUE constraint and add a primary key to an already existing table. As this example shows, you also provide a name for the PRIMARY KEY constraint:

```
CREATE TABLE Friend (
    Name VARCHAR(50) NOT NULL,
    PhoneNo VARCHAR(15),
    CONSTRAINT unq_name UNIQUE(Name));

ALTER TABLE Friend DROP CONSTRAINT unq_name;
ALTER TABLE Friend ADD CONSTRAINT PK_FriendName PRIMARY KEY (Name);
```

You can only create a PRIMARY KEY constraint on a table if the key column doesn't contain any duplicate or NULL values (and, of course, if there isn't already a primary key on that table).

This will work with SQL Server, Oracle, DB2, and Access. However, the syntax for MySQL is a little different. You can only use the ADD/DROP CONSTRAINT syntax with foreign keys. To add or drop a primary key, you use the syntax ADD/DROP PRIMARY KEY, and to add or drop an index (including a UNIQUE index), you use

ADD/DROP INDEX `<column_name>`. In both cases, if you're adding an index or primary key, you need to include the key column(s) in parentheses at the end of the statement. So, to drop the UNIQUE constraint and add a primary key in MySQL, you would use this:

```
ALTER TABLE Friend DROP INDEX Name;
ALTER TABLE Friend ADD PRIMARY KEY (Name);
```

 TIP *You can also use* ALTER TABLE *to change the details of an individual column, such as the data type or whether it can accept* NULL*s.*

Creating Temporary Tables

Temporary tables are tables that exist for a limited period of time or are limited to the current session or transaction. They're particularly useful in triggers or stored procedures when you need to quickly create a table for various tasks. For example, you can use temporary tables when you need to compare a set of data with the current data in the database. If you're thinking of using a cursor but could use a temporary table instead, then it's generally a good idea to use a temporary table (because cursors are bad for performance).

Let's quickly look at a simple example. You'll create a temporary table and fill it with the names of all the students and the average mark they scored over all their exams. You'll then query this table to find the students who did particularly well or particularly badly.

SQL Server

In SQL Server, you create temporary tables just like normal tables except that they have names beginning with # or ##. You use # for local temporary tables (which are visible only to the connection that created them) or ## for global temporary tables (which are visible to all connections).

SQL Server temporary tables are always created in the `tempdb` system database. If a temporary table isn't dropped explicitly by the connection that created it, it's usually dropped automatically as soon as the connection is closed.

Enter and execute the following lines in Query Analyzer:

```
CREATE TABLE #tmp (StudentName VARCHAR(50), AverageMark INT);
INSERT INTO #tmp
   SELECT Student.Name AS StudentName,
          AVG(Mark) AS AverageMark
   FROM StudentExam
      INNER JOIN Student
      ON StudentExam.StudentID = Student.StudentID
   GROUP BY StudentName;

SELECT StudentName, AverageMark FROM #tmp
   WHERE AverageMark < 50;
SELECT StudentName, AverageMark FROM #tmp
   WHERE AverageMark > 70;
```

Here you create a temporary table called #tmp and populate it using the INSERT INTO syntax you saw in Chapter 3, "Modifying Data." You then run two queries against this table, exactly as you would against a normal table:

```
StudentName       AverageMark

---------------   ------------

Gary Burton       48
StudentName       AverageMark
---------------   ------------

Emily Scarlett    80
Maria Fernandez   73
Steve Alaska      71
```

Oracle

In Oracle, you can create a temporary table using the CREATE GLOBAL TEMPORARY TABLE command instead of the usual CREATE TABLE. When you create a temporary table, you can specify whether the data should be preserved for the current session (by specifying an ON COMMIT PRESERVE ROWS clause) or only for the current transaction (ON COMMIT DELETE ROWS). Oracle doesn't automatically allocate space for temporary tables as it does for normal tables: Space will be dynamically allocated as new rows are inserted.

Although the data in Oracle temporary tables is transitory, the tables themselves aren't—after you've created a temporary table, it will remain available until you drop it (using the normal DROP TABLE command).

EXAMPLE: USING TEMPORARY TABLES (ORACLE)

Execute the following query in SQL*Plus:

```
CREATE GLOBAL TEMPORARY TABLE tmp
AS
SELECT Student.Name AS StudentName, AVG(Mark) AS AverageMark
FROM StudentExam
    INNER JOIN Student
    ON StudentExam.StudentID = Student.StudentID
GROUP BY Student.Name;

INSERT INTO tmp
    SELECT Student.Name AS StudentName, AVG(Mark) AS AverageMark
    FROM StudentExam
        INNER JOIN Student
        ON StudentExam.StudentID = Student.StudentID
    GROUP BY Student.Name;

SELECT StudentName, AverageMark FROM tmp WHERE AverageMark < 50;
SELECT StudentName, AverageMark FROM tmp WHERE AverageMark > 70;
```

Again, you create a temporary table called tmp to store the names and average marks of the students. Notice that you don't provide a list of column names and data types to define the table, but you provide a SELECT statement. This statement doesn't, however, fill the table, so you do that using a SELECT INTO statement. You can then query the table to find the students with very good or very poor averages:

StudentName	AverageMark
Gary Burton	48

StudentName	AverageMark
Emily Scarlett	80
Maria Fernandez	73
Steve Alaska	71

DB2

DB2 uses the `DECLARE GLOBAL TEMPORARY TABLE` statement to create a temporary table. You can define the table using either a standard list of columns, as in SQL Server, or a `SELECT` statement, as in Oracle.

When you create a temporary table in DB2, you need to tell DB2 where to put the table; to do this, you have to create a *tablespace*. There are different types of tablespaces in DB2, but to store temporary tables, you need to create a `USER TEMPORARY` tablespace. This type of tablespace can be accessed by users of the database (as opposed to system tablespaces, which can only be accessed by DB2 itself) and will be destroyed once the connection is closed. Tablespaces can be managed either by the system or by the database itself.

EXAMPLE: USING TEMPORARY TABLES (DB2)

Execute the following query in Command Center:

```
CREATE USER TEMPORARY TABLESPACE IUTemp
    MANAGED BY SYSTEM USING ('C:\IUTemp_tbsp');
DECLARE GLOBAL TEMPORARY TABLE tmp (
    StudentName VARCHAR(50), AverageMark INT) IN IUTemp;

INSERT INTO SESSION.tmp
    SELECT Student.Name AS StudentName, AVG(Mark) AS AverageMark
    FROM StudentExam
        INNER JOIN Student
        ON StudentExam.StudentID = Student.StudentID
    GROUP BY Student.Name;
```

```
SELECT StudentName, AverageMark FROM SESSION.tmp WHERE AverageMark < 50;
SELECT StudentName, AverageMark FROM SESSION.tmp WHERE AverageMark > 70;
```

Here you create a system-managed USER TEMPORARY tablespace called IUTemp, specifying that the data files will be stored in the C:\IUTemp_tbsp directory (change this as necessary for your system). This directory doesn't have to exist in advance—DB2 will create it if necessary:

```
CREATE USER TEMPORARY TABLESPACE IUTemp
  MANAGED BY SYSTEM USING ('C:\IUTemp_tbsp');
```

Once you've created the tablespace, you can create the table itself using the DECLARE GLOBAL TEMPORARY TABLE command. In this case, you specify the column definitions for the table explicitly, rather than using the AS SELECT syntax you saw with Oracle. Notice the IN clause, which tells DB2 which tablespace to create the table in:

```
DECLARE GLOBAL TEMPORARY TABLE tmp (
    StudentName VARCHAR(50), AverageMark INT) IN IUTemp;
```

Once you've created the table, you can populate it with an INSERT INTO...SELECT statement. Notice that the table is by default created in the SESSION schema, not the current user's schema, so you prefix the table name with SESSION (SESSION.tmp). You can then query this table as normal:

```
StudentName      AverageMark

---------------  ------------
Gary Burton      48

StudentName      AverageMark
---------------  ------------
Emily Scarlett   80
Maria Fernandez  73
Steve Alaska     71
```

MySQL

MySQL has the simplest syntax—you create temporary tables using the CREATE TEMPORARY TABLE statement, which has the same syntax as a normal CREATE TABLE statement. Temporary tables can be particularly useful in MySQL as a way of getting around the lack of support for subqueries.

EXAMPLE: USING TEMPORARY TABLES (MYSQL)

Execute the following query at the mysql command prompt:

```
CREATE TEMPORARY TABLE tmp (StudentName VARCHAR(50), AverageMark INT);

INSERT INTO tmp
    SELECT Student.Name AS StudentName, AVG(Mark) AS AverageMark
    FROM StudentExam
        INNER JOIN Student
        ON StudentExam.StudentID = Student.StudentID
    GROUP BY Student.Name;

SELECT StudentName, AverageMark FROM tmp WHERE AverageMark < 50;
SELECT StudentName, AverageMark FROM tmp WHERE AverageMark > 70;
```

In this example, you just create a temporary table named tmp with the StudentName and AverageMark columns and populate it using the INSERT INTO...SELECT statement. You then run your two queries against the tmp table:

```
StudentName       AverageMark

---------------   -----------
Gary Burton       48


StudentName       AverageMark
---------------   -----------
Emily Scarlett    80
Maria Fernandez   73
Steve Alaska      71
```

Using Sequences

Sequences are the objects that allow you to simulate autonumbered fields with Oracle. DB2 also support sequences.

A sequence is a database object that, when queried, always returns a new value. By default the sequence has a seed of one and an increment value of one. You can create such a sequence with a simple command like this:

```
CREATE SEQUENCE FriendIDSeq;
```

You create a sequence with an initial value of 1,000 like this:

```
CREATE SEQUENCE FriendIDSeq INCREMENT BY 1 START WITH 1000;
```

You can drop a sequence, like most database objects, using the DROP command:

```
DROP SEQUENCE FriendIDSeq;
```

In order to test the FriendIDSeq sequence, let's re-create the Friend table. This time you have a FriendID integer column as the primary key:

```
CREATE TABLE Friend (
    FriendID INT PRIMARY KEY NOT NULL,
    Name VARCHAR(50),
    PhoneNo VARCHAR(15) DEFAULT 'Unknown Phone');
```

Once the sequence and the new Friend table are in place, insert some new records into Friend like this:

```
INSERT INTO Friend (FriendID, Name, PhoneNo)
            VALUES (FriendIDSeq.NextVal, 'Mike', '123');
INSERT INTO Friend (FriendID, Name, PhoneNo)
            VALUES (FriendIDSeq.NextVal, 'John', '456');
INSERT INTO Friend (FriendID, Name, PhoneNo)
            VALUES (FriendIDSeq.NextVal, 'Cath', '789');
```

Now the Friend table contains something like this:

FriendID	Name	PhoneNo
1000	Mike	123
1001	John	456
1002	Cath	789

If you want to see the last sequence value generated, you can call its CurrVal property. This query displays the last value generated by FriendIDSeq:

```
SELECT FriendIDSeq.CurrVal FROM DUAL;
```

NOTE   *The* DUAL *table is a special table with one row and one column named* DUMMY *of type* CHAR(1). *This table is useful when you want to get quick information not related to any special table but rather from an external source or function, just like you did for querying the current value of the sequence. Another simple example for using* DUAL *is getting the current system value using* SELECT SYSDATE FROM DUAL *or calculating mathematical functions such as* SELECT POWER (2,5) FROM DUAL.

Sequences are particularly useful (in conjunction with triggers) for simulating autonumbering in Oracle. You'll look at how to do this in more detail in Chapter 13, "Triggers," where you look at triggers in depth, but let's look at a simple example here of how to do this in the different database systems.

Using Autonumbered Fields

You saw in Chapter 1, "Understanding SQL and Relational Databases," that database systems provide a way of automatically generating numerical values for columns when you add new records to a table. These auto-generated fields can be (and usually are) used in conjunction with the PRIMARY KEY constraint.

To create such a field, you use the IDENTITY keyword with SQL Server, AUTO_INCREMENT for MySQL, GENERATED AS IDENTITY for DB2, and AUTOINCREMENT for Access.

To test this feature, you'll add a separate primary key field to the `Friend` table, named `FriendID`, of type `INT`. You want the database to automatically supply values to this column whenever you insert new rows to the table. You'll then insert a new row and retrieve and display the last auto-generated ID inserted.

SQL Server

In SQL Server, you use the `IDENTITY` keyword to create an autonumbered column. SQL Server allows you to retrieve the value of the last auto-generated number using the `@@IDENTITY` variable.

EXAMPLE: AUTONUMBERED COLUMNS (SQL SERVER)

This statement creates the table with an autonumbered primary key column for SQL Server:

```
CREATE TABLE Friend (
    FriendID INT IDENTITY PRIMARY KEY NOT NULL,
    Name     VARCHAR(50),
    PhoneNo  VARCHAR(15) DEFAULT 'Unknown Phone');
```

With SQL Server, you can optionally specify a *seed* value (the first value that will be generated), and an *increment* value (which specifies by how much the auto-generated value increases on each iteration). By default, the seed and the increment are both one, but they can be specified as parameters of `IDENTITY` if you want to use other values. This is how you'd create the `Friend` table using a seed of 1,000 and an increment of one:

```
CREATE TABLE Friend (
    FriendID INT IDENTITY (1000, 1) PRIMARY KEY NOT NULL,
    Name     VARCHAR(50),
    PhoneNo  VARCHAR(15) DEFAULT 'Unknown Phone');
```

 NOTE *SQL Server doesn't allow you to supply values for* IDENTITY *columns manually—once you set a field as* IDENTITY, *you must let the database supply its values.*

Now insert a new row into `Friend` using this statement:

```
INSERT INTO Friend (Name, PhoneNo) VALUES ('Mike', '123');
```

This inserts a new row into the Friend table with a FriendID value equal to the identity seed value. In SQL Server, you can retrieve this value by reading the @@IDENTITY variable:

```
PRINT @@IDENTITY;
```

Oracle

As we've mentioned, you need to use triggers in Oracle to perform this. You'll look at this Oracle example in more detail in Chapter 13, "Triggers," but we'll present the basic code here for reference.

A *trigger* is essentially a stored procedure that executes automatically whenever a particular operation is requested, such as the insertion of a new row into the database. You can set up a sequence, use a trigger to retrieve the next value from the sequence whenever a new row is inserted into the Friend table, and use this value as the auto-generated number.

EXAMPLE: AUTONUMBERED COLUMNS (ORACLE)

First, create the Friend table as normal:

```
CREATE TABLE Friend (
    FriendID INT PRIMARY KEY NOT NULL,
    Name     VARCHAR(50),
    PhoneNo  VARCHAR(15) DEFAULT 'Unknown Phone');
```

Second, create the sequence and the trigger:

```
CREATE SEQUENCE SEQ;

CREATE OR REPLACE TRIGGER AUTONUMBER
BEFORE INSERT ON Friend
```

```
FOR EACH ROW
BEGIN
    SELECT SEQ.NEXTVAL
    INTO :NEW.FriendID FROM DUAL;
END;
/
```

You can now insert a new row. You don't need to specify the `FriendID` value because this will be supplied by the trigger before the row is inserted into the table. If you do supply a value for it, the supplied value will be overridden by the auto-generated value and simply ignored:

```
INSERT INTO Friend (Name, PhoneNo) VALUES ('Mike', '123');
```

You can now retrieve the new value by checking the current value of the sequence:

```
SELECT SEQ.CURRVAL FROM DUAL;
```

You use the `WHERE` clause so that you only have one row returned, not one row for every row in the table. The output from this query is as follows:

```
CURRVAL
--------
1
```

DB2

In DB2, you can create autonumbered columns by specifying a GENERATED ALWAYS AS IDENTITY clause. If you do this, the database will always supply an automatically generated value for the identity column and throw an error if you attempt to provide another value manually. You can also use GENERATED BY DEFAULT AS IDENTITY, in which case you're allowed to supply your own values.

EXAMPLE: AUTONUMBERED COLUMNS (DB2)

The DB2 command to create the table is as follows:

```
CREATE TABLE Friend (
    FriendID INT GENERATED ALWAYS AS IDENTITY PRIMARY KEY,
    Name     VARCHAR(50),
    PhoneNo  VARCHAR(15) DEFAULT 'Unknown Phone');
```

Next, insert a new row into the table:

```
INSERT INTO Friend (Name, PhoneNo) VALUES ('Mike', '123');
```

This inserts a new row into the Friend table with a FriendID value of one. You can now retrieve the value using this query:

```
SELECT FriendID FROM Friend
WHERE FriendID = IDENTITY_VAL_LOCAL();
```

You do it this way to ensure that only one row is returned (if you said SELECT IDENTITY_VAL_LOCAL() FROM Friend, then one row would be returned for every row in the Friend table).

The output of this query is as follows:

```
FriendID

---------

1
```

MySQL

With MySQL, you use the AUTO_INCREMENT keyword to create an autonumbered field. MySQL is more permissive than SQL Server, and it allows you to provide your own values for the AUTO_INCREMENT field if you want.

This MySQL statement creates the table:

```
CREATE TABLE Friend (
    FriendID INT AUTO_INCREMENT PRIMARY KEY NOT NULL,
    Name      VARCHAR(50),
    PhoneNo   VARCHAR(15) DEFAULT 'Unknown Phone');
```

Next, insert a new row into the table:

```
INSERT INTO Friend (Name, PhoneNo) VALUES ('Mike', '123');
```

You can now display the value of the auto-generated ID field using this query:

```
SELECT LAST_INSERT_ID();
```

The output from this is as follows:

```
last_insert_id()

----------------
1
```

Access

With Access, you use the AUTOINCREMENT keyword to create an autonumbered column.

 TIP   *With Access,* AUTOINCREMENT *is actually a separate data type rather than a column parameter. As such, when using* AUTOINCREMENT *you're not allowed to specify yet another data type (such as* INT*) as you did in the previous examples.*

This statement creates the table with an autonumbered primary key column for Access:

```
CREATE TABLE Friend (
   FriendID AUTOINCREMENT PRIMARY KEY NOT NULL,
   Name     VARCHAR(50),
   PhoneNo  VARCHAR(15) DEFAULT 'Unknown Phone');
```

Optionally, you can specify as AUTOINCREMENT parameters a *seed* value (the first value that will be generated) and an *increment* value (which specifies by how much the auto-generated value increases on each iteration). By default, the seed and the increment are both one. This is how you'd create the Friend table using a seed of 1,000 and an increment of one:

```
CREATE TABLE Friend (
   FriendID AUTOINCREMENT (1000, 1) PRIMARY KEY NOT NULL,
   Name     VARCHAR(50),
   PhoneNo  VARCHAR(15) DEFAULT 'Unknown Phone');
```

NOTE *Access doesn't allow you to manually supply values for* AUTOINCREMENT *fields.*

Using Indexes

Indexes are database objects designed to increase the overall speed of database operations by creating internal "lookup" tables to allow for very quick searches. They work on the presumption that the vast majority of database operations are read and search operations. Having an index in a table is likely to improve SELECT operations on that table, but it could slow down DELETE, UPDATE, and INSERT operations. In most cases, the gains of having an index on a frequently accessed column will considerably outweigh the drawbacks.

You can create one or more indexes on a particular table, each index working on one column or on a set of columns. When a table is indexed on a specific column, its rows are either indexed or physically arranged based on the values of that column and of the type of index. This allows the database to find information quickly if you perform a search based on the indexed columns. For example, if you have a long friends list in the Friend table, having an index on the Name column would significantly improve searches based on the name. This happens because instead of performing a full-table scan, the index is used to quickly find the requested record.

Indexes can slow down INSERT, UPDATE, and DELETE operations because the internal index structures need to be updated (or the table rows rearranged) each time such an operation occurs. For this reason, having too many indexes can slow down the general performance of the database and therefore should applied carefully.

The general rule of thumb is to set indexes on columns that are frequently used in WHERE or ORDER BY clauses, that are used in table joins, or that have foreign key relationships with other tables. However, especially for big databases, a carefully designed performance-testing plan can reveal the best combination of indexes for your database.

Also, from a performance standpoint, it's worth placing indexes on columns that aren't going to have much duplicated data (they're said to have *high selectivity*) and on columns for which the SELECT statements are likely to be highly restrictive—for example, when you're searching for a *particular* row rather than reading half of the table (in which case having an index may actually slow down the query).

Indexes can be unique or non-unique. Unique indexes don't permit repeating values on the indexed columns.

NOTE *Unique indexes are always created for columns that have* PRIMARY KEY *or* UNIQUE *constraints set.*

Indexes that are automatically created as a result of setting a constraint (PRIMARY KEY or UNIQUE) are removed when the constraint is removed, and they can't be removed separately. They're tied to the constraint that created them.

Creating Indexes

Let's consider the Friend table once again:

```
CREATE TABLE Friend (
    FriendID INT PRIMARY KEY NOT NULL,
    Name VARCHAR(50),
    PhoneNo VARCHAR(15) DEFAULT 'Unknown Phone');
```

If you're planning to do frequent searches on this table based on the name (such as, What is John's phone number?), placing an index on the Name column will improve the performance of your queries.

The command to create a non-unique index on Name is as follows:

```
CREATE INDEX NameIndex ON Friend (Name);
```

For unique indexes, you add the UNIQUE keyword:

```
CREATE UNIQUE INDEX NameIndex ON Friend (Name);
```

Make sure Friend is empty and execute the following INSERT statements:

```
INSERT INTO Friend (FriendID, Name, PhoneNo) VALUES (1,'Mike','1234567');
INSERT INTO Friend (FriendID, Name, PhoneNo) VALUES (2,'Mike','3333333');
INSERT INTO Friend (FriendID, Name, PhoneNo) VALUES (3,'Cath','7654321');
```

If you created a UNIQUE index, the second INSERT will be rejected because it duplicates an existing name.

Having an index on Name will now make queries such as the following much faster (supposing, of course, that the Friend table is filled with far more records than you inserted here):

```
SELECT FriendID, Name FROM Friend WHERE Name='Cath';
```

The same happens for queries returning multiple rows:

```
SELECT FriendID, Name FROM Friend WHERE Name LIKE 'M%';
```

However, there's one catch: Text columns are indexed from left to right. For this reason, queries such as the previous one use the index you created on Name. However, the index isn't used when you're searching for substrings that don't occur at the start of the string (that is, the first character of the search string is a wildcard, as in the following query). In such situations, a normal, full-table scan is performed to find the requested rows:

```
SELECT FriendID, Name FROM Friend WHERE Name LIKE '%ike';
```

Dropping Indexes

The SQL command to drop indexes is DROP INDEX. However, its exact syntax depends on the database vendor.

With SQL Server, you need to prefix the index name with the table name:

```
DROP INDEX Friend.PhoneNoIndex;
```

With Oracle and DB2, you just need to specify the index name:

```
DROP INDEX PhoneNoIndex;
```

With MySQL, you also need to specify both the table name and index name but use a different syntax:

```
DROP INDEX PhoneNoIndex ON Friend;
```

Understanding Declarative Referential Integrity and the FOREIGN KEY Constraint

You learned in Chapter 1, "Understanding SQL and Relational Databases," about the relationships that can exist between data tables; *Declarative Referential Integrity (DRI)* is what makes sure that the rules aren't broken.

You saw that both one-to-many and many-to-many relationships are physically implemented as one-to-many relationships (a many-to-many relationship is composed of two one-to-many relationships). By "declaring" these relationships to the database, you ensure the database will take care of itself and enforce those rules.

You can enforce a one-to-many relationship in the database through foreign keys, which tie the referencing table to the referenced table. To test foreign keys, you'll add something to the Friend scenario: You'll assume that each friend can have any number of phone numbers, thus creating a simple one-to-many scenario.

To implement this, you'll need to store the phone numbers in a separate table named Phone. Phone will have three columns: an ID column named PhoneID, which will be the primary key; a FriendID column, which links to the friend that has the phone number; and a PhoneNo column, which contains the actual phone number. Figure 12-1 shows the relationship between Phone and Friend.

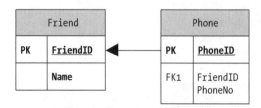

Figure 12-1. The relationship between Phone *and* Friend

The referential integrity in this case is between the FriendID column in the Phone table and the FriendID column in the Friend table. This ensures that each record in the Phone table belongs to a real record of the Friend table.

The arrow in Figure 12-1 shows the nature of the relationship that happens between Friend and Phone. It points to the *one* table of the one-to-many relationship, which is the table whose primary key field is being referenced.

> **NOTE** *The two columns you're connecting with the* FOREIGN KEY *constraint must be of the same (or at least similar) data type.*

The FOREIGN KEY constraint applies on the column in the referencing table—in this case, the FriendID field in Phone. So, let's build the two data tables.

> **TIP** *The basic syntax of specifying* FOREIGN KEY *constraints is the same for all databases. However, with MySQL there are a couple of tricks you need to know first.*

If you're using SQL Server, Oracle, DB2, or Access, create Friend and Phone like this:

```
CREATE TABLE Friend (FriendID INT PRIMARY KEY NOT NULL,
                     Name VARCHAR(50));

CREATE TABLE Phone (
    PhoneID INT PRIMARY KEY NOT NULL,
    FriendID INT,
    PhoneNo VARCHAR(20),
    CONSTRAINT FID_FK FOREIGN KEY(FriendID)
        REFERENCES Friend(FriendID));
```

Let's examine how you create the constraint in Phone. First, you use the CONSTRAINT keyword to supply a name for the new constraint. FOREIGN KEY(FriendID) specifies that you're placing a FOREIGN KEY constraint on the FriendID column in the current table (Phone). You then use the REFERENCES keyword to specify the column that the foreign key points to: In this case, you're referencing Friend(FriendID), which means the FriendID column in the Friend table.

This command creates a FOREIGN KEY constraint named FID_FK, which enforces the one-to-many relationship between Friend and Phone. As usual, if you're not interested in providing a name for the constraint, you can let the database take care of this by not supplying the CONSTRAINT keyword:

```
CREATE TABLE Phone
   (PhoneID INT PRIMARY KEY NOT NULL,
    FriendID INT,
    PhoneNo VARCHAR(20),
    FOREIGN KEY(FriendID) REFERENCES Friend(FriendID));
```

Because SQL is flexible, each database usually supports even more ways to create a FOREIGN KEY constraint. For example, if you're using SQL Server, here's a faster way to create Phone:

```
CREATE TABLE Phone (
   PhoneID INT PRIMARY KEY NOT NULL,
   FriendID INT FOREIGN KEY REFERENCES Friend(FriendID),
   PhoneNo VARCHAR(20));
```

MySQL supports foreign keys only with the InnoDB table type—it's not the first time you've encountered this table type because it's the most advanced table type supported by MySQL (as you saw in Chapter 10, "Transactions," it's the only one that fully supports the ACID transaction properties).

Both the referencing and referenced tables must be InnoDB tables, so don't forget to add TYPE=InnoDB at the end of the CREATE TABLE statement; otherwise, MySQL will simply ignore any FOREIGN KEY constraint you may define.

InnoDB tables also require you to create an index on the column being used as a foreign key. Here's how you create the Phone table with MySQL:

```
CREATE TABLE Phone (
   PhoneID INT PRIMARY KEY NOT NULL,
   FriendID INT,
   PhoneNo VARCHAR(20),
   FOREIGN KEY(FriendID) REFERENCES Friend(FriendID),
   INDEX idx1(FriendID))
TYPE=InnoDB;
```

You can test the relationship by executing the following commands:

```
INSERT INTO Friend (FriendID, Name) VALUES (1, 'Helen');
INSERT INTO Friend (FriendID, Name) VALUES (2, 'Susan');
INSERT INTO Phone (PhoneID, FriendID, PhoneNo)
   VALUES (1, 1, '555-HELEN');
INSERT INTO Phone (PhoneID, FriendID, PhoneNo)
   VALUES (2, 1, '555-HL-WORK');
INSERT INTO Phone (PhoneID, FriendID, PhoneNo)
   VALUES (3, 2, '555-SUZY-Q');
INSERT INTO Phone (PhoneID, FriendID, PhoneNo)
   VALUES (5, 9, '0982734833');
```

The last command will generate an error because you tried to add a phone number for a friend that doesn't exist (a friend with an ID of 9). Because the phone numbers are stored in a separate table, you need to do a table join in order to get a list with your friends and their phone numbers (you learned about table joins in Chapter 7, "Querying Multiple Tables"):

```
SELECT Friend.FriendID, Friend.Name, Phone.PhoneNo
FROM Friend
    INNER JOIN Phone
    ON Friend.FriendID = Phone.FriendID
ORDER BY Friend.Name;
```

The results are as follows:

```
Name                 PhoneNo

------------------   --------------------
Helen                555-HELEN
Helen                555-HELEN-WORK
Susan                555-SUZY-Q
```

 CAUTION *As you might expect, you can't drop a table if it's being referenced from another table.*

Using Database Schemas

Schemas allow you to create tables and to view and grant permissions for objects in a single transaction. Schemas are supported by SQL Server, Oracle, and DB2, and they're created with the CREATE SCHEMA command, which looks like this:

```
CREATE SCHEMA AUTHORIZATION <schema owner>
<schema body>
```

The schema body can contain CREATE TABLE, CREATE VIEW, and GRANT statements. If all statements in the body execute successfully, the transaction is committed. Otherwise, the changes are rolled back.

The individual statements inside the schema body aren't separated by delimiters, such as semicolons. Here's a typical CREATE SCHEMA statement, which creates two data tables for the user Chris and grants access to them to the user Mike:

```
CREATE SCHEMA AUTHORIZATION Chris
CREATE TABLE Friend (
    FriendID INT PRIMARY KEY NOT NULL, Name VARCHAR(50))
CREATE VIEW FriendsNames AS SELECT Name FROM Friend
GRANT SELECT ON FriendsNames TO Alice;
```

Within a schema, the created objects don't have to appear in logical order. To ensure this is true, drop the Friend table and the FriendsNames view and reverse the order of the statements inside the schema body:

```
CREATE SCHEMA AUTHORIZATION System
GRANT SELECT ON FriendsNames TO Alice
CREATE VIEW FriendsNames AS SELECT Name FROM Friend
CREATE TABLE Friend (
    FriendID INT PRIMARY KEY NOT NULL, Name VARCHAR(50));
```

This executes correctly, even though these statements would have generated errors if executed from within a trigger or a stored procedure; you grant access on a view that wasn't created yet, and you create the view "before" creating the table.

Summary

Whew—you've covered a lot of ground in this chapter! Databases are, indeed, complex objects with a life of their own and with rules and problems of their own.

The chapter started by showing how to create and drop databases. Then it continued by providing a closer look at how to create the most important database object—the data table. Data tables are smart objects, too—they know how to take care of their own integrity and know how to relate to other tables using foreign keys.

You also learned about other common objects that live inside a database: indexes, temporary tables, and sequences.

Triggers

TRIGGERS ARE ONE OF THE more complex mechanisms available to you for enforcing business rules, data integrity, and consistency inside a database. A *trigger* is a special kind of stored procedure that's associated with a particular table, and it automatically executes when data in the table is modified.

Using triggers, you can automate the execution of SQL code by having it react to certain events that happen to database tables. In this chapter, you'll learn about the following:

- Understanding what triggers are and how they work

- Logging table activity using AFTER triggers

- Creating triggers that respond to inputting, updating, and deleting data in a table

Because only SQL Server, Oracle, and DB2 support triggers, we won't cover MySQL or Access in this chapter. However, each database platform implements triggers slightly differently, so you'll see the code for creating and working with triggers in three Relational Database Management System (RDBMS)–specific sections.

What Are Triggers?

Triggers are essentially the event handlers of the database. When creating a trigger, you need to specify some important pieces of information.

Triggers are associated with data tables and are executed by reacting automatically to events. When creating a trigger, it's a basic requirement that you associate it with a table and specify the event or events on which it should fire. Do you want the trigger to execute when new rows are added to the table or when rows are deleted or updated? You're allowed to specify any of these actions (INSERT, DELETE, UPDATE) or any combination of them.

> **TIP** *There are scenarios when triggers aren't called, even though it may seem like they should be. For example, a* DELETE *trigger isn't called if the table records are deleted using a* TRUNCATE TABLE *command.* TRUNCATE TABLE *is an unlogged operation; it doesn't fire any triggers and can't be rolled back by transactions.*

Another decision you need to make is when exactly the trigger should fire. Because triggers are executed by events, they can be instructed to execute *before* or *after* those events occur. You can also create a trigger that executes *instead of* the event that fired it.

The final important part of a trigger is the code itself—the SQL procedure that executes when the trigger is fired.

Note that although a trigger is similar to a stored procedure in that it's made up of SQL statements, it can't take any input values or return any values—this makes sense because the trigger is called automatically by the database.

Inside the trigger code, each database has its own ways of telling you why the trigger was raised and which rows are about to be modified, updated, or deleted. In this chapter, you'll examine these details separately for each database.

You can create more than one trigger on a single data table. The actions that happen in a trigger can fire other triggers (in which case they're said to be *nested triggers*), and a trigger can even call itself recursively.

A Variety of Triggers

Based on the number of times a trigger executes when an event that affects multiple rows happens, triggers are categorized in statement-level triggers and row-level triggers:

- **Statement-level triggers**: A statement-level trigger executes only once, even if the INSERT, UPDATE, or DELETE statement that fired the trigger affects multiple rows.

- **Row-level triggers**: These triggers fire for each row affected by an INSERT, UPDATE, or DELETE statement. If an UPDATE affects 100 rows, the trigger will be executed 100 times, once for each row.

You can set both statement-level triggers and row-level triggers to execute *before, after,* or *instead of* the command that triggered them. Based on the time when the trigger executes relative to the event that fired it, there are three kinds of triggers:

BEFORE and AFTER **triggers:** Because triggers are executed by events, they can be set to fire *before* or *after* those events happen. It's important to keep in mind that BEFORE triggers fire before any existing constraints are checked; AFTER triggers only fire after the new rows have actually been modified (which implies that the command has passed the referential integrity constraints defined for the table). For this reason, AFTER triggers are often used in auditing applications (you'll see simple examples in action later in this chapter).

INSTEAD OF **triggers:** These are used when you want to replace the action intended by the user with some other actions—so the code defined in the trigger is executed in place of the statement that was actually issued. This is particularly useful for triggers that are associated with views. When a complex view is updated, you're likely to want its underlying data tables to be updated.

Some databases also support triggers that act on other events, such as table creation or modification, a user login or log out, database startup or shutdown, and so on. Please consult the documentation for your database to find out what it has in store for you in this area.

This chapter discusses each type of trigger, but focuses on the code examples on AFTER triggers because these are probably the most commonly used in day-to-day SQL programming.

Creating Triggers

The SQL-99 command for creating triggers is CREATE TRIGGER. You drop triggers via the DROP TRIGGER command. The SQL-99 syntax for creating triggers looks pretty ugly, and it isn't implemented as such by any database software. However, here it is for reference:

```
CREATE TRIGGER trigger_name
    { BEFORE | AFTER }
    {[DELETE] | [INSERT} | [UPDATE]
    [OF column [,...n]} ON table_name
    [REFERENCING {OLD [ROW] [AS] old_name | NEW [ROW] [AS] new_name
     OLD TABLE [AS] old_name | NEW TABLE [AS] new_name}]
    [FOR EACH { ROW | STATEMENT }]
    [WHEN (conditions)]
<<SQL code block>>
```

It looks rather complex, but as you work through some examples, things will become clearer.

The syntax for dropping a trigger is the same for all platforms:

```
DROP TRIGGER trigger_name;
```

Using Triggers

Triggers are complex beasts, with applications in programming, administration, security, and so on. Typical uses for triggers include the following:

- **Supplementing Declarative Referential Integrity (DRI)**: You know DRI is done using foreign keys. However, there are times when the foreign key isn't powerful enough because there are complex kinds of table relationships it can't deal with (such as the ones that spread across more databases or database servers).

- **Enforcing complex business rules**: When data is being modified in a table, you can use a trigger to make sure that no complex business rules or data integrity rules are broken.

- **Creating audit trails**: In these examples, you'll see how to log all the operations that take place on a data table.

- **Simulating functionality**: They can simulate the functionality of CHECK constraints but across tables, databases, or database servers.

- **Substituting statements**: You can substitute your own statements instead of the action that was intended by the user. This is particularly useful when the user tries to insert data in a view, and you intercept this and update the underlying tables instead.

Yes, triggers are a powerful and versatile feature you can use to control many aspects of your database operation. However, this control comes at the expense of database processing power. Triggers definitely have their place but should not be used where simple constraints, such as foreign keys for referential integrity, will suffice.

In this chapter, you'll implement a simple auditing example using AFTER triggers. This example will use statement-level triggers for SQL Server and row-level triggers for Oracle and DB2.

In the examples, you'll use a simple version of the Friend table. You'll see how to log changes that happen to it using a second table, FriendAudit. For now, remove your existing Friend table and re-create it like this:

```
CREATE TABLE Friend (Name VARCHAR(50) PRIMARY KEY NOT NULL,
                     PhoneNo VARCHAR(15));
```

CAUTION *Remember that if you need to drop* Friend *and it's being referenced from the* Phone *table you created earlier through a* FOREIGN KEY *constraint, you need to drop the* Phone *table first or remove the* FOREIGN KEY *constraint in* Phone.

You'll create a FriendAudit table separately for each database with which you'll work. Figure 13-1 shows its structure.

Figure 13-1. The FriendAudit *table*

The FriendAuditID primary key uniquely identifies each record.

The Operation field will contain "Update", "Insert", or "Delete", depending on the operation you're logging. The other fields will contain details about the specific operation.

For INSERT operations, you'll populate the NewName and NewPhone fields, and OldName and OldPhone will contain NULLs. For DELETE operations, you'll populate the OldName and OldPhone, and NewName and NewPhone will contain NULLs. On UPDATE operations, all fields will be populated, specifying both the old friend values and the new updated ones.

Working with SQL Server Triggers

SQL Server supports only statement-level triggers. It doesn't support row-level triggers. This means that if you issue a DELETE command that deletes 10 rows, the trigger will fire once for the entire statement—not 10 times, once for each deleted row.

SQL Server doesn't support BEFORE triggers, but it supports AFTER (also named FOR) triggers and, starting with SQL Server 2000, INSTEAD OF triggers.

The important difference between AFTER (FOR) triggers and INSTEAD OF triggers is that AFTER triggers are called after any existing constraints have been checked. INSTEAD OF triggers are called immediately, even if the rows being inserted or updated wouldn't pass existing constraints.

Working with SQL Server triggers implies working with two special data tables: Inserted and Deleted. These tables exist only inside the trigger, and they're the means by which SQL Server tells you what happened and why the trigger was called.

When the trigger fires because of an INSERT statement, the row or rows that were inserted (or were going to be inserted, in case of an INSTEAD OF trigger) are saved in the Inserted table. Similarly, when deleted, they're available through the Deleted table. UPDATE operations are regarded as a pair of DELETE and INSERT operations—the old values are saved to Deleted, and the new ones to Inserted.

 TIP Inserted *and* Deleted *have the same structure as the table on which the trigger is created.*

Let's now start playing with some triggers using the scenario introduced earlier.

Logging Table Activity Using AFTER Triggers

Let's first create the FriendAudit table that will record the log data:

```
CREATE TABLE FriendAudit
(FriendAuditID INT IDENTITY PRIMARY KEY NOT NULL,
 Operation VARCHAR(10),
 RecordedOn DateTime DEFAULT GETDATE(),
 OldName VARCHAR(50),
 NewName VARCHAR(50),
 OldPhone VARCHAR(15),
 NewPhone VARCHAR(15));
```

In this code, you supplied a default value of GETDATE() for the RecordedOn field; so whenever you add new values to FriendAudit without specifying a value for RecordedOn, the current date and time will be automatically supplied.

Logging INSERT Operations

Let's start by logging only the INSERT operations that happen to your table. Create LogFriendTrigger like this:

```
CREATE TRIGGER LogFriendTrigger
ON Friend
FOR INSERT
```

```
AS
DECLARE @NewName VARCHAR(50)
DECLARE @NewPhone VARCHAR(15)

SELECT @NewName=Name FROM Inserted
SELECT @NewPhone=PhoneNo FROM Inserted

INSERT INTO FriendAudit (Operation, NewName, NewPhone)
VALUES ('Insert',@NewName,@NewPhone);
```

Let's test the new trigger by inserting some values to Friend:

```
INSERT INTO Friend(Name, PhoneNo) VALUES('Jerry', '001-Jerry')
INSERT INTO Friend(Name, PhoneNo) VALUES('Harrison', '999-Harry');
INSERT INTO Friend(Name, PhoneNo) VALUES('Peter', '223223223');
```

Now let's see what happened to FriendAudit:

```
SELECT * FROM FriendAudit;
```

Figure 13-2 shows the results.

	FriendAuditID	Operation	RecordedOn	OldName	NewName	OldPhone	NewPhone
1	1	Insert	2003-03-10 00:12:35.513	NULL	Jerry	NULL	001-Jerry
2	2	Insert	2003-03-10 00:12:35.633	NULL	Harrison	NULL	999-Harry
3	3	Insert	2003-03-10 00:12:35.633	NULL	Peter	NULL	223223223

Figure 13-2. The FriendAudit *table*

The trigger can be improved (you'll see in a minute why and how), but it works well on most occasions. When creating the trigger, you needed to specify its name, the table it protects, and the action on which it fires:

```
CREATE TRIGGER LogFriendTrigger
ON Friend
FOR INSERT
```

Then the game begins. The body of LogFriendTrigger reads Name and PhoneNo from Inserted (remember that Inserted has the same structure as Friend) and saves them to FriendAudit by using two variables named @NewName and @NewPhone:

```
AS
DECLARE @NewName VARCHAR(50)
DECLARE @NewPhone VARCHAR(15)
```

```
SELECT @NewName=Name FROM Inserted
SELECT @NewPhone=PhoneNo FROM Inserted

INSERT INTO FriendAudit (Operation, NewName, NewPhone)
VALUES ('Insert',@NewName,@NewPhone)
```

The problem with this implementation is that if more rows are inserted using a single SQL statement (say, with INSERT INTO...SELECT), the trigger fires only once, and only one record is added to FriendAudit. In the following exercise, you'll see how to deal with this scenario.

Logging DELETE Operations

Here, not only will you improve your trigger to log DELETE operations, but you'll also improve the way it handles INSERT operations.

For situations when you want to change an existing trigger, instead of dropping and re-creating it, SQL Server provides you with the ALTER TRIGGER command. Execute the following command:

```
ALTER TRIGGER LogFriendTrigger
ON Friend
FOR INSERT, DELETE
AS

IF EXISTS (SELECT 1 FROM Inserted)
  BEGIN
    INSERT INTO FriendAudit (Operation, NewName, NewPhone)
      SELECT 'Insert', Inserted.Name, Inserted.PhoneNo
      FROM Inserted
  END

ELSE IF EXISTS (SELECT 1 FROM Deleted)
  BEGIN
    INSERT INTO FriendAudit (Operation, OldName, OldPhone)
      SELECT 'Delete', Deleted.Name, Deleted.PhoneNo
      FROM Deleted
  END;
```

To test the new trigger, just delete the rows you inserted previously:

```
DELETE FROM Friend;
```

Note that this DELETE statement affects more rows—so using a logging similar to the one used in the first trigger (for INSERT operations) would have only logged a single item, not all the deleted rows. Now if you read the FriendAudit table, you see something like Figure 13-3.

	FriendAuditID	Operation	RecordedOn	OldName	NewName	OldPhone	NewPhone
1	1	Insert	2003-03-10 00:12:35.513	NULL	Jerry	NULL	001-Jerry
2	2	Insert	2003-03-10 00:12:35.633	NULL	Harrison	NULL	999-Harry
3	3	Insert	2003-03-10 00:12:35.633	NULL	Peter	NULL	223223223
4	4	Delete	2003-03-10 00:17:02.600	Harrison	NULL	999-Harry	NULL
5	5	Delete	2003-03-10 00:17:02.600	Jerry	NULL	001-Jerry	NULL
6	6	Delete	2003-03-10 00:17:02.600	Peter	NULL	223223223	NULL

Figure 13-3. The FriendAudit *table*

In the new trigger, first you see the new FOR DELETE clause in its definition:

```
ALTER TRIGGER LogFriendTrigger
ON Friend
FOR INSERT, DELETE
AS
```

Second, using IF clauses, you check if the trigger has been called because a row was inserted or deleted. This detail is important because you need to know from which table to gather the information to save in FriendAudit—from Inserted or from Deleted?

You do this by first verifying if there are any rows in the Inserted table:

```
IF EXISTS (SELECT 1 FROM Inserted)
```

If there are any rows in Inserted, you copy them into FriendAudit with INSERT INTO combined with a SELECT clause. (Remember that you learned about this construct in Chapter 3, "Modifying Data.") For example:

```
IF EXISTS (SELECT 1 FROM Inserted)
   BEGIN
     INSERT INTO FriendAudit (Operation, NewName, NewPhone)
       SELECT 'Insert', Inserted.Name, Inserted.PhoneNo
       FROM Inserted
   END
```

This method has the advantage that it works even when multiple rows have been added to Friend in a single SQL statement.

You then do the same test for Deleted although this time it's not really necessary. Because this is a FOR INSERT, DELETE trigger, if no rows have been inserted, you can be sure it was a DELETE operation that executed the trigger. You use the same technique to extract rows from the Deleted table and append them to FriendAudit:

```
ELSE IF EXISTS (SELECT 1 FROM Deleted)
  BEGIN
    INSERT INTO FriendAudit (Operation, OldName, OldPhone)
      SELECT 'Delete', Deleted.Name, Deleted.PhoneNo
      FROM Deleted
  END
```

Logging UPDATE Operations

When a trigger is fired after an UPDATE operation, both Inserted and Deleted tables are populated. The following example shows the new trigger, which logs INSERT, DELETE, and UPDATE operations to FriendAudit. It also displays a message specifying what kind of operation was logged.

Enter the following code to amend the trigger:

```
ALTER TRIGGER LogFriendTrigger
ON Friend
FOR INSERT, DELETE, UPDATE
AS

IF EXISTS (SELECT 1 FROM Inserted) AND EXISTS (SELECT 1 FROM DELETED)
  BEGIN
    INSERT INTO FriendAudit (Operation, OldName, OldPhone, NewName, NewPhone)
      SELECT 'Update', d.Name, d.PhoneNo, i.Name, i.PhoneNo
      FROM Deleted d JOIN Inserted i
      ON d.Name = i.Name
    PRINT 'Update Logged'
  END
ELSE IF EXISTS (SELECT 1 FROM Inserted)
  BEGIN
    INSERT INTO FriendAudit (Operation, NewName, NewPhone)
      SELECT 'Insert', Inserted.Name, Inserted.PhoneNo
      FROM Inserted
    PRINT 'Insert Logged'
  END
ELSE IF EXISTS (SELECT 1 FROM Deleted)
  BEGIN
    INSERT INTO FriendAudit (Operation, OldName, OldPhone)
```

```
      SELECT 'Delete', Deleted.Name, Deleted.PhoneNo
      FROM Deleted
    PRINT 'Delete Logged'
  END;
```

To test the new trigger, proceed with the following steps. First, clear the Friend and FriendAudit tables (note that the order is important):

```
DELETE FROM Friend;
DELETE FROM FriendAudit;
```

Then perform the following operations on Friend:

```
INSERT INTO Friend(Name, PhoneNo) VALUES('Jerry', '001-Jerry');
INSERT INTO Friend(Name, PhoneNo) VALUES('Harrison', '999-Harry');
INSERT INTO Friend(Name, PhoneNo) VALUES('Peter', '223223223');
UPDATE Friend SET PhoneNo = 'Unknown';
DELETE FROM Friend;
```

Now, if you read the FriendAudit table, you should see something like Figure 13-4.

	FriendAuditID	Operation	RecordedOn	OldName	NewName	OldPhone	NewPhone
1	7	Insert	2003-03-10 00:19:20.057	NULL	Jerry	NULL	001-Jerry
2	8	Insert	2003-03-10 00:19:20.057	NULL	Harrison	NULL	999-Harry
3	9	Insert	2003-03-10 00:19:20.067	NULL	Peter	NULL	223223223
4	10	Update	2003-03-10 00:19:20.077	Harrison	Harrison	999-Harry	Unknown
5	11	Update	2003-03-10 00:19:20.077	Jerry	Jerry	001-Jerry	Unknown
6	12	Update	2003-03-10 00:19:20.077	Peter	Peter	223223223	Unknown
7	13	Delete	2003-03-10 00:19:20.077	Harrison	NULL	Unknown	NULL
8	14	Delete	2003-03-10 00:19:20.077	Jerry	NULL	Unknown	NULL
9	15	Delete	2003-03-10 00:19:20.077	Peter	NULL	Unknown	NULL

Figure 13-4. The FriendAudit *table*

The latest version of the trigger is interesting; take a closer look at the piece of code that logs UPDATE operations:

```
IF EXISTS (SELECT 1 FROM Inserted) AND EXISTS (SELECT 1 FROM DELETED)
  BEGIN
    INSERT INTO FriendAudit (Operation, OldName, OldPhone, NewName, NewPhone)
      SELECT 'Update', d.Name, d.PhoneNo, i.Name, i.PhoneNo
      FROM Deleted d JOIN Inserted i
      ON d.Name = i.Name
    PRINT ''Update Logged'
  END
```

An inner join is used to get the necessary data to populate FriendAudit.

Another Technique with the Same Results

In LogFriendTrigger, you can populate the FriendAudit table with a single query by making a FULL JOIN between Inserted and Deleted—that's good news for lazy fingers. However, by only using the full join, you can't populate the Operation field differently based on the operation being done:

```
ALTER TRIGGER LogFriendTrigger
ON Friend
FOR INSERT, DELETE, UPDATE
AS

INSERT INTO FriendAudit (Operation, OldName, OldPhone, NewName, NewPhone)
  SELECT 'Log', d.Name, d.PhoneNo, i.Name, i.PhoneNo
    FROM Deleted d FULL JOIN Inserted i
    ON d.Name = i.Name;
```

If you want to make sure Operation is correctly filled, the following is a possible approach that also uses IF and CASE statements:

```
ALTER TRIGGER LogFriendTrigger
ON Friend
FOR INSERT, DELETE, UPDATE
AS

DECLARE @Operation TINYINT
SELECT @Operation=0
IF EXISTS (SELECT 1 FROM Inserted) SELECT @Operation = @Operation + 1
IF EXISTS (SELECT 2 FROM Deleted) SELECT @Operation = @Operation + 2

INSERT INTO FriendAudit (Operation, OldName, OldPhone, NewName, NewPhone)
  SELECT CASE @Operation
            WHEN 1 THEN 'Insert'
            WHEN 2 THEN 'Delete'
            WHEN 3 THEN 'Update'
         END,
         d.Name, d.PhoneNo, i.Name, i.PhoneNo
    FROM Deleted d FULL JOIN Inserted i
    ON d.Name = i.Name;
```

Enabling and Disabling Triggers

There are times when,for performance reasons, you want to temporarily disable existing triggers. A common scenario of this is during large data loads into the database, when disabling the triggers can considerably improve performance.

When created, triggers are enabled by default. You can turn off a trigger using the ALTER TABLE command. Here's how you can disable LogFriendTrigger:

```
ALTER TABLE Friend DISABLE TRIGGER LogFriendTrigger;
```

And here's how you enable it again:

```
ALTER TABLE Friend ENABLE TRIGGER LogFriendTrigger;
```

To enable or disable all existing triggers associated with a table, use ALL instead of a specific trigger name.

Working with Oracle Triggers

Oracle triggers are very powerful. Oracle supports BEFORE, AFTER, and INSTEAD OF triggers.

AFTER triggers execute after the intended SQL command executes; they fire only if the SQL command doesn't break any constraints existing on that data table. BEFORE and INSTEAD OF triggers fire before the command executes (so before any constraints are checked), allowing you to perform changes on the actions originally intended by the user.

With Oracle you can have statement-level triggers or row-level triggers. With statement-level triggers, a SQL command that affects multiple rows will execute the trigger only once (just like with SQL Server). In Oracle, statement-level triggers are most often used to enforce various security measures on the actions that can be performed on the data, rather than actually controlling and modifying the data that gets changed, inserted, or deleted.

Row-level triggers are invoked for each row that's affected by the SQL command. If a single query updated 100 rows, the row-level trigger is called 100 times for each inserted row. Inside a row-level trigger, you can refer to the *old* and *new* values of the row for which the trigger was invoked using special accessors. These are called by default :OLD and :NEW, but the CREATE TRIGGER syntax permits changing these default names.

You can access the row being inserted using :NEW and the row being deleted with :OLD. An UPDATE trigger populates both :NEW and :OLD.

TIP *After writing a trigger you may be told that it wasn't correctly compiled. If this is the case, you can use the* SHOW ERRORS *command to see a detailed list with the errors.*

Oracle also supports database-level triggers and schema-level triggers, which are useful for automating database maintenance and audition actions or for providing additional database security monitoring. Schema-level triggers can watch for CREATE TABLE, ALTER TABLE, and DROP TABLE events and react to them. You can set database-level triggers to fire on database events such as errors, logons, log offs, shutdown operations, and startup operations.

Logging Table Activity Using AFTER Triggers

You start by creating the FriendAudit table that will hold the audit information:

```
CREATE TABLE FriendAudit
(FriendAuditID INT PRIMARY KEY NOT NULL,
 Operation VARCHAR(10),
 RecordedOn DATE DEFAULT SysDate,
 OldName VARCHAR(50),
 NewName VARCHAR(50),
 OldPhone VARCHAR(15),
 NewPhone VARCHAR(15));
```

In this code, we supplied the SysDate function as the default value for the RecordedOn field (this has a similar result to using CURRENT_DATE, which you saw in the previous chapter), so whenever you add new values to FriendAudit without specifying a value for RecordedOn, the current date and time will be automatically supplied.

Let's also create a sequence named FriendAuditIDSeq, which you'll use to generate unique ID values for FriendAudit:

```
CREATE SEQUENCE FriendAuditIDSeq;
```

Logging INSERT Operations

So, let's start by creating a simple trigger that logs INSERT operations that happen to Friend.

Create the trigger using the following CREATE TRIGGER command:

```
CREATE TRIGGER FriendAuditTrigger
AFTER INSERT ON Friend
FOR EACH ROW
BEGIN
  INSERT INTO FriendAudit (FriendAuditID, Operation, NewName, NewPhone)
  VALUES (FriendAuditIDSeq.NEXTVAL, 'Insert ', :NEW.Name, :NEW.PhoneNo);
END;
/
```

Remember that you can use SHOW ERRORS to see what happened if anything went wrong.

Let's test the trigger now. Add three records to Friend using the following queries:

```
INSERT INTO Friend(Name, PhoneNo) VALUES('Jerry', '001-Jerry');
INSERT INTO Friend(Name, PhoneNo) VALUES('Harrison', '999-Harry');
INSERT INTO Friend(Name, PhoneNo) VALUES('Peter', '223223223');
```

Now you can query FriendAudit and see that your trigger worked as expected. You created FriendAuditTrigger as an AFTER INSERT, row-level trigger:

```
CREATE TRIGGER FriendAuditTrigger
AFTER INSERT ON Friend
FOR EACH ROW
```

Because it's an AFTER trigger, it's invoked only after all other constraints have been checked and the new row has been introduced. This is what you need because in this case you want to log only the operations that have succeeded—you're not interested in recording failed attempts.

If you wanted to also record failed attempts, you could have used a BEFORE trigger or both BEFORE and AFTER triggers—remember that you're allowed to place multiple triggers on a single table.

The body of the trigger gets data from :NEW and saves it into FriendAudit:

```
BEGIN
  INSERT INTO FriendAudit (FriendAuditID, Operation, NewName, NewPhone)
  VALUES (FriendAuditIDSeq.NEXTVAL, 'Insert ', :NEW.Name, :NEW.PhoneNo);
END;
```

Note that you use the FriendAuditIDSeq sequence to generate a value for the primary key.

Applying Conditions for the Trigger

Oracle permits adding conditions that control whether the trigger should execute. You do this with the WHEN parameter in CREATE TRIGGER.

With Oracle, instead of CREATE TRIGGER, you use CREATE OR REPLACE TRIGGER. With this command, if the trigger already exists, it's simply replaced by the new definition, without requiring you to drop the trigger first. If the trigger already exists, CREATE OR REPLACE TRIGGER has the same effect as SQL Server's ALTER TRIGGER.

The following trigger only logs INSERT operations when the name to be inserted is Peter:

```
CREATE OR REPLACE TRIGGER FriendAuditTrigger
AFTER INSERT ON Friend
FOR EACH ROW
WHEN (NEW.Name='Peter')
BEGIN
  INSERT INTO FriendAudit (FriendAuditID, Operation, NewName, NewPhone)
  VALUES (FriendAuditIDSeq.NEXTVAL, 'Insert ', :NEW.Name, :NEW.PhoneNo);
END;
/
```

In order to test the trigger, let's first clear the Friend and FriendAudit tables:

```
DELETE FROM Friend;
DELETE FROM FriendAudit;
```

Now execute the INSERT statements again:

```
INSERT INTO Friend(Name, PhoneNo) VALUES('Jerry', '001-Jerry');
INSERT INTO Friend(Name, PhoneNo) VALUES('Harrison', '999-Harry');
INSERT INTO Friend(Name, PhoneNo) VALUES('Peter', '223223223');
```

You'll see that only the last insert was logged into FriendAudit. This happens because you added the WHEN parameter when creating the trigger:

```
WHEN (NEW.Name='Peter')
```

This makes the trigger execute only when the Name column of the inserted row has the value of 'Peter'. Note that here you don't place : before NEW.

Logging DELETEs and UPDATEs

Okay, you've learned how to log INSERTS. Let's now complicate the trigger to log all operations: inserts, updates, and deletes. Let's first write the new trigger, and then we'll comment upon it:

```
CREATE OR REPLACE TRIGGER FriendAuditTrigger
AFTER INSERT OR DELETE OR UPDATE ON Friend
FOR EACH ROW
BEGIN
  IF INSERTING THEN
    INSERT INTO FriendAudit (FriendAuditID, Operation, NewName, NewPhone)
    VALUES (FriendAuditIDSeq.NEXTVAL, 'Insert ', :NEW.Name, :NEW.PhoneNo);
  ELSIF DELETING THEN
    INSERT INTO FriendAudit (FriendAuditID, Operation, OldName, OldPhone)
    VALUES (FriendAuditIDSeq.NEXTVAL, 'Delete ', :OLD.Name, :OLD.PhoneNo);
  ELSIF UPDATING THEN
    INSERT INTO FriendAudit (FriendAuditID, Operation,
                               OldName, OldPhone, NewName, NewPhone)
    VALUES (FriendAuditIDSeq.NEXTVAL, 'Update ',
             :OLD.Name, :OLD.PhoneNo, :NEW.Name, :NEW.PhoneNo);
  END IF;
END;
/
```

Let's test the new trigger. First, clear the existing the tables, in this order:

```
DELETE FROM Friend;
DELETE FROM FriendAudit;
```

Second, execute the following operations:

```
INSERT INTO Friend(Name, PhoneNo) VALUES('Jerry', '001-Jerry');
INSERT INTO Friend(Name, PhoneNo) VALUES('Harrison', '999-Harry');
INSERT INTO Friend(Name, PhoneNo) VALUES('Peter', '223223223');
UPDATE Friend SET PhoneNo = 'Unknown';
DELETE FROM Friend;
```

Now if you read the FriendAudit table, you'll see there are three INSERT operations, three UPDATE operations, and finally three DELETE operations logged.

To implement the new functionality, you first instructed the trigger to fire after any INSERT, DELETE, or UPDATE actions:

```
CREATE OR REPLACE TRIGGER FriendAuditTrigger
AFTER INSERT OR DELETE OR UPDATE ON Friend
FOR EACH ROW
```

Inside the trigger you can test the kind of SQL command that caused the trigger to fire using IF conditional statements. If the trigger is fired because of an INSERT operation, you execute the SQL you already know from the previous exercises:

```
IF INSERTING THEN
   INSERT INTO FriendAudit (FriendAuditID, Operation, NewName, NewPhone)
   VALUES (FriendAuditIDSeq.NEXTVAL, 'Insert ', NEW.Name, :NEW.PhoneNo);
```

The trigger has similar behavior for rows that are being deleted or updated. Note that in case of updated rows, you get information from both :OLD and :NEW, and you store the old and new values into the FriendAudit table.

Implementing Autonumbering Functionality Using Triggers

As you can see, when inserting new records into FriendAudit, you always specify a value for FriendAuditID using the FriendAuditIDSeq sequence.

Using a sequence and a trigger, you can simulate in Oracle the autonumbering functionality that's available with SQL Server, DB2, MySQL, and Access.

For the purpose of this example, let's assume that you don't want to manually supply a new value for FriendAuditID when inserting a new row into FriendAudit— you want the database do this for you.

The following code shows how to create the FriendAuditIDSeq sequence and how to use it in a trigger named FriendAuditIDAutonumberTrigger. This is a BEFORE INSERT trigger; it specifies a value for the FriendAuditID before the actual INSERT happens:

```
CREATE SEQUENCE FriendAuditIDSeq;

CREATE OR REPLACE TRIGGER FriendAuditIDAutonumberTrigger
BEFORE INSERT ON FriendAudit
FOR EACH ROW
BEGIN
    SELECT FriendAuditIDSeq.NEXTVAL
    INTO :NEW.FriendAuditID FROM DUAL;
END;
/
```

So, this time you have a BEFORE INSERT trigger. This is a must because you need to supply a value for the ID column before this is added to the database.

The trigger's body sets the FriendAuditID column to the next value of the sequence; it's exactly what you were doing manually in the past, except this time it's all handled by the trigger:

```
SELECT FriendAuditIDSeq.NEXTVAL
INTO :NEW.FriendAuditID FROM DUAL;
```

Note this trigger supplies a new value, without checking if you supplied our own; in other words, if you specify your own ID values, they'll be ignored (or better said, overwritten).

Once the trigger is in place, the technique of finding out the last number generated is still the same: FriendAuditIDSeq.CurrVal returns the current value of the sequence. The following simple query types the current value of the sequence:

```
SELECT FriendAuditIDSeq.CurrVal FROM Dual;
```

After having the autonumbering functionality in place, you don't need to manually specify values when inserting new ID values to FriendAudit. If you do specify any values, they're overridden by FriendAuditIDAutonumberTrigger anyway. In this case, FriendAuditTrigger should look like this:

```
CREATE OR REPLACE TRIGGER FriendAuditTrigger
AFTER INSERT OR DELETE OR UPDATE ON Friend
FOR EACH ROW
BEGIN
  IF INSERTING THEN
    INSERT INTO FriendAudit (Operation, NewName, NewPhone)
    VALUES ('Insert ', :NEW.Name, :NEW.PhoneNo);
  ELSIF DELETING THEN
    INSERT INTO FriendAudit (Operation, OldName, OldPhone)
    VALUES ('Delete ', :OLD.Name, :OLD.PhoneNo);
  ELSIF UPDATING THEN
    INSERT INTO FriendAudit (Operation, OldName, OldPhone, NewName, NewPhone)
    VALUES ('Update ', :OLD.Name, :OLD.PhoneNo, :NEW.Name, :NEW.PhoneNo);
  END IF;
END;
/
```

In this newer version of FriendAuditTrigger you don't specify your own values for the FriendAuditID column anymore. Repeat the tests from the previous test, and you'll see that everything works as expected.

Enabling and Disabling Triggers

There are times when you want to temporarily disable existing triggers. A common scenario for this is during large data loads into the database, when disabling the triggers can considerably improve the performance.

TIP   *When created, triggers are enabled by default.*

To manually enable and disable triggers, you use the ALTER TRIGGER command. Here are the commands that enable and disable FriendAuditTrigger:

```
ALTER TRIGGER FriendAuditTrigger ENABLE;
ALTER TRIGGER FriendAuditTrigger DISABLE;
```

You can also enable and disable triggers on a per-table basis. The following two statements disable, and respectively enable, all the triggers associated with the Friend table. Remember that a table can have more triggers associated with it:

```
ALTER TABLE Friend DISABLE ALL TRIGGERS;
ALTER TABLE Friend ENABLE ALL TRIGGERS;
```

Working with DB2 Triggers

When creating triggers in DB2, you can set them to be NO CASCADE BEFORE, AFTER, and INSTEAD OF.

Similarly to Oracle and SQL Server, AFTER triggers execute after the intended SQL command executes; they always fire if the SQL command doesn't break any constraints existing on that data table. NO CASCADE BEFORE and INSTEAD OF triggers fire before the command executes (so before any constraints are checked), allowing you to perform changes on the actions originally intended by the user. In addition, the NO CASCADE BEFORE trigger prevents the event that fired the trigger from executing any other triggers.

Like Oracle, DB2 supports row-level and statement-level triggers. Row-level triggers are applied once for each affected row, and statement-level triggers are applied once per statement (so even if a large number of rows is affected, the trigger is applied once).

You can also use the REFERENCING clause to specify some temporary variables to store information about the row or table before and after the trigger has been processed. Old rows are specified using OLD AS *old_name*, and new rows are specified using the NEW AS *new_name*, as you'll see in the examples.

Logging Table Activity Using AFTER Triggers

Again, let's create the FriendAudit table, which you'll use to hold audit information:

```
CREATE TABLE FriendAudit
(FriendAuditID INT GENERATED ALWAYS AS IDENTITY PRIMARY KEY NOT NULL,
 Operation VARCHAR(10),
 RecordedOn DATE DEFAULT CURRENT_DATE,
 OldName VARCHAR(50),
 NewName VARCHAR(50),
 OldPhone VARCHAR(15),
 NewPhone VARCHAR(15));
```

Notice that, like SQL Server, you can use a standard built-in function for ensuring that your FriendAuditID is always an automatically generated unique number. Also, you use the CURRENT_DATE function to provide the default value for the RecordedOn field.

Logging INSERT Operations

Let's now create the trigger that runs when you insert values:

```
CREATE TRIGGER InsFriendAuditTrig
AFTER INSERT ON Friend
REFERENCING NEW AS N
FOR EACH ROW MODE DB2SQL
BEGIN ATOMIC
  INSERT INTO FriendAudit (Operation, NewName, NewPhone)
  VALUES ('Insert ', N.Name, N.PhoneNo);
END
```

Take care to change the statement termination character in the command console before executing the statement.

> **TIP** *Note that you must always specify* MODE DB2SQL, *even though* DB2SQL *is the only mode currently available.*

It's time for a test. Run the following statements:

```
INSERT INTO Friend(Name, PhoneNo) VALUES('Jerry', '001-Jerry');
INSERT INTO Friend(Name, PhoneNo) VALUES('Harrison', '999-Harry');
INSERT INTO Friend(Name, PhoneNo) VALUES('Peter', '223223223');
```

Now query FriendAudit to see the results:

```
SELECT * FROM FriendAudit;
```

You should see the following:

```
FRIEND

AUDITID   OPERATION   RECORDEDON    OLDNAME   NEWNAME    OLDPHONE   NEWPHONE
-------   ---------   ----------    -------   -------    --------   ---------
   1       Insert     03/10/2003      -       Jerry         -       001-Jerry
   2       Insert     03/10/2003      -       Harrison      -       999-Harry
   3       Insert     03/10/2003      -       Peter         -       223223223
```

You've created a trigger called InsFriendAuditTrig (you're limited to 18-character names) that fires after an INSERT is performed on the Friend table. Again, because it's an AFTER trigger, it's invoked only after all other constraints have been checked and the new row has been introduced.

In this example, you referenced new rows using the prefix N:

```
REFERENCING NEW AS N
```

This allows you to log the new information in the FriendAudit table:

```
BEGIN ATOMIC
  INSERT INTO FriendAudit (Operation, NewName, NewPhone)
  VALUES ('Insert ', N.Name, N.PhoneNo);
END;
```

Applying Conditions for the Trigger

Like Oracle, DB2 can use conditions to control whether the trigger is executed using the WHEN parameter.

Note that to amend a trigger, you first need to drop the original and replace it with the new trigger. Start by dropping the first trigger you created:

```
DROP TRIGGER InsFriendAuditTrig;
```

Now create the following trigger. This trigger only logs INSERT operations when the name to be inserted is Peter:

```
CREATE TRIGGER InsFriendAuditTrig
AFTER INSERT ON Friend
REFERENCING NEW AS N
FOR EACH ROW MODE DB2SQL
WHEN (N.Name='Peter')
BEGIN ATOMIC
  INSERT INTO FriendAudit (Operation, NewName, NewPhone)
  VALUES ('Insert ', N.Name, N.PhoneNo);
END
```

So, let's test this. Clear the two tables by running the following statements:

```
DELETE FROM Friend;
DELETE FROM FriendAudit;
```

Now execute the INSERT statements again:

```
INSERT INTO Friend(Name, PhoneNo) VALUES('Jerry', '001-Jerry');
INSERT INTO Friend(Name, PhoneNo) VALUES('Harrison', '999-Harry');
INSERT INTO Friend(Name, PhoneNo) VALUES('Peter', '223223223');
```

You'll see that only the last insert was logged into FriendAudit:

```
FRIEND

AUDITID  OPERATION  RECORDEDON  OLDNAME  NEWNAME  OLDPHONE  NEWPHONE
-------  ---------  ----------  -------  -------  --------  ---------
   4       Insert   03/10/2003     -      Peter      -      223223223
```

Again, as you saw with Oracle, you only added one line to this trigger to restrict its functionality:

```
WHEN (N.Name='Peter')
```

Logging DELETEs and UPDATEs

It's time to create triggers that handle deleting and updating data in the Friend table. Before moving on, make sure you have the version of InsFriendAuditTrigger that logs all inserts, not just the ones for Peter. If you need to drop the trigger to recreate it, use the following statement:

```
DROP TRIGGER InsFriendAuditTrig;
```

Now let's create a trigger that handles updates as follows:

```
CREATE TRIGGER UpdFriendAuditTrig
AFTER UPDATE ON Friend
REFERENCING OLD AS O NEW AS N
FOR EACH ROW MODE DB2SQL
BEGIN ATOMIC
  INSERT INTO FriendAudit (Operation, OldName, OldPhone, NewName, NewPhone)
  VALUES ('Update ', O.Name, O.PhoneNo, N.Name, N.PhoneNo);
END
```

And add a trigger to handle deletions as follows:

```
CREATE TRIGGER DelFriendAuditTrig
AFTER DELETE ON Friend
REFERENCING OLD AS O
FOR EACH ROW MODE DB2SQL
BEGIN
  INSERT INTO FriendAudit (Operation, OldName, OldPhone)
  VALUES ('Delete ', O.Name, O.PhoneNo);
END
```

Now, clear all data from the two tables as before:

```
DELETE FROM Friend;
DELETE FROM FriendAudit;
```

You're ready to run some test statements. Enter the following and then check the result in the FriendAudit table:

```
INSERT INTO Friend(Name, PhoneNo) VALUES('Jerry', '001-Jerry');
INSERT INTO Friend(Name, PhoneNo) VALUES('Harrison', '999-Harry');
INSERT INTO Friend(Name, PhoneNo) VALUES('Peter', '223223223');
UPDATE Friend SET PhoneNo = 'Unknown';
DELETE FROM Friend;
```

Performing a simple SELECT against FriendAudit should produce the following results:

FRIEND

AUDITID	OPERATION	RECORDEDON	OLDNAME	NEWNAME	OLDPHONE	NEWPHONE
8	Insert	03/10/2003	-	Jerry	-	001-Jerry
9	Insert	03/10/2003	-	Harrison	-	999-Harry
10	Insert	03/10/2003	-	Peter	-	223223223
11	Update	03/10/2003	Jerry	Jerry	001-Jerry	Unknown
12	Update	03/10/2003	Harrison	Harrison	999-Harry	Unknown
13	Update	03/10/2003	Peter	Peter	223223223	Unknown
14	Delete	03/10/2003	Jerry	-	Unknown	-
15	Delete	03/10/2003	Harrison	-	Unknown	-
16	Delete	03/10/2003	Peter	-	Unknown	-

NOTE *For SQL Server and Oracle, you also saw how to temporarily enable and disable a trigger. DB2 doesn't have built-in support for this feature, but a few workarounds do exist. They're explained in the article "How to Temporarily Disable Triggers in DB2 Universal Database," located at* http://www7b.software.ibm.com/dmdd/library/techarticle/ 0211yip/0211yip.html.

Summary

In this chapter, you looked at how triggers work and how you implement them. There are variations between the different RDBMS platforms in how they're created and which types of trigger are supported, but the end result is the same:

You have the ability to add code that executes when an appropriate table event occurs. You used a simple logging example to demonstrate how the various types of trigger work. Specifically, you learned about the following:

- What triggers are and how they work

- How to create triggers that react to inserting, updating, and deleting data

- How to temporarily disable and enable SQL Server and Oracle triggers

- How to use triggers and sequences in Oracle to implement autonumbering functionality

In the next chapter, you'll look at creating a product catalog case study and extracting and updating information using a variety of statements.

CHAPTER 14

Case Study: Building a Product Catalog

WELCOME TO THE FIRST CASE study of this book! Here you'll analyze the scenario of a simple product catalog, a common requirement for many software products and Web sites today.

The chapter starts by discussing how to create the data tables, their properties (data types, relationships, constraints, and so on), and the relationships between them. Then, after adding some sample data to the database, the chapter discusses how you can perform different kinds of operations on the existing data: You'll see how to get different kinds of reports about your data, how to update product catalog information, and how to search for products.

The product catalog presented in this case study creates the underlying database for a full-featured Web site. In this chapter, you'll concentrate exclusively on the database itself, and you'll have a lot of fun playing with the four data tables that make the simple catalog. This chapter explains all the steps in your journey for the databases covered so far in this book. These steps are as follows:

1. Create the data structures for the product catalog.

2. Populate the product catalog with sample data.

3. Analyze options for retrieving catalog information.

4. Analyze options for updating catalog information.

5. Search the product catalog.

 NOTE *Because the different Relational Database Management Systems (RDBMSs) have different implementations of SQL, this chapter highlights any differences between code as appropriate. Note, though, that MySQL doesn't support nested queries or stored procedures, and Access has trouble running some of the* JOIN *statements presented in this chapter.*

Setting Up the Catalog

Before you even start to think about data tables or any database-specific tasks, you need to clearly understand what you want to achieve. The way you design the product catalog and its data structures depends (as usual) on the client's requirements. For this case study, we'll cheat a little bit and suppose the client wants such a product catalog that allows just enough (but not too many) features to explore in this chapter.

So, what kind of product catalog does your client want? Well, the requirements for the structure of the product catalog are simple enough:

- The product catalog needs to store information about products, product categories, and departments.

- Products, categories, and departments have names and descriptions.

- A product can be on promotion for the entire catalog or only for the departments to which it belongs.

The relationships between products, categories, and departments are as follows:

- A product can belong to at least one category.

- A category can contain zero or more products.

- A category always belongs to a department.

For example, your store will have a Full Costumes department, which will contain a number of categories, such as Exotic Costumes and Scary Costumes. The product catalog will contain products such as Cleopatra Kit and Vampire Disguise. If you were to build an e-commerce store based on your database, the information in these tables might be used to generate a product catalog looking something like Figure 14-1.

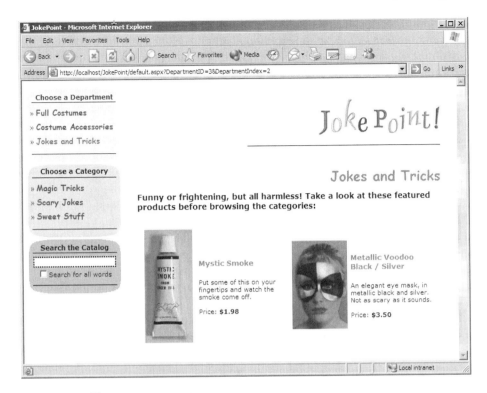

Figure 14-1. The e-commerce store

TIP *Figure 14-1 shows the e-commerce store created in* Beginning ASP.NET E-Commerce, *Second Edition (Apress, 2003).*

You can see the list of departments listed in the left side of the page. Underneath, you can see the list of categories that belong to the currently selected department (which in this case is Jokes and Tricks). The rest of the page is filled with products.

When a department is selected, the page is filled with the products that are on promotion for that department, and its list of categories also appears. When a category is then selected, the page is populated with all the products that belong to that category.

You know a product can also be on catalog promotion. Such a product will be listed in the front page of the site.

To store this information, you'll need at least three data tables: a Department table, a Category table, and a Product table. To decide how to implement these tables and their relationships, let's first try to visualize them using some simple diagrams.

We decided earlier that a department can contain multiple categories, but a category always belongs to a single department. This is a one-to-many relationship, and it can be imagined as in Figure 14-2 (*one* department, *many* categories).

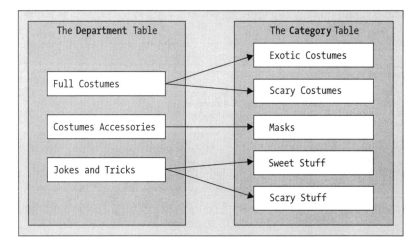

Figure 14-2. The relationship between the Department *and* Category *tables*

Remember that you implement one-to-many relationships by adding a FOREIGN KEY constraint to the table in the *many* side of the relationship, which references the primary key of the other table. In this case, you'd implement the relationship like in Figure 14-3.

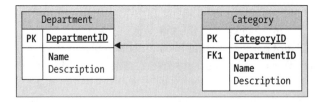

Figure 14-3. Implementing the one-to-many relationship

Both the Department and Category tables contain two properties: Name and Description. For both tables, Name is obligatory, and Description accepts NULLs. The Category table also contains a column named DepartmentID, which references the DepartmentID column in Department.

Between products and categories, you have a different kind of relationship because a product can belong to (relate to) many categories, and also a category can contain (relate to) many products. Figure 14-4 represents how categories and products are related.

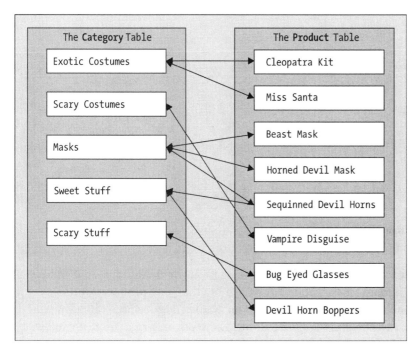

Figure 14-4. The relationship between the Category *and* Product *tables*

Yep, this looks like a many-to-many relationship. You'll recall that many-to-many relationships are physically implemented using a third table, called a ***junction*** table (often referred to as a *mapping table*). In this case, the junction table will be named ProductCategory.

Let's take a look at the complete database diagram now. Notice the two one-to-many relationships between the junction table (ProductCategory) and the Category and Product tables in Figure 14-5.

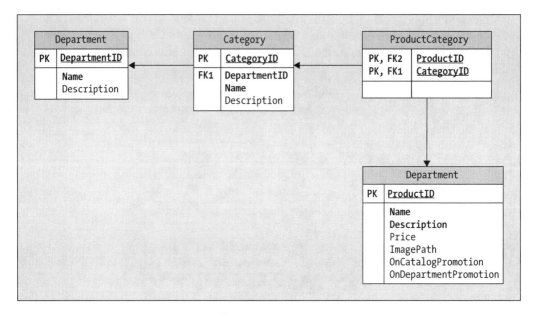

Figure 14-5. The four database tables

ProductCategory has a primary key made from two fields, ProductID and CategoryID (remember that you can't have more than one primary key in a table!). Each record of this table will associate a product with a category. Because the ProductID/CategoryID pair forms the primary key, you're not allowed to have identical entries in this table. In other words, each row in this table uniquely associates one product with one category.

The Product table has more fields than the other tables. The following summarizes each of the fields in the table:

- Price: This field stores the price of the product.

- ImagePath: This field stores the hard disk location (usually a relative path) of a file containing the product's image. This solution is often used instead of storing the image directly into the database because of performance issues. Databases are generally not optimized for storing large binary data.

- OnCatalogPromotion: This field stores a binary value (zero or one), specifying if the product is in promotion for the entire catalog.

- OnDepartmentPromotion: This field is similar to OnCatalogPromotion, but it specifies if the product is on promotion for the departments that contain it.

Using fields such as OnCatalogPromotion and OnDepartmentPromotion is one of the ways of tracking which products are featured on a site and where they're featured. For example, in an e-commerce Web site, on the front page of the site you'd see the products that have the `OnCatalogPromotion` bit set to one. When the visitor is selecting one of the departments, only the products that have the `OnDepartmentPromotion` bit set to one appear. Finally, when a category is selected from one of the departments, all the products in that category are listed.

Creating the Data Structures

So here you are, starting to build the catalog. First, you should create a new database for your product catalog. Create a new database named `ProductCatalog` on your favorite database server using the steps you learned in Chapter 12, "Working with Database Objects."

Let's see again what tables you want to create. Figure 14-6 was created with SQL Server Enterprise Manager.

Figure 14-6. The `ProductCatalog` *database in Enterprise Manager*

None of the diagrams presented so far lists the data types (and other properties) for each column. Most of the times the decision of which data type to use will not be hard to make, and you'll deal with this when you create the tables. Still, there's an issue you should consider before starting to construct the tables: How should you generate new IDs for the primary key column(s) when inserting new data records to the tables? Here are the common solutions to this question:

In many cases (as well as in this case study), you rely on the database to automatically generate new IDs values.

Another common solution is to get the maximum value for the ID column and add one unit in order to generate a new unique value. This solution is straightforward, but it's not a recommended one because problems can appear when multiple users try to add new rows at the same time (which could result in a failed attempt to insert two identical values for the primary key).

Generate a new Globally Unique Identifier (GUID) every time. GUIDs are randomly generated values that are guaranteed to be unique across time and space. There are a number of scenarios (such as replication scenarios) where these prove to be helpful.

In some cases, you'll know beforehand the values for the primary key columns, such in the case of the junction table where, for each record, you need to add an existing product ID and an existing category ID (these two values forming the primary key).

Except for the junction table, you'll use autonumbered columns on the primary key columns of your tables.

Creating the Department Table

The Department table has three columns:

- DepartmentID (autonumbered)

- Name

- Description

Remember that there are different ways to implement autonumber functionality into the data table: You use IDENTITY columns for SQL Server, AUTOINCREMENT for Access, AUTO_INCREMENT columns for MySQL, GENERATED AS IDENTITY columns for DB2, and sequences for Oracle. We covered these in the previous chapters. Let's now create the Department table.

With SQL Server, use the following command to create the Department table:

```
CREATE TABLE Department (
DepartmentID INT IDENTITY NOT NULL PRIMARY KEY,
Name VARCHAR(50) NOT NULL,
Description VARCHAR (200) NULL);
```

This is the similar command for DB2:

```
CREATE TABLE Department (
DepartmentID INT GENERATED ALWAYS AS IDENTITY NOT NULL PRIMARY KEY,
Name VARCHAR(50) NOT NULL,
Description VARCHAR (200));
```

Note that DB2 doesn't let you specify a default value of NULL for the Description field as you've done in the rest of these statements.

Access requires similar syntax:

```
CREATE TABLE Department (
DepartmentID AUTOINCREMENT NOT NULL PRIMARY KEY,
```

```
Name VARCHAR(50) NOT NULL,
Description VARCHAR (200) NULL);
```

With MySQL, you use the InnoDB table type, which supports FOREIGN KEY constraints (the default table type, MyISAM, doesn't). Because of the way categories
relate to departments, you'll need to add a FOREIGN KEY constraint to Category
that will reference the DepartmentID column in Department. Even if only the
Category column has a FOREIGN KEY constraint defined, both tables that take part
in the relationship need to be InnoDB tables. You'll see the other end of this relationship when you create the Category table. Here's the code for creating the
Department table in MySQL:

```
CREATE TABLE Department (
DepartmentID INT AUTO_INCREMENT NOT NULL PRIMARY KEY,
Name VARCHAR(50) NOT NULL,
Description VARCHAR (200) NULL) Type=InnoDB;
```

Because Oracle doesn't have an out-of-the-box way to automatically generate unique numbers like the other platforms, you can't specify that DepartmentID
is an autonumbered column when creating it:

```
CREATE TABLE Department (
DepartmentID INT NOT NULL PRIMARY KEY,
Name VARCHAR(50) NOT NULL,
Description VARCHAR(200) NULL);
```

Instead, you create a sequence and trigger that implements the autonumber
functionality:

```
CREATE SEQUENCE DepartmentIDSeq;

CREATE OR REPLACE TRIGGER DepartmentAutonumberTrigger
BEFORE INSERT ON Department
FOR EACH ROW
BEGIN
  SELECT DepartmentIDSeq.NEXTVAL
  INTO :NEW.DepartmentID FROM DUAL;
END;
/
```

After creating the sequence and trigger, you'll be able to add new rows the
same way as with MySQL and SQL Server.

Creating the Category Table

The Category table is similar to Department except that it has an additional column—DepartmentID—that references the DepartmentID column of the Department table.

Here's how you create this table with SQL Server:

```
CREATE TABLE Category (
CategoryID INT IDENTITY NOT NULL PRIMARY KEY,
DepartmentID INT NOT NULL FOREIGN KEY REFERENCES DEPARTMENT,
Name VARCHAR(50) NOT NULL,
Description VARCHAR (200) NULL);
```

This is the command in Access:

```
CREATE TABLE Category (
CategoryID AUTOINCREMENT NOT NULL PRIMARY KEY,
DepartmentID INT NOT NULL,
Name VARCHAR(50) NOT NULL,
Description VARCHAR (200) NULL,
CONSTRAINT fk_DepartmentID FOREIGN KEY (DepartmentID)
                        REFERENCES Department (DepartmentID));
```

Notice that Access doesn't allow you to use the shorthand constraint syntax that you used for SQL Server.

This is the command that creates the table with DB2:

```
CREATE TABLE Category (
CategoryID INT GENERATED ALWAYS AS IDENTITY NOT NULL PRIMARY KEY,
DepartmentID INT NOT NULL,
Name VARCHAR(50) NOT NULL,
Description VARCHAR (200),
FOREIGN KEY (DepartmentID) REFERENCES Department (DepartmentID));
```

With MySQL, when adding FOREIGN KEY constraints, apart from using the InnoDB table type and defining the FOREIGN KEY constraint, you also need to create an index on the FOREIGN KEY column:

```
CREATE TABLE Category (
CategoryID INT AUTO_INCREMENT NOT NULL PRIMARY KEY,
DepartmentID INT NOT NULL,
Name VARCHAR(50) NOT NULL,
Description VARCHAR (200) NULL,
FOREIGN KEY (DepartmentID) REFERENCES Department (DepartmentID),
INDEX idxDepartmentID (DepartmentID)
) Type=InnoDB;
```

CAUTION   *If you forget to specify* InnoDB *for* Category *or* Department, *no errors will be generated by MySQL when adding the foreign key. Instead, the* FOREIGN KEY *constraint will simply be ignored.*

This is how you create the table on Oracle:

```
CREATE TABLE Category (
CategoryID INT NOT NULL PRIMARY KEY,
DepartmentID INT NOT NULL,
Name VARCHAR(50) NOT NULL,
Description VARCHAR (200) NULL,
FOREIGN KEY (DepartmentID) REFERENCES Department (DepartmentID));
```

After creating the Category table with Oracle, you implement the autonumbering functionality using the same method as before:

```
CREATE SEQUENCE CategoryIDSeq;

CREATE OR REPLACE TRIGGER CategoryAutonumberTrigger
BEFORE INSERT ON Category
FOR EACH ROW
BEGIN
    SELECT CategoryIDSeq.NEXTVAL
    INTO :NEW.CategoryID FROM DUAL;
END;
/
```

Creating the Product Table

With Product, you have a few more values to store than with Department or Category.

You have the OnCatalogPromotion and OnDepartmentPromotion columns, which hold binary values, and you have a Price column, which needs to store monetary values.

With SQL Server, for OnCatalogPromotion and OnDepartmentPromotion you use the BIT data type, which stores zero or one. This is just fine for what you need. Also, you have a specialized MONEY data type that stores monetary data with fixed precision:

```
CREATE TABLE Product (
ProductID INT IDENTITY NOT NULL PRIMARY KEY,
Name VARCHAR(50) NOT NULL,
Description VARCHAR(1000) NOT NULL,
Price MONEY NULL,
ImagePath VARCHAR(50) NULL,
OnCatalogPromotion BIT NULL,
OnDepartmentPromotion BIT NULL);
```

Access uses similar syntax:

```
CREATE TABLE Product (
ProductID AUTOINCREMENT  NOT NULL PRIMARY KEY,
Name VARCHAR(50) NOT NULL,
Description VARCHAR(255) NOT NULL,
Price MONEY NULL,
ImagePath VARCHAR(50) NULL,
OnCatalogPromotion BIT NULL,
OnDepartmentPromotion BIT NULL);
```

Notice that the maximum field length for a VARCHAR in Access is 255 characters. The command you use for DB2 is slightly different here because DB2 doesn't have a MONEY or BIT data type, so you use DECIMAL for the price and SMALLINT for the two Boolean values:

```
CREATE TABLE Product (
ProductID INT GENERATED ALWAYS AS IDENTITY NOT NULL PRIMARY KEY,
Name VARCHAR(50) NOT NULL,
Description VARCHAR(1000) NOT NULL,
Price DECIMAL(7,2),
ImagePath VARCHAR(50),
OnCatalogPromotion SMALLINT,
OnDepartmentPromotion SMALLINT);
```

With MySQL you record monetary data using the DECIMAL data type. You record the description as a VARCHAR(255) instead of VARCHAR(1000) because MySQL doesn't support higher dimensions. The alternative would be to use BLOB (binary large object) fields, which are usually best avoided because of the impact they have on performance:

```
CREATE TABLE Product (
ProductID INT AUTO_INCREMENT NOT NULL PRIMARY KEY,
Name VARCHAR(50) NOT NULL,
Description VARCHAR(255) NOT NULL,
```

```
Price DECIMAL NULL,
ImagePath VARCHAR(50) NULL,
OnCatalogPromotion BIT NULL,
OnDepartmentPromotion BIT NULL) Type=InnoDB;
```

Oracle has the universal NUMBER data type, which you'll use for Price, OnCatalogPromotion, and OnDepartmentPromotion columns. For the binary values, you specify the minimum size for number length and number of decimal places to ensure you occupy the smallest space possible:

```
CREATE TABLE Product (
ProductID INT NOT NULL PRIMARY KEY,
Name VARCHAR(50) NOT NULL,
Description VARCHAR(1000) NOT NULL,
Price NUMBER NULL,
ImagePath VARCHAR(50) NULL,
OnCatalogPromotion NUMBER(1,0) NULL,
OnDepartmentPromotion NUMBER(1,0) NULL);
```

Once again, you create the trigger and sequence:

```
CREATE SEQUENCE ProductIDSeq;

CREATE OR REPLACE TRIGGER ProductAutonumberTrigger
BEFORE INSERT ON Product
FOR EACH ROW
BEGIN
    SELECT ProductIDSeq.NEXTVAL
    INTO :NEW.ProductID FROM DUAL;
END;
/
```

Creating the ProductCategory Table

With ProductCategory, the new challenge is to create the multivalued primary key. You also have two foreign keys that reference the primary keys of the Category and Product tables.

With SQL Server, Access, Oracle, and DB2, here's how you create the ProductCategory table. Note that here you're using the shorter syntax, which doesn't give explicit names to the PRIMARY KEY and FOREIGN KEY constraints:

```
CREATE TABLE ProductCategory (
ProductID INT NOT NULL,
CategoryID INT NOT NULL,
PRIMARY KEY (ProductID, CategoryID),
FOREIGN KEY (ProductID) REFERENCES Product (ProductID),
FOREIGN KEY (CategoryID) REFERENCES Category (CategoryID)
);
```

Alternatively, with SQL Server you can create the foreign keys with the simpler syntax:

```
CREATE TABLE ProductCategory (
ProductID INT NOT NULL FOREIGN KEY REFERENCES PRODUCT,
CategoryID INT NOT NULL FOREIGN KEY REFERENCES CATEGORY,
PRIMARY KEY (ProductID, CategoryID)
);
```

With MySQL, you need to create indexes on the columns used in foreign keys and make sure the table type is `InnoDB`:

```
CREATE TABLE ProductCategory (
ProductID INT NOT NULL,
CategoryID INT NOT NULL,
PRIMARY KEY (ProductID, CategoryID),
FOREIGN KEY (ProductID) REFERENCES Product (ProductID),
INDEX idxProductID (ProductID),
FOREIGN KEY (CategoryID) REFERENCES Category (CategoryID),
INDEX idxCategoryID (CategoryID)
) Type=InnoDB;
```

Adding Sample Data

Now, the good news (which is probably old news for you) is that the commands to insert new rows are identical for the databases covered in this book. In the following sections, you'll add some test values to the tables you created.

There's one catch, though: You don't need to (and in some cases you aren't allowed to) specify values for the ID columns because you want them to auto-number themselves. Although when adding new rows to the tables these values should receive consecutive values, starting with one, this isn't always guaranteed by the database (especially with Oracle because of the way sequences work).

In these examples, the ID columns always started with one and are incremented by one. However, if this isn't the same on your system, you'll need to manually specify the values on the foreign key columns. So be careful when adding rows to the Category and ProductCategory tables because these are the tables on which the FOREIGN KEY constraints are defined.

TIP   *If you want to delete all the rows from a table and reset the auto-increment ID, you should truncate the table, as described in Chapter 12, "Working with Database Objects" (which works just like dropping and re-creating the table). Simply deleting the rows will not reset the auto-increment values.*

If the values you try to insert aren't valid, the database will not accept them because of the referential integrity you established using the foreign keys.

Adding Departments

Let's now insert some values into the Department table:

```
INSERT INTO Department (Name, Description)
    VALUES ('Full Costumes', 'We have the best costumes on the internet!');
INSERT INTO Department (Name, Description)
    VALUES ('Costume Accessories', 'Accessories and fun items for you.');
INSERT INTO Department (Name, Description)
    VALUES ('Jokes and Tricks', 'Funny or frightening, but all harmless!');
```

CAUTION   *Always remember to* COMMIT *the transaction after adding, updating, or deleting table rows if you're working in automatic-transactions mode. This is the default mode for Oracle and DB2. For more information, refer to Chapter 10, "Transactions."*

Adding Categories

In this example, let's assume that the automatically created departments have the IDs 1, 2, and 3. If they have different IDs, you'll need to specify different values for the DepartmentID column when adding the categories:

```
INSERT INTO Category (DepartmentID, Name, Description)
    VALUES (1, 'Exotic Costumes', 'Sweet costumes for the party girl:');
INSERT INTO Category (DepartmentID, Name, Description)
    VALUES (1, 'Scary Costumes', 'Scary costumes for maximum chills:');
```

```
INSERT INTO Category (DepartmentID, Name, Description)
   VALUES (2, 'Masks', 'Items for the master of disguise:');
INSERT INTO Category (DepartmentID, Name, Description)
   VALUES (3, 'Sweet Stuff', 'Raise a smile wherever you go!');
INSERT INTO Category (DepartmentID, Name, Description)
   VALUES (3, 'Scary Stuff', 'Scary accessories for the practical joker:');
```

The new categories should have IDs from 1 to 5. Test to see that you can't reference a nonexistent DepartmentID. For example, the following query will fail if there isn't any department with the ID of 99:

```
INSERT INTO Category (DepartmentID, Name, Description)
   VALUES (99, 'Scary Stuff', 'Scary accessories for the practical joker:');
```

Adding Products

Here are the commands that add a few new products to your database:

```
INSERT INTO Product (Name, Description, Price, ImagePath,
                          OnCatalogPromotion, OnDepartmentPromotion)
VALUES ('Beast Mask',
        'Red-eyed and open-mouthed scary mask guaranteed to scare!',
        5.99, '20214.jpg', 1, 0);

INSERT INTO Product (Name, Description, Price, ImagePath,
                          OnCatalogPromotion, OnDepartmentPromotion)
VALUES ('Cleopatra Kit',
        'Full of Eastern promise. Includes headband, necklace and bracelet.',
        14.99, '20247.jpg', 0, 0);

INSERT INTO Product (Name, Description, Price, ImagePath,
                          OnCatalogPromotion, OnDepartmentPromotion)
VALUES ('Horned Devil Mask',
        'Full devil mask with horns. The perfect Halloween disguise!',
        5.99, '97023.jpg', 0, 1);

INSERT INTO Product (Name, Description, Price, ImagePath,
                          OnCatalogPromotion, OnDepartmentPromotion)
VALUES ('Miss Santa',
        'A stunning red-sequinned Santa dress. Includes dress, belt, cape,
        hat and boot covers. A perfect present.!',
        49.99, '20393.jpg', 0, 1);
```

```
INSERT INTO Product (Name, Description, Price, ImagePath,
                        OnCatalogPromotion, OnDepartmentPromotion)
VALUES ('Vampire Disguise',
        'Vampire Set consisting of wicked wig, fangs, and fake blood.',
        9.99, '325.jpg',  1, 0);


INSERT INTO Product (Name, Description, Price, ImagePath,
                        OnCatalogPromotion, OnDepartmentPromotion)
VALUES ('Sequinned Devil Horns',
        'Shiny red horns for the little devil inside you!',
        3.75, '20017.jpg', 0, 0);


INSERT INTO Product (Name, Description, Price, ImagePath,
                        OnCatalogPromotion, OnDepartmentPromotion)
VALUES ('Devil Horn Boppers',
        'These red glitter boppers are guaranteed to attract attention.
        They will soon be under your spell!',
        2.50, '21355.jpg', 1, 0);


INSERT INTO Product (Name, Description, Price, ImagePath,
                        OnCatalogPromotion, OnDepartmentPromotion)
VALUES ('Bug Eyed Glasses',
        'Bug-eyed glasses to astound and amuse.',
        2.75, '98413.jpg', 0, 1);
```

Connecting Products and Categories

Finally, you add values into the ProductCategory table, which establishes connections between the existing products and categories. We assume the categories and products inserted earlier received consecutive ID values:

```
INSERT INTO ProductCategory (ProductID, CategoryID) VALUES (1,3);
INSERT INTO ProductCategory (ProductID, CategoryID) VALUES (2,1);
INSERT INTO ProductCategory (ProductID, CategoryID) VALUES (2,3);
INSERT INTO ProductCategory (ProductID, CategoryID) VALUES (3,3);
INSERT INTO ProductCategory (ProductID, CategoryID) VALUES (4,1);
INSERT INTO ProductCategory (ProductID, CategoryID) VALUES (5,2);
INSERT INTO ProductCategory (ProductID, CategoryID) VALUES (6,3);
INSERT INTO ProductCategory (ProductID, CategoryID) VALUES (6,4);
```

```
INSERT INTO ProductCategory (ProductID, CategoryID) VALUES (7,4);
INSERT INTO ProductCategory (ProductID, CategoryID) VALUES (8,5);
```

Retrieving Catalog Information

Okay, after populating the data tables, it's time to do some querying against your data.

You'll start with some simple queries on the Product table. You'll continue by seeing how to associate products with their categories using the ProductCategory junction table, and finally you'll see how to associate the products with their departments.

What About the Products?

In the following sections, you'll look at queries that involve the Product table alone, not relating it to Category or Department. Let's start with one of the simplest meaningful queries that you can make of your database.

Getting the Entire List of Products Ordered by Name

A single SELECT statement combined with the ORDER BY clause does the trick in this case; this query should work the same for any existing relational database software:

```
SELECT Name, Description FROM Product ORDER BY Name;
```

As a result of this query, you should see the product names and descriptions you typed earlier when populating the Product table.

Getting the List of Products That Are on Catalog Promotion

This isn't much more complicated than the previous query. This time, you filter the results based on the OnCatalogPromotion field, which needs to have a value of 1. Here's the query:

```
SELECT Name, Description
FROM Product
WHERE OnCatalogPromotion=1
ORDER BY Name;
```

Note that Access will store the `OnCatalogPromotion` value as `-1`, so you'll need to alter the `WHERE` clause appropriately to match the required records.

Based on your sample data, this query should return the following data:

```
Name                    Description

--------------------    --------------------------------------

Beast Mask              Red-eyed and open-mouthed scary mask
                        guaranteed to scare!
Devil Horn Boppers      These red glitter boppers are
                        guaranteed to attract attention. They
                        will soon be under your spell!
Vampire Disguise        Vampire Set consisting of wicked wig,
                        fangs, and fake blood. Spinechilling!
```

Getting the Five Most Expensive Products

For this query, you need to use the `ORDER BY` clause to order the list of products by `Price` in descending order:

```
SELECT Name, Price FROM Product ORDER BY Price DESC;
```

Note that you can use multiple criteria with the `ORDER BY` clause. If, say, you want the products with the same price to be sorted by name in ascending order, you'd add a few bits to the query:

```
SELECT Name, Price FROM Product ORDER BY Price DESC, Name ASC;
```

The `ASC` keyword is optional because ascending is the default order anyway.

Now let's see how you get only the top five most expensive products. In practice, you need to limit the results you get from the previous query. This isn't handled in the same way by each RDBMS, so let's see how you can do that with each of them. In any case, you expect to get this list of results:

Name	Price
Miss Santa	49.9900
Cleopatra Kit	14.9900
Vampire Disguise	9.9900
Horned Devil Mask	5.9900
Beast Mask	5.9900

You may be wondering what would happen if you had asked for the top four most expensive items because you have two items priced at $5.99. Well, the way we've written the following queries, one of the $5.99 items would simply be omitted from the list. We're not going to worry too much about that here, but the way to get around this problem is described in detail, for each database, in Chapter 4, "Summarizing and Grouping Data."

SQL Server

SQL Server and Access support the TOP clause. To get the top five most expensive products, you need this command:

```
SELECT TOP 5 Name, Price
FROM Product
ORDER BY Price DESC, Name ASC;
```

With SQL Server, you can alternatively use SET ROWCOUNT to limit the number of returned rows. Here's an example:

```
SET ROWCOUNT 5;
SELECT Name, Price
FROM Product
ORDER BY Price DESC, Name ASC;
```

Also, you can limit by specifying what percent of the result set to return. The following command returns the top 15 percent of most expensive products:

```
SELECT TOP 15 PERCENT Name, Price
FROM Product
ORDER BY Price DESC, Name ASC;
```

MySQL

MySQL has the LIMIT keyword that has similar functionality. The following is the MySQL command that returns the first five most expensive products:

```
SELECT Name, Price
FROM Product
ORDER BY Price DESC, Name ASC
LIMIT 0,5;
```

As you can see, the LIMIT clause has two parameters. The first one specifies the index of the first returned record (starting with zero), and the second specifies how many rows to return.

Oracle

With Oracle, you use the ROWNUM pseudocolumn to limit the number of returned rows:

```
SELECT Name, Price FROM
     (SELECT Name, Price
      FROM Product
      ORDER BY Price DESC, Name ASC)
WHERE ROWNUM<=5;
```

This technique works only when you restrict the query for a ROWNUM that starts with one (such as ROWNUM <=5). If you try to restrict using another range, such as ROWNUM BETWEEN m and n, where m is greater than one, the query will return no results. You'll see a workaround to this limitation in the next exercise.

ROWNUM is a pseudocolumn that associates a row number to each record returned by a query. What's important to note here is that ROWNUM values are assigned *before* the ORDER BY clause executes. For this reason, you need to use a subselect instead of simply limiting by ROWNUM in the first place, like this:

```
SELECT Name, Price
FROM Product
WHERE ROWNUM<=5
ORDER BY Price DESC, Name ASC
```

This query doesn't return the expected results because the WHERE filter is applied first and takes the first five rows (in a random order). These rows are then ordered by Price and Name (which isn't what you intended to do).

DB2

Using DB2, you can list the top five most expensive products using FETCH FIRST *n*
ROWS ONLY:

```
SELECT Name, Price
FROM Product
ORDER BY Price DESC, Name ASC
FETCH FIRST 5 ROWS ONLY;
```

Browsing Through Products

In real-world scenarios, you frequently need to present the user with lists of
products, categories, and so on. When the list is long enough, a typical practice
is to present a number of products at a time (five in these examples) and let the
user browse the list using Next 5 Products and Previous 5 Products buttons.

In this exercise, you'll see how to retrieve the rows *m* to *n* (say, five to 10) in an
ordered list of products. This time you'll order the products by their IDs.

At the first sight, it may seem that you can simply get the required products
with a simple command such as this:

```
SELECT Name FROM Product WHERE ProductID BETWEEN 5 AND 10
```

However, this method isn't reliable because you aren't guaranteed to have
the ProductIDs in sequential order, so you aren't guaranteed to get five products
back. Additionally, this method is useless if the user wants the list of products
sorted by any other column than ProductID.

For the purpose of these examples, you'll ask for the second group of five
products (products size to 10), but because currently you have only eight products, this is what you should get:

```
ProductID    Name

-------------  --------------------------------------------
6                    Sequinned Devil Horns
7                    Devil Horn Boppers
8                    Bug Eyed Glasses
```

Let's see how you can ask your databases to give you a specific portion of an ordered list of products. The solution is different for each RDBMS, so let's analyze each one individually.

MySQL

With MySQL, this problem turns out to be a piece of cake. With MySQL, you use the LIMIT keyword, just like in the previous example but using different parameters this time:

```
SELECT ProductID, Name
FROM Product
ORDER BY ProductID
LIMIT 5,5;
```

This time you specified 5 as the first parameter (instead of 0), mentioning that you want retrieve rows starting with the sixth record in the result set (remember that the row number is zero-based). The second parameter specifies how many rows you want to retrieve.

Oracle

With Oracle, you use a command similar to the one you saw in the previous example. However, there's a catch—you can't limit the result set based on the ROWNUM pseudocolumn being between *m* and *n* if *m*>1. If you execute the following query, no rows will be returned:

```
SELECT ProductID, Name FROM
      (SELECT ProductID, Name
       FROM Product
       ORDER BY ProductID)
WHERE ROWNUM BETWEEN 6 AND 10;
```

The workaround to this problem is as follows:

```
SELECT ProductID, Name FROM
      (SELECT ProductID, Name, ROWNUM AS rn FROM
            (SELECT ProductID, Name
             FROM Product
             ORDER BY ProductID)
      ) inner
WHERE inner.rn BETWEEN 6 AND 10;
```

Here you "saved" the ROWNUM values in a new row of the subquery, so you could filter correctly the results in the outer query.

Alternatively, and more elegantly, you can use the RANK analytic function, as described in Chapter 4, "Summarizing and Grouping Data":

```
SELECT ProductID, Name FROM
(
SELECT RANK() OVER (ORDER BY ProductID) As Ranking, ProductID, Name
FROM Product
ORDER BY PRODUCTID
)
WHERE Ranking BETWEEN 6 AND 8;
```

SQL Server

SQL Server doesn't provide you with a simple way to achieve your goal. The TOP clause works well as long as you're only interested in the top records of a query. There are a number of workarounds for this limitation.

Let's discuss the most obvious solution first. This uses the SQL-99 syntax (so with some tweaking it works with other databases as well) and uses correlated subqueries (correlated subqueries were discussed in Chapter 6, "Combining SQL Queries"):

```
SELECT ProductID, Name
FROM Product AS P1
WHERE
  (SELECT COUNT(*) FROM Product AS P2
    WHERE P1.ProductID >= P2.ProductID) BETWEEN 6 AND 10
ORDER BY ProductID;
```

 NOTE *This method only works if the list of products is ordered by a unique column. You can't use it, for example, if the products are ordered by price and if there's more than one product with the same price.*

Remember that a correlated subquery executes once for every record of the outer query. In this example, for each product returned by the outer query, the subquery calculates how many products have a lower ID. You're looking for products for which that number is between six and 10.

The second method uses the TOP function. The idea is simple, but the SQL code will look a bit awkward at first. If you want to retrieve products between six and 10, here's a working strategy:

- First, you get the TOP 10 products, ordered by ProductID (ascending). The products you're interested in are the bottom of this list.

- You order the resulting list in descending order by ProductID (so the rows you're interested in will be at the TOP).

- You get the TOP 5 products from list.

- You finally sort the remaining products in ascending order by ProductID.

By using subqueries, you can implement all these steps in a single SQL command:

```
SELECT ProductID, Name
FROM
   (SELECT TOP 5 ProductID, Name
    FROM
       (SELECT TOP 10 ProductID, Name
        FROM Product
        ORDER BY ProductID) AS P1
    ORDER BY ProductID DESC) AS P2
ORDER BY ProductID
```

The last technique I'll present for SQL Server consists of using a temporary table with an IDENTITY column. This solution is versatile so that it can also be implemented for other databases as well. For more information about temporary tables and IDENTITY columns, please read Chapter 12. The code for this solution, presented below, is self-explanatory:

```
/* Create a temporary table named #Product, having an IDENTITY column */
CREATE TABLE #Product
(RowNumber SMALLINT NOT NULL IDENTITY(1,1),
 ProductID INT,
 Name VARCHAR(50))
```

```
/* Populate the temporary table with records from the table we browse through.
   The RowNumber column will generate consecutive numbers for each product.
   We're free to order the list of products by any criteria. */
INSERT INTO #Product (ProductID, Name)
SELECT ProductID, Name
FROM Product
ORDER BY Price DESC

/* Retrieve the requested group or records from the temporary table */
SELECT ProductID, Name
FROM #Product
WHERE RowNumber BETWEEN 6 and 10

/* Drop the temporary table */
DROP TABLE #Product
```

DB2

The first query that was presented for SQL Server (using correlated subqueries) works with no modifications with DB2. Here it is again, for reference:

```
SELECT ProductID, Name
FROM Product AS P1
WHERE
  (SELECT COUNT(*) FROM Product AS P2
   WHERE P1.ProductID >= P2.ProductID) BETWEEN 6 AND 10
ORDER BY ProductID;
```

The second solution is DB2 specific. It uses the ROWNUMBER function in a subquery to generate a "rownumber" fabricated column, which is then used to filter and retrieve the specified range of products:

```
WITH temp AS
  (SELECT ProductID, Name,
          ROWNUMBER() OVER(ORDER BY ProductID) AS row
   FROM Product)
SELECT ProductID, Name FROM temp WHERE row>5 and row<=10
```

ROWNUMBER, RANK, and DENSERANK are three analytical functions supported by DB2 that come in handy when you need to perform tasks that imply record numbering or ranking. The functions RANK and DENSE_RANK are also supported by

Oracle, along with several others. (Chapter 4, "Summarizing and Grouping Data," demonstrates how to use the RANK function.) You'll also see them in action again, later in this case study. For detailed information about the analytic functions supported and how they work, please refer to your vendor's SQL reference manual.

Associated Products and Categories

In the previous exercises, you asked for products without associating them with the existing categories or departments. In reality, most of your queries regarding products will also involve the categories to which they belong.

Selecting Products That Belong to a Specific Category

In real-world scenarios, it's likely that you'll need to gather a list of products that belong to a specific category. In this case, the category of interest will always be identified by its ID (its primary key). You're interested in getting both the Name and Description of the products that belong to a specific category.

If you want only the IDs of the products associated with a specific Category, a simple query like this on ProductCategory solves the problem:

```
SELECT ProductID FROM ProductCategory WHERE CategoryID=3;
```

However, to get the Name and Description, you need to perform an INNER JOIN between Product and ProductCategory. You learned how to join tables in Chapter 7, "Querying Multiple Tables." This query returns all the products that belong to the category with an ID of 3:

```
SELECT Name
FROM Product INNER JOIN ProductCategory
ON Product.ProductID = ProductCategory.ProductID
WHERE ProductCategory.CategoryID = 3;
```

As an alternative syntax, you could use the WHERE clause to join your two tables:

```
SELECT Name
FROM Product, ProductCategory
WHERE Product.ProductID = ProductCategory.ProductID
AND ProductCategory.CategoryID = 3;
```

The results of the query look like this:

```
Name

--------------------
Beast Mask
Cleopatra Kit
Horned Devil Mask
Sequinned Devil Horns
```

Selecting Categories That Contain a Specific Product

Compared to the previous query, this section covers the opposite scenario. Now you know the product, and you need to find the categories associated with it. Here's the query that lists the categories that contain the product with ProductID of 6:

```
SELECT Category.CategoryID, Name
FROM Category INNER JOIN ProductCategory
ON Category.CategoryID = ProductCategory.CategoryID
AND ProductCategory.ProductID = 6;
```

> **CAUTION**   *Access doesn't like this join syntax because it's a bit more picky about how joins are constructed (see Chapter 7, "Querying Multiple Tables" for more information). Instead of using the JOIN syntax, you should use the alternative subquery method supplied here or alter the join appropriately.*

You can achieve the same result using subqueries. The subquery returns the IDs of categories associated with the product you want, and using these results you get the names and descriptions you're interested in:

```
SELECT CategoryID, Name
FROM Category
WHERE CategoryID IN
    (SELECT CategoryID
     FROM ProductCategory
     WHERE ProductCategory.ProductID = 6);
```

CAUTION *Remember that MySQL doesn't support subqueries. None of the examples that include subqueries will run in MySQL.*

Based on the sample data, there are two matching categories for the product for which you were looking:

CategoryID	Name
3	Masks
4	Sweet Stuff

What Products Belong to the Same Categories As Another Product?

This kind of query is useful in situations where you want to find out which products are similar to a specified product. So how do you find out what products belong to the same categories as another product (remember that a product can belong to more than one category)?

After having run the previous two exercises, this should be fairly straightforward. First, remember how you extracted the products that belong to a category:

```
SELECT Name
FROM Product INNER JOIN ProductCategory
ON Product.ProductID = ProductCategory.ProductID
AND ProductCategory.CategoryID = 3;
```

Now you need to determine which products belong to one or more categories, so you'll need to do something like this:

```
SELECT Name
FROM Product INNER JOIN ProductCategory
ON Product.ProductID = ProductCategory.ProductID
WHERE ProductCategory.CategoryID IN ( <list of categories> )
```

All you need to do is substitute *<list of categories>* for the list of categories in which you're interested.

Here's the query that alphabetically lists all the products that belong to the same categories as the product with the ID of 6:

```
SELECT DISTINCT Product.ProductID, Product.Name
FROM Product INNER JOIN ProductCategory
ON Product.ProductID = ProductCategory.ProductID
WHERE ProductCategory.CategoryID IN
    (SELECT Category.CategoryID
    FROM Category INNER JOIN ProductCategory
    ON Category.CategoryID = ProductCategory.CategoryID
    WHERE ProductCategory.ProductID = 6)
ORDER BY Name;
```

Here are the results:

ProductID	Name
1	Beast Mask
2	Cleopatra Kit
7	Devil Horn Boppers
3	Horned Devil Mask
6	Sequinned Devil Horns

Note that you use SELECT DISTINCT to guard against duplicate results. You need this because the subquery might return more categories, and the products that belong to more than one of them would be listed more than once (because, remember, a product can belong to more than one category!).

Unfortunately, the previous statement won't execute on MySQL because MySQL doesn't support nested queries. Access also doesn't like this particular syntax, but in just a moment, you'll see an alternative syntax that does work on Access.

Getting the Same Results Using Table Joins

The solution presented earlier is probably the most commonly used. However, as anticipated, you can obtain the same results using joins, with a much more elegant query. This solution also works with MySQL, which doesn't support subqueries:

```
SELECT DISTINCT P1.ProductID, P1.Name
FROM Product P1
   INNER JOIN ProductCategory PC1
      ON P1.ProductID = PC1.ProductID
   INNER JOIN ProductCategory PC2
      ON PC1.CategoryID = PC2.CategoryID
WHERE PC2.ProductID = 6
ORDER BY Name;
```

TIP *Referring to Figure 14-6 will help you construct join queries. Just follow the path of the table joins in the figure, and everything will become clearer.*

Notice that, in this example, we've used some table aliases to make the SQL code a bit shorter (`ProductCategory` is, after all, quite a long word to type!).

This is the same query, written with the alternate syntax (which works on Access):

```
SELECT DISTINCT P1.ProductID, P1.Name
FROM Product P1, ProductCategory PC1, ProductCategory PC2
WHERE P1.ProductID = PC1.ProductID
   AND PC1.CategoryID = PC2.CategoryID
   AND PC2.ProductID = 6
ORDER BY Name;
```

Wow, you have just joined three tables! And, to add to the confusion, you used two instances of the `ProductCategory` table. The action of joining two instances of the same table is called a *self-join*, and it works just as if they were two separate tables.

Joining the two `ProductCategory` instances on the `CategoryID` field generates a list of `ProductID`/`ProductID` pairs, containing products associated with the same category.

Now that you have this list of products, which are related by their category, the rest is simple: In the right side of the list, you filtered according to the `ProductID` that you were looking for (6 in this case). In this manner, in the left side of the list there remained only the products related to the product with an ID of 6. Finally, in the left side of the list you joined with the `Product` table in order to get the names and descriptions of the resulted products.

Note that you still need the `DISTINCT` keyword to filter duplicate records from products that belong to more than one of the resulting categories.

Getting a List of Categories and Their Products

Because you're expert in table joins by now, let's look at another simple exercise: Say you want to get a list containing categories and their products, like this:

Category Name	Product Name
Exotic Costumes	Cleopatra Kit
Exotic Costumes	Miss Santa
Masks	Horned Devil Mask
Masks	Cleopatra Kit
Masks	Sequinned Devil Horns
Scary Costumes	Vampire Disguise
Scary Stuff	Bug Eyed Glasses
Sweet Stuff	Sequinned Devil Horns
Sweet Stuff	Devil Horn Boppers

If you need to associate categories with products, the path followed by joins is quite clear. You have the ProductCategory table, which contains the IDs of associated categories and products. You join this table on its left and right sides to get the category and product names associated with the IDs. Here's the query that does this for you:

```
SELECT C.Name as "Category Name", P.Name as "Product Name"
FROM Product P
INNER JOIN ProductCategory PC ON P.ProductID = PC.ProductID
INNER JOIN Category C ON PC.CategoryID = C.CategoryID
ORDER BY C.Name, P.Name;
```

The same query, rewritten using WHERE statements instead of JOIN statements, looks like this (and works on Access):

```
SELECT C.Name as "Category Name", P.Name as "Product Name"
FROM Product P, ProductCategory PC, Category C
WHERE P.ProductID = PC.ProductID AND PC.CategoryID = C.CategoryID
ORDER BY C.Name, P.Name;
```

Getting the Same Results Using Correlated Subqueries

This method is less obvious, but it's good to know that there are multiple ways to get the same results with SQL. In this particular scenario, the solution using table joins is likely to be faster, but in practice remember that only a good set of tests can show you what's the best solution for your database:

```
SELECT C.Name as "Category Name", Product.Name as "Product Name"
FROM Product, Category C
WHERE Product.ProductID IN
  (SELECT ProductID FROM ProductCategory
   WHERE ProductCategory.CategoryID = C.CategoryID)
ORDER BY C.Name, Product.Name;
```

This query is a bit more complicated than the previous ones—if you have problems understanding it, please reread the section on correlated subqueries in Chapter 6, "Combining SQL Queries."

What you did was to ask from the start for a category name and product name without specifying anything about the linking table, ProductCategory. In the outer query, you asked only for the columns you were interested in without specifying how they're related. However, for each category, the WHERE clause uses the correlated subquery to filter out only the products that are associated with it.

Remember that correlated subqueries execute for each record of the main query. In this case, for each category returned by the outer query, the correlated subquery executes and returns the products associated with that category. The outer query gets the results back and uses them to compose the list containing category and product names.

The important detail to understand is the way the categories from the outer query are used in the subquery:

```
WHERE ProductCategory.CategoryID = C.CategoryID)
```

This line does the whole trick: The category of the outer query (C.CategoryID) is used in a table join in the correlated subquery. The category ID from the outer query is referenced through the C alias defined for Category.

Getting the Most Expensive Products in Each Category

Say you want to get a list containing all existing categories, along with the most expensive two products for each category. Based on the data you have, the list should contain the following products:

Category	Product	Price
Exotic Costumes	Miss Santa	49.9900
Exotic Costumes	Cleopatra Kit	14.9900
Masks	Cleopatra Kit	14.9900
Masks	Beast Mask	5.9900
Scary Costumes	Vampire Disguise	9.9900
Scary Stuff	Bug Eyed Glasses	2.7500
Sweet Stuff	Sequinned Devil Horns	3.7500
Sweet Stuff	Devil Horn Boppers	2.5000

Let's see how to obtain this list with SQL Server, Oracle, and DB2.

SQL Server

For SQL Server, here's the query that does the trick. You get the top two products for each category using a correlated subquery:

```
SELECT C.Name AS "Category", Product.Name AS "Product",
       Product.Price as "Price"
FROM Product, Category C
WHERE Product.ProductID IN
  (SELECT TOP 2 ProductID FROM ProductCategory
   WHERE ProductCategory.CategoryID = C.CategoryID
   ORDER BY Price DESC)
ORDER BY C.Name, Product.Price DESC;
```

DB2

DB2 doesn't allow you to use FETCH FIRST *n* ROWS ONLY in subqueries, so you can't simply translate the SQL Server version (which uses TOP) to a DB2 equivalent.

The DB2 solution uses the ROWNUMBER function, which you already saw in an earlier example. However, this time you use PARTITION BY in combination with ORDER BY to create a ranking for each product in descending order of its price, for each category in part:

```
WITH tmp (CategoryName, ProductName, ProductPrice, rank)
AS
    (SELECT C.Name, P.Name, P.Price,
            ROWNUMBER() OVER (PARTITION BY C.Name ORDER BY P.Price DESC)
            AS rank
```

```
    FROM Product P
    JOIN ProductCategory PC ON P.ProductID = PC.ProductID
    JOIN Category C ON C.CategoryID = PC.CategoryID)

SELECT CategoryName, ProductName, ProductPrice
FROM tmp
WHERE rank <= 2
ORDER BY CategoryName
```

PARTITION BY C.Name specifies that you want the products ranking created separately for each category. ORDER BY P.Price DESC specifies that, for each category, you want the products sorted in descending order of their price.

ROWNUMBER (or ROW_NUMBER) always returns a unique number for each returned row. DB2 also supports two similar functions, RANK and DENSERANK (or DENSE_RANK). RANK and DENSERANK return the same value for records that are equal in respect to the ORDER BY criterion—in this case, if two or more products of a category have the same price, they'll receive the same ranking. The difference between RANK and DENSERANK is that RANK leaves gaps in rankings when two or more products have the same ranking. Say, for example, if the first three most expensive products have the same price, they'll all receive a ranking of 1. The following product in the list will have a RANK of 4 but a DENSERANK of 2 because DENSERANK leaves no gaps.

Oracle

With Oracle, you apply a similar method as for DB2, except that the syntax is a little different. Oracle supports RANK and DENSE_RANK just like DB2, but it doesn't support ROW_NUMBER. For this reason the Oracle query will not be guaranteed to retrieve a maximum of two products for each category:

```
SELECT CategoryName, ProductName, ProductPrice
  FROM
    (SELECT C.Name as CategoryName,
            P.Name as ProductName,
            P.Price as ProductPrice,
            RANK() OVER (PARTITION BY C.Name ORDER BY P.Price DESC)
            AS rank
    FROM Product P
    JOIN ProductCategory PC ON P.ProductID = PC.ProductID
    JOIN Category C ON C.CategoryID = PC.CategoryID)
WHERE rank <= 2
ORDER BY CategoryName;
```

What About Products and Their Departments?

Here you take things one step further and analyze how you can get different product listings based on the departments to which they belong. The queries become a bit more complicated because a fourth table, Department, comes into play.

Selecting Products That Belong to a Specific Department

Say you know the ID of a department, and you want to get all the products that belong to it.

In the previous exercises, you learned how to extract the products in a specific category. Now, instead of looking for the products in a category, you're looking for the products that belong to a list of categories (more specifically, the list of categories in the department for which you're looking).

Using subqueries, you use the IN keyword to filter the results based on a list of category IDs. Here's the SQL query that does the trick for you:

```
SELECT Product.ProductID, Product.Name
FROM Product INNER JOIN ProductCategory
ON Product.ProductID = ProductCategory.ProductID
WHERE ProductCategory.CategoryID IN
    (SELECT CategoryID
    FROM Category
    WHERE DepartmentID = 1)
 ORDER BY Product.Name;
```

This query outputs these records:

ProductID	Name
2	Cleopatra Kit
4	Miss Santa
5	Vampire Disguise

Getting the Same Results Using Table Joins

Using table joins, you need to join the Product, ProductCategory, and Category tables. You don't need to also join the Department table because you don't need

anything from it (its name or description). You filter the results based on the
DepartmentID field of the Category table:

```
SELECT Product.ProductID, Product.Name
FROM Product
    INNER JOIN ProductCategory
    ON Product.ProductID = ProductCategory.ProductID
    INNER JOIN Category
    ON ProductCategory.CategoryID = Category.CategoryID
WHERE Category.DepartmentID = 1
ORDER BY Product.Name;
```

The same query, without using JOIN, looks like this (note that this form will
work on Access and pre-9i versions of Oracle):

```
SELECT Product.ProductID, Product.Name
FROM Product, ProductCategory, Category
WHERE Product.ProductID = ProductCategory.ProductID
    AND ProductCategory.CategoryID = Category.CategoryID
    AND Category.DepartmentID = 1
ORDER BY Product.Name;
```

Getting a List of the Departments and Their Products

Now, what if you want to see a list containing the departments and the products
that belong to them: For example:

Department	Product
Costume Accessories	Beast Mask
Costume Accessories	Cleopatra Kit
Costume Accessories	Horned Devil Mask
Costume Accessories	Sequinned Devil Horns
Full Costumes	Cleopatra Kit
Full Costumes	Miss Santa
Full Costumes	Vampire Disguise
Jokes and Tricks	Bug Eyed Glasses
Jokes and Tricks	Devil Horn Boppers
Jokes and Tricks	Sequinned Devil Horns

This time, apart from the Product, ProductCategory, and Category tables, you'll also need the Department table. You need it to extract the department names.

Using table joins, you can extract this list using the following query. To get a list with products and departments, you make the usual trip starting with the Product table and ending with Department. This trip walks through the tables that have relationships: Product...ProductCategory...Category...Department. If you follow this road, what the query does becomes quite obvious:

```
SELECT Department.Name AS "Department",
       Product.Name AS "Product"
FROM Department
   INNER JOIN Category
   ON Department.DepartmentID = Category.DepartmentID
   INNER JOIN ProductCategory
   ON Category.CategoryID = ProductCategory.CategoryID
   INNER JOIN Product
   ON ProductCategory.ProductID = Product.ProductID
ORDER BY Department.Name, Product.Name;
```

You ordered departments by name, and for each department the products are also ordered by name.

Here is the same query using the alternate syntax that works on Access, as well as the other platforms:

```
SELECT Department.Name AS "Department",
       Product.Name AS "Product"
FROM Product, ProductCategory, Category, Department
WHERE Product.ProductID = ProductCategory.ProductID
  AND ProductCategory.CategoryID = Category.CategoryID
  AND Category.DepartmentID = Department.DepartmentID
ORDER BY Department.Name, Product.Name;
```

Getting the Same List with a Correlated Subquery

If you prefer using correlated subqueries, this is the way to go:

```
SELECT D.Name AS "Department", P.Name AS "Product"
FROM Product P, Department D
WHERE ProductID IN
      (SELECT ProductID
       FROM ProductCategory INNER JOIN Category
       ON ProductCategory.CategoryID = Category.CategoryID
       WHERE Category.DepartmentID = D.DepartmentID)
ORDER BY D.Name, P.Name;
```

On the outer query, you only specify the fields in which you're interested and enforce the relationships between them using the subquery. The correlated (inner) subquery is called for each department returned by the outer query, and it returns the ProductIDs associated with that department.

Note that you have flexibility to write the subquery in any number of ways, including using another subquery instead of table joins, like this:

```
SELECT D.Name AS "Department", Product.Name AS "Product"
FROM Product, Department D
WHERE ProductID IN
      (SELECT ProductID from ProductCategory
       WHERE ProductCategory.CategoryID IN
               (SELECT CategoryID FROM Category
                WHERE D.DepartmentID = DepartmentID))
ORDER BY D.Name, Product.Name;
```

You'll rarely want to complicate your queries like this, but it demonstrates how flexible SQL can be.

What About Departments That Have No Products?

In the previous queries, when you retrieved a list of departments and their products, you always assumed that each department had at least one product. Just for the fun of it, let's add a new department now:

```
INSERT INTO Department (Name) VALUES ('Books');
```

With this new department in place, run the previous SQL queries again. Maybe you'll be surprised to see that the new department doesn't show up, but this behavior is quite correct.

If you want to have all the departments listed, regardless of whether they have products, you'll need to modify the first query to use outer joins instead of inner joins. Chapter 7, "Querying Multiple Tables," presented outer joins. Here's the updated query:

```
SELECT Department.Name AS "Department",
       Product.Name AS "Product"
FROM Department
   LEFT JOIN Category
   ON Department.DepartmentID = Category.DepartmentID
   LEFT JOIN ProductCategory
   ON Category.CategoryID = ProductCategory.CategoryID
   LEFT JOIN Product
   ON ProductCategory.ProductID = Product.ProductID
ORDER BY Department.Name, Product.Name;
```

The result of this query is as follows:

```
Department                    Product

----------------------        ------------------------
Books                         NULL
Costume Accessories           Beast Mask
Costume Accessories           Cleopatra Kit
Costume Accessories           Horned Devil Mask
Costume Accessories           Sequinned Devil Horns
Full Costumes                 Cleopatra Kit
Full Costumes                 Miss Santa
Full Costumes                 Vampire Disguise
Jokes and Tricks              Bug Eyed Glasses
Jokes and Tricks              Devil Horn Boppers
Jokes and Tricks              Sequinned Devil Horns
```

You used left outer joins in this example to make sure all departments are returned. If you used right outer joins instead, you would have to make that all products were listed instead—including the ones that don't belong to any department.

Remember that an outer join *always takes all the rows* in one side of the join (left or right) and tries to match with rows from the other side of the join. If no match is made, NULL is assumed instead.

This is different from the inner join (the default type of join), which is exclusive—it only returns rows that have matches in both sides of the join. The opposite is the full join (FULL OUTER JOIN), which includes all the rows in both sides of the join.

How Many Products Belong to Each Department?

If you managed to find out how to get a list of products for each department, you're only one step away from counting how many products exist in each department. You do this using the GROUP BY clause and using the COUNT aggregate function:

```
SELECT Department.Name AS "Department",
       COUNT(Product.Name) AS "Products"
FROM Product
    INNER JOIN ProductCategory
    ON Product.ProductID = ProductCategory.ProductID
```

```
   INNER JOIN Category
   ON ProductCategory.CategoryID = Category.CategoryID
   INNER JOIN Department
   ON Category.DepartmentID = Department.DepartmentID
GROUP BY Department.Name
ORDER BY Department.Name;
```

Recall that we discussed the GROUP BY clause and aggregate functions in Chapter 4, "Summarizing and Grouping Data."

Here's the results list:

Department	Products
Costume Accessories	4
Full Costumes	3
Jokes and Tricks	3

If you wanted to count only those products that are on promotion for each department, you'd simply need to filter the products:

```
SELECT Department.Name AS "Department",
       COUNT(Product.Name) AS "Featured Products"
FROM Product
   INNER JOIN ProductCategory
   ON Product.ProductID = ProductCategory.ProductID
   INNER JOIN Category
   ON ProductCategory.CategoryID = Category.CategoryID
   INNER JOIN Department
   ON Category.DepartmentID = Department.DepartmentID
WHERE Product.OnDepartmentPromotion = 1
GROUP BY Department.Name
ORDER BY Department.Name;
```

The results should look like this:

Department	Featured Products
-------------------	------------------
Costume Accessories	1
Full Costumes	1
Jokes and Tricks	1

Getting the Same List with Correlated Subqueries

You can obtain the same results using correlated subqueries. There are two main ways you can rewrite the previous queries using correlated subqueries.

In the first example, you first group the products by department using GROUP BY and perform a COUNT for each group:

```
SELECT D.Name AS "Department", COUNT(P.Name) AS "Products"
FROM Department D, Product P
WHERE ProductID IN
      (SELECT ProductID
       FROM ProductCategory INNER JOIN Category
       ON ProductCategory.CategoryID = Category.CategoryID
       WHERE Category.DepartmentID = D.DepartmentID)
GROUP BY D.Name
ORDER BY D.Name;
```

In the second solution, you use a subquery to calculate the number of products for each department instead of using GROUP BY to group by departments. Note that the subquery is still a correlated subquery, and it executes once for each department selected by the outer query:

```
SELECT D.Name AS "Department",
       (SELECT COUNT(ProductID)
        FROM ProductCategory INNER JOIN Category
        ON ProductCategory.CategoryID = Category.CategoryID
        WHERE Category.DepartmentID = D.DepartmentID) AS "Products"
FROM Department D;
```

What Is the Average Price of Products in Each Department?

Suppose you want to see the average price for all the products in each department. You can do this quickly now because it is similar to the query that counted the number of products in each department:

```
SELECT Department.Name AS "Department",
       AVG(Product.Price) AS "Average Price"
FROM Product
   INNER JOIN ProductCategory
   ON Product.ProductID = ProductCategory.ProductID
   INNER JOIN Category
   ON ProductCategory.CategoryID = Category.CategoryID
   INNER JOIN Department
   ON Category.DepartmentID = Department.DepartmentID
GROUP BY Department.Name;
```

After executing this query, you see that the Full Costumes department has the most expensive products:

Department	Average Price
Costume Accessories	7.6800
Full Costumes	24.9900
Jokes and Tricks	3.0000

You can complicate things a bit more and ask, for example, for the average price in each department but only for those departments having at least three products. Also, you can request the results listed in descending order of the average department price:

```
SELECT Department.Name AS "Department",
       COUNT(Product.Name) AS "Products",
       AVG(Product.Price) AS "Average Price"
FROM Product
   INNER JOIN ProductCategory
   ON Product.ProductID = ProductCategory.ProductID
   INNER JOIN Category
   ON ProductCategory.CategoryID = Category.CategoryID
   INNER JOIN Department
   ON Category.DepartmentID = Department.DepartmentID
GROUP BY Department.Name
HAVING COUNT(Product.Price)>=3
ORDER BY AVG(Product.Price) DESC;
```

Because all departments have at least three products, you'll receive all of them back; this time, they're listed in descending order of their average price:

```
Department                    Products            Average Price


--------------------          -----------         ----------------------
Full Costumes                    3                   24.9900
Costume Accessories              4                    7.6800
Jokes and Tricks                 3                    3.0000
```

Updating Catalog Information

In this section, you'll look at some of the most common operations that insert, update, or delete catalog records. We won't attempt to list all queries that would be required in a complete solution because many of them are similar.

In this case study, you're more interested in the statements themselves, rather than the way they're packaged: In most cases, where possible, the statements should be saved as stored procedures into the database. This is a good practice that keeps the code clean and also brings some other benefits, as you learned in Chapter 9, "Using Stored Procedures." We'll first present the statements and then show how to package them as SQL Server, Oracle, and DB2 stored procedures.

Almost any command that updates information has input parameters, which define how to update, insert, or delete catalog information. When presenting the statements without including them in stored procedures, we'll replace the input parameters with general identifiers, such as <<ProductID>> or <<DepartmentName>>.

These should be replaced by stored procedure parameters if you're using stored procedures or by values if you're executing the commands directly on the database.

These will be most useful for MySQL users because MySQL doesn't support stored procedures. With Access queries, the stored procedure parameters aren't separately declared; instead they're used directly in the statements, written between square brackets. For more information, see Chapter 9, "Using Stored Procedures."

Let's start with something simple. . . .

Updating a Department

When you want to modify or delete a single record, you always identify it by its primary key. This ensures that you only affect a single record or no records at all. For example, the following is a typical command that updates the name of the department with an ID of 1:

```
UPDATE Department
SET Name = 'Weird Stuff'
WHERE DepartmentID = 1;
```

As you can see, you don't attempt to change the department's ID because you have no reason to do that. Moreover, changing the value of an ID column might break the referential integrity, established through foreign keys, with existing categories.

A command that updates a department's information looks like this if you're executing the command directly in the database:

```
UPDATE Department
SET Name = <<DepartmentName>>,
    Description = <<DepartmentDescription>>
WHERE DepartmentID = <<DepartmentID>>;
```

Packaged as a SQL Server stored procedure, the query looks like this:

```
CREATE PROCEDURE UpdateDepartment
(@DepartmentID int,
@DepartmentName varchar(50),
@DepartmentDescription varchar(1000))

AS
UPDATE Department
SET Name = @DepartmentName,
    Description = @DepartmentDescription
WHERE DepartmentID = @DepartmentID;
```

The same procedure looks like this for Oracle:

```
CREATE PROCEDURE UpdateDepartment
(DeptID IN integer,
DepartmentName IN varchar2,
DepartmentDescription IN varchar2)

AS
  BEGIN
    UPDATE Department
    SET Name = DepartmentName,
        Description = DepartmentDescription
    WHERE DepartmentID = DeptID;
  END;
/
```

TIP *Remember to use the* SHOW ERRORS *command, which comes in handy when writing stored procedures in SQL*Plus.*

And the DB2 equivalent is as follows:

```
CREATE PROCEDURE DB2ADMIN.UpdateDepartment
(i_DepartmentID INT,
 i_DepartmentName VARCHAR(50),
 i_DepartmentDescription VARCHAR(1000))

P1: BEGIN
    UPDATE Department
    SET Name = i_DepartmentName,
        Description = i_DepartmentDescription
    WHERE DepartmentID = i_DepartmentID;
END P1
```

Once you have stored a stored procedure, you can execute it using the EXECUTE command. Let's look at how you can call UpdateDepartment inside a transaction and then roll back the transaction: This allows you to test that the stored procedure works okay, without damaging the existing department data. (Chapter 10, "Transactions," covered transactions.)

Here's the SQL Server version of the code:

```
BEGIN TRANSACTION
EXECUTE UpdateDepartment 1, 'Strange new name',
                            'Strange new description'
SELECT * FROM Department
ROLLBACK TRANSACTION;
```

The same script looks a bit different with Oracle:

```
EXECUTE UpdateDepartment (1, 'Strange new name',
                            'Strange new description');
SELECT * FROM Department;
ROLLBACK WORK;
```

The DB2 version is similar to the Oracle syntax, except that you use the CALL keyword instead of EXECUTE:

```
CALL UpdateDepartment (1, 'Strange new name',
                              'Strange new description');
SELECT * FROM Department;
ROLLBACK WORK;
```

In all cases, you rolled back the changes, so none of your amendments were actually applied. However, you've verified that the procedure works as expected.

Adding a New Category

The SQL query that adds a new category is simple, and the way you package it as a stored procedure is just as in the previous example. The query looks like this:

```
INSERT INTO Category (DepartmentID, Name, Description)
VALUES (<<DepartmentID>>, <<CategoryName>>,
        <<CategoryDescription>>);
```

Because `CategoryID` is an autonumbered field, you don't specify values for it when inserting new rows into `Category`.

Deleting a Department

When deleting departments, you're faced a new issue: The department you want to delete might have categories associated with it, so trying to delete it can break the referential integrity rules.

So how do you deal with this problem? How do you make sure you don't generate any database exceptions? Well, the answer relates to how the application is architected.

For example, you might simply want not to avoid database exceptions and handle the errors within the application's code. So, you might simply remove the department, without caring if you break any existing integrity constraints:

```
DELETE FROM Department
WHERE DepartmentID = <<DepartmentID>>;
```

This would be a perfectly fine stored procedure if the application were meant to handle the database errors itself. In this scenario, you rely on the database to throw an error if you attempt to delete a department that has any related categories and on the software application to catch these errors and respond accordingly.

If you want to avoid any errors, you need to test if there are any categories that belong to the department that you're trying to delete. So, you first issue a SQL command that tests if any related categories exist, like this:

```
SELECT Name FROM Category
WHERE DepartmentID = <<DepartmentID>>;
```

If no rows are returned, you can delete the department:

```
DELETE FROM Department
WHERE DepartmentID = <<DepartmentID>>;
```

You can package these two commands as a SQL Server stored procedure; here we've used NOT EXISTS, but you could very well use other techniques, such as using COUNT to see how many categories belong to that department:

```
CREATE PROCEDURE DeleteDepartment
(@DepartmentID int)
AS
IF NOT EXISTS
    (SELECT Name FROM Category WHERE DepartmentID = @DepartmentID)
DELETE FROM Department
WHERE DepartmentID = @DepartmentID;
```

Let's now see the Oracle version of the DeleteDepartment stored procedure. Notice that NOT EXISTS is used in a slightly different manner here:

```
CREATE PROCEDURE DeleteDepartment
(DeptID IN integer)
AS
  BEGIN
    DELETE FROM Department
    WHERE DepartmentID = DeptID
    AND NOT EXISTS (SELECT Name FROM Category WHERE DepartmentID = DeptID);
  END;
/
```

Finally, you have the following for DB2:

```
CREATE PROCEDURE DB2ADMIN.DeleteDepartment
(i_DepartmentID INT)
P1: BEGIN
```

```
   IF NOT EXISTS (SELECT Name FROM Category
                    WHERE DepartmentID = i_DepartmentID)
   THEN
      DELETE FROM Department
      WHERE DepartmentID = i_DepartmentID;
   END IF;
END P1
```

Assigning a Product to a Category

To assign a product to a category, you need to execute a simple INSERT command
that inserts a pair of rows into the ProductCategory table:

```
INSERT INTO ProductCategory (ProductID, CategoryID)
VALUES (<<ProductID>>, <<CategoryID>>);
```

Let's see the SQL Server procedure that does the same thing:

```
CREATE PROCEDURE AssignProductToCategory
(@ProductID int, @CategoryID int)
AS

INSERT INTO ProductCategory (ProductID, CategoryID)
VALUES (@ProductID, @CategoryID)
RETURN;
```

Its Oracle version looks like this:

```
CREATE PROCEDURE AssignProductToCategory
(ProdID IN integer,
 CategID IN integer)

AS
   BEGIN
      INSERT INTO ProductCategory (ProductID, CategoryID)
      VALUES (ProdID, CategID);
   END;
/
```

And the DB2 version looks like this:

```
CREATE PROCEDURE DB2ADMIN.AssignProductToCategory
(i_ProductID INT,
 i_CategoryID INT )
P1: BEGIN
   INSERT INTO ProductCategory (ProductID, CategoryID)
   VALUES (i_ProductID, i_CategoryID);
END P1
```

These stored procedures assume that the supplied CategoryID and ProductID values are valid. However, you can use the techniques you saw in the previous example to verify this.

Creating a New Product and Automatically Assigning It to a Category

This isn't a difficult task, but it's got a catch. There are basically two operations that you need to perform: adding a new product to the Product table and then associating this product with the appropriate category by adding a record into ProductCategory.

The catch is that product IDs are automatically generated by the database (because you designed them this way), so you need a way to find these IDs.

The first of the two operations is a simple INSERT into the Product table:

```
INSERT INTO Product (... fields ...)
VALUES (... values ...)
```

The second operation that you need to perform is an INSERT into ProductCategory:

```
INSERT INTO ProductCategory (ProductID, CategoryID)
VALUES (<<ProductID>>, <<CategoryID>>);
```

Let's see these two operations as a SQL Server stored procedure:

```
CREATE PROCEDURE CreateProductToCategory
(@CategoryID int,
 @ProductName varchar(50),
 @ProductDescription varchar(1000),
 @ProductPrice money,
 @ProductImage varchar(50),
 @OnDepartmentPromotion bit,
 @OnCatalogPromotion bit)
AS
```

```
DECLARE @ProductID int

INSERT INTO Product (Name, Description, Price,
                        ImagePath, OnDepartmentPromotion, OnCatalogPromotion)
VALUES (@ProductName, @ProductDescription, CONVERT(money,@ProductPrice),
          @ProductImage, @OnDepartmentPromotion, @OnCatalogPromotion)

SELECT @ProductID = @@Identity

INSERT INTO ProductCategory (ProductID, CategoryID)
VALUES (@ProductID, @CategoryID)
RETURN;
```

With SQL Server, you use the @@Identity system variable, which returns the last-generated ID. You need to save its value to a local variable (@ProductID in this case) immediately after you issue the INSERT command because SQL Server resets its value automatically.

With Oracle, you use sequences to automatically generate ID values—the sequence that generates the value is the one that can tell you what the current value is. With the DepartmentIDSeq sequence, you call DepartmentIDSeq.NextVal to get the next value of the sequence. To get the current value, you call DepartmentID.CurrVal:

```
CREATE PROCEDURE CreateProductToCategory
(CategoryID integer,
 ProductName IN varchar2,
 ProductDescription IN varchar2)
AS
BEGIN
  INSERT INTO Product (Name, Description)
  VALUES (ProductName, ProductDescription);

  INSERT INTO ProductCategory (ProductID, CategoryID)
  VALUES (ProductID.CurrVal, CategoryID);
END;
/
```

The DB2 version of this procedure looks as follows:

```
CREATE PROCEDURE DB2ADMIN.CreateProductToCategory
(i_CategoryID INT,
 i_ProductName VARCHAR(50),
 i_ProductDescription VARCHAR(1000),
```

```
    i_ProductPrice DECIMAL(7,2),
    i_ProductImage VARCHAR(50),
    i_OnDepartmentPromotion SMALLINT,
    i_OnCatalogPromotion SMALLINT)

P1: BEGIN
    DECLARE pid INT;
    INSERT INTO Product
                (Name, Description, Price, ImagePath,
                 OnDepartmentPromotion, OnCatalogPromotion)
    VALUES (i_ProductName, i_ProductDescription,
            i_ProductPrice, i_ProductImage,
            i_OnDepartmentPromotion, i_OnCatalogPromotion);

    SET pid = IDENTITY_VAL_LOCAL();

    INSERT INTO ProductCategory (ProductID, CategoryID)
    VALUES (pid, i_CategoryID);

END P1
```

Because DB2 supports autonumbered fields, you can use the `IDENTITY_VAL_LOCAL()` function to retrieve the next available ID and assign it to your new product.

We can't provide a similar example with MySQL because it doesn't support stored procedures, but it does have something similar to SQL Server's @@Identity—it's the `LAST_INSERT_ID()` function, which also returns the last automatically generated value. You can display its value like this:

```
SELECT LAST_INSERT_ID();
```

After inserting a product into the Product table in MySQL, you can populate ProductCategory like this:

```
INSERT INTO ProductCategory (ProductID, CategoryID)
VALUES (LAST_INSERT_ID(), <<CategoryID>>);
```

Removing a Product

Imagine that you want to remove a product from the database. The problem you have is that the product can belong to a number of categories, and you need to remove the ProductCategory entries before removing the product.

You want to create a stored procedure or script with the following function-ality: You provide as parameters a product ID and a category ID. The script will first remove the product from the category by deleting a ProductCategory record. Then, if no more categories are left for this product, the product is removed from the Product table as well. In other words, you make sure there are no products that don't have an associated category: As soon as you detach the product from its last category, the product is removed altogether.

This functionality is simple to implement as a number of separated SQL statements. First, you delete the product from the mentioned category:

```
DELETE FROM ProductCategory
WHERE CategoryID=<<CategoryID>> AND ProductID=<<ProductID>>;
```

Second, you count how many categories are associated with the product:

```
SELECT COUNT(*) FROM ProductCategory
WHERE ProductID=<<ProductID>>;
```

If you get a value higher than zero, you leave the product alone. Otherwise, you remove the product from the Product table:

```
DELETE FROM Product where ProductID=<<ProductID>>;
```

Okay, the theory is simple. Let's see how to put it in practice in a SQL Server procedure:

```
CREATE PROCEDURE RemoveProduct
(@ProductID int, @CategoryID int)
AS

DELETE FROM ProductCategory
WHERE CategoryID=@CategoryID AND ProductID=@ProductID

IF (SELECT COUNT(*) FROM ProductCategory
                    WHERE ProductID=@ProductID) = 0
    DELETE FROM Product WHERE ProductID=@ProductID;
```

Here's one implementation of the same procedure in Oracle:

```
CREATE OR REPLACE PROCEDURE RemoveProduct
(ProdID int, CategID int)
AS
```

```
BEGIN
  DECLARE
    CategoriesCount integer;
  BEGIN
    DELETE FROM ProductCategory
    WHERE CategoryID = CategID AND ProductID = ProdID;

    SELECT COUNT(*) INTO CategoriesCount FROM ProductCategory
      WHERE ProductID = ProdID;

    IF CategoriesCount = 0 THEN
      DELETE FROM Product WHERE ProductID = ProdID;
    END IF;
  END;
END;
/
```

Finally, let's take a quick look at the DB2 equivalent:

```
CREATE PROCEDURE DB2ADMIN.RemoveProduct
( i_ProductID INT,
  i_CategoryID INT)

P1: BEGIN
    DELETE FROM ProductCategory
    WHERE CategoryID = i_CategoryID AND
          ProductID = i_ProductID;
    IF (SELECT COUNT(*) FROM ProductCategory
        WHERE ProductID = i_ProductID) = 0
    THEN
        DELETE FROM Product WHERE ProductID = i_ProductID;
    END IF;
END P1
```

Searching the Catalog

You'll now see a way to search the product catalog for products containing a number of words in their name or description. You can do either an all-words search or an any-words search in the catalog.

In an all-words search, you're looking for products containing all the words in the search string. In any-words search, you're looking for products containing any of the words in the search string.

NOTE *Each database product has special features and options for doing advanced full-text searches, with ranking, word similarities, and other complex options. Full-text searches are usually done using the* CONTAINS *keyword, but it works only if the table is full-text indexed. Full-text searching and indexing is a database-specific feature that isn't part of SQL-99 and isn't covered in this book.*

The Basics

The following query searches for *devil mask* with an all-words search. This means you're searching for products having both words (*devil* and *mask*) in their name.:

```
SELECT Name, Description
FROM Product
WHERE (Description LIKE '%devil%' OR Name LIKE '%devil%')
  AND (Description LIKE '%mask%' OR Name LIKE '%mask%');
```

Using the sample data presented earlier in the chapter, this query generates the following:

Name	Description
Horned Devil Mask	Full devil mask with horns. The perfect Halloween disguise!

Note the percent wildcard character, which replaces any string of zero or more characters. The expression Description LIKE '%devil%' returns true for any description that contains the word *devil*.

You can shorten the previous SQL query a bit by using a neat trick: You can concatenate Description and Name and search for the words in the resulted string. String concatenation is performed differently by databases. Here's how to do it with SQL Server:

```
SELECT Name, Description
FROM Product
WHERE (Description + Name LIKE '%devil%')
  AND (Description + Name LIKE '%mask%');
```

With Oracle and DB2, you use || instead of +:

```
SELECT Name, Description
FROM Product
WHERE (Description || Name LIKE '%devil%')
  AND (Description || Name LIKE '%mask%');
```

MySQL uses the CONCAT function:

```
SELECT Name, Description
FROM Product
WHERE (CONCAT(Description, Name) LIKE '%devil%')
  AND (CONCAT(Description, Name) LIKE '%mask%');
```

There are alternative ways of achieving the same result. For example, with MySQL you can use the INSTR function, which returns the position of the first occurrence of a substring in a string. Here's how to use it:

```
SELECT Name, Description
FROM Product
WHERE INSTR(CONCAT(Description, Name), 'devil') > 0
  AND INSTR(CONCAT(Description, Name), 'mask') > 0;
```

So far we've presented examples with all-words searches. For any-words searches, you just need to use OR instead of AND in the WHERE clause:

```
SELECT Name, Description
FROM Product
WHERE (Description LIKE '%devil%' OR Name LIKE '%devil%')
  OR (Description LIKE '%mask%' OR Name LIKE '%mask%');
```

Using this sample data, this returns the following:

Name	Description
Beast Mask	Red-eyed and open-mouthed scary mask guaranteed to scare!
Horned Devil Mask	Full devil mask with horns. The perfect Halloween disguise!
Sequinned Devil Horns	Shiny red horns for the little devil inside you!
Devil Horn Boppers	These red glitter boppers are guaranteed to attract attention. They will soon be under your spell!

The SearchCatalog Stored Procedure

The previous statements work fine, but they need to be dynamically generated by the application and sent to the database as such. If you want to store them as stored procedures, things become a bit more complicated.

First, you need to get the words to search for as stored procedure parameters. You can optionally receive a single string and split it into separate words, but this would typically result in a messy, slow, and database-specific stored procedure.

In the following stored procedures, you receive a parameter named AllWords that specifies whether you do an all-words or an any-words search. You also take five string parameters, having a default value of NULL (so you don't have to specify values for all of them when calling the procedure), which will contain the words for which you're looking. It's simple to add more parameters and allow the stored procedure to handle more input parameters.

 TIP *Some people think it's dangerous to pose this kind of limitation to the end user (such as not processing more than a fixed number of words from the search string). Well, this may be true, but this limitation doesn't stop people from using Google (which has a limitation of 10 words).*

SQL Server

The following is the SQL Server version of the SearchCatalog stored procedure. The @AllWords parameter is a BIT data type, so it can receive values of 0 or 1:

```
CREATE PROCEDURE SearchCatalog
(@AllWords bit,
@Word1 varchar(15) = NULL,
@Word2 varchar(15) = NULL,
@Word3 varchar(15) = NULL,
@Word4 varchar(15) = NULL,
@Word5 varchar(15) = NULL)
AS

IF @AllWords = 0
    SELECT Name, Description
    FROM Product
    WHERE (Name + Description LIKE '%'+@Word1+'%')
        OR (Name + Description LIKE '%'+@Word2+'%' AND @Word2 IS NOT NULL)
        OR (Name + Description LIKE '%'+@Word3+'%' AND @Word3 IS NOT NULL)
        OR (Name + Description LIKE '%'+@Word4+'%' AND @Word4 IS NOT NULL)
        OR (Name + Description LIKE '%'+@Word5+'%' AND @Word5 IS NOT NULL)

IF @AllWords = 1
    SELECT Name, Description
    FROM Product
    WHERE (Name + Description LIKE '%'+@Word1+'%')
      AND (Name + Description LIKE '%'+@Word2+'%' OR @Word2 IS NULL)
      AND (Name + Description LIKE '%'+@Word3+'%' OR @Word3 IS NULL)
      AND (Name + Description LIKE '%'+@Word4+'%' OR @Word4 IS NULL)
      AND (Name + Description LIKE '%'+@Word5+'%' OR @Word5 IS NULL);
```

Although it's quite lengthy, the stored procedure isn't complicated. The important thing to understand is the logic of the SELECT statements. In an any-words search, because the conditions are tied with OR, you need to make sure they return False for the NULL words. Also, note that you require at least one word to be provided:

```
SELECT Name, Description
FROM Product
WHERE (Name + Description LIKE '%'+@Word1+'%')
    OR (Name + Description LIKE '%'+@Word2+'%' AND @Word2 IS NOT NULL)
    OR (Name + Description LIKE '%'+@Word3+'%' AND @Word3 IS NOT NULL)
    OR (Name + Description LIKE '%'+@Word4+'%' AND @Word4 IS NOT NULL)
    OR (Name + Description LIKE '%'+@Word5+'%' AND @Word5 IS NOT NULL)
```

In an all-words search, this is exactly the opposite. You do require at least
a matching word, and the rest of the conditions need to return true for the NULL
words (the words that haven't been specified by the calling program):

```
SELECT Name, Description
FROM Product
WHERE (Name + Description LIKE '%'+@Word1+'%')
   AND (Name + Description LIKE '%'+@Word2+'%' OR @Word2 IS NULL)
   AND (Name + Description LIKE '%'+@Word3+'%' OR @Word3 IS NULL)
   AND (Name + Description LIKE '%'+@Word4+'%' OR @Word4 IS NULL)
   AND (Name + Description LIKE '%'+@Word5+'%' OR @Word5 IS NULL);
```

It's interesting to see how you dealt with the all-words search, where all
words except the first one are also checked if they're NULL. This is required; otherwise, the logical condition will return false if you have NULL words (which is their
default value), and the stored procedure wouldn't return any results.

Now let's search for the words *devil* and *mask* using an all-words search:

```
EXECUTE SearchCatalog 1, 'devil', 'mask';
```

Using the sample data provided earlier, the results should look like this:

```
Name                          Description

--------------------          -----------------------------------------
Horned Devil Mask             Full devil mask with horns. The perfect
                                       Halloween disguise!
```

Now let's do an any-words search using the same words:

```
EXECUTE SearchCatalog 0, 'devil', 'mask';
```

The results look like this:

Name	Description
Beast Mask	Red-eyed and open-mouthed scary mask guaranteed to scare!
Horned Devil Mask	Full devil mask with horns. The perfect Halloween disguise!
Sequinned Devil Horns	Shiny red horns for the little devil inside you!
Devil Horn Boppers	These red glitter boppers are guaranteed to attract attention. They will soon be under your spell!

Oracle

As you learned in Chapter 9, "Using Stored Procedures," you'll create a package that'll help you return records from the stored procedure. Create the Types package like this:

```
CREATE OR REPLACE PACKAGE Types
AS
    TYPE CursorType IS REF CURSOR;
END;
/
```

Next, create the SearchCatalog stored procedure like this:

```
CREATE OR REPLACE PROCEDURE SearchCatalog
(retCursor IN OUT Types.CursorType,
 AllWords IN NUMBER := 0,
 Word1 IN VARCHAR := NULL,
 Word2 IN VARCHAR := NULL,
 Word3 IN VARCHAR := NULL,
 Word4 IN VARCHAR := NULL,
 Word5 IN VARCHAR := NULL)
AS
```

```
BEGIN
  IF AllWords <> 1 THEN
    OPEN retCursor FOR
    SELECT Name, Description
    FROM Product
    WHERE (Name||Description LIKE '%'||Word1||'%')
       OR (Name||Description LIKE '%'||Word2||'%' AND Word2 IS NOT NULL)
       OR (Name||Description LIKE '%'||Word3||'%' AND Word3 IS NOT NULL)
       OR (Name||Description LIKE '%'||Word4||'%' AND Word4 IS NOT NULL)
       OR (Name||Description LIKE '%'||Word5||'%' AND Word5 IS NOT NULL);
  ELSE
    OPEN retCursor FOR
    SELECT Name, Description
    FROM Product
    WHERE (Name||Description LIKE '%'||Word1||'%')
      AND (Name||Description LIKE '%'||Word2||'%' OR Word2 IS NULL)
      AND (Name||Description LIKE '%'||Word3||'%' OR Word3 IS NULL)
      AND (Name||Description LIKE '%'||Word4||'%' OR Word4 IS NULL)
      AND (Name||Description LIKE '%'||Word5||'%' OR Word5 IS NULL);
  END IF;
END;
/
```

To execute an all-words search, execute the procedure and list the results using the following commands in SQL*Plus:

```
VARIABLE C RefCursor
EXEC SearchCatalog (:C, 1, 'Devil', 'Mask')
PRINT C;
```

To do an any-words search, execute the stored procedure like this:

```
VARIABLE C RefCursor
EXEC SearchCatalog (:C, 0, 'Devil', 'Mask')
PRINT C;
```

DB2

The following is the DB2 version of the SearchCatalog stored procedure. The @AllWords parameter in this case is a SMALLINT data type because DB2 doesn't have a BIT type:

```
CREATE PROCEDURE DB2ADMIN.SearchCatalog
(i_AllWords SMALLINT,
 i_Word1 VARCHAR(15),
 i_Word2 VARCHAR(15),
 i_Word3 VARCHAR(15),
 i_Word4 VARCHAR(15),
 i_Word5 VARCHAR(15))

RESULT SETS 1
P1: BEGIN

DECLARE curs1 CURSOR WITH RETURN FOR
   SELECT Name, Description FROM Product
   WHERE (Name || Description LIKE '%' ||i_Word1|| '%')
      OR (Name || Description LIKE '%' ||i_Word2|| '%'
                              AND i_Word2 IS NOT NULL)
      OR (Name || Description LIKE '%' ||i_Word3|| '%'
                              AND i_Word3 IS NOT NULL)
      OR (Name || Description LIKE '%' ||i_Word4|| '%'
                              AND i_Word4 IS NOT NULL)
      OR (Name || Description LIKE '%' ||i_Word5|| '%'
                              AND i_Word5 IS NOT NULL);

DECLARE curs2 CURSOR WITH RETURN FOR
   SELECT Name, Description FROM Product
   WHERE (Name || Description LIKE '%' ||i_Word1|| '%')
     AND (Name || Description LIKE '%' ||i_Word2|| '%'
                              OR i_Word2 IS NULL)
     AND (Name || Description LIKE '%' ||i_Word3|| '%'
                              OR i_Word3 IS NULL)
     AND (Name || Description LIKE '%' ||i_Word4|| '%'
                              OR i_Word4 IS NULL)
     AND (Name || Description LIKE '%' ||i_Word5|| '%'
                              OR i_Word5 IS NULL);

IF i_AllWords = 0 THEN
   OPEN curs1;
ELSE
   OPEN curs2;
END IF;

END P1
```

Because you can't explicitly set the search terms to NULL in your stored procedure, you need to enter NULL for any clause that isn't used when the procedure is called. To call this procedure, you can open Command Console and enter the following code:

```
CALL SearchCatalog(0, 'Devil', 'Mask', NULL, NULL, NULL)
```

Summary

Here you are, at the end of what was quite a long and intense case study. We hope you had fun with it and were able to reinforce your understanding of many of the subjects presented throughout the book.

The chapter started by creating the data structures to hold product catalog information. There were only four data tables, but as you could see, they were just enough for your purposes.

The chapter continued by presenting a range of SELECT statements on your data. You could see the same results being returned using table joins, subqueries, and correlated subqueries.

The next step was to update catalog information. You saw how to add, remove, and update different pieces of data in your catalog. You also saw how to save these statements as SQL Server, Oracle, and DB2 stored procedures. The case study ended by showing a simple method of searching catalog products.

Case Study: Implementing Role-Based Security

THIS CHAPTER WALKS YOU through a case study examining how to use SQL and stored procedures to implement role-based security. You can implement the case study on any back-end relational database that supports stored procedures, such as SQL Server, DB2, or Oracle, and for any kind of application, be it e-commerce, intranet, or anything else.

 NOTE *The code download for this chapter includes separate scripts that will allow you to create the required tables and stored procedures on SQL Server, DB2, and Oracle.*

The goal of this case study is to show you a flexible, extensible solution and explain how we came to the conclusions used to build the solution. By the end of the chapter, you should have a firm grasp on key concepts such as roles, permissions, and users, and you should know what kinds of features must be made available to an application to support role-based security.

What Is Role-Based Security?

Role-Based Security (RBS) is a system by which users are granted permissions *implicitly* by being assigned various roles. A *role* is a collection of *permissions,* or access points. Each permission indicates an ability to perform some action. The permission might be something as vague as Administration or as detailed as Create New Orders. Each role is *granted* a list of permissions, and the permissions *inherited* by the user are the list of all permissions granted to all of the roles to which the user belongs.

Why Implement Role-Based Security?

The main advantage of RBS is in the maintenance of systems employing the technique. The typical example is that you have a system of some kind that contains thousands of different users, possibly a human resources Web site for your corporate intranet. You want some users to be able to maintain their own information while you want a portion of other users to not have permission to write over existing files (or data in a database) or to access those files or data at all. In addition, you want to be able to grant to other users the ability to maintain information related to the corporate hierarchy, departments, organizational charts, and more.

So, in this sample, several different types of users exist within the system. Each type of user will need a different set of permissions in order to do their job. A user higher up in an organization might be granted more permissions than someone in the lower level of the organization. For example, the "department-head" type of user might have 50 different permissions while a "team-lead" type of user might only have 20 permissions. If the system has 10,000 users, think about the amount of time required to maintain each set of permissions individually for each user.

A more maintainable solution would be to first identify the various types of users in the system. Each "type" of user is a role. Then determine the permissions that belong to each role. Maintaining the system then becomes exponentially easier because all you have to do is map users to roles, rather than spending the painstaking time mapping individual permissions to each user.

Implementing Role-Based Security

Now that we've discussed *why* you want to use RBS, let's get on to *how* you're going to use it. In this case study, we'll build the security system in two basic stages:

- **Database tables**: We'll build the tables needed to support the users and the required roles and permissions.

- **Stored procedures**: We'll build the stored procedures required to allow you to create, alter and query these users, roles and permissions.

However, before you get started with the actual implementation of your database, we need to discuss some of the basic assumptions that underpin this implementation as well as some essential background information. In this case study, you're going to store and use bitmasked values to determine how a particular permission is mapped to a role. Therefore, we'll discuss some of the technology and math you're going to use for *bitmasked access modes*, as well as the naming convention you'll use for all of your stored procedures.

Understanding Bitmasked Access Modes

Before talking about a bitmasked access mode, we need to define what a *bitmask* actually is. As you know, the computer stores numbers in binary, which are all just long runs of zeros and ones. A bitmask uses the run of zeros and ones as the meaningful characteristic of that number rather than its decimal value.

For example, let's say you have the following value, in binary:

```
001100
```

In decimal, that value is 12. The value 12 has no meaning to you in terms of a bitmask. What you're actually looking at is a series of Boolean values. Each of the places in the binary number is actually going to be used as a Boolean value, or a *flag*. Rather than reading it in binary, you can look at the previous number as follows:

```
False False True True False False
```

So, instead of being able to store the single numeric value 12 in an integer-type data column, what you're actually storing is a large number of Boolean flags, or *bits*.

You might be thinking: Why would you use an `Integer` field to store a collection of bit flags when your database server allows you to create single columns that contain small fields that can be used as Booleans? After all, eight columns of the type `Bit` are going to take up just as much space as a single column of the type `Byte`, and each can store eight Boolean flags. So, why would you go to all the trouble of using a complex number that you have to perform bitwise operations on to figure out the Boolean values? Two words: extensibility and flexibility.

Extensibility and Flexibility

Let's say that for a sample Web site, you want users to have the following permission flags:

- Create

- Retrieve

- Update

- Delete

You're confident that the users are never going to need more permission assignments than this because this list covers the four basic types of operations you can perform on data. However, what happens if, six months after you build the application, you have to modify this list of flags so that there's a distinction between single items and batch items? In this system, you'd have to add four new columns to the database (Create Batch, Retrieve Batch, Update Batch, and Delete Batch), as well as add all of the extra stored procedure code to handle it. The programmers would probably have a fairly difficult task upgrading all of their code to work with the new data structure.

However, if you have a single column called Mode (or something similar) that was an integer, then in your database, if you have a 4-byte integer (32 bits), you actually have room to store up to 32 different permission flags (one for each bit) without having to worry about changing the data structure. Other database servers might have different size numeric value types available. You can create a column that will hold as many bits as you need flags for your security system. In addition, it's easier for programmers to pass around a single integer than it is to pass around a collection of Boolean values.

For the RBS system you're building in this case study, which could easily be the security system for an intranet or e-commerce Web site, you'll store permission grants on roles with a *mode*. Table 15-1 describes the bitmask values with which you're going to start.

Table 15-1. Bitmask Values

Mode	Bitmask Value	Description
Create	$1\ (2^0)$	This permission mode allows the grantee to create a new item. What kind of item is determined by the permission granted—for example, a new user, new product, and so on.
Transmit	$2\ (2^1)$	This permission mode allows the grantee to create copies of one or more items in a portable transfer format, such as Extensible Markup Language (XML).
Read	$4\ (2^2)$	This permission mode allows the grantee to examine an item. Typically this means that the grantee is allowed to view lists of the item as well as individual items.
Update	$8\ (2^3)$	This permission mode allows the grantee to modify data belonging to a previously existing item.
Delete	$16\ (2^4)$	This permission mode allows the grantee to modify data belonging to a previously existing item.

As you can see, you're only using five out of a potential 32 values. This gives you plenty of room to expand if you need to later. If you remember a little bit about binary math, a role that has Create, Transmit, and Delete permissions is going to have a mode value of 19 (simply add the numeric value assigned to Create(1), Transmit(2), and Delete(16) for the total). Note that there's no way of summing any of the other permission values to come up with a value of 19, so the combination of access modes is guaranteed to be unique.

Naming Conventions

A non-uniform naming convention will come back to haunt you. How many of you have created a suite of procedures for a particular application and later had someone else create more procedures for another application, which shared the same database, using a different naming convention? The result is confusion. For this case study, all stored procedures are prefixed with RBS_ (because this is a case study on RBS). Immediately following the RBS_ prefix is a description of the *type* of stored procedure, such as Select (multiple retrieve), Load (single retrieve), Update, Create, and Delete.

For example, a stored procedure to create a user might be called RBS_CreateUser, and a procedure to retrieve a list of users might be called RBS_SelectUsers.

Oracle has the concept of *packages*, which allow you to create logical groupings for your stored procedures and functions. So, in Oracle you could create a package called RBS and not need the prefix on the stored procedure names. You would refer to the stored procedures in such a package as RBS.CreateUser or RBS.SelectUsers. Other database servers have their own ways of distinguishing stored procedures for different applications.

Stage 1: Creating the Database Tables

Now that we've covered the basics of permission modes and discussed the naming convention, let's get to the meat of creating this database. Figure 15-1 shows what the whole thing is going to look like.

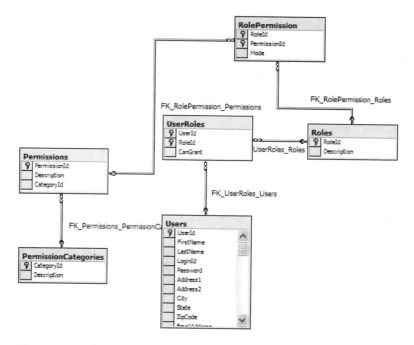

Figure 15-1. The RBS database

The first thing to do is identify the most basic type of data to be stored in the database. As you can see, there are four key storage tables:

- Users: This stores all the relevant information about your application users.

- Roles: Each role defines a specific collection of permissions (a typical role might be Administrator).

- Permissions: A permission is a point of access into the system (a typical permission might be Document).

- PermissionCategories: This allows you to define certain types of permission, such as Tax Documents.

There are also two mapping tables:

- UserRoles: This allows you to map roles to users.

- RolePermission: This allows you to map permissions to roles.

In this case, everything is going to revolve around the Users table, so let's determine what kind of information you need to store about users.

Users

In this example, you're targeting the database at a Web site application, so you'll need some kind of unique identifier for the user, as well as a login/password combination that you can use to authenticate the user. In addition, you need to keep some contact information on the user. In summary, you'll need to store the following:

- Name

- Address

- Login ID

- Password

- E-mail address or other contact details

In this example, you're not going to support international addresses because the topic of storing international addresses in a database is probably big enough for its own chapter. The only tricky part of this is the password. How do you store the password in such a way that the following conditions are true:

- The customers are guaranteed privacy (your employees can't get at customer passwords).

- There's privacy over the wire so that communication between the application and the database server is never disclosing a private password?

Well, you could use encryption or some form of hashing. When designing the database, you don't need to worry too much about how the programmers accomplish the hashing or encryption. You'll simply be storing raw binary bytes for the user's password. If your database server doesn't have a convenient way of storing raw binary data, you can simply use a string column (such as VARCHAR) and store the "hexified" ASCII version of the binary data. The assumption for this case study is that the application will be encrypting the password into some arrangement of binary data. That binary data is the only thing that the database is ever going to see. The user validation attempts will be performed against encrypted passwords, and users will be created and modified with encrypted passwords. This provides the maximum level of security for the user because you're adhering to the following rule: Private data is never transmitted between applications, application components, or physical environments without first being encrypted.

Creating the Users Table

With the previous in mind, let's look at the design of the Users table (see Table 15-2).

Table 15-2. The Users *Table*

Name	Data Type	Size	Description
UserId	INT	4	This is the unique numeric ID of the user. It is an ID field (auto-incrementing) and the primary key.
FirstName	VARCHAR	40	The first name of the user.
LastName	VARCHAR	40	The last name of the user.
LoginId	VARCHAR	10	The login ID of the user.
Password	BINARY	20	The password of the user. To provide maximum security, it's stored in its encrypted format as a set of raw bytes.
Address1	VARCHAR	80	First line of the user's address.
Address2	VARCHAR	80	Second (optional) line of the user's address.
City	VARCHAR	30	User's city.
State	VARCHAR	2	User's state (two-character abbreviation).
ZipCode	VARCHAR	10	User's ZIP code (dashes removed from extended ZIP codes).
EmailAddress	VARCHAR	255	The user's e-mail address.

There really aren't any surprises or complex columns in the Users table, with the exception of the Password column, which is stored in binary. The thing to keep in mind is that SQL allows you to compare a set of raw bytes just as easily as you can compare strings, so you won't have to do anything special to provide authentication services for your users with encrypted passwords. Oracle also allows the comparison of raw binary data (in fact, all string comparisons in Oracle end up as raw binary comparisons eventually). If your underlying database doesn't support binary, then you can store the data as a string as long as you can ensure that the database doesn't attempt to convert byte values more than 127 into something printable.

Let's look at the SQL script for creating the Users table in SQL Server, Oracle, and DB2.

SQL Server

The script should look fairly straightforward to you if you've worked through Chapter 12, "Working with Database Objects." UserID is the primary key column, so you define it as an identity column, with values starting at one and incrementing by one each time:

```
CREATE TABLE Users (
    UserId int IDENTITY (1, 1) NOT NULL ,
    FirstName varchar (40)  NOT NULL ,
    LastName varchar (40) NOT NULL ,
    LoginId varchar (10) NOT NULL ,
    Password binary (20) ,
    Address1 varchar (80) NOT NULL ,
    Address2 varchar (80) NULL ,
    City varchar (30) NOT NULL ,
    State varchar (2) NOT NULL ,
    ZipCode varchar (10) NOT NULL ,
    EmailAddress varchar (255) NOT NULL
);
```

You then define UserID as the primary key column:

```
ALTER TABLE Users ADD
    CONSTRAINT PK_Users PRIMARY KEY
    (
        UserId
    );
```

> **NOTE** *In the code download for this chapter, there's a separate script that creates all necessary constraints for every table.*

Oracle

The code to create the UserID table in Oracle is pretty similar. Oracle doesn't use the binary data type, so we've stored the password in a varchar field although you could also use a raw type:

```
CREATE TABLE Users
(
    UserId int NOT NULL ,
```

```
      FirstName varchar (40)  NOT NULL ,
      LastName varchar (40) NOT NULL ,
      LoginId varchar (10) NOT NULL ,
      Password varchar(20),
      Address1 varchar (80) NOT NULL ,
      Address2 varchar (80) NULL ,
      City varchar (30) NOT NULL ,
      State varchar (20) NOT NULL ,
      ZipCode varchar (10) NOT NULL ,
      EmailAddress varchar (255) NOT NULL
);
ALTER TABLE Users
    ADD CONSTRAINT PK_Users PRIMARY KEY (UserID);
```

We've used the varchar type to maintain as much consistency in the code as possible. This code will work on Oracle, but you should note that the varchar is a deprecated type and it's advised that you use varchar2 instead.

You need to create a sequence and a trigger, as described in Chapter 12, "Working with Database Objects," to automatically supply unique values to the primary key field:

```
CREATE SEQUENCE userid_seq;

CREATE OR REPLACE TRIGGER Users_AUTONUMBER
BEFORE INSERT ON Users
FOR EACH ROW
BEGIN
SELECT userid_seq.NEXTVAL
INTO :NEW.UserID FROM DUAL;
END;
/
```

DB2

Again, the code for DB2 is similar. In the absence of a binary data type, you store the password in a simple varchar field:

```
CREATE TABLE Users
(
    UserId int GENERATED ALWAYS AS IDENTITY,
...<etc.>...
    Password varchar(20),
...<script cropped>...;
```

```
ALTER TABLE Users
    ADD CONSTRAINT PK_Users PRIMARY KEY (UserID);
```

Roles

With the Users table designed in the database, you can move on to other things. Now we're going to talk about roles. What is a role? A *role* is just a placeholder for a collection of permissions. You also know that you want to keep this database in the appropriate normal form to keep it scalable and easily manageable, so you're not going to use columns to map roles to permissions. Instead, you just need a single table to maintain roles (you'll learn about relating roles and permissions a little later).

For now, let's figure out what information you need to store about a role:

- Identifier

- Description

That's about it. Really all you need is the unique identity of the role and some verbose description of the role such as "administrator" or "middle management."

Creating the Roles Table

Let's look at the design for the Roles table (see Table 15-3).

Table 15-3. The Roles *Table*

Name	Data Type	Size	Description
RoleId	INT	4	The primary key of the Roles table, the unique numeric identifier for a role
Description	VARCHAR	50	The description of the role

The following is the SQL script used to generate the Roles table in SQL Server (this is taken from SQL by right-clicking the database, choosing All Tasks, and then selecting Generate Script):

```
CREATE TABLE Roles (
    RoleId int IDENTITY (1, 1) NOT NULL ,
```

```
    Description varchar (50) NOT NULL
);
ALTER TABLE Roles
    ADD CONSTRAINT PK_Roles PRIMARY KEY (RoleID);
```

In DB2, you create the identity column as follows:

```
RoleID int GENERATED ALWAYS AS IDENTITY,
```

In Oracle you have to create a sequence and a trigger, exactly as described in the "Creating the Users Table" section.

Permissions

A *permission* is a point of access into the system. Remember that we're making a big distinction between a permission and a permission mode. An example of a permission might be Document. When that permission is granted to a role, it might be granted with a mode indicating read/update/delete access.

Therefore, with that distinction made, the following is really the only information you need to store about permissions:

- Identifier

- Description

However, there's a bit of extra information that you can add to a permission. In complex systems with many different kinds of data and resources that need protecting, managing all of the different permissions can be a complicated task. To make things easier for administrators, you're going to provide the ability to categorize permissions. Therefore, you're going to have something called a *permission category*. This also only needs a description because the majority of the work comes from the mapping of a permission to its parent category. A permission category might group sets of permissions with the type of data they relate to, such as Files, Tax Data, Legal Data, and so on.

Creating the PermissionCategories Table

The PermissionCategories table is a simple table that is defined in Table 15-4.

Table 15-4. The PermissionCategories *Table*

Name	Data Type	Size	Description
CategoryId	INT	4	This is the primary key and identity field. Unique numeric identifier for a permission category.
Description	VARCHAR	50	Description of the permission category.

The SQL Server script for the PermissionCategories table is as follows:

```
CREATE TABLE PermissionCategories (
    CategoryId int IDENTITY (1, 1) NOT NULL ,
    Description varchar (50) NOT NULL
);

ALTER TABLE PermissionCategories
    ADD CONSTRAINT PK_PermCategories PRIMARY KEY (CategoryID);
```

By now you can easily convert the table code to DB2 and Oracle, and then you can create the appropriate sequence and trigger for Oracle.

Creating the Permissions Table

The Permissions table is defined in Table 15-5.

Table 15-5. The Permissions *Table*

Name	Data Type	Size	Description
PermissionId	INT	4	This is the primary key and identity field. Unique numeric identifier for a permission.
Description	VARCHAR	50	Description of the permission.
CategoryId	INT	4	Foreign key (PermissionCategories). This is the category to which the permission belongs.

The SQL Server script for the Permissions table is as follows:

```
CREATE TABLE Permissions (
    PermissionId int IDENTITY (1, 1) NOT NULL ,
    Description varchar (50) NOT NULL ,
    CategoryId int NOT NULL
)
```

In addition to the primary key, this time you also create a foreign key on the CategoryID column, which references the same column in PermissionCategories:

```
ALTER TABLE Permissions
    ADD CONSTRAINT PK_Permissions PRIMARY KEY (PermissionID);
```

```
ALTER TABLE Permissions
    ADD CONSTRAINT FK_Perms_PermCats FOREIGN KEY (CategoryID)
    REFERENCES PermissionCategories (CategoryID)
        ON DELETE CASCADE;
```

Notice that you enforce cascading deletes in the relationship between this table and the PermissionCategories table so that on a delete operations, all related items are removed.

Mapping Tables

So far, we've covered the design for the Users, Roles, Permissions, and PermissionCategories tables. Each of these has been basically stand-alone data with no relation to any other data in the system. Now we're going to cover the tables you need to create the mappings and relationships that will finish up the database design for the RBS system.

Creating the UserRoles Table

The first thing you're going to look at is the ability to assign roles to users. Table 15-6 defines the UserRoles table.

Table 15-6. The UserRoles *Table*

Name	Data Type	Size	Description
UserId	Int	4	User ID to which the role is mapped. This is part of the primary key.
RoleId	Int	4	Role ID assigned to the user.
CanGrant	BIT	1	Indicates whether that user may grant the role to others if they also have the ability to edit security within the application.

Here's the script for the UserRoles table:

```
CREATE TABLE UserRoles (
    UserId int NOT NULL ,
    RoleId int NOT NULL ,
    CanGrant bit NOT NULL
);
```

For Oracle and DB2, you can use a smallint data type for the CanGrant column in place of bit.

 NOTE *As we explain shortly, you actually want the* CanGrant *column to take a default value of zero. In DB2, it's best to do that when you actually create the table.*

You create the primary key as usual. Note that this time, though, you're using a composite primary key. The values in the UserID and RoleID columns *together* will uniquely identify each row:

```
ALTER TABLE UserRoles
    ADD CONSTRAINT PK_UserRoles PRIMARY KEY (UserID, RoleID);
```

This next ALTER command creates two foreign keys on the UserRoles table. One key references RoleID from the Roles table, and the other key references the UserID from the Users table. Because this table has foreign keys pointing at both the User and Role table, it should be impossible to create a mapping between any role or user that doesn't exist. The database will also not allow the removal of a user or a role that contains a mapping in this table. The following is the code for Oracle and DB2:

```
ALTER TABLE UserRoles
    ADD CONSTRAINT FK_UserRoles_Roles FOREIGN KEY (RoleID)
    REFERENCES Roles (RoleID) ON DELETE CASCADE
    ADD CONSTRAINT FK_UserRoles_Users FOREIGN KEY (UserID)
    REFERENCES Users (UserID) ON DELETE CASCADE;
```

The code for SQL Server is only slightly different:

```
ALTER TABLE UserRoles
    ADD CONSTRAINT FK_UserRoles_Roles FOREIGN KEY (RoleId)
    REFERENCES Roles (RoleId) ON DELETE CASCADE,
    CONSTRAINT FK_UserRoles_Users FOREIGN KEY
    (UserId) REFERENCES Users (UserId) ON DELETE CASCADE;
```

You might've noticed the CanGrant flag on this mapping table. One thing it was necessary to include in the RBS was the ability to prevent administrators from giving out permissions they're not allowed to give. For example, let's say an administrator has the ability to modify users, but they don't have the Middle Management role. The system needs to be able to make sure that the user can't grant roles they aren't supposed to be granting as a way of circumventing the security system. The default data would be set up to allow the System user to grant all roles, with the regular administrator allowed to grant everything but the System role. It can be used to create the equivalent of a Unix root user or the SQL Server sa user.

So, let's now alter the CanGrant column so that it takes a default value of zero. In SQL Server, you do it like this:

```
ALTER TABLE UserRoles ADD
    CONSTRAINT DF_UserRoles_CanGrant DEFAULT (0) FOR CanGrant;
```

In Oracle, you can use this:

```
ALTER TABLE UserRoles
    MODIFY (CanGrant smallint DEFAULT 0);
```

In DB2, you create the DEFAULT constraint when you create the table:

```
CREATE TABLE UserRoles (
    UserID int NOT NULL,
    RoleID int NOT NULL,
    CanGrant smallint NOT NULL DEFAULT 0
);
```

Creating the RolePermission Table

The next table, RolePermission, takes care of assigning permissions to roles, the guts of allowing users to perform any secured task in the application (see Table 15-7). Obviously, you need to store the RoleID and the PermissionID. This is also where you're going to make use of the bitmasked access mode discussed earlier in the chapter, so you need a field to contain all 32-bits of the bitmask flags.

Table 15-7. The RolePermission *Table*

Name	Data Type	Size	Description
RoleId	Int	4	This is the role ID to which the permission is mapped.
PermissionId	INT	4	This is the permission ID mapped to the role.
Mode	INT	4	This indicates how this permission is mapped to the role. This is a bitmasked value and can contain multiple flags.

This is the script for the RolePermission table:

```
CREATE TABLE RolePermission (
    RoleId int NOT NULL ,
    PermissionId int NOT NULL ,
    Mode int NOT NULL
);
```

Interestingly, Mode is a reserved word in Oracle, so you need to use a different column name (such as PermMode).

You define a composite primary key:

```
ALTER TABLE RolePermission
    ADD CONSTRAINT PK_RolePermission
    PRIMARY KEY (RoleID, PermissionID);
```

Much like for the previous mapping table, the RolePermission table maps roles to permissions. As such, you create a foreign key referencing the Permissions table (on the RolePermissionID column) and another foreign key on the Roles table (on the RolesID column). For Oracle and DB2, you use the following:

```
ALTER TABLE RolePermission
    ADD CONSTRAINT FK_RolePermission_Permissions
      FOREIGN KEY(PermissionId)
      REFERENCES Permissions (PermissionId
        ON DELETE CASCADE
    ADD CONSTRAINT FK_RolePermission_Roles
      FOREIGN KEY (RoleId)
      REFERENCES Roles (RoleId)
        ON DELETE CASCADE;
```

For SQL Server, simply replace the second ADD keyword with a comma.

Now that you have the tables taken care of, let's take a look at the stored procedures that are going to use these table and relations.

Starting Again

If at any point you want to drop all of the tables and start over, the following is the script that will do it:

```
DROP TABLE UserRoles;
DROP TABLE Users;
DROP TABLE RolePermisison;
DROP TABLE Roles;
DROP TABLE Permissions;
DROP TABLE Permissioncategories;
```

Stage 2: Creating the Stored Procedures

You can conveniently subdivide the stored procedures into those that work on each of the four core storage tables and those that work on one of the mapping tables.

Users Stored Procedures

You'll start by examining the stored procedures that will allow you to do the following:

- Create a new user

- Update an existing user

- Delete a user

- Query for a list of all users

- Load the details for an individual user

- Validate a user's login credentials

Creating a User

The RBS_CreateUser stored procedure will create a new user in the system. The procedure accepts as input parameters all relevant user details, including the user's password (which is passed as a 20-byte binary parameter) and then inserts a new user into the database based on these values. It passes as an output parameter the UserID value for the newly created user.

SQL Server

You use a simple INSERT statement to create the new user and then return the newly assigned identity column value from that table with the SQL constant @@IDENTITY:

```
CREATE PROCEDURE RBS_CreateUser
@loginid varchar(10),
@FirstName varchar(40),
@LastName varchar(40),
@Password binary(20),
@Address1 varchar(80),
@Address2 varchar(80),
@City varchar(30),
@State varchar(20),
@ZipCode varchar(10),
```

```
@EmailAddress varchar(255),
@NewUserId int output
AS
    INSERT INTO Users(loginid, firstname, lastname, password,
                        address1, address2, city, state, zipcode,
                      emailaddress)
                VALUES(@loginid, @FirstName, @LastName, @Password,
                        @Address1, @Address2, @City, @State, @ZipCode,
                        @EmailAddress)

    SET @NewUserId = @@IDENTITY
```

Because this example is small and just a case study, you can get away with using @@IDENTITY. There are some issues with this constant that might make it inappropriate if you're using it in a high-volume system. For example, the value returned by @@IDENTITY *may not actually be the value given to your row*. If a row is inserted between the time you performed your insert and the time you retrieve the value of @@IDENTITY, you'll retrieve the wrong value. You can easily fix this by wrapping your CREATE functions in isolated transactions.

Oracle

The code for Oracle is somewhat different:

```
CREATE OR REPLACE PROCEDURE RBS_CreateUser
(
i_loginid IN varchar,
i_FirstName IN varchar,
i_LastName IN varchar,
i_Password IN varchar,
i_Address1 IN varchar,
i_Address2 IN varchar,
i_City IN varchar,
i_State IN varchar,
i_ZipCode IN varchar,
i_EmailAddress IN varchar,
o_NewUserId OUT int
)
AS
BEGIN
INSERT INTO Users(loginid, firstname, lastname, password,
                    address1, address2, city, state, zipcode,
                    emailaddress)
```

```
                VALUES(i_loginid, i_FirstName, i_LastName, i_Password,
                      i_Address1, i_Address2, i_City, i_State, i_ZipCode,
                      i_EmailAddress)
;

select userid_seq.currval into o_NewUserId from dual;

END;
/
```

You insert the current sequence value into your output parameter by selecting it from the DUAL dummy table.

DB2

The only real difference between the code for DB2 and that from Oracle is the way in which you insert the new UserID value into your output parameter:

```
CREATE PROCEDURE RBS_CreateUser (
    i_LoginID varchar(10),
    i_FirstName varchar(40),
    i_LastName varchar(40),
    i_Password varchar(20),
    i_Address1 varchar(80),
    i_Address2 varchar(80),
    i_City varchar(30),
    i_State varchar(20),
    i_ZipCode varchar(10),
    i_EmailAddress varchar(255),
    OUT o_NewUserId int)
BEGIN
INSERT INTO Users(loginid, firstname, lastname, password,
                  address1, address2, city, state, zipcode,
                  emailaddress)
            VALUES(i_loginid, i_FirstName, i_LastName, i_Password,
                  i_Address1, i_Address2, i_City, i_State, i_ZipCode,
                  i_EmailAddress)
;

    SET o_NewUserID = IDENTITY_VAL_LOCAL();
END
```

In terms of minor coding differences between Oracle and DB2, you'll notice that in DB2, the following are true:

- You can't use the CREATE OR REPLACE syntax.

- You're able to declare the size of your input and output parameters.

- You declare an output parameter by placing the OUT keyword *before* rather than after the parameter name.

- You don't use the AS keyword before BEGIN.

Deleting a User

The procedure responsible for deleting a user from the system is remarkably simple. In SQL Server, it looks like this:

```
CREATE PROCEDURE RBS_DeleteUser
@UserID int
AS
    DELETE Users WHERE UserId = @UserId
```

In DB2 and Oracle, it looks like this (bold indicates additions for the Oracle version):

```
CREATE OR REPLACE PROCEDURE RBS_DeleteUser (i_UserID int)
AS
BEGIN
    DELETE FROM Users WHERE UserID = i_UserID;
END;
/
```

The cascading delete options you've chosen on the foreign keys will ensure that related data in the database will be deleted as this procedure is executed.

Updating a User

The RBS_UpdateUser stored procedure will modify an existing user record. It takes as parameters the unique identifier for the user and all of that user's information including the password. A common limitation on many Web sites is that the e-mail address of the user is used as the primary key, so users often can't change their own e-mail addresses without creating a new account. This is cumbersome and often annoying to users. In this implementation, neither the login ID nor the e-mail address is restricted, and users can modify both of them as they choose. The key piece of information you use to identify a user in this stored procedure is their automatically assigned numeric ID.

SQL Server

In SQL Server, the code looks like this:

```
CREATE PROCEDURE RBS_UpdateUser
@UserId int,
@loginid varchar(10),
@Password binary(20),
@FirstName varchar(40),
@LastName varchar(40),
@Address1 varchar(80),
@Address2 varchar(80),
@City varchar(30),
@State varchar(2),
@ZipCode varchar(10),
@EmailAddress varchar(255)
AS
    UPDATE Users SET
        loginid = @loginid,
        Password = @Password,
        FirstName = @FirstName,
        LastName = @LastName,
        Address1 = @Address1,
        Address2 = @Address2,
        City = @City,
        State = @State,
        ZipCode = @ZipCode,
        EmailAddress = @EmailAddress
    WHERE UserId = @UserID
```

DB2 and Oracle

In DB2, the code is virtually identical to the previous code (add the code in bold for Oracle and remember to remove the data type sizes):

```
CREATE OR REPLACE PROCEDURE RBS_UpdateUser
(
    i_UserID int,
    i_LoginID varchar(10),
    i_FirstName varchar(40),
```

```
          i_LastName varchar(40),
          i_Password clob(20),
          i_Address1 varchar(80),
          i_Address2 varchar(80),
          i_City varchar(30),
          i_State varchar(20),
          i_ZipCode varchar(10),
          i_EmailAddress varchar(255))
AS
BEGIN
UPDATE Users SET
loginid = i_loginid,
Password = i_Password,
FirstName = i_FirstName,
LastName = i_LastName,
Address1 = i_Address1,
Address2 = i_Address2,
City = i_City,
State = i_State,
ZipCode = i_ZipCode,
EmailAddress = i_EmailAddress
WHERE UserId = i_UserID;
END;
/
```

Querying Users

In keeping with the naming convention, you know that this particular procedure, RBS_SelectUsers, retrieves more than one user. In this case, it retrieves all of
the users in the system in no particular order. Because you don't exactly know
what kind of code is being written for this application, we're providing this procedure as part of a set of default services just in case the application needs this
to load a cache or some other function.

SQL Server

The code in SQL Server is simple:

```
CREATE PROCEDURE RBS_SelectUsers
AS
    SELECT FirstName, LastName, LoginId, UserId FROM Users
    ORDER BY Lastname, FirstName
```

Oracle

In Oracle, things are a little more complicated. You return your rows into a special PL/SQL construct called a *cursor*, which you handle using a package (see Chapter 9, "Using Stored Procedures," for details). In the package specification, you declare your cursor (UserCur) along with the procedure (GetUsers) that are contained in the package body and will populate your cursor with the rows of users. The output parameter from the procedure is of type REF CURSOR and is called o_UserCur:

```
CREATE OR REPLACE PACKAGE RBS_SelectUsers_pkg
AS
TYPE
UserCur IS REF CURSOR;
PROCEDURE GetUsers(o_userCur OUT userCur);
END RBS_SelectUsers_pkg
;
/
```

In the package body, you open the cursor and load it with the rows of data:

```
CREATE OR REPLACE PACKAGE BODY RBS_SelectUsers_pkg
AS
PROCEDURE GetUsers(o_userCur OUT userCur)
IS
BEGIN
OPEN o_userCur FOR
SELECT FirstName, LastName, LoginId, UserId FROM Users;
END Getusers;
END RBS_SelectUsers_pkg;
/
```

DB2

In DB2 you again return the rows into a cursor, but the code is more straight-forward:

```
CREATE PROCEDURE RBS_SelectUsers()
RESULT SETS 1
BEGIN
    DECLARE curUsers CURSOR WITH RETURN FOR
        SELECT FirstName, LastName, LoginID, UserID FROM Users
        ORDER BY LastName, FirstName;
    OPEN curUsers;
END
```

Loading an Individual User

Chances are fairly good that the application will be loading details for a single user at some point. This will more than likely be done right after a user's login/password combination is validated successfully. The assumption of this stored procedure is that the client code has already retrieved a list of user ID or an individual user ID via a login validation procedure. That numeric user ID is passed to this stored procedure as the key to load a user. Based on this validated user ID, the RBS_LoadUser procedure retrieves all details (except the password) from the Users table and returns them in output parameters.

SQL Server

The code is as follows:

```
CREATE PROCEDURE RBS_LoadUser
@UserId int,
@Loginid varchar(10) output,
@FirstName varchar(40) output,
@LastName varchar(40) output,
@Address1 varchar(80) output,
@Address2 varchar(80) output,
@City varchar(30) output,
@State varchar(2) output,
@ZipCode varchar(10) output,
@EmailAddress varchar(255) output
AS
    SELECT
        @LoginId = loginid,
        @FirstName = FirstName,
        @LastName = LastName,
        @Address1 = Address1,
        @Address2 = Address2,
        @City = City,
        @State = State,
        @ZipCode = ZipCode,
        @EmailAddress = EmailAddress
    FROM Users
    WHERE
        UserId = @UserId
```

Oracle

Again, the code here is similar:

```
CREATE OR REPLACE PROCEDURE RBS_LoadUser
(
o_UserId int,
o_Loginid OUT varchar,
o_FirstName OUT varchar,
o_LastName OUT varchar,
o_Address1 OUT varchar,
o_Address2 OUT varchar,
o_City OUT varchar,
o_State OUT varchar,
o_ZipCode OUT varchar,
o_EmailAddress OUT varchar
)
AS
BEGIN
SELECT loginid, FirstName, LastName, Address1,
       Address2, City, State, ZipCode, EmailAddress
INTO
       o_LoginId, o_FirstName, o_LastName,o_Address1,
       o_Address2, o_City, o_State, o_ZipCode,
       o_EmailAddress
FROM Users
WHERE UserId = o_UserId;
END;
/
```

DB2

And finally for DB2, this is the code:

```
CREATE PROCEDURE RBS_LoadUser (
    i_UserID int,
    OUT o_LoginID varchar(10),
    OUT o_FirstName varchar(40),
    OUT o_LastName varchar(40),
    OUT o_Address1 varchar(80),
    OUT o_Address2 varchar(80),
    OUT o_City varchar(30),
```

```
    OUT o_State varchar(20),
    OUT o_ZipCode varchar(10),
    OUT o_EmailAddress varchar(255))
BEGIN
SELECT loginid, FirstName, LastName, Address1,
        Address2, City, State, ZipCode, EmailAddress
INTO
        o_LoginId, o_FirstName, o_LastName,o_Address1,
        o_Address2, o_City, o_State, o_ZipCode,
        o_EmailAddress
FROM Users
WHERE UserId = o_UserId;
END;
/
```

Validating User Login

The following stored procedure, RBS_ValidateLogin, will validate a user's login
and password combination. The LoginID and Password are sent as input parameters to the stored procedure. The output parameters are the FirstName and
LastName. In addition, the stored procedure returns a numeric value that indicates whether the login was successful. Again, note that the user's password
should be encrypted before it's even passed as a parameter to the database. You
first perform a SELECT statement, looking to retrieve the row from the Users table
that matches the LoginID and Password. If no such row exists, the login fails and
the stored procedure returns -1. Otherwise, the stored procedure returns the
numeric ID of the user, as well as that user's first and last name. The numeric ID
of the user must be retained by the client application in some way because it's
used as the key parameter in many other procedures.

It is fairly common practice for Web sites and applications to provide some
kind of greeting in the application to display to authenticated users. Rather than
require the application to make an additional round trip to the database to retrieve
the first and last name of a user after they've logged in, you simply return that
information as output parameters from this procedure for optimal performance.

SQL Server

The following is the code for the SQL Server version of RBS_ValidateLogin:

```
CREATE PROCEDURE RBS_ValidateLogin
@loginid varchar(10),
@password binary(20),
```

```
@FirstName varchar(40) output,
@LastName varchar(40) output
AS

    DECLARE @UserId int

    SELECT @UserId = UserId, @FirstName = firstname, @LastName = lastname
    FROM Users
    WHERE loginid = @loginid AND password = @password

    IF @UserId IS NOT NULL
        RETURN @UserId
    ELSE
        RETURN -1
```

Oracle

You can't get return values from Oracle stored procedures, so you simply define your UserID as an output parameter:

```
CREATE OR REPLACE PROCEDURE RBS_ValidateLogin
(
i_loginid varchar,
i_password varchar,
o_FirstName OUT varchar,
o_LastName OUT varchar,
o_UserID OUT int
)
AS
BEGIN

SELECT UserID, firstname, lastname
INTO o_UserID, o_FirstName, o_LastName
FROM Users
WHERE loginid = i_loginid
AND password = i_password;

IF o_UserId IS NULL
THEN
      o_userid := -1;
END IF;
END;
/
```

However, if you do want to actually return the UserID, you can re-create the procedure as a stored *function*:

```
CREATE OR REPLACE FUNCTION RBS_ValidateLogin_FUNC
(
i_loginid varchar,
i_password raw,
o_FirstName OUT varchar,
o_LastName OUT varchar
)
RETURN int
AS
o_UserID int;
BEGIN

SELECT UserID, firstname, lastname
INTO o_UserID, o_FirstName, o_LastName
FROM Users
WHERE loginid = i_loginid
AND password = i_password;

IF o_UserId IS NOT NULL
THEN
RETURN o_userID;
ELSE
Return -1;
END IF;
END;
/
```

DB2

The code for DB2 is more similar to what you used for SQL Server:

```
CREATE PROCEDURE RBS_ValidateLogin
(
i_LoginID varchar(10),
i_password clob(20),
OUT o_FirstName varchar(40),
OUT o_LastName varchar(40))
BEGIN
    DECLARE l_UserID int;
```

```
    SELECT UserID, FirstName, LastName
    INTO l_UserID, o_FirstName, o_LastName
    FROM Users
    WHERE LoginID = i_LoginID;

    IF l_UserID IS NOT NULL THEN
        RETURN l_UserID;
    ELSE
        RETURN -1;
    END IF;
END
```

Roles Stored Procedures

Let's take a look at the stored procedures you're going to create to provide application services dealing with roles.

Creating a Role

The RBS_CreateRole procedure creates a new role with the supplied description and returns the identity of the newly inserted row.

In SQL Server, you use the @@IDENTITY constant to return the RoleID for the newly inserted row:

```
CREATE PROCEDURE RBS_CreateRole
@Description varchar(50),
@NewRoleId int output
AS
    INSERT INTO Roles(Description) VALUES(@Description)

    SET @NewRoleId = @@IDENTITY
```

In addition to the minor differences noted earlier, in place of the @@IDENTITY constant, for Oracle you use the following:

```
select roleid_seq.currval into o_NewRoleId from dual;
```

And for DB2 you use the following:

```
SET o_NewRoleID = IDENTITY_VAL_LOCAL();
```

Deleting a Role

This procedure deletes an existing role. Note that there's no additional checking to make sure the role exists before it's deleted. Foreign keys and cascading rules will allow all data related to the role to be automatically deleted when the role is deleted. The procedure will simply return without error if an attempt to delete a nonexistent role is made:

```
CREATE PROCEDURE RBS_DeleteRole
@RoleId int
AS
    DELETE Roles WHERE RoleId = @RoleId
```

For DB2 and Oracle, you have the following:

```
CREATE OR REPLACE PROCEDURE RBS_DeleteRole (i_RoleID int)
AS
BEGIN
    DELETE FROM Roles WHERE RoleID = i_RoleID;
END;
/
```

Updating a Role

This procedure will modify the description of an existing role. It takes as input parameters the unique identifier for the role and the description. In SQL Server, you have the following:

```
CREATE PROCEDURE RBS_UpdateRole
@RoleId int,
@Description varchar(40)
AS
    UPDATE Roles SET Description = @Description WHERE RoleId = @RoleId
```

In DB2 the code looks like this (for Oracle, add the bold code and don't specify the size of the description parameter):

```
CREATE OR REPLACE PROCEDURE RBS_UpdateRole
(i_RoleID int, i_Description varchar(40))
AS
```

```
BEGIN
    UPDATE Roles
    SET Description = i_Description
    WHERE RoleID = i_RoleID;
END;
/
```

Loading a Role

This procedure will load the description of an existing role into an output parameter. In SQL Server, use the following:

```
CREATE PROCEDURE RBS_LoadRole
@RoleId int,
@Description varchar(40) output
AS
    SELECT @Description = Description
    FROM Roles
    WHERE RoleId = @RoleId
```

In DB2 (for Oracle, add the bold code, remove the parameter size, and move the OUT keyword to after the parameter name):

```
CREATE OR REPLACE PROCEDURE RBS_LoadRole
(
i_RoleId int,
OUT o_Description varchar(40)
)
AS
BEGIN
    SELECT Description
    into o_Description
    FROM Roles
    WHERE RoleId = i_RoleId;
END;
/
```

Selecting Roles

The following procedure will retrieve a list of all of the roles in the database, sorted by the name of the role. In SQL Server, use the following:

```
CREATE PROCEDURE RBS_SelectRoles
AS
    SELECT RoleId, Description FROM Roles ORDER BY Description
```

In Oracle, as for the RBS_SelectUsers procedure, you load the rows into a cursor and handle this using a package:

```
CREATE OR REPLACE PACKAGE RBS_SelectRoles_pkg
AS
TYPE
RoleCur IS REF CURSOR;
PROCEDURE GetRoles(o_roleCur OUT roleCur);
END RBS_SelectRoles_pkg
;
/

CREATE OR REPLACE PACKAGE BODY RBS_SelectRoles_pkg
AS
PROCEDURE GetRoles(o_roleCur OUT roleCur)
IS
BEGIN
OPEN o_roleCur FOR
SELECT RoleId, Description FROM Roles ORDER BY Description;
END GetRoles;
END RBS_SelectRoles_pkg;
/
```

In DB2, you have this:

```
CREATE PROCEDURE RBS_SelectRoles()
RESULT SETS 1
BEGIN
    DECLARE curRoles CURSOR WITH RETURN FOR
        SELECT RoleID, Description FROM Roles
        ORDER BY Description;
    OPEN curRoles;
END
```

Permissions Stored Procedures

Now you'll look at the stored procedures that deal with permissions. Once again, you'll see how to create, update, and delete a permission as well as how to load an individual permission and query for a list of all permissions.

Creating a Permission

This procedure will create a new permission. It takes a description as an input parameter, and the new ID of the permission created is placed in an output parameter. The SQL Server script is as follows:

```
CREATE PROCEDURE RBS_CreatePermission
@Description varchar(50),
@NewPermissionId int output
AS

    INSERT INTO Permissions(Description) VALUES(@Description)

    SET @NewPermissionId = @@IDENTITY
```

You can convert this to DB2 and Oracle in the same manner as you did for the RBS_CreateUser and RBS_CreateRoles procedures.

Updating a Permission

The following procedure will modify the description and category of an existing permission. Some applications may require that you not be able to change the category of a permission once it has been created, but you'll leave it up to the application to enforce that business rule because it won't violate any of the data rules to allow that. For SQL Server, you have the following:

```
CREATE PROCEDURE RBS_UpdatePermission
@PermissionId int,
@Description varchar(50),
@CategoryId int
AS
    UPDATE Permissions
    SET
        Description = @Description,
        CategoryId = @CategoryId
    WHERE

        PermissionId = @PermissionId;
```

In DB2, use the following (for Oracle, add the bold code and remove the size attribute from the i_Description parameter):

```
CREATE OR REPLACE PROCEDURE RBS_UpdatePermission
(i_PermissionID int,
i_Description varchar(50),
i_CategoryID int
)
AS
BEGIN
    UPDATE Permissions
    SET Description = i_Description, CategoryID = i_CategoryID
    WHERE PermissionID = i_PermissionID;
END;
/
```

Deleting a Permission

The following procedure is responsible for removing a permission from the database. The cascading rules on the foreign keys will take care of removing any related data for you. In SQL Server, the code is as follows:

```
CREATE PROCEDURE RBS_DeletePermission
@PermissionId int
AS
    DELETE Permissions
    WHERE
        PermissionId = @PermissionId;
```

Again, here is the DB2/Oracle code:

```
CREATE OR REPLACE PROCEDURE RBS_DeletePermission
(
i_PermissionID int
)
AS
BEGIN
    DELETE FROM Permissions
    WHERE PermissionID = i_PermissionID;
END;
/
```

Loading a Permission

The following procedure will load an individual permission and return its data in output parameters. It makes use of an inner join to return the name and description of the category to which the permission belongs as well as the category ID:

```
CREATE PROCEDURE RBS_LoadPermission
@PermissionId int,
@Description varchar(50) output,
@CategoryName varchar(50) output,
@CategoryId int output
AS
    SELECT @Description = p.Description,
           @CategoryId = p.CategoryId,
           @CategoryName = pc.Description
  FROM
   Permissions p
   INNER JOIN  PermissionCategories pc
   ON p.CategoryId = pc.CategoryId
   WHERE p.PermissionId = @PermissionId;
```

In DB2, you have the following:

```
CREATE PROCEDURE RBS_LoadPermission
(i_PermissionID int,
OUT o_Description varchar(50),
OUT o_CategoryName varchar(50),
OUT o_CategoryID int)
BEGIN
    SELECT p.Description, p.CategoryID, pc.Description
    INTO o_Description, o_CategoryID, o_CategoryName
    FROM Permissions p
    INNER JOIN PermissionCategories pc
    ON p.CategoryID = pc.CategoryID;
END
```

In Oracle, the query has been written to run on all Oracle versions (only 9i and later support the `INNER JOIN` syntax):

```
CREATE OR REPLACE PROCEDURE RBS_LoadPermission
(
i_PermissionId int,
o_Description OUT varchar,
o_CategoryName OUT varchar,
o_CategoryId OUT int
)
```

```
AS
  BEGIN
    SELECT p.Description, p.CategoryId, pc.Description
    INTO o_Description, o_CategoryId, o_CategoryName
    FROM Permissions p, PermissionCategories pc
    WHERE p.CategoryId = pc.CategoryId
    AND p.PermissionId = i_PermissionId;
  END;
/
```

Querying Permissions

The following stored procedure will return a list of permissions. If a category is supplied, then the list of permissions will be a list of permissions that belong to that category. If a -1 is supplied in place of a category ID, then the list of permissions returned will be unfiltered. All results are ordered by the category name and then by the permission name. In SQL Server, the code is as follows:

```
CREATE PROCEDURE RBS_SelectPermissions
@CategoryId Int
AS

  IF @CategoryId = -1
    SELECT p.PermissionId, p.CategoryId,  p.Description,
            pc.Description as CategoryName
    FROM Permissions p
    INNER JOIN PermissionCategories pc
      ON p.CategoryId = pc.CategoryId
    ORDER BY pc.Description, p.Description
  ELSE
    SELECT p.PermissionId, p.CategoryId, p.Description,
            pc.Description as CategoryName
    FROM Permissions p
    INNER JOIN PermissionCategories pc
      ON p.CategoryId = pc.CategoryId
    WHERE p.CategoryId = @CategoryId
    ORDER BY p.Description;
```

In DB2, you load the results into a cursor as follows:

```
CREATE PROCEDURE RBS_SelectPermissions(i_CategoryID int)
RESULT SETS 1
BEGIN
DECLARE cursor1 CURSOR WITH RETURN FOR
    SELECT p.PermissionID, p.CategoryID, p.Description,
            pc.Description AS CategoryName
        FROM Permissions p
        INNER JOIN PermissionCategories pc
        ON p.CategoryID = pc.CategoryID
        ORDER BY pc.Description, p.Description;
DECLARE cursor2 CURSOR WITH RETURN FOR
    SELECT p.PermissionID, p.CategoryID, p.Description,
            pc.Description AS CategoryName
        FROM Permissions p
        INNER JOIN PermissionCategories pc
        ON p.CategoryID = pc.CategoryID
        WHERE p.CategoryID = i_CategoryID
        ORDER BY p.Description;
IF i_CategoryID = -1 THEN
    OPEN cursor1;
ELSE
    OPEN cursor2;
END IF;
END
```

In Oracle, you have the usual package specification and body:

```
CREATE OR REPLACE PACKAGE RBS_SelectPerms_pkg
AS
TYPE permCur IS REF CURSOR;
PROCEDURE Getperms(i_CategoryID IN int, o_permCur OUT permCur);
END RBS_SelectPerms_pkg
;
/

CREATE OR REPLACE PACKAGE BODY RBS_SelectPerms_pkg
AS
PROCEDURE Getperms
(
i_CategoryID IN int, o_permCur OUT permCur
)
IS
```

```
BEGIN
IF i_CategoryId = -1
THEN
OPEN o_permCur FOR
SELECT p.PermissionId, p.CategoryId,  p.Description, pc.Description as
CategoryName
FROM Permissions p, PermissionCategories pc
WHERE p.CategoryId = pc.CategoryId
ORDER BY pc.Description, p.Description;

ELSE
OPEN o_permCur FOR
SELECT p.PermissionId, p.CategoryId, p.Description, pc.Description as
CategoryName
FROM Permissions p, PermissionCategories pc
WHERE p.CategoryId = pc.CategoryId
AND p.CategoryId = i_CategoryId
ORDER BY p.Description;
END IF;
END Getperms;
END RBS_SelectPerms_pkg;
/
```

Stored Procedures for the Mapping Tables

Finally, let's look at the stored procedures that are going to work with the mapping tables. From here on, we present only the SQL Server code. However, the conversion techniques have been fully covered in previous samples, and the code download for this chapter includes full scripts for all three databases.

Setting the Role's Permission Mode

The following procedure will create an entry in the RolePermission table. It assigns a permission to a role with a particular numeric mode value. The first thing you do is check to see if a mapping already exists. If it does, then you'll update that mapping with the new mode value. If it doesn't exist, then you'll create a new mapping with the supplied mode value. Note that the change to the role permission mode isn't additive. Therefore, the client application will be responsible for determining the previous value and adding access modes if that's the desired behavior. However, this type of stored procedure lends itself well to an application that provides a form with a list of data-bound checkboxes that can be submitted to invoke this procedure:

```
CREATE PROCEDURE RBS_SetRolePermissionMode
@PermissionId int,
@RoleId int,
@Mode int
AS
    DECLARE @Count int

    SELECT @Count  = Count(PermissionId) FROM RolePermission WHERE
        RoleId = @RoleId AND PermissionId = @PermissionId

    IF @Count = 0
        INSERT INTO RolePermission(RoleId, PermissionId, Mode)
        VALUES(@RoleId, @PermissionId, @Mode)
    ELSE
        UPDATE RolePermission
        SET
            Mode = @Mode
        WHERE
            PermissionId = @PermissionId AND
            RoleId = @RoleId;
```

Querying the Permissions Assigned to a Role

The following procedure will return a list of permissions that are assigned to
a given role, which is ordered by the name of the permission category and then
by the name of the permission to produce an alphabetic list of permissions:

```
CREATE PROCEDURE RBS_SelectRolePermissions
@RoleId int
AS
    SELECT p.PermissionId, p.Description, pc.Description as CategoryName, rp.Mode
    FROM Permissions p
    INNER JOIN PermissionCategories pc
    ON p.CategoryId = pc.CategoryId
        INNER JOIN RolePermission rp
        ON p.PermissionId = rp.PermissionId
    WHERE rp.RoleId = @RoleId
    ORDER BY pc.Description, p.Description;
```

Querying the User's Effective Permission List

This next procedure is essentially the entire meat of the RBS system. The bottom
line is that roles exist for organization and maintenance purposes. Although it

might be nice to display to the user or to administrators which roles are assigned to a user, that isn't the data you need.

The data you really need is a list of all of the tasks that a given user can perform. This list is a composition of all of the permissions granted to all of the roles that are assigned to that user and the modes associated with that user.

There's a slight twist you need to be aware of before you start writing your procedure, though. Think about this example: A user is a member of the Network Administrators role, and they're also a member of the Computer Administrators role. The Network Administrators role grants complete and full access to Users, and the Computer Administrators role grants only read access on Users. Which access does the user have if they've been granted two different modes of the same permission? Thankfully, because you chose to use simple integers rather than a pile of columns to indicate all of your mode flags, your choice is easy. You can make it additive. The result will be the *most* flags available. In other words, all you have to do is select the MAX() of the mode of each permission in a GROUP BY clause:

```
CREATE PROCEDURE RBS_SelectEffectivePermissions
@UserId int
AS

    SELECT RolePermission.PermissionId,
           Max(Mode) as Mode,
           Description
FROM RolePermission
    INNER JOIN UserRoles On RolePermission.RoleId = UserRoles.RoleId
    INNER JOIN Permissions ON RolePermission.PermissionId =
Permissions.PermissionId
    WHERE UserRoles.UserId = @UserId
    GROUP BY RolePermission.PermissionId, Permissions.Description;
```

Figure 15-2 shows an execution of the stored procedure (from within SQL Server's query tool), retrieving the list of effective permissions belonging to user 1, a full administrator in the sample database.

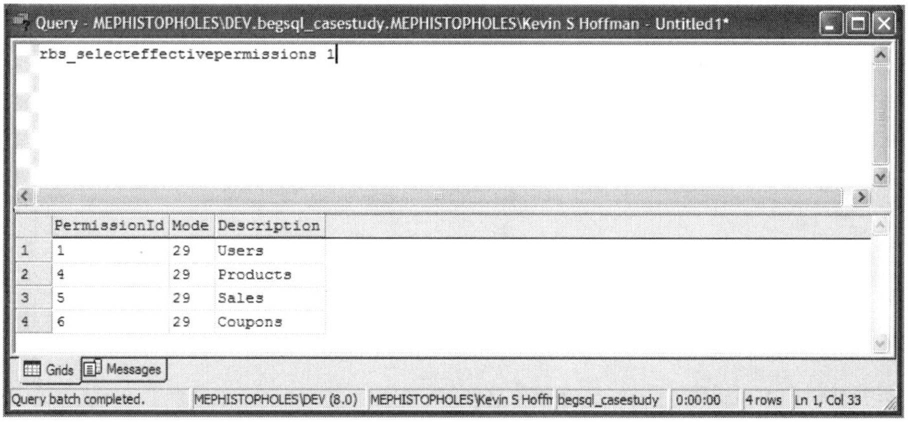

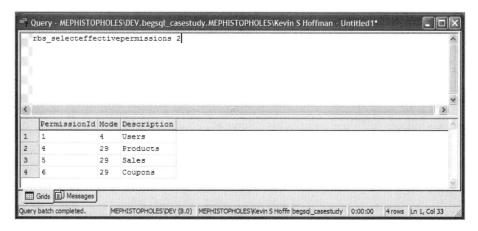

Figure 15-2. Retrieving a list of effective permissions for User 1

Figure 15-3 shows an execution of selecting the effective permission list for the second user in the database, which does not have quite as much power as the administrator (user 1).

Figure 15-3. Selecting the effective permissions for User 2

To rehash what we were illustrating about bitmasking, a Mode value of 29 given the bitmask key indicates that Create, Read, Update, and Delete are all *true*, and a Mode value of 4 indicates that only Read is available on the user's permission, as shown in Table 15-8.

Table 15-8. Permission Assignments for User 2

Permission	Create	Read	Update	Delete
Users	No	Yes	No	No
Products	Yes	Yes	Yes	Yes
Sales	Yes	Yes	Yes	Yes
Coupons	Yes	Yes	Yes	Yes

Querying a User's Assigned Roles

This procedure allows your application to retrieve all of the roles that have been assigned to a given user and whether that user is allowed to grant those roles to others (assuming they can modify user permissions to begin with):

```
CREATE PROCEDURE RBS_SelectUserRoles
@UserId int
AS

    SELECT UserRoles.RoleId, Description, CanGrant FROM UserRoles
    INNER JOIN Roles ON UserRoles.RoleId = Roles.RoleId
    WHERE UserId = @UserId
    ORDER BY Description;
```

Figure 15-4 illustrates how you execute the stored procedure to retrieve the list of roles that are assigned to a user and whether the user can grant that role to other users (assuming they can modify user security settings).

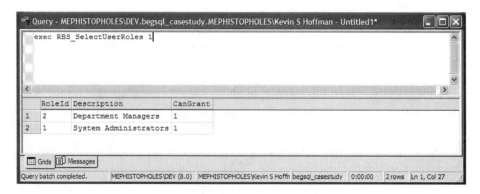

Figure 15-4. Retrieving the list of roles assigned to a user

Summary

This case study has been all about building a RBS system. At the beginning of the chapter, we talked about how implementing a RBS system provides you with an easier way to maintain security than if permissions were mapped individually to each user. We also talked about how providing a Mode value gives you the ability to extend and scale your system to meet additional security demands without having to modify your data structure or severely impact the code of an application written against your system.

When you got into the implementation of the system, you saw the data structures that make up the system you're building, and you looked at all of the stored procedures that you needed to create in order to provide a full set of services to any application written against your database.

By now you should have a firm grasp of the functionality and features involved in building RBS systems, as well as some of the SQL data design and query techniques that get that job accomplished. The sample presented in this chapter should serve as a good starting point for any RBS system that you might want to implement in your own solution.

APPENDIX A

Executing SQL Statements

THROUGHOUT THIS BOOK, we've been assuming that you're entering and executing the example SQL statements in the simplest way possible—using the SQL editing tools provided by the database. These tools vary considerably in their complexity, and it's not the purpose of this book to examine them in detail; however, we do need to show how we're expecting you to execute the examples!

Entering SQL Statements

Because each database vendor provides its own tools for entering and executing SQL statements on the fly, this appendix covers each of the systems in turn. It provides step-by-step instructions for connecting to the InstantUniversity database and executing SQL statements. You'll examine the InstantUniversity database in Appendix B, "Setting Up the InstantUniversity Database."

SQL Server

The easiest way to execute SQL statements against a SQL Server (7.0 or higher) database is using Query Analyzer. Open Query Analyzer from the Start menu (Programs ➤ Microsoft SQL Server ➤ Query Analyzer), and you'll be prompted to enter the connection details for the database server you want to connect to, as shown in Figure A-1.

Figure A-1. Connecting to SQL Server

The SQL Server instances running on your network should all appear in the SQL Server drop-down box, so select the appropriate one (or type the name if it doesn't appear). Next, select the authentication mode used to connect to your server. Windows authentication uses the accounts of users on the domain or the local Windows computer to authenticate users, and SQL Server authentication uses special logon accounts created and managed by SQL Server itself.

If you select Windows authentication, SQL Server will use the username and password you're currently using to log on to Windows; otherwise, you'll need to enter a SQL Server login name and password.

Once you've entered the connection details, click OK, and Query Analyzer will open. Select the InstantUniversity database from the drop-down box on the toolbar to ensure that queries are executed against this database. You can then type SQL queries directly into the Query window and execute them by clicking the green arrow to the left of the database drop-down list, as shown in Figure A-2.

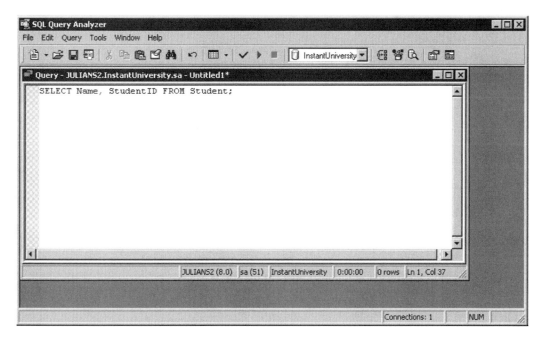

Figure A-2. Executing queries in Query Analyzer

Any results will be displayed in a new pane in the Query window, as shown in Figure A-3.

	Name	StudentID
1	John Jones	1
2	Gary Burton	2
3	Emily Scarlett	3
4	Bruce Lee	4
5	Anna Wolff	5
6	Vic Andrews	6
7	Steve Alaska	7
8	Julia Picard	8

Figure A-3. The results from a SQL Server query

Oracle

The standard utility for entering queries against an Oracle database is SQL*Plus, which in appearance is a simple text editor, similar to a command prompt. When you open SQL*Plus, you're prompted to enter connection details, as shown in Figure A-4.

Log On

User Name:	InstSql
Password:	******
Host String:	(DESCRIPTION=(ADDRESS

OK   Cancel

Figure A-4. Connecting to Oracle from SQL*Plus

As well as the username and password for the user you want to log on as, you must supply the service name of the database to which you want to connect. If Oracle can't resolve the service name, you may need to supply a complete TNS descriptor for the database. For example:

```
(DESCRIPTION=(ADDRESS_LIST=(ADDRESS=(PROTOCOL=TCP)
(HOST=servername)(PORT=1521)))(CONNECT_DATA=
(SERVICE_NAME=servicename)))
```

NOTE *You can get the TNS descriptor from the General tab for the database in Oracle Enterprise Manager Console.*

Once SQL*Plus has loaded, you can type queries directly into the editor; any results will appear immediately after the query, as shown in Figure A-5.

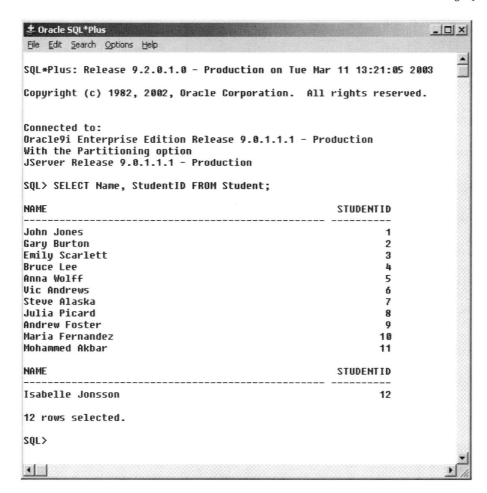

*Figure A-5. Executing queries in SQL*Plus*

For single SQL statements, the query will execute as soon as you enter a line ending in the semicolon termination character. For multistatement queries (for example, CREATE PROCEDURE), which can contain semicolons, you need to mark the end of the statement using the / character:

```
BEGIN
    -- Multiple SQL statements
END;
/
```

DB2

DB2 provides a number of tools that allow you to enter and execute SQL statements, but for this book, we'll assume you're using Command Center.

Command Center has two tabs where you can enter SQL statements, the Interactive and Script tabs. The Script tab allows you to save multiquery scripts, and the SQL window is more generously proportioned, so we'll use that, as shown in Figure A-6.

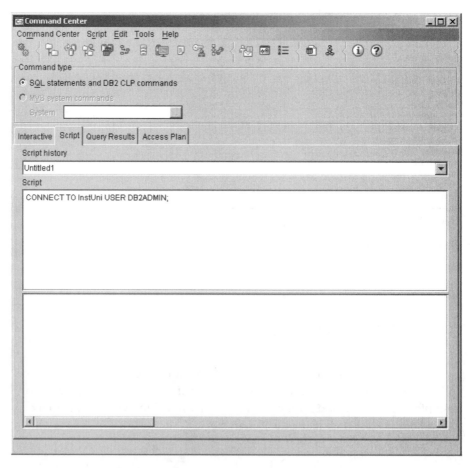

Figure A-6. The Script tab in DB2 Command Center

Because Command Center doesn't prompt you for connection details when it loads, you need to execute a CONNECT statement before you can access the database. You'll see the precise format of this command later in this appendix, but the basic syntax is as follows:

```
CONNECT TO database USER username USING password;
```

You execute statements in the Script window by selecting Script ➤ Execute from the main menu. You don't need to provide a USING clause for the CONNECT statement. For example:

```
CONNECT TO InstSql USER DB2ADMIN;
```

If you don't provide a password, DB2 will prompt you to enter one, as shown in Figure A-7.

Figure A-7. Providing a password to connect to DB2

Any output from SELECT statements, stored procedures, and so on appears in the pane below the SQL pane, as shown in Figure A-8.

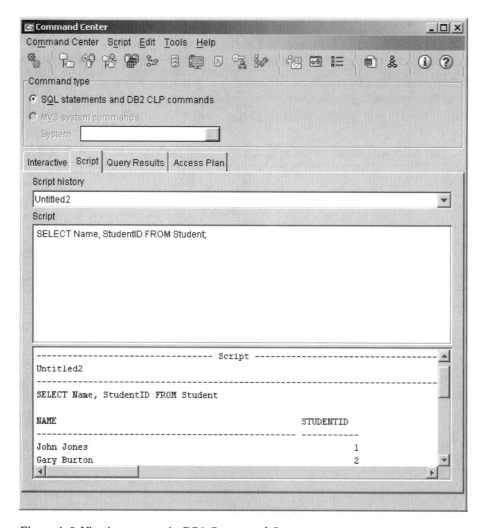

Figure A-8. Viewing output in DB2 Command Center

By default, Command Center will assume that any semicolons it encounters mark the end of a statement. If you want to execute multistatement queries (for example, in a BEGIN ATOMIC...END block), you need to change the default statement termination character to something else so Command Center will send the whole query, not just the part up to the first semicolon. You can do this in the Tools ➤ Tools Settings dialog box, as shown in Figure A-9.

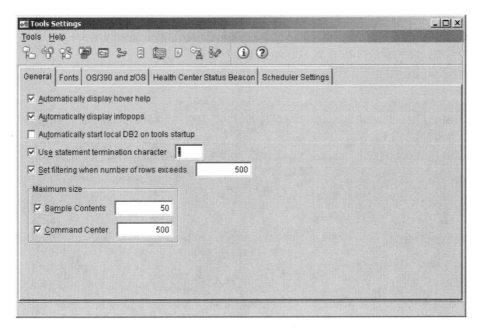

Figure A-9. The Tool Settings dialog box

MySQL

MySQL doesn't, by default, come with any specific editors for entering SQL queries (although many third-party management products are available for MySQL). Instead, you use the mysql command-line tool.

This utility allows you to specify many command-line options, but the key ones are as follows:

- -u *username*, --username=*username*: This is the username to use to log on to the database. Notice that you don't specify the @hostname part of the user-name because this is supplied automatically.

- --password=*password*: This is the password to use to log on to the database. If no password is provided in the mysql command-line instruction, mysql will prompt you for one.

- The database name: You supply this after any other options.

For example, to log on to the InstantUniversity database as Alice@localhost using the password simplepassword, you could use this command:

```
mysql -u Alice --password=simplepassword InstantUniversity
```

Once you've logged on to MySQL, you can just type SQL statements at the command prompt, and they'll execute immediately. Any output appears directly in the command window, as shown in Figure A-10.

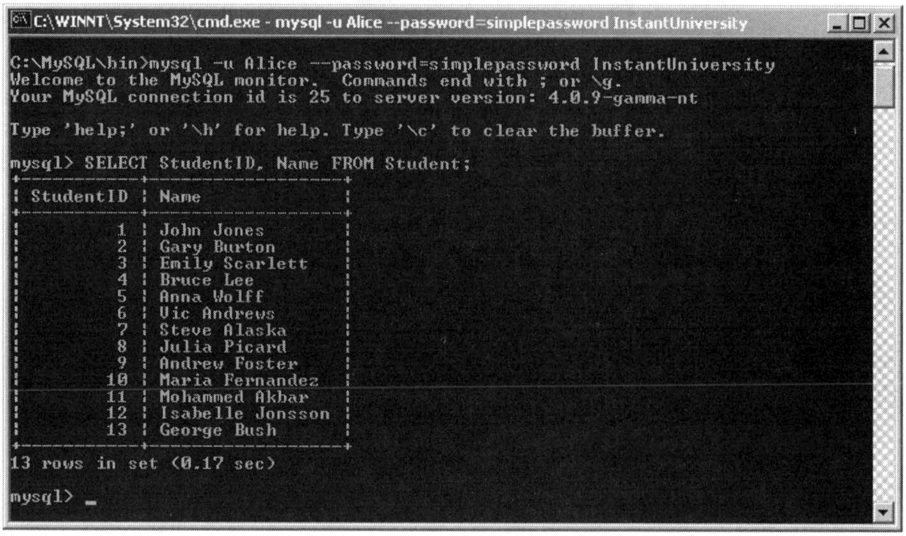

Figure A-10. Viewing MySQL output in the command window

Access

To run queries against the Access version of the database, open the database by double-clicking the InstantUniversity.mdb file in Windows. Access will display a list of the tables in the database, as shown in Figure A-11.

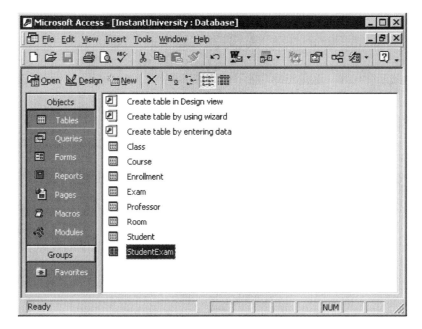

Figure A-11. The tables in Access

To execute SQL statements against your database, you need to create a new query. To do this, select Insert ➤ Query from the main menu. Access will ask you how you want to create the query, as shown in Figure A-12.

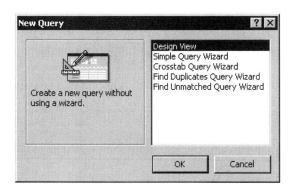

Figure A-12. Creating a new query in Access

Ensure that the Design View option is highlighted, and click OK. Access will present the design view, which allows you to create queries visually rather than by writing the SQL statements by hand, as shown in Figure A-13.

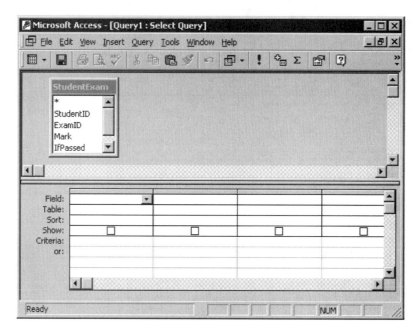

Figure A-13. The design view in Access

However, this is a SQL book, so you don't want to do that! Select View ➤ SQL View from the main menu. Access generates the skeleton of a simple SELECT statement, based on the table highlighted when you inserted the query, as shown in Figure A-14.

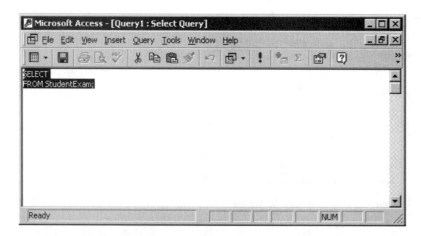

Figure A-14. The skeleton SELECT *statement generated by Access*

Replace this with the query you want to execute and click the ! icon on the toolbar. Access replaces the current window with the results from the query, as shown in Figure A-15.

StudentID	Name
1	John Jones
2	Gary Burton
3	Emily Scarlett
4	Bruce Lee
5	Anna Wolff
6	Vic Andrews
7	Steve Alaska
8	Julia Picard
9	Andrew Foster
10	Maria Fernandez
11	Mohammed Akbar
12	Isabelle Jonsson

Figure A-15. The results from an Access query

When you close the results window, you'll be asked if you want to save the query. If you select Yes, this query will be available to execute as a stored query.

Connecting to Databases Using SQL

As well as installing the InstantUniversity database, you'll need to connect to it in order to execute SQL statements against it. If you're using the SQL editing tools that you looked at previously, this may be done for you. However, if you're using a command-line interpreter or a less sophisticated graphical interface, you'll need to be explicit about what database you're using and provide the correct security credentials to do so, based on the security setting in your Relational Database Management System (RDBMS). You may also need to supply these details should you want to reconnect to a different database.

Three databases—Oracle, DB2, and SQL Server—support the SQL CONNECT statement in some form, which allows you to connect remotely to a specific database. The basic syntax for this is as follows:

```
CONNECT TO [database] USER [user_name];
```

Oracle

The syntax for connecting to a database using SQL*Plus is as follows:

```
CONNECT username@servicename/password
[AS SYSOPER | AS SYSDBA];
```

If Oracle can't resolve the servicename, you'll receive an ORA-12154 error:

```
ORA-12154: TNS:could not resolve service name
```

Again, if this happens, you can supply a complete TNS descriptor instead. For example:

```
CONNECT InstSql@(DESCRIPTION=(ADDRESS_LIST=(
    ADDRESS=(PROTOCOL=TCP)(HOST=servername)(PORT=1521)))
    (CONNECT_DATA=(SERVICE_NAME=servicename)))/password;
```

If you need to connect with SYSDBA or SYSOPER privileges rather than as a normal user, you can specify AS SYSDBA or AS SYSOPER.

You can close the connection in SQL*Plus by executing the DISCONNECT statement.

DB2

The DB2 version of CONNECT follows the standard basic syntax:

```
CONNECT TO database [USER user [USING password]];
```

You can connect using either the actual name of the database or its alias (if this is different). If no password is supplied with the USING clause, you'll be prompted for one when you execute the statement.

Finally, you can close the connection using the command CONNECT RESET.

SQL Server

SQL Server supports CONNECT TO only in Embedded SQL (ESQL) statements. ESQL statements are Transact-SQL statements embedded into C programs. However, Microsoft won't support this Application Programming Interface (API) beyond SQL Server 2000, so it's probably advisable to use a data-access technology such as ODBC or OLE DB in preference to ESQL.

The ESQL syntax for CONNECT TO is as follows:

```
EXEC SQL CONNECT TO database USER user
```

Here *database* is the name of the database to connect to, which will be InstantUniversity or will be *MyServer*.InstantUniversity if you're accessing the database remotely. The *user* is the name of the user account to connect with, which may include a password in the format *username.password*.

You can issue the DISCONNECT command to close the connection; again, you can use this only from ESQL.

Setting Up the InstantUniversity Database

BECAUSE THIS BOOK IS designed to explain how to construct SQL statements on numerous Relational Database Management Systems (RDBMSs), we decided that instead of using one of the database vendor standard databases (such as the pubs SQL Server database, for example), we'd use a custom database as the central example for this book.

The InstantUniversity sample database is designed to model a fictitious university, attended by students and professors, with courses, exams, and so on. Figure B-1 shows a visual model of the database.

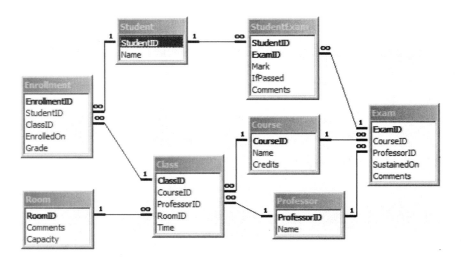

Figure B-1. The InstantUniversity *sample database*

Over the course of this appendix, you'll look through the design for each table in the database and the SQL code that's used to create each table. Finally, you'll look at some of the data used to populate the database. Where appropriate, we'll highlight differences between RDBMS-specific code.

NOTE *The code for creating this database is available for free download from the Downloads section of the Apress Web site (*http://www.apress.com*).*

Creating the Database

To start with, the most basic command for creating the empty sample database is as follows:

```
CREATE DATABASE InstantUniversity;
```

On each of the different database platforms (except for Access), this command creates a new database with the default set of properties assigned to it. For more information, see Chapter 14, "Working with Database Objects."

Note that Access can't create a new database in this manner, so to create the new database in Access, you need to select File ➤ New from the main menu. Then you need to create a new blank database, as shown in Figure B-2.

Microsoft Access 2000

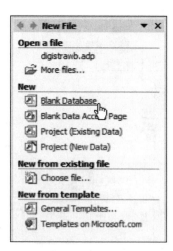

Microsoft Access XP

Figure B-2. Creating a new database

Once the database is created, you need to create the tables and relationships. In just a moment you'll look at the design for each table and the code needed to create each table.

It's worth noting that because you'll be using transactions in some of the chapters in this book, the code for creating tables in MySQL is slightly different from that used on other RDBMSs. When working with MySQL, you need to specify a table type that supports transactions and referential integrity: InnoDB. Also, when creating fields that have a data type suitable for storing dates and times, in SQL Server you refer to the data type as DATETIME, but other database platforms use the DATE data type. We'll highlight differences as you encounter them.

Creating the Professor Table

The first table you need to create is the Professor table. This table stores information about the professors at the fictitious university. Table B-1 shows the Professor table definition.

Table B-1. The Professor Table

Column	Data Type	Required?	Primary Key
ProfessorID	INTEGER	Yes	Yes
Name	VARCHAR(50)	Yes	No

The SQL code used to create this table is as follows:

```
CREATE TABLE Professor (
    ProfessorID INT NOT NULL PRIMARY KEY,
    Name        VARCHAR(50) NOT NULL);
```

As mentioned previously, you need to specify the InnoDB table type when working with MySQL, so you should add one last clause to the statement before executing it:

```
CREATE TABLE Professor (
    ProfessorID INT NOT NULL PRIMARY KEY,
    Name        VARCHAR(50) NOT NULL)
TYPE = InnoDB;
```

Creating the Course Table

The Course table stores information on each of the available courses at the university, as shown in Table B-2.

Table B-2. The Course *Table*

Column	Data Type	Required?	Primary Key
CourseID	INTEGER	Yes	Yes
Name	VARCHAR(50)	No	No
Credits	INTEGER	No	No

The code for creating this table is as follows:

```
CREATE TABLE Course (
    CourseID INT NOT NULL PRIMARY KEY,
    Name     VARCHAR(50),
    Credits  INT);
```

The only platform difference to this example is for MySQL, where you specify the InnoDB table type:

```
CREATE TABLE Course (
    CourseID INT NOT NULL PRIMARY KEY,
    Name     VARCHAR(50),
    Credits  INT)
TYPE = InnoDB;
```

Creating the Room Table

The Room table stores information on the available rooms in the university that can be used for teaching courses or for sitting exams, as shown in Table B-3.

Table B-3. The Room *Table*

Column	Data Type	Required?	Primary Key
RoomID	INTEGER	Yes	Yes
Comments	VARCHAR(50)	No	No
Capacity	INTEGER	No	No

The SQL used for creating this table is as follows:

```
CREATE TABLE Room (
    RoomID    INT NOT NULL PRIMARY KEY,
    Comments VARCHAR(50),
    Capacity INT);
```

Again, you specify the InnoDB table type when using MySQL:

```
CREATE TABLE Room (
    RoomID    INT NOT NULL PRIMARY KEY,
    Comments VARCHAR(50),
    Capacity INT)
TYPE = InnoDB;
```

Creating the Class Table

The Class table stores information on where and when a course is being held and who is taking the class. This table relies on the Professor, Course, and Room tables, as shown in Table B-4.

Table B-4. The Class *Table*

Column	Data Type	Required?	Primary Key
ClassID	INTEGER	Yes	Yes
CourseID	INTEGER	Yes	No
(Foreign key, table: Course)			
ProfessorID	INTEGER	Yes	No
(Foreign key, table: Professor)			
RoomID	INTEGER	Yes	No
(Foreign key, table: Room)			
Time	VARCHAR(50)	No	No

NOTE   *We've used a data type of* VARCHAR (50) *for the* Time *field. This allows you to enter text to describe when a class is taking place and for how long, rather than entering just a time.*

The code for creating this table on platforms other than MySQL is as follows:

```
CREATE TABLE Class (
    ClassID     INT NOT NULL PRIMARY KEY,
    CourseID    INT NOT NULL,
    ProfessorID INT NOT NULL,
    RoomID      INT NOT NULL,
    Time        VARCHAR(50),

    CONSTRAINT  FK_Course FOREIGN KEY (CourseID)
                REFERENCES Course(CourseID),

    CONSTRAINT  FK_Prof FOREIGN KEY (ProfessorID)
                REFERENCES Professor(ProfessorID),

    CONSTRAINT  FK_Room FOREIGN KEY (RoomID)
                REFERENCES Room(RoomID));
```

Note that for Access, if you're creating this table using this SQL statement, you need to enclose Time in square brackets (because Time is a reserved word):

```
...
    [Time]          VARCHAR(50),
...
```

The code for creating this table on MySQL is a bit different:

```
CREATE TABLE Class (
    CourseID    INT NOT NULL,
    ProfessorID INT NOT NULL,
    RoomID      INT NOT NULL,
    ClassID     INT NOT NULL PRIMARY KEY,
    Time        VARCHAR(50),

    INDEX       course_index(CourseID),
    CONSTRAINT  FK_Course FOREIGN KEY (CourseID)
                REFERENCES Course(CourseID),

    INDEX       prof_index(ProfessorID),
    CONSTRAINT  FK_Prof FOREIGN KEY (ProfessorID)
                REFERENCES Professor(ProfessorID),
```

```
    INDEX       room_index(RoomID),
    CONSTRAINT  FK_Room FOREIGN KEY (RoomID)
                REFERENCES Room(RoomID)
) TYPE = InnoDB;
```

Note that all foreign keys in the table must be indexed when creating an InnoDB table. This topic is covered in more detail in Chapter 14, "Working with Database Objects."

Creating the Student Table

The Student table stores basic information about the students who attend the university, as shown in Table B-5.

Table B-5. The Student Table

Column	Data Type	Required?	Primary Key
StudentID	INTEGER	Yes	Yes
Name	VARCHAR(50)	No	No

To create the Student table, use the following SQL code:

```
CREATE TABLE Student (
    StudentID INT NOT NULL PRIMARY KEY,
    Name      VARCHAR(50) NOT NULL);
```

And to specify the table type in MySQL, alter the end of the statement as follows:

```
CREATE TABLE Student (
    StudentID INT NOT NULL PRIMARY KEY,
    Name      VARCHAR(50) NOT NULL
) TYPE = InnoDB;
```

Creating the Exam Table

The Exam table stores information on the course on which the exam is based, the professor who is marking the exam, the date when the exam is to be held, and any extra comments about the contents of the exam, as shown in Table B-6.

Table B-6. The Exam *Table*

Column	Data Type	Required?	Primary Key
ExamID	INTEGER	Yes	Yes
CourseID	INTEGER	Yes	No
(Foreign key, table: Course)			
ProfessorID	INTEGER	Yes	No
(Foreign key, table: Professor)			
SustainedOn	DATE	No	No
Comments	VARCHAR(255)	No	No

The code for creating this table is as follows:

```
CREATE TABLE Exam (
    ExamID      INT NOT NULL PRIMARY KEY,
    CourseID    INT NOT NULL,
    ProfessorID INT NOT NULL,
    SustainedOn DATE,
    Comments    VARCHAR(255),

    CONSTRAINT  FK_ExamCourse FOREIGN KEY (CourseID)
                REFERENCES Course(CourseID),

    CONSTRAINT  FK_ExamProf FOREIGN KEY (ProfessorID)
                REFERENCES Professor(ProfessorID));
```

Note that SQL Server uses DATETIME instead of DATE:

```
...
    SustainedOn DATETIME,
...
```

And, again, MySQL has extra indexes and a table type definition:

```
...
    INDEX       examcourse_index(CourseID),
    CONSTRAINT  FK_ExamCourse FOREIGN KEY (CourseID)
                REFERENCES Course(CourseID),
```

```
    INDEX      examprof_index(ProfessorID),
    CONSTRAINT  FK_ExamProf FOREIGN KEY (ProfessorID)
                REFERENCES Professor(ProfessorID)
) TYPE = InnoDB;
```

Creating the Enrollment Table

The Enrollment table describes which students attend which classes. Of course, a student will attend more than one class, and each class will have more than one student, as shown in Table B-7.

Table B-7. The Enrollment Table

Column	Data Type	Required?	Primary Key
EnrollmentID	INTEGER	Yes	Yes
StudentID	INTEGER	Yes	No
(Foreign key, table: Student)			
ClassID	INTEGER	Yes	No
(Foreign key, table: Class)			
EnrolledOn	DATE	No	No
Grade	VARCHAR(255)	No	No

You can create this table with the following code:

```
CREATE TABLE Enrollment (
    EnrollmentID INT NOT NULL PRIMARY KEY,
    StudentID   INT NOT NULL,
    ClassID     INT NOT NULL,
    EnrolledOn  DATE,
    Grade       INT,

    CONSTRAINT  FK_EnrollStudent FOREIGN KEY (StudentID)
                REFERENCES Student(StudentID),

    CONSTRAINT  FK_EnrollClass FOREIGN KEY (ClassID)
                REFERENCES Class(ClassID));
```

Make sure to change DATE to DATETIME for SQL Server:

```
...
   EnrolledOn    DATETIME,
...
```

Again, MySQL has a couple of extra indexes to add, along with the table type:

```
...
   INDEX        enrollstudent_index(StudentID),
   CONSTRAINT   FK_EnrollStudent FOREIGN KEY (StudentID)
                REFERENCES Student(StudentID),

   INDEX        enrollclass_index(ClassID),
   CONSTRAINT   FK_EnrollClass FOREIGN KEY (ClassID)
                REFERENCES Class(ClassID)
) TYPE = InnoDB;
```

Creating the StudentExam Table

This joining table makes a note of which exams were taken by which students, the grades achieved by each student for each exam taken, and whether the exam was passed (subject to moderation), as shown in Table B-8.

Table B-8. The StudentExam *Table*

Column	Data Type	Required?	Primary Key
StudentID	INTEGER	Yes	Yes
(Foreign key, table: Student)			
ExamID	INTEGER	Yes	Yes
(Foreign key, table: Exam)			
Mark	INTEGER	Yes	No
IfPassed	DATE	No	No
Comments	VARCHAR(255)	No	No

To create the table, use the following SQL:

```
CREATE TABLE StudentExam (
    StudentID  INT NOT NULL,
    ExamID     INT NOT NULL,
    Mark       INT,
    IfPassed   SMALLINT,
    Comments   VARCHAR(255),

    CONSTRAINT PK_StudentExam PRIMARY KEY (StudentID, ExamID),

    CONSTRAINT FK_Student FOREIGN KEY (StudentID)
               REFERENCES Student(StudentID),

    CONSTRAINT FK_Exam FOREIGN KEY (ExamID)
               REFERENCES Exam(ExamID));
```

And, if you're using MySQL, add the following:

```
...
    INDEX      student_index (StudentID),
    CONSTRAINT FK_Student FOREIGN KEY (StudentID)
               REFERENCES Student(StudentID),

    INDEX      exam_index (ExamID),
    CONSTRAINT FK_Exam FOREIGN KEY (ExamID)
               REFERENCES Exam(ExamID)
) TYPE = InnoDB;
```

Inserting Data into the Database

The process of inserting data into the database is also RDBMS specific in many cases, and as such, we'll flag vendor differences when they arise. We won't list the full set of INSERT statements in this appendix because they're quite lengthy. For the full set, download the code from the Downloads section of the Apress Web site (http://www.apress.com).

Professor

Insert the following data into the Professor table:

```
INSERT INTO Professor (ProfessorID,Name)
VALUES (1,'Prof. Dawson');

INSERT INTO Professor (ProfessorID,Name)
VALUES (2,'Prof. Williams');

INSERT INTO Professor (ProfessorID,Name)
VALUES (3,'Prof. Ashby');
...
```

Course

Insert the following data into the Course table:

```
INSERT INTO Course (CourseID,Name,Credits)
VALUES (1,'Mediaeval Romanian',5);

INSERT INTO Course (CourseID,Name,Credits)
VALUES (2,'Philosophy',5);

INSERT INTO Course (CourseID,Name,Credits)
VALUES (3,'History of Computing',5);
...
```

Room

Insert the following data into the Room table:

```
INSERT INTO Room (RoomID,Comments,Capacity)
VALUES (1,'Main hall',500);

INSERT INTO Room (RoomID,Comments,Capacity)
VALUES (2,'Science Department',200);

INSERT INTO Room (RoomID,Comments,Capacity)
VALUES (3,'Science Room 1',100);
...
```

Class

Insert the following data into the Class table:

```
INSERT INTO Class (ClassID,CourseID,ProfessorID,RoomID,Time)
VALUES (1,1,1,6,'Mon 09:00-11:00');

INSERT INTO Class (ClassID,CourseID,ProfessorID,RoomID,Time)
VALUES (2,2,1,5,'Mon 11:00-12:00, Thu 09:00-11:00');

INSERT INTO Class (ClassID,CourseID,ProfessorID,RoomID,Time)
VALUES (3,3,2,3,'Mon 14:00-16:00');
...
```

Student

Insert the following data into the Student table:

```
INSERT INTO Student (StudentID,Name)
VALUES (1,'John Jones');

INSERT INTO Student (StudentID,Name)
VALUES (2,'Gary Burton');

INSERT INTO Student (StudentID,Name)
VALUES (3,'Emily Scarlett');
...
```

Exam

Note that the format you use to enter the date may vary between RDBMS. The following format is one of the most commonly used formats (*YYYY-MM-DD*). You may find that Oracle, for example, prefers dates in this format to be prefixed by the word DATE, for example, DATE '2003-05-03'. Alternatively, you could provide them in the format 03-May-2003.

Insert the following data into the Exam table:

```
INSERT INTO Exam
    (ExamID,CourseID,ProfessorID,SustainedOn,Comments)
VALUES (1,1,1,'2003-03-12','A difficult test that should last an hour');
```

```
INSERT INTO Exam
    (ExamID,CourseID,ProfessorID,SustainedOn,Comments)
VALUES (2,2,1,'2003-03-13','A simple two hour test');

INSERT INTO Exam
    (ExamID,CourseID,ProfessorID,SustainedOn,Comments)
VALUES (3,3,2,'2003-03-11','1 hour long');

INSERT INTO Exam (ExamID,CourseID,ProfessorID,SustainedOn)
VALUES (4,4,3,'2003-03-18');
...
```

Enrollment

Again, take care when inserting date information:

```
INSERT INTO Enrollment
    (EnrollmentID,StudentID,ClassID,EnrolledOn,Grade)
VALUES (1,1,1,'2002-09-23',62);

INSERT INTO Enrollment
    (EnrollmentID,StudentID,ClassID,EnrolledOn,Grade)
VALUES (2,1,2,'2002-09-30',70);

INSERT INTO Enrollment
    (EnrollmentID,StudentID,ClassID,EnrolledOn,Grade)
VALUES (3,2,3,'2003-09-23',51);
...
```

StudentExam

Insert the following data into the Exam table:

```
INSERT INTO StudentExam
    (StudentID,ExamID,Mark,IfPassed,Comments)
VALUES (1,1,55,1,'Satisfactory');

INSERT INTO StudentExam
    (StudentID,ExamID,Mark,IfPassed,Comments)
VALUES (1,2,73,1,'Good result');
```

```
INSERT INTO StudentExam
    (StudentID,ExamID,Mark,IfPassed,Comments)
VALUES (2,3,44,1,'Scraped through');

INSERT INTO StudentExam
    (StudentID,ExamID,Mark,IfPassed,Comments)
VALUES (2,5,39,0,'Failed, and will need to retake this one later in the year');
...
```

Testing the Database Installation

Once all the data has been input into the database, you should test the installation to check whether it worked. One of the simplest tests you can do for quick 'n' dirty testing is to use the following universal command:

```
SELECT * FROM Table;
```

This statement will simply list all available data in the selected table. However, if you want to use something a bit more refined, you can try out the following examples.

EXAMPLE: TESTING THE DATA 1

You can use this example to test whether the sample data has been inserted correctly:

```
SELECT Course.Name AS Course, Student.Name AS Student,
    Professor.Name AS Professor
FROM Student
    INNER JOIN (Professor
        INNER JOIN (Course
            INNER JOIN (Class
                INNER JOIN Enrollment
                ON Class.ClassID = Enrollment.ClassID)
            ON Course.CourseID = Class.CourseID)
        ON Professor.ProfessorID = Class.ProfessorID)
    ON Student.StudentID = Enrollment.StudentID
ORDER BY Course.Name;
```

If you used the INSERT statements available for download from the Apress Web site, then you should see the following results:

COURSE	STUDENT	PROFESSOR
Applied Mathematics	Gary Burton	Prof. Williams
Applied Mathematics	Maria Fernandez	Prof. Williams
Applied Mathematics	Bruce Lee	Prof. Williams
Core Mathematics	Bruce Lee	Prof. Jones
Core Mathematics	Maria Fernandez	Prof. Jones
Core Mathematics	Steve Alaska	Prof. Jones
Electronics	Gary Burton	Prof. Ashby
Electronics	Maria Fernandez	Prof. Ashby
Electronics	Steve Alaska	Prof. Ashby
Electronics	Vic Andrews	Prof. Ashby
History of Computing	Gary Burton	Prof. Williams
History of Computing	Julia Picard	Prof. Williams
History of Computing	Vic Andrews	Prof. Williams
Human Biology	Emily Scarlett	Prof. Patel
Human Biology	Andrew Foster	Prof. Patel
Mediaeval Romanian	John Jones	Prof. Dawson
Mediaeval Romanian	Julia Picard	Prof. Dawson
Mediaeval Romanian	Anna Wolff	Prof. Dawson
Metallurgy	Vic Andrews	Prof. Hwa
Metallurgy	Andrew Foster	Prof. Hwa
Modern English Literature	Anna Wolff	Prof. Dawson
Modern English Literature	Julia Picard	Prof. Dawson
Organic Chemistry	Emily Scarlett	Prof. Ashby
Organic Chemistry	Andrew Foster	Prof. Ashby
Philosophy	John Jones	Prof. Dawson
Philosophy	Anna Wolff	Prof. Dawson

This example will test a table with a date in it to ensure that differences between date syntax haven't led to any errors:

```
SELECT Student.Name AS Student,
       Course.Name AS Course,
       Enrollment.EnrolledOn AS EnrollmentDate,
       Enrollment.Grade AS Grade
FROM Course
   INNER JOIN (Class
      INNER JOIN (Student
         INNER JOIN Enrollment
         ON Student.StudentID = Enrollment.StudentID)
      ON Class.ClassID = Enrollment.ClassID)
   ON Course.CourseID = Class.CourseID
ORDER BY Student.Name;
```

You should see something like the following (depending on the time zone settings on your machine):

STUDENT	COURSE	ENROLLMENTDATE	GRADE
Andrew Foster	Organic Chemistry	9/23/2002	68
Andrew Foster	Human Biology	9/23/2002	66
Andrew Foster	Metallurgy	9/30/2002	68
Anna Wolff	Mediaeval Romanian	9/23/2002	33
Anna Wolff	Modern English Literature	9/23/2002	65
Anna Wolff	Philosophy	9/23/2002	63
Bruce Lee	Applied Mathematics	9/20/2002	60
Bruce Lee	Core Mathematics	9/20/2002	70
Emily Scarlett	Human Biology	9/30/2002	80
Emily Scarlett	Organic Chemistry	9/30/2002	78
Gary Burton	Electronics	9/23/2003	68
Gary Burton	History of Computing	9/23/2003	51
Gary Burton	Applied Mathematics	9/23/2003	41
John Jones	Mediaeval Romanian	9/23/2002	62

John Jones	Philosophy	9/30/2002	70
Julia Picard	Mediaeval Romanian	9/23/2002	70
Julia Picard	History of Computing	9/23/2002	53
Julia Picard	Modern English Literature	9/30/2002	42
Maria Fernandez	Core Mathematics	9/20/2002	75
Maria Fernandez	Applied Mathematics	9/20/2002	66
Maria Fernandez	Electronics	9/20/2002	76
Steve Alaska	Electronics	9/20/2002	82
Steve Alaska	Core Mathematics	9/20/2002	66
Vic Andrews	Metallurgy	9/23/2002	54
Vic Andrews	History of Computing	9/23/2002	78
Vic Andrews	Electronics	9/23/2002	71

APPENDIX C

Data Types

THIS APPENDIX LISTS THE available data types for each Relational Database Management System (RDBMS) and briefly describes the most commonly used types for each database platform.

RDBMS Data Types

Table C-1 summarizes the column data types available in the various RDBMSs used in this book.

Table C-1. Column Data Types

Category	Access	SQL Server	Oracle	MySQL	DB2
Binary Object	OLE Object, Memo	binary, varbinary, Image	bfile, BLOB, long raw	blob, text	blob
Bit	Yes/No (synonyms for tinyint(1))	bit	byte	bit, bool	N/A
Character	Text, Memo	char, nchar, varchar, nvarchar, text, ntext	char, nchar, long, varchar, nvarchar, CLOB	char, nchar, varchar, nvarchar, mediumtext, longtext	char, varchar, longvarchar, CLOB
Currency	Currency	money, smallmoney	N/A	N/A	N/A
Numeric	Number	bigint, decimal, float, int, numeric, real, smallint, tinyint	number (decimal, numeric, double precision, float, integer, smallint)	bigint, decimal, double, int, mediumint, numeric, real, smallint, tinyint	bigint, decimal/ numeric, double/float, integer, smallint, real
Temporal	Date/Time	datetime, smalldatetime	date	datetime, time, timestamp, year	date, time, timestamp
Unique	AutoNumber	unique identifier	N/A	N/A	N/A

SQL Server Data Types

Table C-2 describes the SQL Server data types.

Table C-2. SQL Server Data Types

Category	Data Types	Description
Binary Object	binary, varbinary	The binary type stores fixed-length binary data with a maximum length of 8,000 bytes. varbinary is a variable-length equivalent.
	Image	Variable-length binary data that can store up to $2^{31} - 1$ bytes.
Bit	bit	Integer data, storing either 0 or 1.
Character	char, varchar	char stores fixed-length non-Unicode data up to 8,000 characters. varchar is the variable-length equivalent.
	nchar, nvarchar	nchar is the Unicode equivalent of char, with a maximum length of 4,000 characters. nvarchar is the variable-length equivalent.
	text, ntext	Variable-length non-Unicode character data up to $2^{31} - 1$ characters. ntext stores Unicode character data up to $2^{30} - 1$ characters.
Currency	money, small money	Both store monetary values. Range of acceptable values are: money: -2^{63} to $2^{63} - 1$ smallmoney: -214,748.3648 to 214,748.3647 Both are accurate to one ten-thousandth of a unit.
Numeric	bigint, int, smallint, tinyint	All used for storing integers of varying sizes: bigint: -2^{63} to $2^{63} - 1$ int: -2^{31} to $2^{31} - 1$ smallint: -2^{15} to $2^{15} - 1$ tinyint: 0 to 255
	decimal, numeric	Fixed-precision and scale-numeric data in the range: $-10^{38} + 1$ to $10^{38} - 1$ Both are functionally equivalent.
	float, real	Floating-point precision numbers with ranges: float: $-1.79E + 308$ to $-2.23E - 308$, 0 and $2.23E + 308$ to $1.79E + 308$. real: $-3.40E + 38$ to $-1.18E - 38$, 0 and $1.18E - 38$ to $3.40E + 38$.

Table C-2. SQL Server Data Types (continued)

Category	Data Types	Description
Temporal	datetime, smalldatetime	Both store date and time data. Values range from: datetime: 01/01/1752 to 12/31/9999 smalldatetime: 01/01/1900 to 06/06/2079 datetime is accurate to 3.33 milliseconds, and smalldatetime is accurate to one minute.
Unique	unique identifier	A Globally Unique Identifier (GUID).

Oracle Data Types

Table C-3 describes the Oracle data types.

Table C-3. Oracle Data Types

Category	Data Types	Description
Binary Object	bfile	Contains a locator to a large external binary file of up to 4 gigabytes (GB).
	BLOB	A binary large object of up to 4GB.
	long raw	Raw binary data of up to 2GB.
	raw	Raw binary data of up to 2,000 bytes.
Bit	byte	Stores one byte
Character	char	Stores fixed-length non-Unicode character data up to 2,000 bytes.
	nchar, nvarchar	nchar is the Unicode equivalent of char, with a maximum length of 2,000 characters. nvarchar is the variable-length equivalent, but with a maximum length of 4,000 bytes.
	long, CLOB, NCLOB	long stores variable-length character data up to 2GB. CLOB stores up to 4GB of single-byte characters. Supports fixed- and variable-width character sets. NCLOB is the Unicode equivalent.
	rowid	A hexadecimal string value that represents the address of a row in a table.
	urowid	A hexadecimal string value that represents the logical address of a row in a table ordered by index.
	varchar	Variable-length character data of up to 4,000 bytes.

Table C-3. Oracle Data Types (continued)

Category	Data Types	Description
Numeric	number	The number data type stores all kinds of numbers, both fixed and floating point, positive, negative, and zero. All numeric types are essentially numbers, but with varying scale and precision. When used directly, number can store values in the range of 10^-130 and 10^126 – 1.
	integer, smallint	Both are equivalent and store integer values in the range -10^38 to 10^38.
	decimal, numeric	Both are synonyms for number.
	float, real	Both are identical and store floating-point precision numbers with range of -10^38 to 10^38.
	double precision	Floating-point precision number with a binary precision of 126.
Temporal	date	Stores a date and time between 01/01/4712 BC to 12/31/9999 AD.
	timestamp	Used to represent the year, month, day, hour, minute, or second component of a date.
	interval year to month	Stores the period of time between two dates in years and months.
	interval day to second	Stores the period between two times in days, hours, minutes, and seconds.

DB2 Data Types

Table C-4 describes the DB2 data types.

Table C-4. DB2 Data Types

Category	Data Types	Description
Binary Object	BLOB	Contains a variable-length binary string of up to 2GB.
	vargraphic	Variable-length graphic string of up to 16,336 characters.
Character	char	Fixed-length character data of up to 254 characters.
	clob	Variable-length character data of up to 2GB.
	dbclob	A variable-length character large object of up to 1,073,741,823 characters.
	varchar	Variable-length character data of up to 32,672 bytes.

Table C-4. DB2 Data Types (continued)

Category	Data Types	Description
External Data	datalink	Represents a link to an external data source.
Numeric	bigint	An 8-byte integer in the range -9,223,372,036,854,775,808 to 9,223,372,036,854,775,807.
	integer	A 4-byte integer in the range -2,147,483,648 to 2,147,483,647.
	smallint	A 2-byte integer in the range -32,768 to 32,767.
	decimal	An exact decimal value with fixed precision and scale in the range $-10^{31}+1$ to $10^{31}-1$.
	real	A single-precision floating-point number in the range -3.402E+38 to -1.175E-37, zero, or 1.175E-37 to 3.402E+38.
	double	A double-precision floating-point number in the range -1.79769E+308 to -2.2250738585072014E-308, zero, or 2.225E-307 to 1.79769E+308.
Temporal	Date	Represents a date between 01/01/0001 and 12/31/9999.
	Time	Represents a time in hours, minutes, and seconds.
	Timestamp	Represents a date and time, including a fractional microsecond component.

MySQL Data Types

Table C-5 describes the MySQL data types.

Table C-5. MySQL Data Types

Category	Data Types	Description
Binary Object	longtext/longblob	A variable-length text or BLOB field with a maximum of 4,294,967,295 characters.
	mediumtext/ mediumblob	A variable-length text or BLOB field with a maximum of 16,777,215 characters.
	text/blob	A variable-length text or BLOB field with a maximum of 65,535 characters.
	tinytext/tinyblob	A variable-length text or BLOB field with a maximum of 255 characters.
Bit	tinyint	An integer in the range -128 to 127 (signed) or 0 to 255 (unsigned).

Table C-5. MySQL Data Types (continued)

Category	Data Types	Description
Character	char	A fixed-length string in the national character set.
	varchar	A variable-length string in the national character set.
Composite Types	enum	A string object that can have one out of a number of possible values.
	set	A string object that can have none, one, or more values out of a number of possible values.
Numeric	bigint	An integer in the range -9,223,372,036,854,775,808 to 9,223,372,036,854,775,807 (signed) or 0 to 18,446,744,073,709,551,615 (unsigned).
	decimal	An unpacked floating-point number (stored as a string).
	double	A double-precision floating-point number in the range -1.7976931348623157E+308 to -1.175494351E-38, zero, or 2.2250738585072014E-308 to 1.7976931348623157E+308.
	float	A floating-point value. This can represent either single- or double-precision numbers.
	int	An integer in the range -2,147,483,648 to 2,147,483,647 (signed) or 0 to 4,294,967,295 (unsigned).
	mediumint	An integer in the range -8,388,608 to 8,388,607 (signed) or 0 to 16,777,215 (unsigned).
	smallint	An integer in the range -32,768 to 32,767 (signed) or 0 to 65,535 (unsigned).
Temporal	date	A date in the range 01/01/1000 to 12/31/9999.
	datetime	A combined date and time value.
	time	A time in the range '-838:59:59' to '838:59:59'.
	timestamp	A timestamp value reflecting the number of seconds since midnight on January 1, 1970.
	year	A year in two- or four-digit format.

Access Data Types

Table C-6 shows the Access field types listed with JET SQL equivalents.

Table C-6. Access Field Types

Category	Data Types	Description
Binary Object	**OLE Object** (longbinary)	A variable-length text or BLOB field with a maximum of 4,294,967,295 characters. Longbinary is the Jet name for this data type.
Boolean	**Yes/No** (boolean)	Stores values of -1 for yes/true, 0 for no/false. Any non-zero value input into this field is stored as -1.
Character	**Text** (char, varchar, string)	Can store up to 255 characters. Jet equivalents of a Text field are alphanumeric, char, varchar, and string.
	Memo (longtext, longchar, memo, note)	Can store up to 64,000 characters of alphanumeric data.
Numeric	**Number** (byte, int / integer, single, long, double)	The number field can be defined as one of the Jet types of byte, int, integer, single, double, and long. Sizes are: byte: 1 byte int, integer: 2 bytes single, long: 4 bytes double: 8 bytes
Currency	**Currency** (currency, money)	Precision up to 4 decimal places. Eight bytes.
Unique	**Autonumber** (counter, autoincrement, GUID)	counter and autoincrement use a long field type with a unique constraint and autonumbering functionality. Size: 4 bytes. This is the default size when generating an autonumbering field in Access table design view. GUID stores up to 16 bytes.
Other	**Hyperlink** (longtext, longchar, memo, note)	Stores up to 2,048 bytes of Uniform Resource Locator (URL) data.

Index